CAMBRIDGE

Brighter Thinking

MW00782852

The Making of Modern Britain, 1951–2007

A/AS Level History for AQA Student Book

David Dutton, Lucien Jenkins and Richard Kerridge

Series Editors: Michael Fordham and David Smith

CAMBRIDGE
UNIVERSITY PRESS

University Printing House, Cambridge CB2 8BS, United Kingdom

Cambridge University Press is part of the University of Cambridge.

It furthers the University's mission by disseminating knowledge in the pursuit of education, learning and research at the highest international levels of excellence.

www.cambridge.org
Information on this title: www.cambridge.org/9781107573086 (Paperback)
www.cambridge.org/9781107573130 (Cambridge Elevate enhanced edition)

First published 2016
First edition 2016

A catalogue record for this publication is available from the British Library

ISBN 9781107573086 Paperback
ISBN 9781107573130 Cambridge Elevate enhanced edition

Additional resources for this publication at www.cambridge.org/education

This textbook has been approved by AQA for use with our qualification. This means that we have checked that it broadly covers the specification and we are satisfied with the overall quality. Full details of our approval process can be found on our website.

We approve textbooks because we know how important it is for teachers and students to have the right resources to support their teaching and learning. Please note, however, that the publisher is ultimately responsible for the editorial control and quality of this book.

Please note that when teaching the course, you must refer to AQA's specification as your definitive source of information. While this book has been written to match the specification, it cannot provide complete coverage of every aspect of the course.

A wide range of other useful resources can be found on the relevant subject pages of our website: www.aqa.org.uk

Contents

About this Series

Cambridge A/AS Level History for AQA is an exciting new series designed to support students in their journey from GCSE to A Level and then on to possible further historical study. The books provide the knowledge, concepts and skills needed for the two-year AQA History A-Level course, but it is our intention as series editors that students recognise that their A-Level exams are just one step on to a potential lifelong relationship with the discipline of history. The book is thus littered with further readings, extracts from historians' works and links to wider questions and ideas that go beyond the scope of an A-Level course. With this series, we have sought to ensure not only that the students are well prepared for their examinations, but also that they gain access to a wider debate that characterises historical study.

The series is designed to provide clear and effective support for students as they make the adjustment from GCSE to A Level, and also for teachers, especially those who are not familiar with teaching a two-year linear course. The student books cover the AQA specifications for both AS and A Level. They are intended to appeal to the broadest range of students, and they offer not only challenge to stretch the top end but also additional support for those who need it. Every author in this series is an experienced historian or history teacher, and all have great skill both in conveying narratives to readers and asking the kinds of questions that pull those narratives apart.

In addition to quality prose, this series also makes extensive use of textual primary sources, maps, diagrams and images, and offers a wide range of activities to encourage students to address historical questions of cause, consequence, change and continuity. Throughout the books there are opportunities to critique the interpretations of other historians, and to use those interpretations in the construction of students' own accounts of the past. The series aims to ease the transition for those students who move on from A Level to undergraduate study, and the books are written in an engaging style that will encourage those who want to explore the subject further.

Icons used within this book include:

- Key terms
- Speak like a historian
- Voices from the past/Hidden voices
- Practice essay questions
- Taking it further
- Thematic links
- Chapter summary

About Cambridge Elevate

Cambridge Elevate is the platform which hosts a digital version of this Student Book. If you have access to this digital version you can annotate different parts of the book, send and receive messages to and from your teacher and insert weblinks, among other things.

We hope that you enjoy your AS or A Level History course, as well as this book, and wish you well for the journey ahead.

Michael Fordham and David L. Smith
Series editors

Introduction

This book covers just over half a century of British history. Yet the ever-increasing pace of change means that the Britain of 1951 was very unlike that of 2007 or 2016. The differences are apparent at many levels. Britain in 1951 still looked upon itself, and was widely regarded by others, as the third greatest country on the planet, outranked only by the two superpowers, the United States of America and the Soviet Union. Still glorying in its status as a victor in the Second World War, Britain's Empire remained a reality. The country was still one of the world's leading industrial powers. Britain counted. Not that times were easy – at least by the standards of the 21st century. The War may have been over for six years, but the years of post-war austerity persisted and rationing was still in force as the new Conservative government took office at the end of 1951. Many of the things we now take for granted in our everyday lives were either unheard of, or cherished rarities. Only a minority of homes boasted a television (just one channel, of course). Cars, washing machines and refrigerators were the preserve of the comfortably off middle class. The world of personal computers, smartphones and tablets lay not so much in the distance, as in the realms of a science fiction future. And in 1951 no one would have described Britain as a multicultural society.

So, there is a basic paradox about the half-century covered in these pages. While Britain has slipped steadily down the international league table, its citizens have become richer and more comfortable. That is because the country's decline has been 'relative' and not 'absolute'. Britain has progressed, but several other countries have progressed faster and, in the process, overtaken Britain. This book seeks to guide you, the student, through a period of kaleidoscopic change. Its approach is broad. We consider the country's domestic history and its role in the wider world. We look at the high politics of the period, but we also consider social and economic developments and how they affected ordinary people. Inevitably, we have been faced by problems of compression. There is so much history to cover within the limited number of pages available. On occasion, no doubt, our judgements are too stark and insufficiently nuanced. We hope that you will do something to correct this, through further reading and discussion.

It was once usual to describe all history since 1945 as 'post-War history'. But, to continue using this term would be lazy, unimaginative and unhelpful. There had to come a time when the Second World War would be an inappropriate baseline of historical enquiry! Perhaps it is more appropriate to divide the period under review into two, almost equal, halves: 1951–79 and 1979–2007. In the first half, British governments, both Conservative and Labour, sought to develop and consolidate an essentially social democratic settlement that had grown out of the War. That settlement was based on an interventionist state and a managed economy, its founding fathers the civil servant William Beveridge and the economist John Maynard Keynes. After 1979, much of that settlement was dismantled. The policy-making elite lost much of their confidence in the beneficent effects of an interventionist state; Keynesian economics surrendered much of its authority. Again, both Conservative and Labour governments played their part in this process. In many ways the post-1979 era saw a return to ideas that had been popular in the pre-war period and even during the 19th century. The terminal date of this book – 2007 – is perhaps appropriate. The international financial crisis of the following year may yet come to be seen as the starting point of another new era, with its own distinctive ideas and priorities.

The politics of the years 1951 to 1979 were distinctly different from those of 1979 to 2007 in another way that provides further justification for sub-dividing our period in two. In the general election of 1951 almost 97% of those who cast a vote gave their support to the Conservative and Labour parties. By 2005 that figure had dropped to under 68%. Not only had there been a revival in the fortunes of the once formidable Liberal party, now renamed the Liberal Democrats, there had also been a decline in the concept of United Kingdom politics. Notwithstanding some ups and downs, the rise of nationalism in Scotland and Wales could not be ignored, while the Unionists in Northern Ireland had become a force in their own right, no longer a political appendage of the Conservatives.

It is in no way to denigrate the importance of studying earlier periods of history to suggest that the recent past has obvious attractions, in terms of helping us to understand the world in which we now live. But, as history comes ever closer to the present day, it poses particular problems of which the student must be aware. In studying the most recent past, the historian must show more than usual caution and humility. All historical judgements are provisional, as each generation reinterprets the past in the light of its own beliefs and preoccupations. Inevitably, this process can only be at its beginning when, as is the case with the latter part of this book, less than one generation has elapsed since the events being considered. For example, Britain's military intervention in Afghanistan and Iraq is seen in a different light in 2016 from that which existed immediately after the rapid collapse of the Taliban and of Saddam Hussein's regime. But that does not end matters. The much-delayed Chilcot Report on the Iraq War, likely to change perspectives on Britain's participation, may well appear before the publication of this book. Interpretations will probably change again, depending on the way the long-term struggle against Islamic extremism eventually plays out. Similarly, Gordon Brown's ten-year stewardship of the Exchequer, widely praised at the time, inevitably looks less impressive following the world financial crisis of 2008 and the resulting years of painful austerity. Likewise, Tony Blair's impact on the Labour Party, once judged irreversible, has taken on a different complexion with the election of Jeremy Corbyn to the party leadership in 2015. The recent past is best seen as an ongoing process, rather than a clearly defined period of history with a beginning and a known end. Writing history from 'within' can be particularly difficult. Are the problems of Northern Ireland definitively over? What will be the ultimate outcome of Britain's troubled relationship with the European Union?

It is also important to bear in mind that 'contemporary history' will generally have been written by people who lived through the period themselves. That experience is likely to create strongly held opinions and interpretations which, notwithstanding a correct professional aspiration for objectivity, it is often difficult to dislodge at a later date, even in the face of compelling new evidence that points in a different direction. Put simply, those writing about Margaret Thatcher are more likely to feel 'involved' than those charting the career of Benjamin Disraeli. Furthermore, the documentary evidence, upon which historical assessment is rightly based, will inevitably grow as time passes. The vast majority of government documents are not normally available for historical inspection until after the passage of 30 years. Academic historians are sometimes said to be judged by the quality of their footnotes. Those who chronicle the most recent past must often restrict themselves to such enigmatic references as 'private information', or 'the testimony of a senior [unnamed] minister'.

Recognise then that you are participating in – and contributing to – an ongoing process. We hope you find it a rewarding experience.

PART 1: BUILDING A NEW BRITAIN, 1951–1979

1 The Affluent Society, 1951–1964

In this section we will study the developing affluence of British society between 1951 and 1964. We will look into:

- Conservative governments and reasons for their political dominance: Churchill, Eden, Macmillan and Douglas-Home as political leaders; domestic policies; internal Labour divisions; reasons for Conservatives' fall from power.
- Economic developments: post-war boom; balance of payments issues and 'stop-go' policies.
- Social developments: rising living standards; the impact of affluence and consumerism; changing social attitudes and tensions; class and 'the Establishment'; the position of women; attitudes to immigration; racial violence; the emergence of the 'teenager' and youth culture.
- Foreign relations: EFTA and attempts to join the EEC; relations with, and policies towards, USA and USSR; debates over the nuclear deterrent; Korean War; Suez; the 'Winds of Change' and decolonisation.

Conservative governments and reasons for political dominance

Churchill, Eden, Macmillan and Douglas-Home as political leaders

Electoral Politics

At first sight the general election of October 1951 offered a slender foundation for 13 years of Conservative rule. The party and its allies secured a narrow margin (17 seats) over all other parties combined. Yet the victory was very much a function of Britain's **first-past-the-post electoral system** and a demonstration of the distortions of the popular will it can create. The Labour Party had received 13.95 million votes, nearly a quarter of a million more than the Conservatives. Indeed, seen in historical perspective, 1951 was something of a Labour triumph, even though they lost office. The party's 48.8% of the vote was a higher proportion than ever before – or since. The improved Conservative performance, since the last election in February 1950, essentially resulted from a reduction in the number of Liberal candidates and the Conservatives' success in capturing the support of former Liberal voters. The contemporary belief in the 'natural swing' of the electoral pendulum – a movement in one party's favour would normally be corrected at the next election – suggested that the Conservatives would be a one-term government, with Labour returning to power within four or five years. Having joined Churchill's wartime coalition back in 1940, several Labour figures had been in office continuously for more than a decade and welcomed a period of comparative rest. Hugh Dalton, a former Labour Chancellor, described the election's outcome as 'wonderful'.[1]

The Conservatives, however, defied the 'natural swing' theory and went on to strengthen their parliamentary position. In May 1955 they increased their majority to 60 and then, in October 1959, increased it again to 100. This electoral performance was unique in 20th century history. Indeed, so baffled were many observers by the developing political landscape, that they devised a new theory to explain it. Experts wrote of the 'embourgeoisement' of the electorate, which meant that more people in an increasingly prosperous society aspired to, and reached, the status of 'middle class'. They then took on the habits and characteristics of their new class, including a tendency to vote Conservative.

The embourgeoisement thesis, if valid, was, of course, very bad news for Labour. Assuming that the country would generally continue to grow richer, the size of Labour's **core vote** from the manual working class was likely to diminish, and Labour might never again be able to form a government. But the thesis is crude and lost much of its credibility after Labour returned to power in 1964. Furthermore, class-based voting has become less conspicuous in recent decades. Nonetheless, statistics do reveal a long-term decline in the Labour vote and the evidence suggests that the party is most likely to succeed at the polls when, as under Tony Blair, it pitches its appeal beyond its 'natural' supporters.

During the 13 years of Conservative government, the party had four different Prime Ministers. All came from the upper reaches of British society and were in the long-standing tradition of Tory paternalism.

ACTIVITY 1.1

As you work through this chapter, create a set of parallel timelines to chart who was Prime Minister, Chancellor of the Exchequer and Foreign Secretary at any given time. You may like to add a fourth line/column for notes of other key personalities.

Key terms

first-past-the-post electoral system: voting system whereby the individual who tops the poll in each constituency is elected and no account is taken of the percentage of the poll secured by each party in the region or country as a whole.

core vote: that section of the electorate upon which a party can reliably count for support, often associated with a particular class or social group.

Speak like a historian

D. Butler and D. Stokes

From their book *Political Change in Britain*.

Particularly in the wake of the Conservatives' third successive victory in 1959 it was thought that middle-class consumption levels might be eroding the industrial worker's identification with the working class and, with it, his commitment to the Labour Party … The collapse of Conservative strength in the early 1960s dealt a rude blow to the embourgeoisement hypothesis.[2]

Discussion points

1. Does this analysis match your own understanding of the electoral politics of this period?
2. Is the final sentence in the extract wholly convincing, or should it be qualified?

The political leaders

Winston Churchill (1874–1965) was born in Blenheim Palace, and was a grandson of the 7th Duke of Marlborough. He was 76 years of age when he came to office, and not in good health. Some have suggested that he was unfit to resume the reins of government. However, Anthony Seldon, in his pioneering study *Churchill's Indian Summer* (1981), based largely on the oral testimony of surviving contemporaries, produced a nuanced and convincing picture. Churchill, Seldon suggests, proved a relatively successful Prime Minister, at least until a severe stroke in June 1953. The key to his success was his willingness to delegate, while reserving his energies for the fields of foreign and defence policy where he felt most engaged. In his early career Churchill had been a reforming Liberal. Since then his views had undoubtedly moved significantly to the right, partly because of his innate anti-socialism. However, his choice of ministers in 1951 suggested a readiness to accept a form of Conservatism that placed his party firmly in the political centre ground.

Anthony Eden (1895–1977) came from the minor aristocracy of northern England. After a career dominated by overseas policy (he had served three times as Foreign Secretary), his views on domestic politics were not easily discerned. He had given some support to Butler's repositioning of Conservative policy in the late 1940s and was widely associated with, though he had not coined, the progressive-sounding phrase 'a property-owning democracy'. Ironically, his premiership hit the rocks over an issue of foreign policy (the Suez Crisis) where he was supposed to have unrivalled expertise. Even so, his period as Prime Minister offers little evidence of any desire to challenge the moderate Conservatism of his senior colleagues.

Harold Macmillan (1894–1986) was of humbler birth, a member of the celebrated publishing family, who improved his social status by marrying a daughter of the Duke of Devonshire, delighting in his newly acquired aristocratic credentials. He had cut his political teeth in the 1920s and 1930s as MP for the working-class constituency of Stockton-on-Tees. Few Conservatives of his generation and class had such a good rapport with the less well-off in society. A politician to his fingertips, Macmillan succeeded in taking his party further to the left than any Conservative leader in history. A believer in the power of government to do good for its citizens, he respected the cross-party consensus to keep unemployment low and had no desire to reverse most of the reforms enacted by the Labour governments of 1945–51.

Alec Douglas-Home (1903–95) was genuinely aristocratic: he began his premiership as the 14th Earl of Home, one of the greatest Scottish landowners. He only disclaimed his title under newly enacted legislation in order to resume his Commons career. Douglas-Home's instincts were less interventionist and more sceptical about ever-higher levels of government expenditure than those of his predecessors. However, out of the Commons for more than a decade and with little recent experience of domestic politics, he was never likely to move his party away from the prevailing centrist approach that had held sway since the late 1940s. This was, not least, because he took office as Prime Minister knowing that a general election could not be delayed beyond the autumn of 1964. That said, his government was responsible for one important measure that anticipated the more free market approach of later Conservative leaders. Under Douglas-Home, Resale Price Maintenance, the system whereby manufacturers could fix the price at which their goods were sold to the public, was abolished.

Eden, Macmillan and Home were all products of Eton; Churchill attended Harrow (somewhat unsuccessfully). More significantly, all four sought to locate their party in the centre ground of British politics. Churchill may have nurtured some reactionary views, particularly on social and racial questions; Home may have been more right-wing in general outlook than the other three. However, none showed much evidence of the more overtly ideological right-wing stance of some later Conservative leaders. This was important in helping their party appeal to the sort of centre ground 'swing voter' who usually determines the outcome of British elections.

Domestic policies

Continuity and consensus

The most striking feature of the new government's domestic policies was the absence of abrupt change from those pursued by the outgoing Labour administration. Labour had built their election campaign around the proposition that a Conservative victory would involve the large-scale dismantling of Labour's economic and social achievements. This proved not to be the case. Churchill was never going to be the same sort of dynamic chief executive as during the Second World War. His selection of cabinet ministers was, therefore, of particular importance. Three figures will be considered here: Butler, Macmillan and Monckton.

As Chancellor, Churchill appointed R.A. Butler ('Rab Butler'), a man who held high office (though never the premiership) throughout the Conservatives' 13 years in power. Butler was Conservative MP for Saffron Walden from 1929 to 1965. He enjoyed one of the longest ministerial careers of the 20th century. An unapologetic appeaser, he survived the fall of Neville Chamberlain in 1940 and, as President of the Board of Education 1941–45, was responsible for the Education Act of 1944, which formed the basis of post-war schools policy, including selection at the age of 11. He led the way in modernising Conservative policy in the years 1945–51 and was rewarded with the Exchequer when the Tories returned to government. Twice passed over for the premiership in 1957 and 1963, he held high office as Home Secretary and Foreign Secretary until his party lost office. A strong representative of a compassionate and progressive brand of Conservatism, he probably damaged his chances of the premiership with his notorious indiscretions and a tendency to sit on the fence.

Butler epitomised the moderate, centre ground politics, often referred to as **One Nation Conservatism**, dominant at this time. He had played a leading part in the modernisation of party policy during the years of opposition and was prepared to accept much of the programme enacted by the post-war Labour government. Butler had no intention of creating the full-blooded capitalist economy that critics had anticipated and that was eagerly awaited by figures on the Tory right. Nonetheless, such was the economic crisis that Butler inherited, that he offered his backing when, in 1952, Treasury officials came up with a scheme code-named 'Robot', which would have abandoned the pound's fixed exchange rate, allowing it to find its own level in

Key terms

One Nation Conservatism: the name, appropriated from Disraeli, was used by a small group of new Conservative MPs in 1950 to describe their support for the sort of moderate, reforming Toryism, which encouraged social cohesion and avoided divisive policies. Now used more generally to describe the left wing of the Conservative Party.

the markets. 'Robot' would certainly have led to a significant rise in unemployment and, in the face of strong opposition from other cabinet ministers, it was dropped. This decision was a key moment in setting the tone of 1950s Conservatism. Later, when unemployment did show signs of rising, the government prepared highly interventionist schemes to hold it down. Such measures had hitherto been associated with the political left. In 1955 the monthly average figure of registered unemployed dropped to just 232 000, around 1% of the workforce. Notwithstanding one or two blips, the Conservatives generally managed to contain unemployment within acceptable limits during their time in office.

Nationalisation

One of the key changes enacted by Attlee's government had related to the state's role in running British industry. A large number of public service organisations had come into public ownership, including: the Bank of England (1946); coal (1947); electricity, gas and the railways (1948); and steel (1951). Tory governments of the 1980s and 1990s would return such activities to the **private sector**, but the Conservatives of 1951–64 only tinkered with the dividing line between state and private ownership laid down by Labour. Steel, which had been included in Labour's nationalisation agenda at the behest of the party conference, but against the advice of the leadership, was denationalised (or privatised as we would say today). Returning steel to private hands proved relatively uncontroversial and the Conservatives also managed to find buyers for part of the road haulage industry, but denationalisation went no further. Here lies strong evidence that the Conservative leadership now accepted the notion of the 'mixed economy' – the idea that, alongside a flourishing private sector, government should have responsibility for running other industries, particularly the utilities and natural monopolies which might struggle to create profits in the marketplace, but which were vital in the life of the nation.

Butskellism

It was not surprising that, in 1954, sensing an essential continuity between Butler and his Labour predecessor, Hugh Gaitskell, the *Economist* invented the composite figure Mr Butskell, combining the names of the two chancellors. The concept of 'Butskellism' has been at the heart of a historiographical debate over the existence at this time of a **political consensus** between the leading parties. Butler and Gaitskell were not identical in their policies and objectives. As we have seen, Butler backed the 'Robot' plan. Gaitskell was readier than Butler to use the annual budget as an instrument of economic control and the two men had different long-term visions of how wealth should be distributed. Some writers have gone further and suggested that circumstances, rather than conviction, underlay the move towards consensus. The Conservative reluctance to initiate major changes was probably due to their narrow 1951 victory; to their realisation that they had made few inroads into Labour's core working-class vote; and to a determination to dispel fears of any significant reversal of the popular achievements Labour had highlighted in their 1951 campaign. However, if 'consensus' is taken to imply a broad measure of agreement about the way Britain should be run, based on a mixed economy and **Keynesian** demand management, it remains a useful tool of historical analysis. Certainly, there is a marked contrast with the far more polarised stances taken up by Labour and the Conservatives in the 1970s and 1980s.

Housing

Churchill installed Harold Macmillan at the Ministry of Housing – something of a poisoned chalice. Churchill had ambitiously promised that a Tory administration would build 300 000 houses in a single year. If he fulfilled it, Macmillan's standing in the party would be considerably strengthened; if he failed, his political career might be over. In the event the target was reached in 1953, leaving Macmillan set fair for ministerial promotion. 'You were disappointed at the time [of appointment]', Churchill later reminded Macmillan, 'but it made you P.M.'[3]

Key terms

private sector: that part of the economy that is owned and run by private interests, rather than the state, usually along capitalist lines.

political consensus: significant overlap, or similarity, in the policies of the leading parties (or, more usually, their leaders) producing a noticeable continuity in governmental practice.

Keynesian economics: economic theory based on the writings of the Cambridge economist, J.M. Keynes, which dominated thinking from the Second World War until the 1970s. In essence, it involves a belief that government should use economic policy to iron out the fluctuations of the market, in order to control the level of employment and maximise productive efficiency. Regulating demand can encourage growth when necessary, or hold it back when there is danger of the economy overheating.

Voices from the past

Richard Crossman

Richard Crossman was Labour MP for Coventry East.

[Boothby] and Junor both described Lyttelton's anger at being fobbed off with the Colonies, and Boothby said, 'Rab Butler Chancellor! Why, that's Gaitskell all over again, but from Cambridge.' … the real free enterprisers and deflationists seem to have been kept out and there is a good deal in the view that the general make-up of the Churchill Cabinet means that it will be only very slightly to the right of the most recent Attlee Cabinet. Just as Attlee was running what was virtually a coalition policy on a Party basis, so Churchill may well do the same.[4]

Diary, 31 October 1951.

Discussion points

1. What does this extract add to the debate about a political consensus in 1950s Britain?
2. How important is the political stance of the diary writer?
3. How does this extract relate to the concept of 'Butskellism'?

Again, Conservative and Labour policies were not identical. The former stressed the private sector's role in building the required homes; the latter favoured public provision and wanted to protect tenants from exploitation in the private rented sector. The Tories' Rent Act (1957) showed a clear division of purpose in lifting controls over the rents of 400 000 houses, provoking angry Labour opposition. In general, however, Conservative housing policy was part of a humane concern for the needs of the people that characterised their economic and social policies at this time. Important progress was made in the field of slum clearance, though much remained to be done by the time the Conservatives lost office.

Figure 1.1: Some of the 'improvements' planned, and some that were achieved, paid too much attention to the ideas of architects and planners, in terms of high-rise accommodation and the destruction of existing communities, at the expense of the wishes of the citizens directly affected.

Industrial relations

Churchill's third key appointment in 1951 was of Walter Monckton to the Ministry of Labour (a government department more recently known as Employment and, currently, Work and Pensions). In opposition the Conservative spokesman, David Maxwell-Fyfe, had hinted that his party would introduce legislation limiting trade union power. Such a confrontational stance was, however, not part of Monckton's brief. Instead, he consistently tried to bring the two sides of industry together and to avoid strike action. The price of such harmony was often paid by granting inflationary pay awards. Later Conservatives would be highly critical of Monckton's non-confrontational way of kicking a major problem into the political long grass. Nevertheless, Monckton's ability to maintain industrial peace won him the nickname of the 'oilcan', lubricating away potential strife. Those who feared that his spilt oil would create a slippery slope towards economic decline were, as yet, a minority.

Health and education

Labour's creation of the National Health Service (NHS) in 1948 had probably been its single most important domestic achievement. It remains the country's most popular institution and its founding principle, that healthcare should be available to all, free at the point of use, is deeply entrenched in the national psyche. Again, Labour argued that a Conservative government would lead to the erosion, if not the dismantling, of Labour's creation. True, in his first budget, Butler was obliged to introduce some health service charges, but the 'free at the point of use' principle had already been breached by Labour in 1951 in relation to false teeth and spectacles. Reporting in 1956, the Guillebaud Committee concluded that the NHS provided good value for money and urged additional funding. The government accepted these findings. As the economy strengthened, the Conservatives actually increased spending on the social services, including the NHS. Total NHS spending roughly doubled between 1951 and 1962. Successive Tory Ministers of Health successfully buried the notion that they wished to destroy what Labour had built. Then, in the early 1960s, Health Minister Enoch Powell embarked on an ambitious programme of hospital building. Meanwhile, education seemed likely to be a further illustration of broad consensus between the parties, as the Tories continued to implement the provisions of the wartime Butler Education Act (1944). Gradually, however, the divisive effects of segregation at the age of 11 and the poor performance of many secondary modern schools persuaded many in the Labour Party that a comprehensive system was the way forward.

Labour divisions

The Conservatives' policies together with growing popular affluence consolidated the party's position in the electorate's esteem. Typical floating voters saw little reason for transferring their allegiance elsewhere. The Liberals were now little more than a fringe party while for Labour, despite its strong 1951 electoral performance, the following decade was a troubled time. Beset by internal difficulties, it seldom looked convincing as a government-in-waiting. Its problems began, in the dying days of the Labour government, with the resignation of three ministers, Aneurin Bevan, Harold Wilson and John Freeman, over the introduction of NHS charges. Consequently, the early 1950s were dominated by ongoing struggles between the party's left and right wings. Labour conferences witnessed bitter disputes over the movement's soul and future direction. Douglas Jay remembered the 1952 gathering in Morecambe as 'one of the most unpleasant experiences I ever suffered in the Labour Party. The town was ugly, the hotels forbidding, the weather bad, and the Conference, at its worst, hideous.'[5] No agreement existed over the party's way forward. Should the **'socialist'** achievements of 1945–51, particularly the nationalisation programme, be savoured and consolidated, or seen merely as the first step towards a genuinely socialist state? In addition, the left was irritated by Labour's failure to articulate a foreign policy recognisably different from that of the Tories and called for a socialist alternative, although it was never entirely clear what this entailed.

Internal divisions largely determined the changes in the party's leadership during this period. Attlee remained leader until 1955, primarily to thwart the ambitions of his deputy, Herbert Morrison, and of the left-winger, Bevan. He enjoyed some success in keeping a lid on Labour's internal dissension. By the time of the 1955 general election, however, Attlee was 72 years old and unconvincing as an alternative Prime Minister, especially as the Conservatives were now led by the popular and relatively youthful Eden. When Attlee finally stepped down, after two decades at the helm, he was succeeded by Hugh Gaitskell. However, Gaitskell, a man of genuine intellectual ability and political integrity, was unequivocally associated with a faction within the party – its right wing. Many on the left hated him. His leadership was therefore characterised, notwithstanding a personal reconciliation with Bevan, by renewed conflict, particularly over nuclear disarmament and **Clause IV**. The issue of nuclear weapons is covered in more detail in the section on 'The nuclear deterrent' towards the end of this chapter.

Labour entered the 1959 general election campaign with some confidence. However, any hope of victory was lost when the party committed itself to a number of expenditure pledges, such as a rise in the basic state pension, while insisting that these would not necessitate an increase in general taxation. Not for the last time, Labour's electoral prospects were thwarted by its economic policy's lack of credibility.

ACTIVITY 1.2

Draw a Venn diagram to summarise the ways in which Conservative policies after 1951 overlapped with previous Labour policies. Using information here and from your own research, identify where the Conservative government rejected previous Labour policies, and/or initiated its own. Can you explain why they might have done this?

Key terms

Socialism: a political philosophy holding that economic activity should be communally owned and geared towards the needs of society as a whole, rather than the individual. In the British tradition the necessary transformation has generally been seen as a gradualist, rather than revolutionary, process.

Clause IV: a clause in the Labour Party constitution that committed Labour to the common ownership of the means of production, distribution and exchange – in other words, the progressive nationalisation of British industry.

It remains doubtful whether Gaitskell could ever have fully united his party and this may have remained an insuperable barrier to Labour's return to power. In the event, the dilemma was removed by his sudden, unexpected and premature death in January 1963. In choosing Harold Wilson as his successor, rather than the able, but erratic and unpredictable, George Brown, the party laid the foundation of its own electoral salvation. Wilson's particular skill was to unite Labour's contending factions. His credentials as a man of the left were hard to dispute, not least because of his association with Bevan, but his policies were of the centre ground and he attracted considerable support from the right. Rather like Tony Blair in the 1990s, Wilson understood that, to win elections, Labour needed to appeal far beyond its core vote. For perhaps the first time since 1951, Labour seemed ready to return to government, especially when Wilson found himself opposed after October 1963 by the aristocratic Douglas-Home. Wilson appeared dynamic and progressive, embracing the modern world and its challenges – some even likened him to the American President, John F. Kennedy – in contrast to the Conservatives' ex-earl, whose public image remained stubbornly one of privilege and the grouse moor.

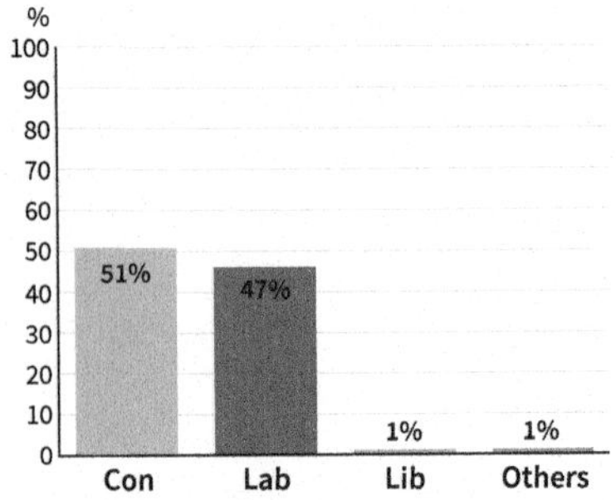

Figure 1.2: Seats in the House of Commons won in the 1951 British general election; percentages have been adjusted to the nearest whole number. Ulster Unionist figures are included in Conservative totals.

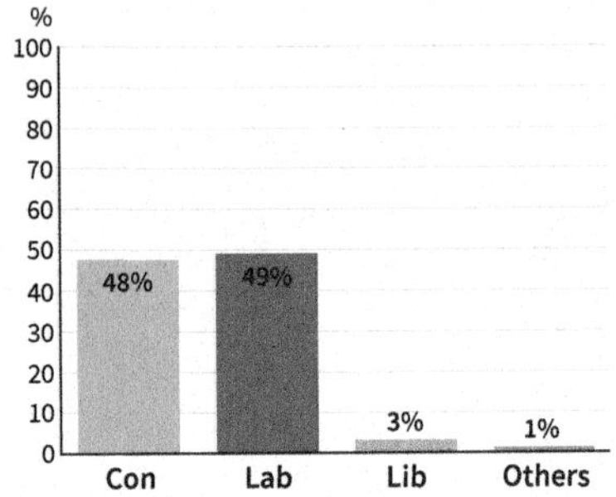

Figure 1.3: Votes won in the 1951 British general election; percentages have been adjusted to the nearest whole number. Ulster Unionist figures are included in Conservative totals.

The Conservatives in decline

In a democracy there is a natural tendency, over time, for the electorate to opt for change. It would have been an astonishing achievement for the Conservatives to have secured a fourth successive victory in 1964. 'I fear the truth is that after ten years of unparalleled prosperity, the people are bored', judged Macmillan in March 1962.[6] But, if we accept that the period of Tory rule was coming to its natural end, a number of other factors, in addition to Labour's new-found credibility, contributed to the government's defeat. In the first instance, the early 1960s witnessed problems with a number of the government's policies. Most importantly, its reputation for economic competence came into question. The government seemed unable to combine economic growth with stable prices. Repeated **balance of payments** crises afforded a clear indication that Britain was failing to pay its way in the world. Signs that the economy was overheating obliged the government to apply the brakes with deflationary measures, such as increases in the **bank rate** and restrictions on hire-purchase. This became particularly characteristic of the Chancellorship of Selwyn Lloyd (1960–62), when commentators wrote of an era of 'stop-go'. Lloyd was dismissed alongside a third of the cabinet in Macmillan's infamous 'Night of the Long Knives' in July 1962. The Prime Minister, renowned for his unflappability – the resignations of the Treasury team in 1958 had been passed off as 'little local difficulties' – had been panicked into a desperate attempt to revitalise the government's image. Increasingly, however, it was Macmillan himself, out of touch with the modern world, who appeared to have exceeded his shelf life, an impression which intensified once Harold Wilson assumed the Labour leadership. Macmillan found himself being ridiculed in a new wave of satire on the stage and television, something that would have been unthinkable only a few years before.

Macmillan suffered a very personal policy setback when General de Gaulle, the French president, vetoed Britain's first application to join the European Economic Community (EEC) in January 1963. The Prime Minister viewed British membership as essential to maintaining the country's position on the world stage and, arguably, he never recovered his personal authority thereafter. In 1960 the Blue Streak missile, designed to take Britain's independent nuclear deterrent into the next generation, was cancelled. Macmillan then had to go cap in hand to President Kennedy to secure an American-built alternative – in many ways a striking illustration of the Prime Minister's adroit diplomacy, but it cast further doubts over the country's international standing. In 1951 Britain had been unequivocally recognised as the world's third greatest power, behind only the United States and Soviet Russia. By the early 1960s this status was far less certain.

Key terms

balance of payments: the relationship between the value of a country's exports and imports, measured in terms of goods and services. A 'favourable balance' is achieved if the value of exports exceeds that of imports.

bank rate: the rate of interest at which the Bank of England lends money, which in turn determines the rate at which the high street banks lend to the public. Increasingly used in the 1960s to cool an overheating economy.

If these policy setbacks were essentially of the government's own making, in other respects it was the victim of sheer bad luck. The early 1960s saw Britain rattled by a succession of spy and sex scandals that had little to do with the government's competence, or lack of it, but which, cumulatively, helped undermine its position. The Vassall case in 1962 involved a homosexual British spy linked with a junior minister. The latter was obliged to resign. Allegations of a relationship between the two men were, in fact, unfounded. More serious was the case of John Profumo, Macmillan's Minister of War, caught up in a seamy tale of high society sex, centred on the activities of the prostitute Christine Keeler. Profumo's indiscretions were compounded by the fact that Keeler was also in a relationship with Captain Ivanov, an official at the Soviet embassy, which raised the possibility of a breach of national security, and by the minister's denial in parliament of any impropriety. Profumo's career came to an abrupt end and the Prime Minister was also damaged by his readiness to accept Profumo's word as that of a gentleman and by his, somewhat pathetic, excuse that he did not 'live among young people'.[7]

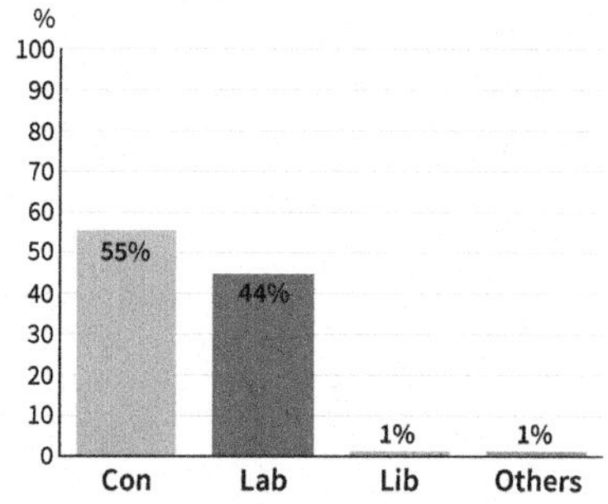

Figure 1.4: Seats in the House of Commons won in the 1955 British general election; percentages have been adjusted to the nearest whole number. Ulster Unionist figures are included in Conservative totals.

Even the circumstances surrounding Macmillan's own resignation and replacement inflicted damage upon his party. He could not be blamed for the sudden (but, as it turned out, far from terminal) illness which struck him down in October 1963. His successor, Douglas-Home, was widely seen to lack legitimacy, not just because he had to be plucked from relative obscurity in the House of Lords, but because of the behind-the-scenes manoeuvres preceding his 'emergence' as Conservative leader. Two senior ministers, Iain Macleod and Enoch Powell, refused to serve under Home. The former penned a devastating indictment in the *Spectator* of how the ailing Macmillan had orchestrated the succession from his sickbed. Unsurprisingly, Home was the last Conservative leader chosen by the 'customary processes', in which informal soundings within the party led to the choice of a new leader, without recourse to a formal election. All his successors have gained the leadership after some form of election.

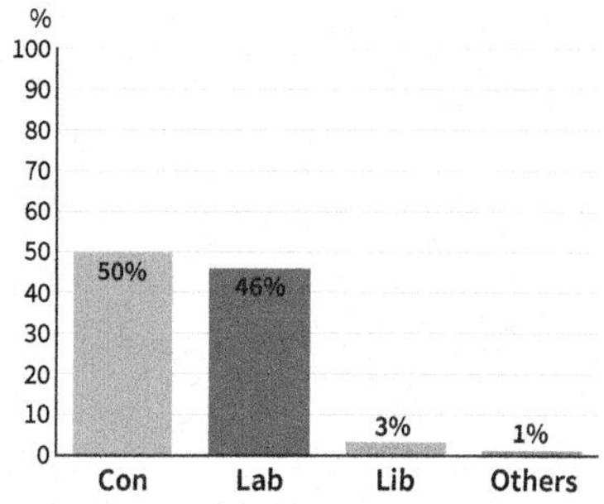

Figure 1.5: Votes won in the 1955 British general election; percentages have been adjusted to the nearest whole number. Ulster Unionist figures are included in Conservative totals.

'How we can be expected in 1964 to go forward to victory under the 14th Earl of Home passes all understanding'.[8] So judged Paul Channon, Parliamentary Private Secretary to R.A. Butler. In all the circumstances, Douglas-Home did surprisingly well in taking his party tantalisingly close to a fourth successive triumph. He was frequently wrong-footed in the Commons by the intellectually nimble Wilson, was hampered by the way he looked on television (even his make-up artist despaired of him), acknowledged his own relative incompetence when it came to economics and was inept in dealing with a hostile audience on the **hustings**. Yet Douglas-Home's defeat was by the narrowest of margins. Indeed, it has been calculated that as few as 900 extra votes, perfectly distributed through key marginal constituencies, could have produced a Conservative win. Labour's vote share scarcely improved from 1959. The party squeezed back into government on the basis of Tory votes lost to the Liberals – something of a reversal of what had happened in 1951. Whatever his defects, and they were fairly obvious, Douglas-Home came across as straightforward and honest. It must be concluded that under his leadership the Conservatives enjoyed a partial recovery from the low point reached by the end of Macmillan's premiership.

> **Key terms**
>
> **hustings:** literally, the platform from which a candidate gives his election address. Now used more generally to describe election campaign activity.
>
> **New Right:** term used to describe those Conservatives who followed Margaret Thatcher and Keith Joseph in their belief that the party should abandon much of the post-war settlement and re-establish its free market, small state credentials, giving priority to the elimination of inflation, even if this meant higher unemployment.

Economic developments

The post-war boom

The economic history of the Conservative governments has aroused debate and controversy. For many the 1950s were something of a golden age, to be looked back on with nostalgia and affection, the beginning of a post-war boom that lasted until the oil price shock of the 1970s. This period saw unprecedented rises in living standards and lifestyle changes that materially improved the lot of millions of ordinary people. Others, particularly of the **New Right** of the 1970s and 1980s, criticised the Conservative governments of 1951–64 for accepting Labour's post-war settlement and complacently presiding over an economy beset by underlying problems. Mounting

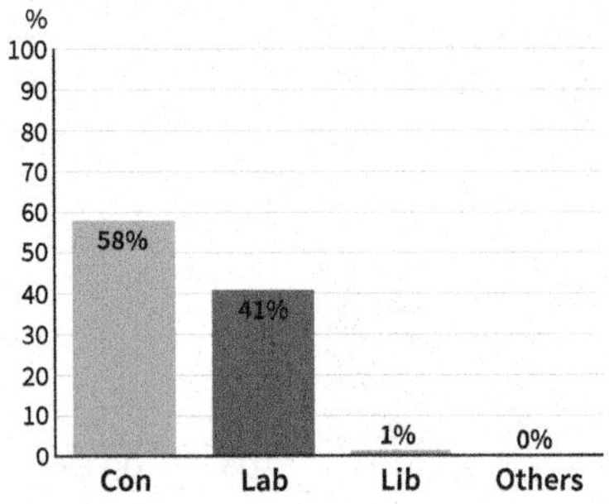

Figure 1.6: Seats in the House of Commons won in the 1959 British general election; percentages have been adjusted to the nearest whole number. Ulster Unionist figures are included in Conservative totals.

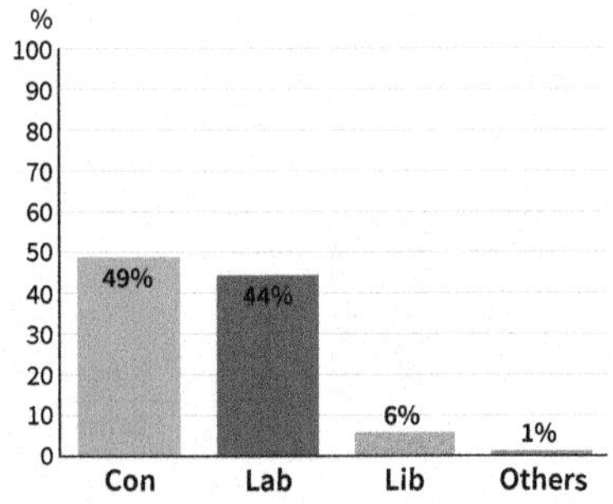

Figure 1.7: Votes won in the 1959 British general election; percentages have been adjusted to the nearest whole number. Ulster Unionist figures are included in Conservative totals.

inflation, insufficient investment, low productivity, antiquated industrial relations and an overvalued pound sterling were not tackled, but swept under the carpet, rendering more difficult the task of a later generation facing an inevitable day of reckoning. Successive governments misdirected the nation's wealth into short-term **consumerism** at the expense of the long-term reconstruction of British industry. Both interpretations are too extreme; but each contains more than an element of truth. Kevin Jefferys has written intriguingly of the 'paradoxical relationship between affluence and "economic decline"'.[9]

Given the bankrupt state of the British economy in 1945 after six years of warfare, compounded thereafter by the costs of reconstruction, the Labour governments of 1945–51 could claim almost heroic achievements. If the 'New Jerusalem'[10] had yet to be fully realised, Labour had still managed to create the Welfare State, maintain full employment and uphold a significant role on the world stage. Nonetheless, it would be hard to deny that the Conservatives' inheritance was an unenviable one. Defence spending had risen alarmingly with involvement in the Korean War and the new government's first months in office were overshadowed by a balance of payments crisis, judged by the Chancellor as more serious than any since the end of the War. In such circumstances, with the currency under pressure and a formal **devaluation** a real possibility, ministers were forced to consider the Treasury's drastic 'Robot' remedies.

By the end of 1952, however, the situation was improving quite markedly. The end of the Korean War in 1953 led to a dramatic fall in world raw material prices. This, in turn, produced a favourable transformation in Britain's 'terms of trade', the relationship between the cost of imports (largely raw materials) and the value of exports (mostly manufactured goods), which enabled Britain to secure a windfall profit on its trading activities. By 1953 the country could afford to buy 13% more imports by value for the same amount of exports. It thus gained around £400m per annum in extra spending power, as a result of developments in the world economy. The government could claim little credit for this, but it was, inevitably, the electoral beneficiary of these changed circumstances, not least when it could finally end food rationing in 1954. The economic climate favoured both full employment and an expansion of the social services. Eden's personal statement to the electorate in 1955 boasted of a record of positive achievements. 'We have seen new houses and new schools and new factories built and building, and soon we shall see new hospitals too. We have seen the social services extended and improved.'[11] Eden confidently predicted that Britain could now double its standard of living within 25 years.

A minor world recession in 1957–58 was the trigger for a second, if less dramatic, reduction in commodity prices. Luck is an important, sometimes essential, factor in political success and the Conservatives had their share of it in the 1950s.

By this time Macmillan had delivered his famous 'never had it so good' speech.

Problems in the economy

Yet all was not well. The Conservatives seemed incapable of securing a reasonably stable economic climate. The calling of the 1955 general election just days into Eden's premiership partly resulted from his knowing there were harder times just around the corner. After a giveaway budget in the spring, Butler was obliged, by a rapidly deteriorating balance of payments situation, to introduce emergency measures in October to reduce local authority building programmes and increase indirect taxation. Too often, especially during Macmillan's premiership, economic policy appeared to be compromised by blatantly political considerations. The government's 1959 election victory was again partly engineered by a generous spring budget, cutting taxes and increasing capital spending. The mounting cynicism of the electorate towards politics in recent decades has some of its origins in this earlier period.

Key terms

Consumerism: an economic situation founded on the continuing sale and purchase of consumer goods.

devaluation: a formal move taken by government in a period of fixed exchange rates to reduce the value of its currency in relation to those of other countries. It has the practical effect of making exports more competitive. The pound was devalued in this way in 1949 and 1967.

Cross-reference *The Suez Crisis*

Eden gave signs towards the end of his premiership that he understood the need to tackle inflationary trends but, overwhelmed by the Suez Crisis, made no real progress in this direction. Macmillan's first Chancellor, Peter Thorneycroft, soon became concerned about ever-rising government expenditure and the growing risk of **inflation**. Some historians have seen in his warnings an anticipation of the Thatcherite rhetoric of later decades. In January 1957 Thorneycroft told the cabinet that 'for many years we have had the sorry spectacle of a Government which spends too much, drifts into inflation, then seeks to cure the situation by fiscal and budgetary measures. These attempts in turn lead to flagging production, taxes are reduced, and demand is stimulated; but we shrink from the measures necessary to cut expenditure decisively and inflation starts again.'[12] Underlying tension between Chancellor and Prime Minister persisted throughout the year and when in January 1958 Macmillan failed to back his proposed package of spending cuts, Thorneycroft and his two junior ministers resigned.

The next two Chancellors, Derick Heathcoat-Amory and Selwyn Lloyd, shared some of Thorneycroft's concerns but, in the last resort, lacked the political clout to prevail against Macmillan. The latter remained haunted, not by inflation, but by the consequences of deflation, the underuse of resources, in his working-class constituency during the inter-war slump. It was not that Macmillan failed to recognise the dangers of inflation. He was reluctant to admit that, to tackle it, the government might need to accept a significantly higher level of unemployment and the sacrifice of some of the gains in living standards secured since 1945. Yet it was less clear that he had a coherent and credible alternative policy to curb the remorseless rise in prices. Lloyd found it impossible to pursue policies of sustained growth without dangerously overheating the economy. An expansionist budget in 1961 led, only a few months later, to a deflationary package that included a pay pause. This was particularly unpopular with nurses and teachers who enjoyed a substantial measure of public support. With Labour making capital out of the slogan 'stop-go', Lloyd lost his job. Macmillan was no nearer finding a solution to the underlying weaknesses of the national economy. He may have found his last Chancellor, Reginald Maudling, the most congenial, but Maudling's policies did little to tackle long-term difficulties. His so-called 'dash for growth' had the unlooked-for effect of sucking in imports, exacerbating the balance of payments situation and stoking up the fires of future inflation.

By the early 1960s the population struggled to make sense of the national economy. Objectively, many, if not most, were better off than ever before. However, they worried about rising prices and were concerned that they were not as prosperous as

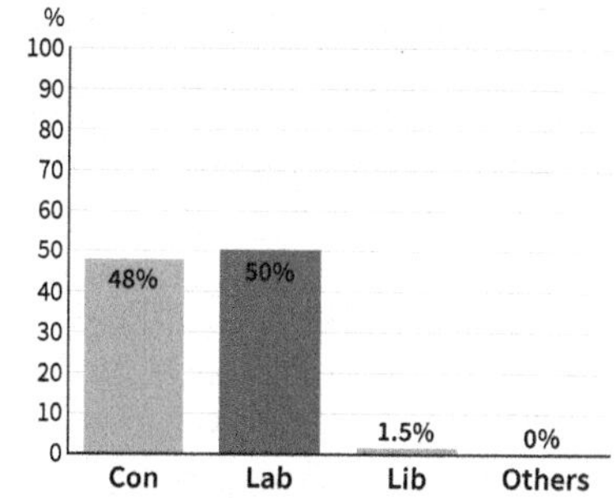

Figure 1.8: Seats in the House of Commons won in the 1964 British general election; percentages have been adjusted to the nearest whole number. Ulster Unionist figures are included in Conservative totals.

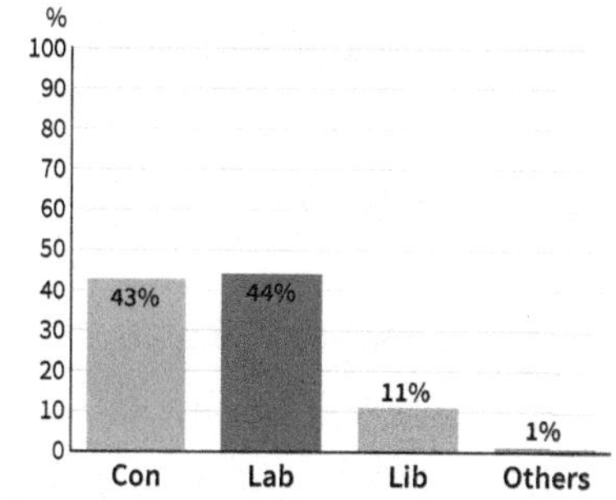

Figure 1.9: Votes won in the 1964 British general election; percentages have been adjusted to the nearest whole number. Ulster Unionist figures are included in Conservative totals.

Voices from the past

Harold Macmillan

This speech, widely remembered for the catchphrase 'never had it so good', was delivered to the voters of Bedford. The full speech makes it clear that he intended to warn of the dangers of complacency. But it was the single phrase that was remembered. Indeed, as far as the majority of British people were concerned, it was true.

Let's be frank about it; most of our people have never had it so good. Go around the country, go to the industrial towns, go to the farms, and you will see a state of prosperity such as we have never had in my lifetime – nor indeed ever in the history of this country. What is beginning to worry some of us is "Is it too good to last?" For, amidst all this prosperity, there is one problem that has troubled us … ever since the war. It's the problem of rising prices.[13]

Discussion point

1. What do you think was the purpose of Macmillan's speech?

they should be. If few voters had actually read Michael Shanks's work *The Stagnant Society*,[14] many more would have been familiar with the book's ominous title. Many were also aware that, in international terms, the country had done less well than some of its competitors and, indeed, might be entering a period of relative decline. The economic performance of France and West Germany, linked in many minds to their founder membership of the EEC, enabled voters to view Britain's economic achievements in a revealing perspective.

A convert to Keynesian economics before these ideas became the prevailing orthodoxy, Macmillan was more committed than any other leading Tory to the goal of full employment and believed that economic policy should be geared to achieving it. As Chancellor (1955–57) and especially Prime Minister (1957–63), Macmillan did more than anyone else to entrench the Conservative Party in the centre ground of British politics, championing growth and full employment even at the price of mounting inflation. Chancellors who questioned his priorities discovered that their tenure of office had limited duration. By the early 1960s the Conservatives were adopting a more interventionist approach to the economy than at any previous time in their history. 'So far as I am concerned', wrote Macmillan to Selwyn Lloyd, 'I have no fear of [greater state direction] because these are the policies that I recommended before the war.'[15] The creation in 1962 of the National Economic Development Council (Neddy) and the National Incomes Commission (Nicky), the introduction of an incomes policy and advocacy of regional policy were all initiatives that might have been expected of a Labour government, introduced now by the Conservatives and backed by the Federation of British Industries.

Key terms

inflation: a process of continual price rises and of the falling value of money, usually measured by the Retail Price Index and, more recently, by the Consumer Prices Index.

ACTIVITY 1.3

Study the election results shown in Figures 1.2–1.9.

Write a short summary explaining what you think happened in these elections.

Social developments

Rising living standards

Despite the problems of government economic policy, the years of Conservative administration were a time of widespread affluence. The celebrated American economist J.K. Galbraith wrote in 1958 of *The Affluent Society* to describe changes taking place across the western world; the pioneering work on Britain, *The Age of Affluence*, edited by Bogdanor and Skidelsky, appeared 12 years later. After the austerity and deprivations of the war years and immediate post-war era, Britain experienced a period of **conspicuous consumption**.

More and more relatively ordinary people could now afford the trappings of what had previously been regarded as a middle-class lifestyle – home ownership, annual holidays (sometimes even abroad), televisions, washing machines and refrigerators. The number of motor cars on Britain's roads went up from 2.5 m in 1951 to 3.3 m in 1955. Over the same period, ownership of televisions grew four-fold to more than four million. Many older people still remember the coronation of Elizabeth II (1953) as their first experience of television, viewed in an atmosphere of amazement and awe on their family's newly acquired set, or on that of a friend or neighbour. Writing in the *Listener* in 1959, Abrams noted that an increasing amount of money was being spent on household goods and that ownership of washing machines had gone up as much as tenfold. '[F]or the first time in modern British history the working-class home, as well as the middle-class home, has become a place that is ... pleasant to live in.'[16]

Hidden voices

In his book ***The Stagnant Society***, subtitled ***A Warning***, Michael Shanks pointed out that Britain's rate of economic growth had been steadily falling behind that achieved by the country's competitors. He suggested that the reasons for this problem were to be found less in economic factors, than in Britain's social structure and way of life. He called for drastic change in the country's industrial and class relations to remove these divisions, which impeded growth and economic efficiency.

If possible, read Shanks's book and assess how convincing you find his arguments.

The impact of affluence and consumerism

Yet Kevin Jefferys cautions against adopting the image of a universally prosperous society.[17] By 1960, although the majority of homes boasted a television, four out of five working-class families still lacked a car, two out of three a washing machine and nearly nine out of ten a refrigerator. The poorest sectors of society still had few material comforts and many northern towns failed to share the advances made further south. For all that, if not everyone now enjoyed the tangible benefits of consumerism, many

Key terms

conspicuous consumption: economic situation in which non-essential goods are being bought in greater numbers and value than is the norm.

more could realistically aspire towards a better lifestyle. The advent of commercial television (1955), with its regular advertisements, fuelled a desire to move up the social ladder, often using the dubious vehicle of **hire-purchase agreements**. If not everyone was yet 'having it so good', many more now believed that they could, and should, improve their lot.

Key terms

hire-purchase agreements: means of buying goods through a series of part-payments over a period of time, generally at a higher overall cost than for ordinary purchase.

It is still common to point to the 1950s as a golden age of social mobility, a time when children of humble birth could rise up the social ladder and achieve a status and prosperity never secured, or even imagined, by their parents. The vehicle for their advance was, of course, the grammar school. Many people were likely to know of someone who had succeeded in this way, even if they had not done so themselves. Yet a focus upon these genuine success stories can obscure, or ignore, the experience of the majority of the population, the roughly 75% whose fate was effectively sealed by selection at age 11. Their subsequent second-class education in a secondary modern school produced career prospects limited to a working life in a factory or, at best, routine office administration. Indeed, in some ways the grammar school tended to confirm, rather than break, the country's existing class structure. Children had a far greater chance of securing a grammar school place if they came from middle-class rather than working-class households. One 1954 report suggested that a third of those children of unskilled or semi-skilled parents, who did succeed in reaching the grammar school – and, therefore, the opportunity of a decisive change in their social status – did not stay on until the sixth form. Their priority, or perhaps their parents' priority, was to leave school, get a job and contribute to the family income.

Changing social attitudes and tensions

Britain in the 1950s remained a society deeply divided along class lines. It was something that any newcomer to this country soon noticed. Middle- and working-class communities remained largely separated – by the jobs they did, the lifestyles they enjoyed, the schools their children attended, the clothes they wore, the pub rooms they frequented and even the language (accents and vocabulary) they used. People would often be classified by their listeners as soon as they opened their mouths. You could discern a person's social standing by knowing whether they ate 'dinner and tea' or 'lunch and dinner/supper'. Nancy Mitford's 1955 attempt to distinguish between 'U' and 'non-U' speech may strike us, six decades on, as quaint and slightly amusing.[18] At the time, however, it reflected a socially partitioned society. Even the nation's sport was partly class-based. Cricketers were divided into 'gentlemen' (amateurs) and 'players' (professionals), the latter referred to only by their surnames. Rugby union and rugby league might appear relatively similar on the pitch, but a huge social chasm separated the two codes' participants and spectators. A lifetime ban might await a union player who ventured into the rival game.

Large numbers of people were overly conscious of their status in society. This meant that broad social groupings tended to be sub-divided, at least in the eyes of those who fell within them. Condescension was a characteristic phenomenon. For many working-class people, asserting that you were somehow 'better' than those beneath you in the social scale was of considerable importance. The temptation to dismiss those deemed to be of a lower order as 'common' was uncomfortably strong. Though objective criteria are not always agreed upon, the 1951 census suggested that around 28% of the population belonged to the middle class, but surveys of the same period which asked individuals to categorise themselves produced figures of 40% or more. Perhaps the explanation for the discrepancy was provided by one housewife, who suggested that 'the chief value of the middle classes is that their way of life represents a standard which the working class can emulate'.[19]

No society is ever entirely static. That said, except in the most turbulent times, change is likely to be incremental, evolutionary, often all but imperceptible. Furthermore, social analysis involves generalisation on a massive scale. Individuals not following a perceived overall trend can be numbered in their millions. However, there is much to be said for David Kynaston's judgement that British society was, indeed, frozen during the decade after 1945 with most people, 'following the shake-up of the war', experiencing 'an instinctive retreat to familiar ways, familiar rituals, familiar relations, all in the context of only very slowly lifting austerity and uncomfortably limited material resources'.[20] The subtext of this assessment is that those factors bringing about significant change in society later in the decade, for example: the emergence of a recognisable youth culture; mass migration from the Commonwealth; higher disposable incomes, did not have a profound impact on early-1950s Britain. The later fifties should be seen as a springboard for the altogether more dynamic decade that would follow.

The majority of the male population was working long hours in British industry. Women were still seen, and largely saw themselves, as 'homemakers'. For leisure, men usually drank in a pub, and more women now did the same, without the social stigma that would have been attached before the War. The cinema, though past its heyday, remained popular. The young still flocked to dance halls, at least before they got married. A bet on a horse offered a frisson of excitement to many mundane lives, though bookmakers' shops remained illegal. A weekly flutter on the football pools offered a safer option. A weekend might be enlivened by a place on the terrace for a man, and perhaps his son, to support the local football team. Those whose wages were sufficient for a small weekly sum to be put away could reap the benefit with an annual week or fortnight's family holiday at the seaside. It all suggests a simpler, less sophisticated, lifestyle than has since become the norm.

Class and the Establishment

Britain's divided society remained overtly hierarchical and often deferential. At the top was the monarchy, deeply respected by most, especially while its private activities remained better protected from public scrutiny than in later decades. Yet, somewhat surprisingly, a BBC survey discovered that 59% of the population objected to the corporation's cancellation of scheduled programmes during the ten days of mourning following George VI's death in 1952. Beneath the monarchy people began to identify, from the mid-1950s onwards, an 'Establishment' – a group whose precise identity was unclear, but which consisted of what might later be called 'the great and the good'. It included leading politicians and churchmen, landowners and aristocrats, the heads of prominent cultural organisations, the captains of industry and the bosses of the major financial institutions. Here was a sort of self-perpetuating ruling elite – 'invisible' but 'ubiquitous', according to Reginald Bevins, a Tory minister of humble origins – sustained by a largely unseen network of family and social relationships. Underpinning it was the British educational system, or rather its exclusive peak. An astonishingly high percentage of the Establishment were products of the leading public schools and the ancient universities of Oxford and Cambridge.

By the early 1960s attitudes towards the Establishment began to change. Hostility grew towards a system that seemed to resist penetration by outsiders and which valued the talented amateur at the expense of the more accomplished newcomer who lacked the necessary background and upbringing. Was it really the case that an Oxbridge 'first' in 'Greats' was ideally equipped to take up the reins of government or industry, rather than pontificate on knotty problems of ancient Greek? It took money, rather than brains, to get into Eton, but this seemed no barrier to a future exalted position in the City or civil service. Was not the answer a genuine meritocracy, in which people advanced on the basis of ability and nothing else?

This changing attitude towards the Establishment fed into the growing contemporary feeling of the early 1960s that there was something fundamentally wrong about Britain and the way it was governed. The increasing criticism was part of an insistent agenda at this time.

It was no coincidence that Harold Wilson, elected Labour leader in 1963, had such an instant appeal. Here was a man from a relatively humble background in Huddersfield who, in contrast to Macmillan and Douglas-Home, was not part of the Establishment but a true meritocrat. In cultivating a working-class image, the pipe smoking Wilson (in private he preferred cigars) went out of his way to conceal the powerful intellect of one who had been an Oxford economics don before the War.

Position of women

If Britain was a deeply divided society in the 1950s, those divisions looked unlikely to translate into serious unrest or conflict. Most people seemed reasonably content with their lot, as part of the natural order of things. Attitudes remained fundamentally 'conservative'. Despite several 'causes célèbres', this was a country that still sanctioned the death penalty and criminalised homosexuality. Nothing, however, testifies better to the essentially conservative nature of British society than the continuing subordinate status of women. The War, of course, had acted as a catalyst for significant social change. Out of sheer necessity, women took on many roles previously regarded as preserves of the male workforce. But concentration on what happened between 1939 and 1945 obscures the extent to which social and cultural life reverted to pre-war patterns once the struggle against Hitler was won. According to Evelyn Home, the much-read agony aunt of *Woman* magazine, 'most women, once they have a family, are more contented and doing better work in the home than they could find outside it'.[21] That average female wages were less than two-thirds those of men was less surprising than the fact that this was widely held, not least by women themselves, to be right and proper. Women worked for 'pin-money', to enable the household to afford the 'little luxuries' that made life more agreeable. But it was indubitably a man's responsibility to provide for his family. Writing in 1955, one as yet unmarried correspondent to *Woman's Own* voiced the contentment which many of her sex found in a life of domesticity: 'If a man cannot support a wife, he doesn't deserve one. I don't mind cooking, sewing and cleaning for him – so long as the place he asks me to do it in isn't too small – but I will not go out and work for him, too'.[22]

Figure 1.10: A Mass Observation survey in 1957 found that a large majority of working-class men opposed the idea of married women going out to work, with the simple maxim that 'a woman's place is in the home' the most frequent explanation of their point of view.

Between 1951 and 1961 the percentage of women in the workforce did rise, but only from 26 to 35%. The Victorian notion of 'separate spheres' remained strong. Very few women made it into senior positions in industry, commerce, politics or the civil service. Women MPs, particularly in the Conservative Party, constituted a tiny minority. The young Margaret Thatcher, turned down as candidate for the safe Tory seat of Orpington, largely because the local party doubted whether she could look after two young children *and* stand for election, concluded that her political ambitions should be put on hold for several years.

Voices from the past

Anthony Sampson

Sampson's influential book *Anatomy of Britain* (1962) sought to dissect and understand the country's ruling elite, and produced a damning verdict:

Briefly it is that the old privileged values of aristocracy, public schools and Oxbridge which still dominate government today have failed to provide the stimulus, the purposive policies and the keen eye on the future which Britain is looking for, and must have . . . The old fabric of the British governing class, while keeping its social and political hold, has failed to accommodate or analyse the vast forces of science, education or social change which (whether they like it or not) are changing the face of the country'.[23]

Discussion points

1. Why does Sampson link the country's educational system and its social structure?
2. How convincing do you find his critique of Britain in the early 1960s?

Immigration

Immigration from the New Commonwealth was a factor that changed or – in the minds of some – threatened, the structure and stability of British society. At the end of the War it was estimated that between 20 000 and 30 000 non-whites were living in Britain, mostly in port areas such as Liverpool and Cardiff's Tiger Bay. The Labour government's British Nationality Act (1948) was never intended to sanction mass immigration. However, largely inadvertently, it opened up the possibility of substantial numbers from the New Commonwealth exercising their newly enshrined right to settle permanently in the United Kingdom. In a well-chosen phrase, David Kynaston has described the act as a 'fine example of liberalism at its most nominal'.[24] Very soon afterwards, to the dismay of ministers and officials in the Ministry of Labour, the former German troop carrier, the *Empire Windrush*, docked at Tilbury with just under 500 passengers from Jamaica.

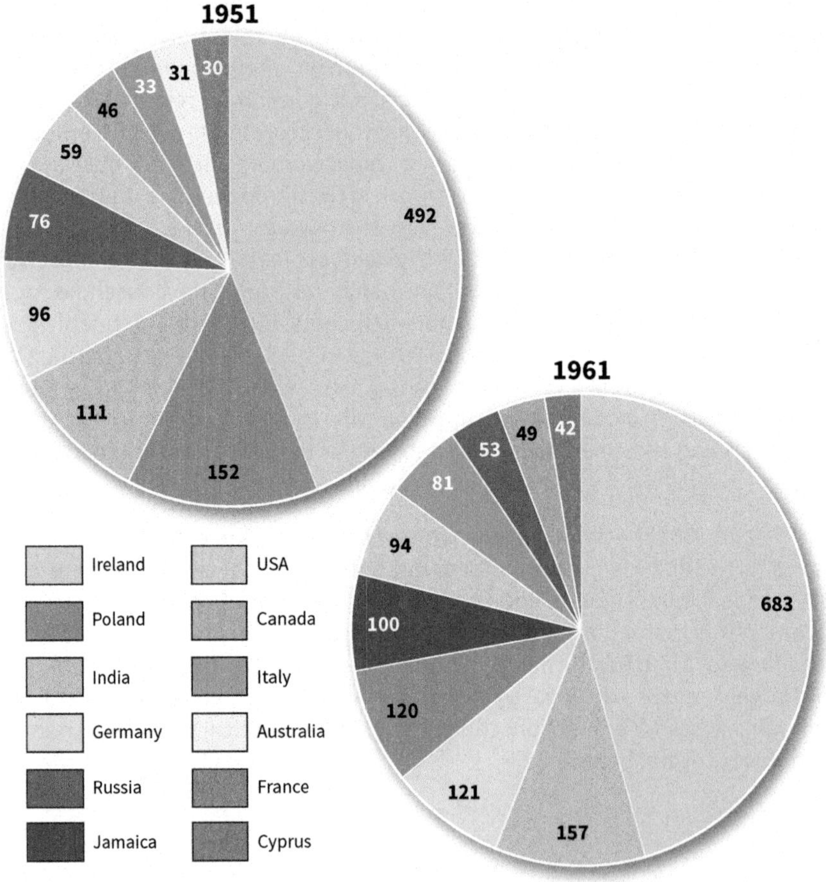

Figure 1.11: Countries of birth for residents in England and Wales born outside the UK (in thousands). In 1951 the total was 4.3% of the overall population, which was 43.7 million. In 1961 the total was 5% of the overall population, which was 46 million.

The anxiety aroused within government, and society more generally, was disproportionate to the scale of this 'influx', dwarfed as it was by an ongoing, but largely unnoticed, arrival of migrant workers from Europe. The anxiety says much about an underlying racial prejudice within British society. A 1951 survey concluded that 'antipathy to coloured [the usual description at this time rather than 'black'] people in this country is probably considerable among at least one-third of the population'.[25] Responding directly to the arrival of the *Windrush*, a group of concerned Labour MPs were blunter: 'an influx of coloured people … is likely to impair the harmony, strength and cohesion of our public and social life and to cause discord and unhappiness among all concerned'.[26] Despite a characteristically measured response from Prime Minister Attlee, it is now clear that the Labour government, in great secrecy, did seriously consider introducing legislation to limit migration from the Commonwealth. It finally decided in February 1951 not to do so, but it was agreed to keep a careful watch on the situation, with future legislation not ruled out.

By the time the Conservatives took office it was estimated that about 5000 migrants had arrived from the New Commonwealth, mostly from the West Indies. Over the next decade this figure increased substantially, not least because of the improving British economy and labour market. Around 2000 arrived from the Caribbean in 1953, but 11 000 in 1954 and 27 000 in 1955. The Churchill and Eden governments also held back from legislation. This was largely because of the difficulty of differentiating between those arriving, for example, from Australia or Canada (the Old Commonwealth), where arguments of 'kith and kin' were compelling, and immigration by natives of the 'new' Commonwealth countries – all were British subjects. Churchill himself was inherently hostile to this 'new' immigration – 'PM thinks "Keep England White" a good slogan' noted Macmillan – but the issue was not one to which he gave priority.[27] Within the cabinet of this time, Lord Salisbury was convinced that only new restrictions could avoid future racial strife. His arguments resonate with debates in our own time over European 'freedom of movement'. Attributing the 'sudden influx of blacks' to the attractions of the Welfare State, he continued: 'So long as the antiquated rule obtains that any British subject can come into the country without any limitation at all, these people will pour in to take advantage of our social services and other amenities, and we shall have no protection at all.'[28]

Historians, including Richard Lamb, have written, perhaps unfairly, of a missed opportunity to introduce restrictive legislation in the mid-1950s.[29] A 1957 report by Lord Hailsham, the Lord President of the Council, expressed further concern and noted the social problems arising in certain towns and cities. Once again, however, the cabinet decided against immediate legislation, noting that public opinion was still insufficiently concerned to justify government action. In the event it was not until 1961 that the Home Secretary, R.A. Butler, introduced the Commonwealth Immigrants Bill to limit the number of 'new' immigrants. Immigration peaked at over 100 000 in 1961 and 1962. Butler's legislation required most immigrants to possess a work permit or employment voucher in order to enter Britain, ending the 'open door' policy that had existed since 1948. By 1961 Labour vehemently opposed such curbs, notwithstanding its own earlier examination of a similar response to what had then been a much smaller problem.

Racial prejudice and violence

By the time of Butler's bill, the government had abundant evidence of the extent of racial prejudice and its capacity to inflame social tensions. Prejudice and discrimination tended to be less obvious than in the southern United States – though opponents of immigration often pointed to America to illustrate what Britain might face in the future – and was often based purely on ignorance and a lack of experience. Many had never before come across people of a different colour. Immigrants later recalled being closely examined by members of the indigenous population, keen to know whether their blackness would rub off! Not all prejudice was based purely on colour. On properties to let, signs proclaiming 'no coloureds' were often accompanied by the complementary exclusion 'no Irish'. For all that, in areas as varied as employment, accommodation, clubs and even, occasionally, the Church, Britain did harbour a significant measure of colour-based prejudice. In June 1952 Bishop Barnes of Birmingham suggested that, in districts where there were significant foreign elements, 'neither moral standards nor social behaviour are satisfactory'.[30]

A television documentary in January 1955 revealed considerable evidence of a British colour bar. Robert Reid, who introduced the documentary, was told by one disgruntled viewer, 'you and your black friends ought to be put up against a wall and shot'.[31] For many people, sexual relations and – for still more – marriage between members of different races were particularly unacceptable. This attitude was justified by the widespread conviction that the practices were 'unnatural' or 'against the Bible', or else by the self-perpetuating argument that children of such liaisons would incur hostility they had done nothing to deserve.

Eliminating such prejudice by legislation would not be easy, but ministers could not ignore outbreaks of racially motivated violence. The late summer of 1958 witnessed Britain's first significant examples of such activity in Nottingham and in Notting Hill, West London. There were ugly scenes – labelled 'nigger-hunts' in the language of the time – prompted primarily by competition for housing in inner city areas. Butler told the cabinet that it would be necessary to give further consideration to the circumstances that had produced interracial violence. For the time being, the government preferred to try to control the rate of immigration without recourse to legislation. Before long, however, Butler became convinced that only pre-emptive action could head off a future rise in racial tension. The Commonwealth Immigrants Bill was his response.

Youth culture

According to Arthur Marwick, the 1960s saw 'the rise to positions of unprecedented influence of young people, with youth culture having a steadily increasing impact on the rest of society'.[32] This trend, whose origins lay in the previous decade, is thought to have had a revolutionary effect on the British way of life. The thesis has some merit, but should be treated with caution. The literary and theatrical output of the so-called 'angry young men' (some of whom were, in fact, approaching middle age) certainly added to the picture of a culture being taken forward by people of a younger age than ever before. It is also true that the 1950s saw an increasing tendency among older people to regard youth itself as a problem. The description 'teenager', invented in 1930s America, came into common use, often with disapproving connotations. But the association of youth with a nation's supposed falling standards is a characteristic attitude among older people, not restricted to any particular decade. Indeed, the word 'hooligan' had been invented at the end of Queen Victoria's reign.

Young people, benefiting from the improving national economy, certainly enjoyed more opportunities and greater affluence than their pre-war forebears. It has been estimated that by 1960 there were around five million teenagers in Britain (defined as those in the 15–25 age range), accounting for 10% of the population's personal income. More significantly, their patterns of consumption were markedly different from those of their elders. They prioritised luxuries and entertainment, and manufacturers and providers soon sought to cater for this new market. This could provoke hostility from those who had grown up in more austere times. The young were seen to have too much time on their hands (especially after the end of **National Service** in 1960) and too much money in their pockets.

Popular music

Not for the first – or last – time, music helped define the generations. Rock and roll first hit Britain in 1954, led by the Americans Bill Haley and Elvis Presley. By the later 1950s, home-grown musicians Tommy Steele, Marty Wilde and Cliff Richard had become important figures in the fast-growing pop music market. Affluent teenagers bought records: all but the poorest could afford a gramophone and the 'singles' market grew twelve-fold between 1955 and 1960. The older generation generally reacted with suspicion and hostility to a musical genre associated with black America and sexual freedom. There was understandable horror when Haley's film *The Blackboard Jungle* was accompanied by violence and vandalism in the country's cinemas. By 1960, however, rock and roll itself, challenged first by 'skiffle', was being subsumed within a wide range of musical traditions. No straight line connected the stars of the 1950s to the 'Beatlemania' that hit Britain in the summer of 1963. Many rock stars were turning,

Hidden voices

Angry Young Men

Phrase coined by *The Times* and used to describe an essentially disparate group of young novelists and dramatists such as Colin Wilson, John Osborne and Kingsley Amis, whose writings gave voice to an alienated generation that wanted to challenge accepted norms and social conventions.

Key terms

National Service: a peacetime continuation of conscription into the armed forces. The National Service Act (1947) originally provided for 18 months of service, but this was raised to two years in 1950.

in fact, to more traditional ballads. The early Cliff Richard had been condemned by the *New Musical Express*. 'His violent hip-swinging was revolting, hardly the performance any parent could wish her children to see.'[33] By the new decade, however, his image was more that of the 'boy next door', a first step towards the 'national treasure' status of his later career. Teenagers dominated the record buying public, but plenty of the works figuring in the 'charts' were also popular with older generations.

Figure 1.12: Bill Haley and the Comets.

Youth and crime

Young people were an easy scapegoat for Britain's rising crime rate. The 'teddy boys' of the early 1950s, with their velvet collars, drainpipe trousers and pointed black shoes, caused widespread alarm, even without the flick-knives many were thought to carry. As Dominic Sandbrook has put it, the 'juvenile delinquent became a metaphor for the supposed collapse of standards throughout society'.[34] Admittedly, violent crime just about doubled between 1955 and 1960, but crime itself had gone up as soon as the War ended. This rise was probably attributable to the removal of the sense of inter-dependent community engendered by the War. The main problem, as so often in social analysis, lies with careless generalisation. The activities of a small minority may have captured the headlines, but they were not necessarily representative of the younger age group as a whole. Indeed, there is evidence that the majority of 1950s teenagers were, like their parents, essentially conservative in their attitudes and behaviour and not the advance guard of some imminent cultural revolution. Like their elders, they were divided by class and never acted as a homogenous whole. Again, Dominic Sandbrook strikes the right note: 'Young people were … never much of a threat to the conventions of British life. They were neither as radical nor as violent as many observers feared'.[35]

Foreign relations

Foreign policy offers the most striking illustration of continuity between the Conservative governments of 1951–64 and their Labour predecessors. It was during Attlee's administration that most of the key decisions that would shape post-war British foreign policy were taken. Anthony Eden, Churchill's Foreign Secretary, agreed in most matters with Ernest Bevin, Foreign Secretary for most of the Labour

Hidden voices

Bill Haley (1925–81)

This American pioneer of rock and roll music began his career as a country music singer. He and his band, the Comets, achieved fame with 'Rock Around the Clock', which featured in the subsequent film ***The Blackboard Jungle***. Other hits included 'Shake, Rattle and Roll' and 'See You Later Alligator'.

ACTIVITY 1.4

Using information from this section of the chapter, draw up a table to show which social changes affected which age-groups. What age would you have chosen to be in 1951, and why?

Key terms

North Atlantic Treaty Organisation (NATO): a military alliance created following the Second World War to counter the threat of the USSR and its allies and retain the involvement of the USA in Europe.

Voices from the past

Winston Churchill

What is this sovereign remedy? It is to re-create the European family, or as much of it as we can, and provide it with a structure under which it can dwell in peace, in safety and in freedom. We must build a kind of United States of Europe … The first step in the recreation of the European family must be a partnership between France and Germany … In all this urgent work, France and Germany must take the lead together. Great Britain, the British Commonwealth of Nations, mighty America, and I trust Soviet Russia – for then indeed all would be well – must be friends and sponsors of the new Europe and must champion its right to live and shine.

Speech in Zurich, 19 September 1946.

Discussion points

What conclusions do you draw from this speech about Churchill's attitude towards:

1. European integration?
2. Britain's role in this process?

Key terms

Eurosceptic: individuals doubting the value of EEC membership, regarding it as a threat to national sovereignty and prosperity.

Benelux countries: a shorthand way of referring to Belgium, the Netherlands and Luxembourg.

government. Bevin set the tone of reserved scepticism towards the process of European integration which, arguably, persists to this day. Labour ensured a leading role for Britain by opting firmly for the United States' side in the evolving Cold War, and had decided that Britain should become a founder member of the **North Atlantic Treaty Organisation (NATO)**, which remains the cornerstone of the country's defence strategy. Indeed, a group of senior Labour ministers – from which leading left-wingers had been consciously excluded – gave the go-ahead to develop Britain's own nuclear deterrent as an indispensable symbol of the country's continuing great power status. In Bevin's celebrated words, 'We have got to have this thing over here whatever it costs … We've got to have the bloody Union Jack flying on top of it'[36] and it was Labour that later accepted the siting of long-range American atomic bombers on British soil.

Cross-reference foreign affairs timeline, Activity 1.7

European integration

Over time, Ernest Bevin had become sceptical about supranational integration, and Labour held aloof from French proposals to pool sovereignty over the coal and steel industries of six West European countries (France, West Germany, Italy, The Netherlands, Belgium, Luxembourg). Yet the European Coal and Steel Community (ECSC), proved to be a trial run for the altogether more significant EEC, set up seven years later.

Churchill, however, emerged as a leading figure in the movement for European Union. His sweeping declarations calling for, but never fully defining, a 'United States of Europe', provoked a response that was emotional rather than intellectual, but nevertheless struck a chord with a growing mood on the continent. He may not really have envisaged Britain being part of an integrated Europe, and there was more continuity in policy towards Europe after 1951 than might have been expected.

Churchill chose to leave Europe to Foreign Secretary Eden, whose focus was on defence, rather than political or economic union. He proposed a Western European Union (WEU), a defensive alliance without supranational implications, which allowed West Germany to rearm, but avoided stirring up memories of German militarism. It represented a major triumph for Eden and won him much prestige.

Europe, however, went on regardless. For failing to see the direction in which Europe would travel and perhaps throwing away possible British leadership of this process, Eden has been much criticised, emerging as a prototype Conservative **Eurosceptic**. In fact, he fully understood the significance of the continental developments – and rejected them. As he noted, 'the experiment of the six cannot succeed without federation … in the sense of one Parliament, one foreign policy, one currency etc … I do not want to become part of such a federation.'[37] Speaking at Columbia University in 1952 Eden confronted head-on the issue of federation, ducked by so many who followed him. The idea of Britain joining a European federation was 'something which we know, in our bones, we cannot do'.[38] Britain's horizons were fixed beyond Europe. Most people in Britain would have had family and friends who had sought a new life in Canada, Australia or New Zealand. Eden once reflected that, in a typical English village's postbag, 90% of letters coming from abroad would be from beyond Europe, from countries where British troops had been stationed or where Britons had relatives living.

EEC and EFTA

The Messina Conference in the spring of 1955, called by the **Benelux countries**, made quick progress in extending the principles of ECSC into other sectors of the economy.

From it emerged the Spaak Committee, which undertook detailed discussions on the twin issues of a Common Market and collaboration over nuclear energy. Britain withdrew its representation from these discussions in November 1955. To head off the drive to federation, Britain proposed a free trade area which, unlike the emerging Common Market, would have no common external tariff against the rest of the world.

Cross-reference *The Suez Crisis*

France, however, annoyed by Britain's unilateral abandonment of the Suez expedition, made a decisive move towards a federal future. In March 1957 the six European countries signed the Treaty of Rome, creating the EEC. British hopes of attaching the EEC to a wider free trade area soon collapsed, so Britain went ahead with the inter-governmental European Free Trade Association (EFTA), consisting of Austria, Denmark, Norway, Portugal, Sweden, Switzerland and the United Kingdom.

Figure 1.13: Membership of the EEC and of EFTA in the early 1960s.

Influential opinion in Britain soon began to change. The new decade saw a growing belief that the country's economic difficulties flowed, in part, from the pattern of its trade, orientated too much towards the Commonwealth at the expense of dynamic markets in western Europe. Senior civil servants concluded in 1960 that the case for joining EEC was now strong. The leading broadsheet newspapers soon voiced their support. Most significantly, Macmillan concluded that membership would actually strengthen Britain's world position and its partnership with the United States. Eisenhower and Kennedy had both made clear their support for Britain joining, in part to provide a counterweight to the neutralist tendencies of the French President, Charles de Gaulle.

Without any great sense of enthusiasm and certainly without a preliminary drive to convince the British people, Macmillan told parliament that Britain would apply for membership. Negotiations made good progress, but were abruptly terminated by a unilateral French veto in January 1963. De Gaulle's hostility towards the Anglo-American axis went back to supposed snubs during the Second World War. Yet his public statement rejecting Britain's application bore more than an element of truth. 'England in fact is insular, maritime, bound by her trade, her markets, her supplies, to countries that are very diverse and often very far away ... How can England, as she lives, as she produces, as she trades, be incorporated in the Common Market?'[39]

ACTIVITY 1.5

Which factors do you think support de Gaulle's analysis of Britain's position in the 1950s and early 1960s?

Relations with the superpowers

Although Churchill left most of the detailed administration of foreign policy to Eden, he set the broad parameters of that policy and there were key areas within it that he reserved for himself, most importantly relations with the superpowers, America and the Soviet Union. Churchill's outlook was shaped by his vision of Britain's global position within a complex of three interlinking circles – its ongoing role as a great imperial power; the Atlantic community based upon Churchill's treasured 'Special Relationship' with the United States; and (least important in Churchill's scheme) the country's leadership of western Europe. The Prime Minister believed that his own status as one of the wartime 'Big Three' offered unique opportunities to deploy Britain's power and authority at the highest level of international diplomacy.

This starry-eyed vision was riddled with problems. If Britain remained one of the world's three great powers in 1945, it did so as the least of the three – the gap between Britain and the other two in wealth, military power and global influence could only increase. Furthermore, Churchill greatly overestimated the United States' willingness to recreate the sort of relationship with Britain that had existed during the War. The Americans found the old man's romantic nostalgia irritating. He was tolerated but, in the last resort, ignored. This was particularly apparent at talks in Bermuda in 1953, when observers noted Eisenhower's impatience with Churchill's rambling flights of fancy. The Empire remained an asset, but it was a waning one. Its self-governing components in the Commonwealth, such as Australia and Canada, had long shown their determination to go their own way in the world. Meanwhile, the dependent territories in Africa and Asia would reach independence much sooner than Churchill envisaged. The concept of British leadership of western Europe could only become a reality if Britain engaged from the outset in moves towards integration in both political and economic terms, which the government was not prepared to do.

There was always something rather forlorn about Churchill's personal diplomacy. Though his government decided that Britain should move on to the next stage of nuclear weaponry and construct its own hydrogen bomb, the Prime Minister became haunted by the nightmare of thermonuclear warfare. With his global prestige, he believed himself uniquely placed to save the world from self-destruction, if only he could bring the competing sides in the Cold War together in a summit conference.[40] However, Churchill faced significant opposition. The Americans believed that little could be achieved by what they regarded as a diplomatic stunt. Even leading members of the government, including Eden, remained sceptical, not least because of doubts over whether Churchill still possessed the intellectual strength to successfully handle such a gathering. Churchill persisted, partly because this last crusade offered repeated opportunities to postpone his long-promised retirement. However, no summit conference took place, at least until after his retirement, when leaders of the great powers gathered in Geneva in 1955 to negotiate a belated peace treaty with Austria.

As Foreign Secretary Eden secured a number of significant diplomatic successes, not least in bringing a (temporary) resolution to the crisis in South-East Asia, where the end of French colonial control had led to threats of American military intervention and even talk of a third world war. On the European stage Eden's patient skills helped resolve a diplomatic impasse over the rearming of West Germany and laid the groundwork for its admission to NATO. Eden's attitude towards the United States was altogether more hard-headed than Churchill's. Even so, the Foreign Secretary's successes, underpinned by national pride in such diverse events as: the royal coronation, the conquest of Everest by a British-led expedition and even the regaining of the Ashes by England's cricket team – all of which encouraged talk of a new 'Elizabethan Age'– may have led him to an unrealistic view of Britain's world position and its capacity to pursue its interests independently of even its most important allies. As Prime Minister, during the Suez Crisis of 1956, he allowed Anglo-American relations to reach a low point unequalled in the post-war era. The damage was speedily repaired, but a lasting legacy of Suez was the realisation of the difficulties Britain would face in the future in pursuing a major foreign policy objective without, at least tacit, American support.

Figure 1.14: The coronation of Queen Elizabeth II, 1953.

Taking it further

Research the diplomatic impasse over the rearming of West Germany, then set up a class debate on the following motion: 'This house believes West Germany should be admitted to NATO.'

Despite his own deep involvement in the Suez fiasco, Macmillan saw it as his primary foreign policy goal as Prime Minister to restore the Special Relationship to its former intimacy. Events worked in his favour. Reconciliation with the Americans had not been possible under Eden, but Macmillan was able to build upon his wartime friendship with Eisenhower to ensure that international bridges were rebuilt. The two men struck up a renewed rapport when meeting in Bermuda in March 1957. Indeed, the personal factor remained important throughout Macmillan's premiership and, somewhat surprisingly, an equally warm relationship developed post-1961 with Eisenhower's successor, J.F. Kennedy, notwithstanding a 23-year age gap between President and Prime Minister.

Macmillan had no ambition to rein in Britain's pretensions to great power status. The Special Relationship remained at the heart of his vision, but in what became known as his 'Grand Design' Macmillan also envisaged Britain assuming a leading role in the EEC. He personally sought to maintain a high profile on the world stage, his Moscow visit in 1959 being particularly successful, though more in terms of enhancing his credentials as a world statesman than in any tangible reduction in Cold War tension. Like Churchill, he advocated a summit conference and achieved this goal in Paris in 1960. Unfortunately for Macmillan, the atmosphere at the summit was poisoned by the recent shooting down of an American spy plane over Soviet territory. Nonetheless, Macmillan successfully persuaded Kennedy to supply Polaris nuclear missiles to maintain Britain's 'independent' nuclear deterrent and the country took part in the 1963 Test Ban Treaty, perhaps the last time that the pretence of equality with the superpowers was maintained.

Anglo-Russian timeline

July–August 1945	Last top-level wartime meeting with Soviet leaders at Potsdam Conference.
October 1951	Churchill becomes Prime Minister.
October 1952	Britain tests its first atomic bomb.

March 1953	Death of Stalin.
August 1953	Soviet Union tests its first hydrogen bomb.
April 1954	Opening of Geneva Conference on South-East Asia with Anglo-Soviet co-chairmen.
July 1955	Geneva Summit Conference. First meeting of heads of government since 1945.
October 1955	British and Soviet warships exchange courtesy visits.
February 1956	Khrushchev announces 'de-Stalinisation'.
April 1956	Khrushchev and Bulganin visit to Britain overshadowed by 'Crabb incident'.
November 1956	Soviet forces crush Hungarian uprising.
November 1956	Bulganin threatens Britain over invasion of Egypt.
October 1957	Soviet Union launches world's first space satellite.
October 1958	Conference opens in Geneva on suspension of nuclear tests. Concern was growing about fallout in the earth's atmosphere.
February 1959	Macmillan makes official trip to Moscow.
December 1959	Anglo-Soviet cultural agreement signed.
May 1960	Paris Summit Conference collapses after U-2 incident.
August 1961	Berlin Wall erected.
August 1963	Partial Test Ban Treaty signed, banning surface tests, but not those underground.
October 1964	Fall of Khrushchev.

Taking it further

Some entries shown in the Anglo-Russian relations timeline are not covered in this chapter. Use them as prompts for research to deepen your understanding of this period.

Douglas-Home's short premiership, dominated by the inevitability of the forthcoming general election, saw few new foreign policy developments. In any case, he was not looking to change the main lines of policy laid down by his predecessors. A visit to Washington in February 1964 for talks with the President was only partially successful. The personal factor, so important during the Macmillan years, had evaporated following Kennedy's assassination in November 1963. His successor, Lyndon Johnson, felt no particular fraternity with Britain. The atmosphere at the talks was friendly enough, but tension developed over Britain's decision not to block the sale of British Leyland buses to Cuba and the wording of the end of conference communiqué was, at best, anodyne. Britain did not know it, but advice given to Johnson before Douglas-Home's arrival drew attention to the essential truth about the Special Relationship. Whereas the 'close US–UK association [was] the most important single factor in British foreign policy', for America Britain's friendship was valuable but not pre-eminent.[41] In short, the relationship was far more special for Britain than for the United States.

The nuclear deterrent

British universities were at the forefront of experimental work in the 1930s on splitting the atom and understanding the process of nuclear fission. Scientific work done by refugee scientists in Britain in the early part of the War, and Britain's participation in the secret Manhattan Project to produce the world's first atomic bomb, facilitated ending the struggle against Japan. In September 1944 Churchill and Roosevelt agreed that full atomic collaboration should continue once the War ended. Following Roosevelt's death in April 1945, however, his successor Truman went back on this agreement. The American Atomic Energy Act of August 1946, promoted by Senator McMahon, even made the communication of classified atomic information to any foreign power punishable by life imprisonment or even death. By this time the Attlee government had begun considering a British nuclear programme. Nuclear capacity was seen as key to 'great power' status. The government accepted that the bomb's deterrent effect offered the best available protection against attack from the Soviets, particularly if, as after the First World War, the United States withdrew at some future time from the defence of western Europe. Precisely the same combination of national identity and national interests determined the approach of Churchill and the Conservatives. Britain's first atomic test was carried out off the coast of north-west Australia in October 1952.

Almost immediately, however, the exacting problems of competing in the super league of world powers were revealed. A month after the successful British test, the Americans detonated the substantially more powerful hydrogen bomb, followed by the Soviets in August 1953. Having made the fundamental decision that Britain should not be excluded from this arms race, the government had little alternative but to follow suit. As Churchill put it: 'We must do it; it is the price we pay to sit at the top table.'[42] By the end of 1957 Britain had, with some American technical assistance, managed to test its first megaton thermonuclear bomb, with a destructive capacity 75 times that of the atomic device exploded five years earlier. The strain placed on the British economy in attempting to stay in touch with the two superpowers was considerable, though reliance on a nuclear defence, as set out by Duncan Sandys in a white paper of April 1957, did permit significant savings in the nation's bill for conventional forces.

Taking it further

Deliberately appointed Minister of Defence by Macmillan in 1957 because of his 'no-nonsense' reputation for getting things done, Duncan Sandys wasted no time in presenting a thorough review of British defence strategy, incorporating the lessons of the Suez adventure. His white paper made the nuclear deterrent the unequivocal centrepiece of Britain's national security.

Find out more about the arguments used for and against Britain's participation in the nuclear arms race.

In the long term, however, it was apparent that any pretence of a British nuclear deterrent was dependent on increased American collaboration, even if this undermined the principle of supposed 'independence'. Macmillan led this modification to British strategy. In March 1957 he agreed to the stationing of 60 American intermediate range ballistic missiles (IRBM) on British soil under an arrangement which, theoretically, required both countries' consent before the weapons could be used. The following year saw the repeal of the McMahon Act and an agreement on technical exchanges that would prove crucial for Britain's future nuclear programme. The fruits of the Prime Minister's diplomacy became apparent after the cancellation in 1960 of Britain's own IRBM, Blue Streak, on grounds of cost and questionable capability. Britain hoped it would be replaced by America's Skybolt programme, but this was abandoned and in December 1962 Macmillan persuaded Kennedy to supply Britain with Polaris missiles for use from British-built nuclear submarines. In this instance, at least, the Special Relationship was a reality. The American concession was not offered to any other country and enabled Britain to maintain a deterrent at a vastly lower cost than would have been possible independently.

Britain's nuclear strategy also proved troublesome for the Labour opposition. Many on the left never reconciled themselves to weapons capable of destroying civilisation itself. Morally, they saw a qualitative difference between nuclear and conventional forces and questioned the practical value of a defence strategy that could invite massive and cataclysmic retaliation. The Labour leadership, however, regarded the bomb as an unfortunate necessity, until such time as the superpowers accepted the principle of multilateral disarmament. Aneurin Bevan came close to expulsion from the party in 1955 when he opposed the leadership's support for developing a British hydrogen bomb. However, he experienced a change of heart and, as Shadow Foreign Secretary, surprised and appalled former left-wing colleagues by warning the 1957 party conference of the dangers of unilateralism and the folly of sending a British Foreign Secretary 'naked into the Conference Chamber'.[43] The Campaign for Nuclear Disarmament (CND) was formed in 1958. Though theoretically non-party, it attracted considerable support from Labour's left and, by 1960, was calling for Britain to leave NATO. That year's Labour conference passed unilateralist resolutions, against strong opposition from the leadership. These were reversed in 1961 after a passionate campaign by Gaitskell. It was probably fortunate for Labour's incoming government in 1964 that much of CND's momentum had by then evaporated.

The Korean War

Among the unwelcome overseas problems bequeathed to the Conservatives by the outgoing Labour government, the Korean War was probably the most serious. Korea had been 'temporarily' partitioned along the 38th parallel at the end of the Second World War. In the north, Stalin established a hard-line Communist state under the dictator, Kim Il-sung; to the south the Americans sponsored the right-wing Republic of Korea, led by the autocratic Syngman Rhee. Koreans on both sides spoke of reunification, but were restrained by their superpower mentors. In 1950, however, and with backing from the newly established communist government in China, Stalin's attitude changed. On 25 June the North Koreans launched a surprise attack, which soon had the South Korean army in disarray. By 2 July, as part of a UN response to this aggression, British frigates were in action against North Korean gunboats; air attacks on North Korean targets soon followed. Britain's rapid deployment is best seen in Anglo-American, rather than UN terms. Indeed, the United States was only able to secure a Security Council resolution authorising a UN multinational force because of the temporary absence of the Soviet delegate in protest at the UN's failure to recognise the legitimacy of the Communist government in Peking (Beijing). The Labour government felt obliged to join the Americans in the UN cause, not least because of its overriding determination to secure a long-term American commitment to western European defence. Ever since, British governments have felt bound to act as loyal allies at the United States' side, even if the scale of British military support might be irrelevant in securing American objectives. Britain's 27th Brigade was despatched from Hong Kong in August, followed by the reserve 29th Brigade. Thirty-two Royal Navy warships took part in operations over the next three years, while British aircraft carriers formed the core of UN naval forces operating on the western side of the Korean peninsula.

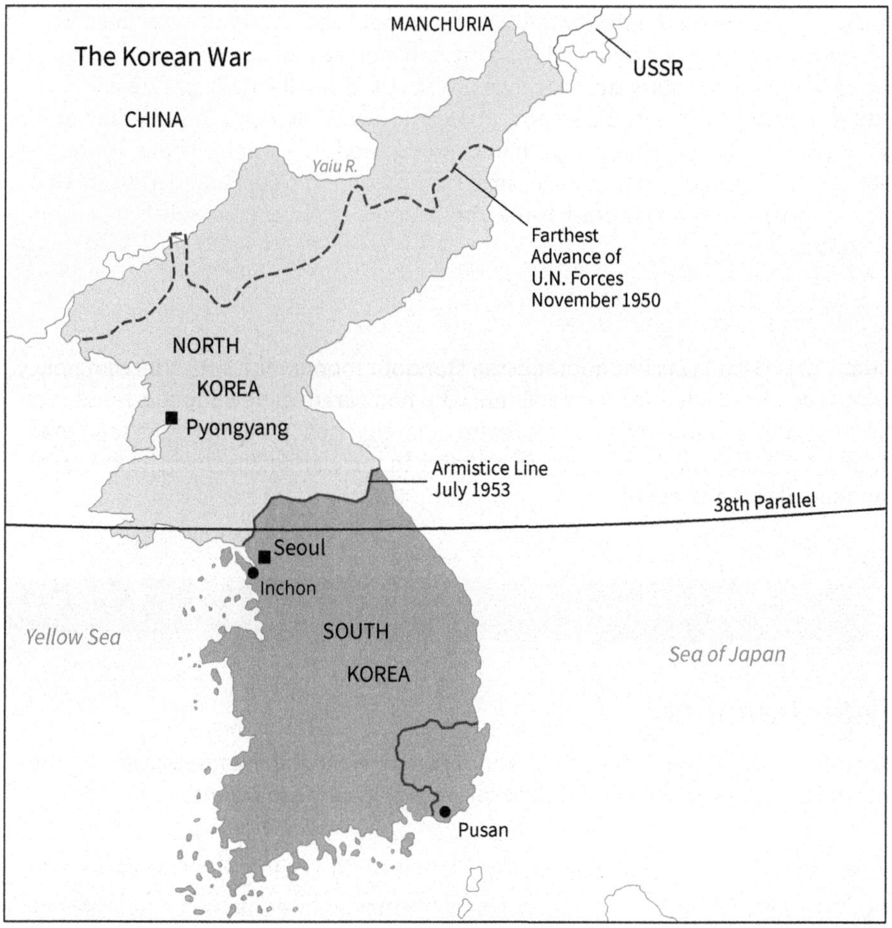

Figure 1.15: The partition of Korea along the 38th Parallel. The line around Pusan shows the furthest advance of North Korean forces, September 1950.

The Churchill government accepted the basic rationale behind British participation and there was no significant change in policy. The conflict, however, placed an enormous strain on Britain's resources, military and economic. The country's strategic 'overstretch', a feature of the entire post-war era, was dramatically revealed as Britain struggled to deploy even its two brigades and dashed any hope of a reduction in defence spending, a long-term post–Second World War 'peace dividend'. In January 1951 planned expenditure over the following three years was increased to £4 700 m, a rise from 8 to 14% of **gross national product**, and higher *per capita* than even the USA. By 1952 defence spending stood at 25.9% of total government expenditure. Meanwhile, National Service was increased from 18 months to two years, a striking decision for a country with a long-held suspicion of standing armies.

Britain was operating very much as a subordinate to the United States, even compared with the latter stages of the Second World War. There were significant disagreements between British and American commanders and, throughout the war, Britain was concerned to prevent the conflict spilling beyond the Korean peninsula and alarmed by aggressive pronouncements from the American commander-in-chief, Douglas MacArthur. Famously, Attlee had visited Washington in December 1950 to impress upon President Truman Britain's objections to any use of battlefield nuclear weapons.

Key terms

gross national product: the total value of all the goods and services produced in one year by the residents of a country, including income from overseas investments. 'Gross Domestic Product' excludes overseas investments.

The Cold War could not be allowed to escalate into an atomic 'hot' war, even if periods of conventional armed conflict were unavoidable.

Notwithstanding intervention by Communist China, armistice talks opened in 1951. They might have reached an early conclusion had the American and British Commonwealth representatives not insisted that no prisoners of war should be returned against their wishes – a condition designed to encourage individual Chinese and Koreans to show their hostility towards their countries' communist regimes. By 1953, however, neither side believed that outright victory was possible and, under mounting financial pressure, the armistice negotiations finally made progress. After three years of undeclared war, hostilities formally ceased on 27 July. Albeit at considerable cost, Britain's objectives had been secured. The war had been contained, nuclear conflict averted and the Anglo-American partnership confirmed. Despite this, the problems posed by an isolated, brutal, belligerent and unpredictable North Korea remain to this day.

The Suez Crisis

The Suez Crisis (1956) was undoubtedly the standout moment of British foreign policy in the period 1951–64. It is ironic that Eden, who had carefully developed a reputation for expertise and understanding in the realm of foreign policy, should have seen that reputation destroyed, and his country's standing in the world brought to its knees, by his handling of this one event.

Speak like a historian

Peter Hennessy

Though much of the damage was soon repaired, Hennessy has well captured the enormity of the crisis in which Eden's premiership came to an end:

> He had succeeded in alienating not just the Arab world, but President Eisenhower, the bulk of the Commonwealth and most of the major players at the United Nations. He had also succeeded in splitting his country, dividing his Cabinet and party, and causing the near collapse of the pound, while leaving Soviet influence uncurbed and an untoppled Nasser's prestige in the Arab world hugely enhanced.[44]

Discussion points

Investigate the Suez Crisis further and then try to explain:

1. why Eden acted as he did
2. why the consequences of his actions were catastrophic.

Key terms

bi-partisan: common to the two leading political parties.

The problem began when, on 26 July 1956, Colonel Nasser, the Egyptian dictator, nationalised the Anglo-French Suez Canal Company, the body responsible for operating a vital waterway in Britain's line of communication with its far-eastern Empire. Nasser was responding to the decision of America and Britain to terminate funding for Egypt's major civil engineering project to build a high dam on the Nile at Aswan. The response in Britain to Nasser's action was almost universally hostile and seemed, at first, to represent a typically **bi-partisan** approach from the country's politicians. Many compared Nasser to Mussolini and Hitler before the Second World War. This was an exaggeration. Nasser never posed a threat comparable to that of the 1930s dictators. But, for Eden the parallel proved irresistible – and tragic. His reputation had been founded on his supposed opposition to appeasement in the 1930s; he could not afford to buckle in the face of aggression now, especially as many were comparing him unfavourably with his predecessor, Churchill, while the *Daily Telegraph* called for 'the smack of firm government'.[45]

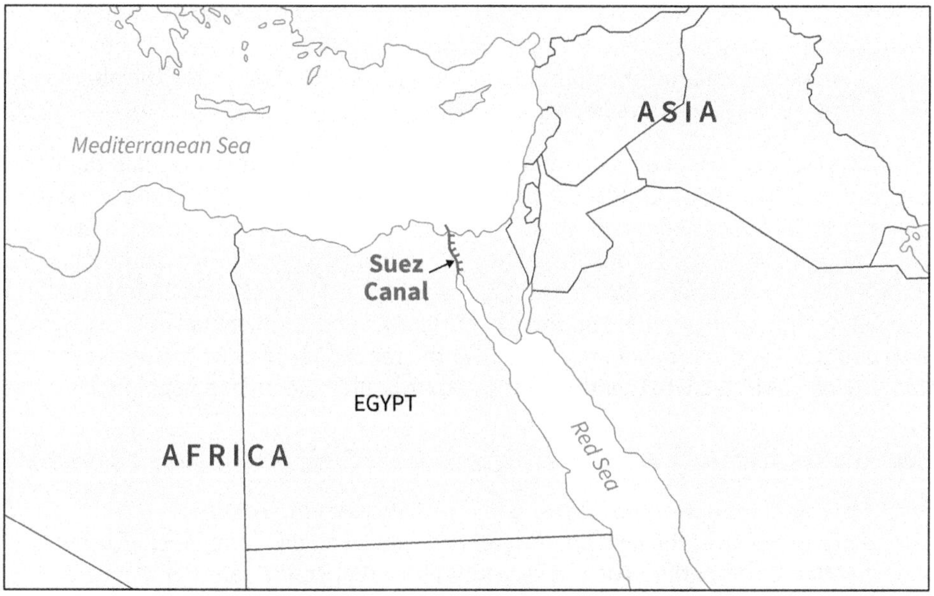

Figure 1.16: The Suez Canal. By 1955 oil was a significant proportion of its traffic, and more than half of the petroleum used in Europe passed through the canal. It was nicknamed the British Empire's 'jugular vein'.

A military response from Britain required lengthy preparations, and the delay proved fatal. Passions died down, the Egyptians proved perfectly capable of running the Canal themselves and majority opinion moved towards a UN-sponsored negotiated settlement. By the autumn such a conclusion was in sight, but Eden was plotting with France and Israel. Under the secret Protocol of Sèvres, Israel would invade Egypt as part of its ongoing conflict with the Arab world; Britain and France, in a mood of feigned outrage, would call upon both sides to cease fire and withdraw ten miles either side of the Canal. Israel would accept this demand and Egypt almost certainly reject it, providing the justification for an Anglo-French invasion to 'protect' the Canal and topple Nasser. Eden believed the plot could be kept secret and went to his grave never having admitted the truth. Ignoring repeated warnings from Eisenhower that America strongly opposed military action, he accepted assurances from Macmillan, recently returned from the United States, that the Americans would be annoyed, but would acquiesce in Britain's aggression. This was a catastrophic misreading of the American position.

Eden's conduct at this time has never been satisfactorily explained. Almost certainly his health was a key factor, though it hardly explains the unequivocal support offered by senior ministers such as Macmillan and Home. Eden had never fully recovered from a botched operation in 1953 and his doctors had been prescribing a combination of stimulants and sedatives that would not be contemplated today. This treatment may well have led to erratic and uncharacteristic behaviour on Eden's part.

The Anglo-French invasion went ahead as planned. Militarily, it proved reasonably successful, though there were no signs of Nasser's fall from power. Diplomatically, however, the expedition was an unqualified disaster. American opposition was genuine. At the UN Security Council Britain used its veto for the first time ever, to block a hostile resolution. On 2 November Britain and France were outvoted 65 to 5 at the General Assembly in a call for a ceasefire and the withdrawal of British, French and

Israeli forces from Egypt. Only Australia, New Zealand and Israel itself supported the European aggressors. In the Commons there was uproar. Gaitskell, now determined that the UN should take control, denounced a 'disastrous folly'.[46] Many Conservative MPs were shocked and bewildered by their government's behaviour. Many more nurtured doubts and uncertainty. On 5 November the Soviet premier, Bulganin, sent warning notes to Britain, France and Israel. Meanwhile, the threatening presence of the American Sixth Fleet symbolised the complete collapse of the Special Relationship. There was mounting pressure on the pound, orchestrated by the US, which began selling sterling, threatening its international exchange value. Eden had little alternative but to accept a ceasefire at midnight on 6 November.

While Eden sought rest and recuperation in Jamaica, his senior ministers had to pick up the pieces of an episode still seen as the low point of post-war British diplomacy. Eden's political future seemed compromised, but, in any case, his doctors insisted in early January 1957 that his constitution was no longer equal to the demands of his office. For the Conservative government it was a difficult time. Though Eden's actions enjoyed considerable popular support, much 'liberal' and 'intellectual' opinion had been alienated and was never recovered over the remaining years of Tory government. Many, in fact, doubted whether the Conservatives could hold on to power much longer.

Decolonisation

Britain emerged from the Second World War with its vast empire shaken, but essentially intact. Over the next quarter-century, however, the imperial edifice was almost entirely dismantled. The process, though neither continuous nor at first coherently planned, left only a few intractably problematic dependencies and a scattering of island territories, too small, remote or underdeveloped for independence. Independence for the Indian sub-continent (1947–48), and abandoning the League of Nations/UN mandate over Palestine (1948) – little more than an undignified scuttle –

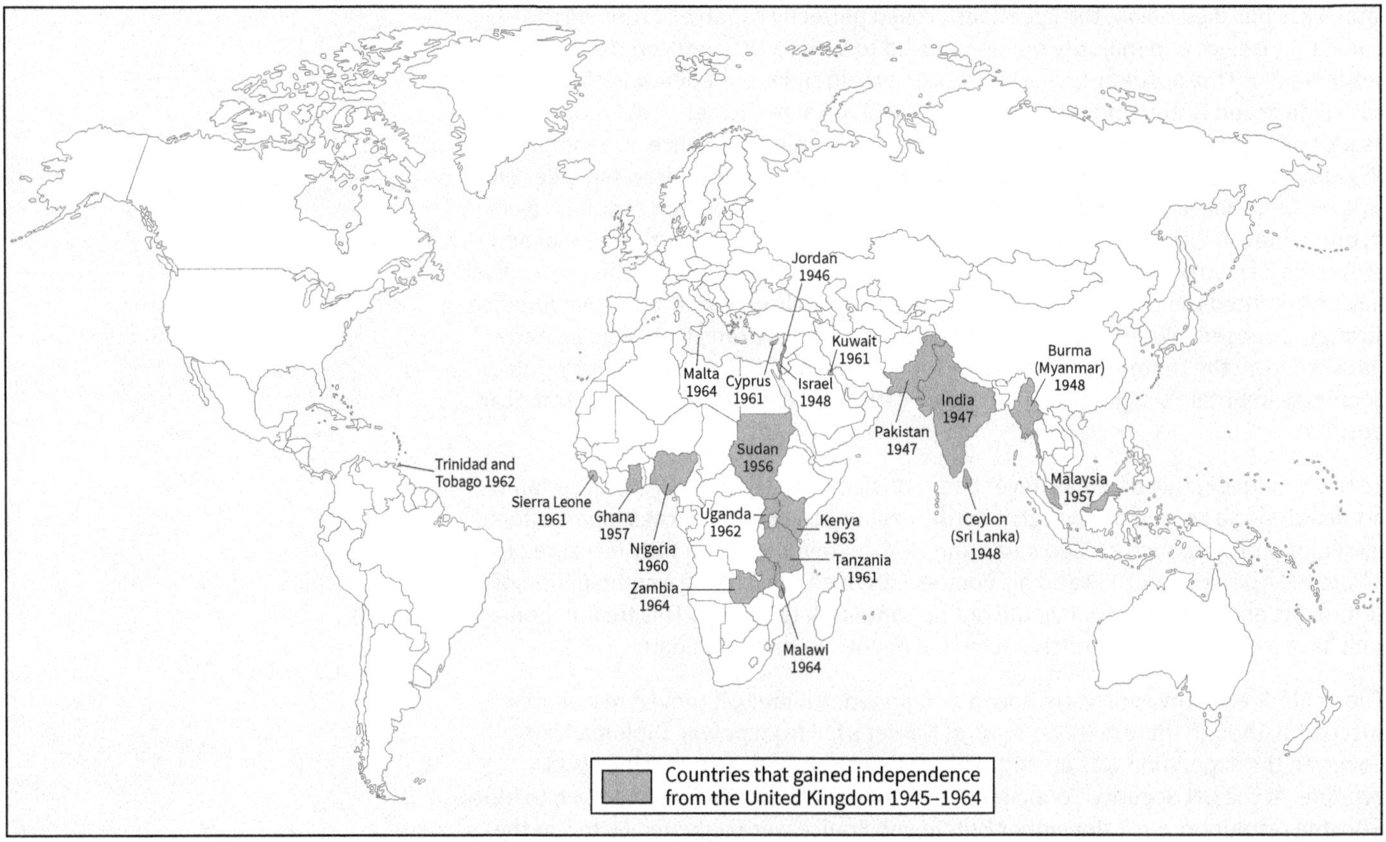

Figure 1.17: The decolonisation of the British Empire 1945–1964.

were both pragmatically necessary, as there were insuperable obstacles to continued British rule. Labour hoped that independence would not lead to the end of British influence. After all, the independent dominions had decided of their own will to join the war effort of the 'mother country', and their support was still a fresh memory. An independent India within the Commonwealth would be part of a 'body confidently expected in Whitehall to grow eventually into a surrogate empire bolstering British prestige on the international stage'.[47]

In places where British strategic and economic interests were involved, the Labour government tried to hold back the tides of decolonisation and maintain imperial control, so when the Conservatives returned to power there was more continuity than might have been expected. Churchill's views had been shaped in the Victorian era, and he bitterly opposed Indian independence. However, the majority of leading Tories accepted that the days of the Raj had come to an inevitable end. One Labour minister recalled that it was Eden's job 'to keep Churchill away from the House while the [Indian independence] Bill went through'.[48] In the dependent colonial territories both Labour and Conservative governments made minor constitutional concessions to assuage nationalist unrest, but were not afraid to use force to preserve British authority. In Kenya following the Mau-Mau insurrection, in Cyprus in response to the EOKA (Ethniki Organosis Kyprion Agoniston) independence movement and in Malaya against the ongoing communist insurgency, British forces used oppressive measures, with varying success, to maintain control.

ACTIVITY 1.6

Using the information in this chapter and your own research, establish a timeline showing which countries gained independence from the British Empire between 1945 and 1964.

The 'wind of change'

The real change came with Macmillan's premiership. The new Prime Minister immediately commissioned a 'profit and loss' audit for each remaining colony. It had long been understood that, whatever the Empire's economic benefits, its maintenance imposed a heavy burden on the Treasury. Though the findings of this survey proved inconclusive, Macmillan embarked on a new phase in Britain's imperial history. Between January 1957 and October 1964, 20 colonies secured their independence. This represented a conscious shift of policy in London. The change of direction was most marked after Iain Macleod's appointment as Colonial Secretary in October 1959. Indeed, Macleod announced that he hoped to be the last ever occupant of this office. (In fact, this distinction fell to Labour's Fred Lee in 1966.)

The motivation of Macmillan and Macleod was multi-layered. If the cost/benefit analysis had not offered an overwhelming case for the government's policy, the changing pattern of British trade did. The percentage of trade with Empire and Commonwealth countries almost halved during the 1960s; that with Europe significantly increased. In a celebrated speech to the South African parliament in February 1960, Macmillan declared that the 'wind of change' was blowing through the African continent. 'Whether we like it or not', he added, 'the growth of national consciousness is a political fact.' Yet it would be wrong to interpret the process of decolonisation as primarily a response to the growth of national sentiment, although the existence of heavyweight and credible national leaders such as Nkrumah (the Gold Coast), Nyerere (Tanganyika) and Banda (Nyasaland) did facilitate the actual handover of power. Rather, the wind of change was blowing through Whitehall and much of the British establishment. The perils of trying to hang on to colonial possessions too long, demonstrated by France in Indo-China and Algeria, Belgium in the Congo or Portugal in Mozambique and Angola, were plain to see. International opinion was united in opposition to imperialism. American hostility dated back at least to the Second World War; Soviet antagonism was entangled in its Cold War strategy to increase influence in the developing world. The age of imperialism proved much shorter than earlier generations had anticipated. Some remnants of Empire – Southern Rhodesia, the Falkland Islands, Hong Kong and Gibraltar – continued to cause difficulties in the decades ahead. Overall, however, the process of decolonisation was carried out relatively well, at least in comparison to that of other leading imperial powers.

ACTIVITY 1.7

1. Study the timeline. Events have been put into separate columns: which would you move to a different column and why?
2. Which developments have been omitted from the table that you think should be included? Explain why.

Timeline 1950–64

Government and politics	Economics	Date	Society	Foreign affairs
		1950		Outbreak of Korean War
Conservatives secure narrow victory at general election. Churchill Prime Minister; Eden Foreign Secretary; Butler Chancellor		1951		April: Treaty of Paris establishes European Coal and Steel Community
September: Labour Party divisions emerge at Morecambe Conference	Plan Robot considered, but rejected by cabinet	1952		April: NATO comes formally into being October: first British Atomic Bomb test
June: coronation of Queen Elizabeth II Churchill suffers severe stroke		1953	Conservatives meet 300 000 houses per annum target	July: hostilities cease in Korea. December: Eisenhower and Churchill meet in Bermuda
	February: Economist coins phrase 'Butskellism' July: food rationing ended	1954		April: Geneva Conference on South-East Asia October: WEU created
April: Churchill retires; Eden becomes Prime Minister; Macmillian Foreign Secretary May: Conservatives' majority up to 85 seats December: Macmillian replaces Butler as Chancellor; Atlee retires; Gaitskell becomes Labour leader	April: Butler's 'giveaway' pre-election budget October: emergency 'pots and pans' budget	1955	February: plans for atomic power stations announced September: start of commercial television	June: Messina Conference
		1956	Gulliebaud Committee endorses NHS	October–November: Anglo–French invasion of Egypt
January: Eden resigns; Macmillian becomes Prime Minister; Thorneycroft Chancellor; Selwyn Lloyd Foreign Secretary Bevan speaks in favour of nuclear weapons	July: Macmillian's 'never had it so good' speech in Bedford September: bank rate raised to 7%	1957	March: Homocide Act retains death penalty for 'capital' murder Rent Act relaxes rent controls April: end of National Service announced June: first Premium Bond draw	March: Gold Coast becomes independent as Ghana March: Macmillan and Eisenhower meet in Bermuda March: Treaty of Rome sets up European Economic Community April: Sandys Defence Review May: first British hydrogen bomb test

Government and politics	Economics	Date	Society	Foreign affairs
January: Thorneycroft replaced as Chancellor by Amory February: CND founded	January: Clash between Prime Minister and Chancellor over government expenditure leads to resignation of Treasury ministers	1958	August: race riots in Nottingham and Notting Hill	
October: general election, Conservatives increase majority to 100 seats Macleod appointed Colonial Secretary		1959	December: Crowther Report recommends raising school leaving age to 16	
July: Lord Home becomes Foreign Secretary	Selwyn Lloyd becomes Chancellor (until 1962); era of 'stop-go'	1960	National Service ends June: House of Commons rejects Wolfenden Committee report	February: Macmillian's 'Wind of Change' speech in South African parliament May: European Free Trade Association launched; Paris Summit Conference
		1961	May: first legal betting shops *The Stagnant Society* published	August: Britain makes first application for EEC membership
July: Macmillan's 'Night of the Long Knives'; third of the cabinet sacked	National Economic Development Council and National Incomes Commission established Reginald Maudling becomes Chancellor (until 1964) Unsuccessful 'dash for growth'	1962	July: Commonweath Immigrants Act becomes law	December: Macmillan negotiates purchase of Polaris missiles from USA
January: death of Gaitskell February: Harold Wilson becomes Labour leader October: Macmillan resigns; Dougles-Home 'emerges' as Prime Minister; Buter Foreign Secretary; Maudling Chancellor		1963	March: Beeching Report on British Railways publishing October: Robbins Report on higher education	January: DeGaulle vetoes Britain's EEC application August: Partial Test Ban Treaty
October: narrow Labour win in general election; end of 13 years of Conservative government	Resale Price Maintenence abolished	1964		February: Douglas-Home visits Washington for talks with Johnson

Further reading

A number of recent writers have succeeded in synthesising the political, economic and social history of this period. See, in particular, Peter Hennessy, *Having It So Good: Britain in the Fifties* (London, 2006), David Kynaston, *Family Britain 1951–57* (London, 2009) and *Modernity Britain 1957-62* (London, 2013–14), and Dominic Sandbrook, *Never Had It So Good: A History of Britain from Suez to the Beatles* (London, 2005). The approach of Kevin Jefferys, *Retreat from New Jerusalem: British Politics 1951–64*

(London, 1997) is narrower, but it provides a concise and perceptive introduction to the politics of these years.

Practice essay questions

1. 'There remained a broad measure of agreement between the Conservative and Labour Parties in the years 1951 to 1964.' Explain why you agree or disagree with this view.
2. 'British society in the 1950s remained fundamentally conservative and resistant to change.' Assess the validity of this view.
3. 'The Suez Crisis clearly showed that Britain was no longer a Great Power'. Explain why you agree or disagree with this view.
4. With reference to the sources and your understanding of the historical context, which of these two sources is more valuable in explaining Britain's failure to join the European Common Market?

Source A

Source: Earl of Kilmuir (Home Secretary 1951–54 and Lord Chancellor 1954–62), ***Political Adventure***. London: Weidenfeld and Nicolson; 1964. p. 188

The breakdown of the Brussels negotiations early in 1963, which occurred after I had left the Government, had its roots in 1951–52. Had we taken our proper part in those years in associating ourselves warmly with European Union, our economic and political authority in the free world would have been enormously increased and also, I believe, the benefits would not have been confined to one side. The humiliation of Brussels in 1963 was, in modern parlance, the 'pay-off' for our faint-heartedness and apparent duplicity in 1951–52. European unity never meant abandonment of the Commonwealth, but the hesitation and pusillanimity shown by both major parties in the 'fifties gave the opportunity for the shrill xenophobia of the Beaverbrook press and others to arouse fears and anxieties which were groundless.

Source B

Source: Sir Anthony Eden. ***Full Circle***. London: Cassell & Co; 1960. p. 32

I had no quarrel with the conception of a European Defence Community ... I liked the idea, for I have never thought that my country need have any apprehension on account of a closer union between the nations of continental Europe. We have suffered too much from the lack of it, and the trend these days should be towards larger units. My reservation arose from other causes ... it seemed to attempt too much, to ask more of the nations concerned than they could freely give and then the outcome might be disillusion, leaving Europe in disarray. On the other hand, I was prepared to admit that I could be wrong in this judgment, which might be the result of our English preference for taking our changes in doses rather than at a gulp.

Chapter summary

At the end of this chapter you should be able, taking account of the views of different historians of this period of British history, to form your own views regarding:

- the consensus policies of the Conservative governments during this period, and how well successive leaders honoured the electors' confidence in them
- the variations in economic performance by the British economy during this period
- how the new sense of affluence gave rise to changes for women and young people, and in attitudes to class, and how Britain reacted to increased immigration
- Britain's relationship with her European neighbours and with the USA and USSR, and the reduction in the role of the UK in worldwide politics.

Endnotes

1 Pimlott B. (ed.) *The Political Diary of Hugh Dalton*. London: Jonathan Cape; 1986. p. 567.

2 Butler D and Stokes D. *Political Change in Britain*. London: Macmillan; 1974. p. 106–7.

3 Catterall P. (ed.) *The Macmillan Diaries, vol. II*. London: Macmillan; 2011. p. 598.

4 Morgan J. (ed.) *The Backbench Diaries of Richard Crossman*. London: Hamish Hamilton and Jonathan Cape; 1981. p. 30.

5 Jay D. *Change and Fortune: a Political Record*. London: Hutchinson; 1980. p. 223.

6 Catterall P. (ed.) *The Macmillan Diaries, vol. II*. London: Macmillan; 2011. p. 462.

7 House of Commons Debates, 5th Series, vol. 679, col. 65.

8 Jefferys K. *Retreat from New Jerusalem: British Politics 1951–1964*. Basingstoke: Macmillan; 1997. p. 184.

9 Jefferys K. *Retreat from New Jerusalem: British Politics 1951–1964*. Basingstoke: Macmillan; 1997. p. 5.

10 Jefferys K. *Retreat from New Jerusalem: British Politics 1951–1964*. Basingstoke: Macmillan; 1997.

11 Shepherd R. *Iain Macleod*. London: Hutchinson; 1994. p. 100.

12 Ramsden J. *The Winds of Change: Macmillan to Heath, 1957–75*. London: Longman; 1996. p. 32.

13 Macmillan H. *Riding the Storm*. London: Macmillan; 1971. p. 350–51.

14 Shanks M. *The Stagnant Society*. London: Penguin; 1961.

15 Turner J. *Macmillan*. Harlow: Longman; 1994. p. 244.

16 Jefferys K. *Retreat from New Jerusalem: British Politics 1951–1964*. Basingstoke: Macmillan; 1997. p. 156.

17 Jefferys K. *Retreat from New Jerusalem: British Politics 1951–1964*. Basingstoke: Macmillan; 1997. p. 156.

18 For Mitford's differentiation between acceptable and unacceptable vocabulary, see Mitford N. The English Aristocracy. *Encounter*. 1955; September 24. p. 5–11.

19 Kynaston D. *Family Britain*. London: Bloomsbury; 2010. p. 147.

20 Kynaston D. *Family Britain*. London: Bloomsbury; 2010. p. 133–34.

21 Kynaston D. *Family Britain*. London: Bloomsbury; 2010. p. 572.

22 Kynaston D. *Family Britain*. London: Bloomsbury; 2010. p. 578–79.

23 Sampson A. *Anatomy of Britain*. London: Hodder and Stoughton; 1962. p. 637–38.

24 Kynaston D. *Austerity Britain*. London: Bloomsbury; 2008. p. 274.

25 Kynaston D. *Austerity Britain*. London: Bloomsbury; 2008. p. 519.

26 Kynaston D. *Austerity Britain*. London: Bloomsbury; 2008. p. 275.

27 Catterall P. (ed.) *The Macmillan Diaries, vol. II*. London: Macmillan; 2011. p. 382.

28 Hennessy P. *Having It So Good: Britain in the Fifties*. London: Penguin; 2006. p. 223.

29 Lamb R. *The Failure of the Eden Government*. London: Sidgwick & Johnson; 1987. p. 15–24.

30 Kynaston D. *Family Britain*. London: Bloomsbury; 2010. p. 100.

31 Kynaston D. *Family Britain*. London: Bloomsbury; 2010. p. 448.

[32] Marwick A. *The Sixties: Cultural Revolution in Britain, France, Italy, and the United States, c. 1958–c. 1974*. Oxford: Oxford University Press; 1998. p. 17.

[33] Sandbrook D. *Never Had It So Good: a History of Britain from Suez to the Beatles*. London: Little, Brown; 2006. p. 474.

[34] Sandbrook D. *Never Had It So Good: a History of Britain from Suez to the Beatles*. London: Little, Brown; 2006. p. 445.

[35] Sandbrook D. *Never Had It So Good: a History of Britain from Suez to the Beatles*. London: Little, Brown; 2006. p. 450–51.

[36] Bullock A. *Ernest Bevin: Foreign Secretary*. London: Heinemann; 1983. p. 352.

[37] Self R. *British Foreign and Defence Policy since 1945*. Basingstoke: Palgrave Macmillan; 2010. p. 120.

[38] Young JW. (ed.) *The Foreign Policy of Churchill's Peacetime Administration, 1951–1955*. Leicester: Leicester University Press; 1988. p. 85.

[39] George S. *An Awkward Partner: Britain in the European Community*. Oxford: Oxford University Press; 1998. p. 34.

[40] For more on this, see Young JW. *Winston Churchill's Last Campaign: Britain and the Cold War 1951–5*. Oxford: Clarendon Press; 1996.

[41] Dutton D. *Douglas-Home*. London: Haus; 2006. p. 73.

[42] Self R. *British Foreign and Defence Policy since 1945*. Basingstoke: Palgrave Macmillan; 2010. p. 201.

[43] Campbell J. *Nye Bevan and the Mirage of British Socialism*. London: Weidenfeld and Nicolson; 1987. p. 337.

[44] Hennessy P. *The Prime Minister: the Office and its Holders Since 1945*. London: Penguin; 2001. p. 217–18.

[45] *Daily Telegraph*. 3 January 1956.

[46] Brivati B. *Hugh Gaitskell*. London: Richard Cohen; 1996. p. 273.

[47] Self R. *British Foreign and Defence Policy since 1945*. Basingstoke: Palgrave Macmillan; 2010. p. 45.

[48] Lapping B. *End of Empire*. London: Paladin; 1985. p. 87.

2 The Sixties, 1964–1970

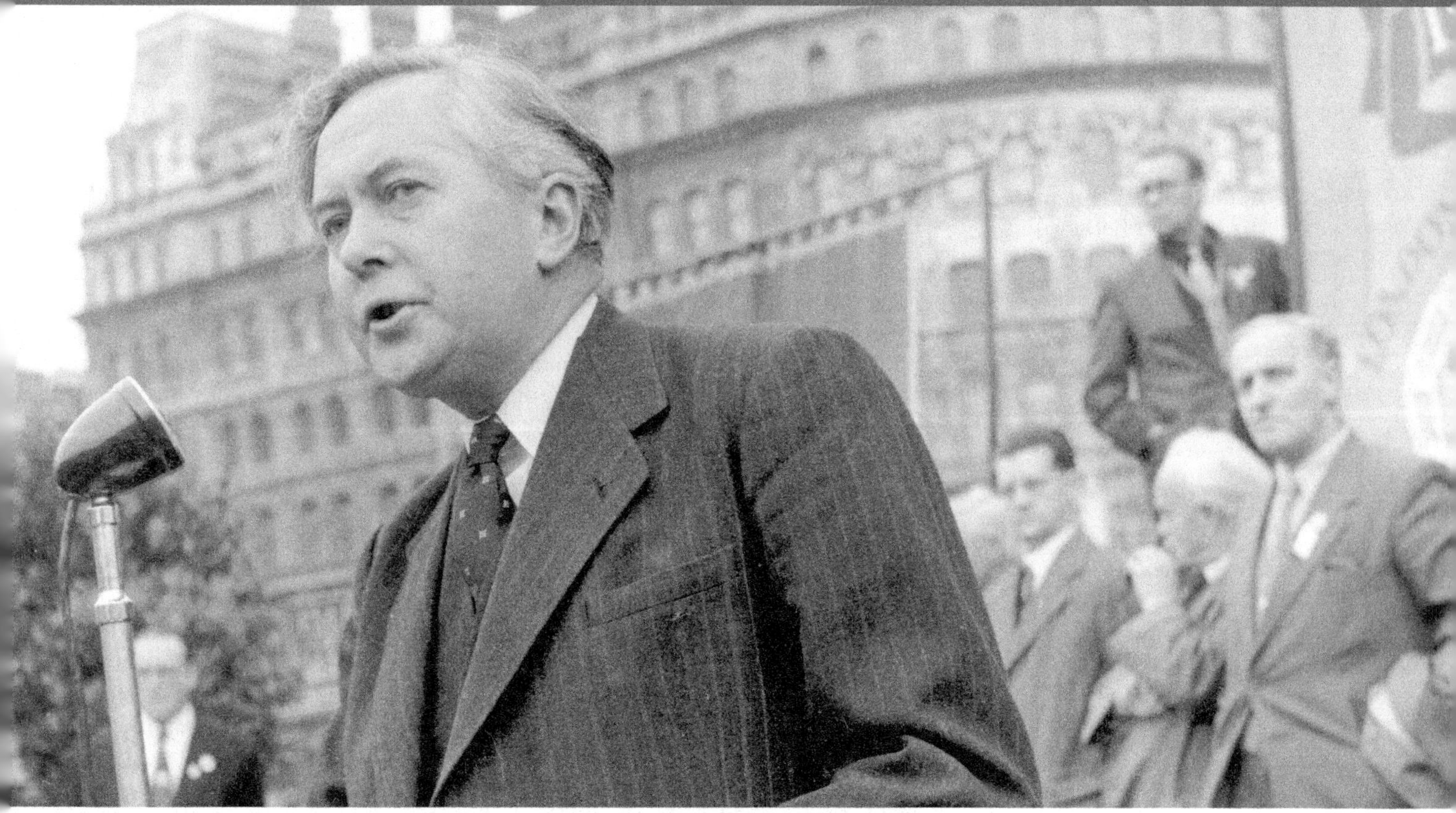

In this section, we will be focusing on the 1960s, an iconic period of change in Britain and in the wider world. There were many challenges, both political and economic, facing Britain and countries around the world. These were happening in tandem with radical social and technological developments that were changing the way people not only lived, but also thought. In particular, we will look into:

- Wilson and the Labour governments: Wilson's ideology and leadership; economic policies and problems; devaluation; industrial relations; the trade unions; other domestic policies; Labour divisions; the beginning of the 'Troubles' in Northern Ireland; the end of post-war consensus; loss of 1970 election.
- Liberal reforming legislation: private members' bills and the end of capital punishment; divorce reform; the legalisation of abortion; the legalisation of homosexual relations; educational reform.
- Social and cultural change: the expansion of the mass media; growth in leisure activities; the impact of scientific developments; the reduction in censorship; progress towards female equality; changes in moral attitudes; youth culture and the 'permissive society'; anti-Vietnam war riots; issues of immigration and race.
- Relations with, and policies towards, the USA, particularly the issue of Vietnam; response to world affairs and relations with Europe; decolonisation including 'withdrawal East of Suez' and Rhodesia.

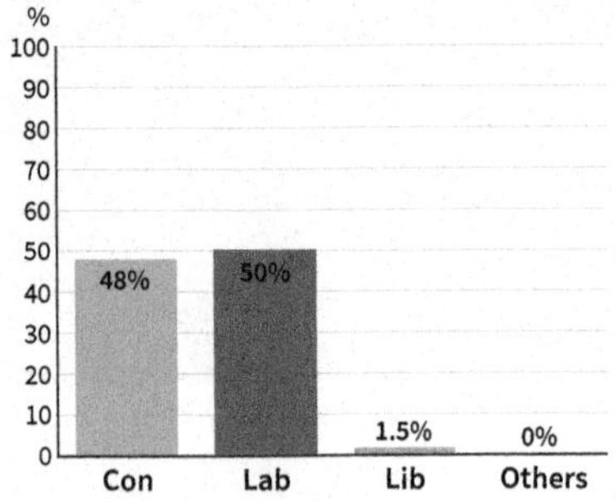

Figure 2.1: Seats in the House of Commons won in the 1964 British general election; percentages have been adjusted to the nearest whole number. Ulster Unionist figures are included in Conservative totals.

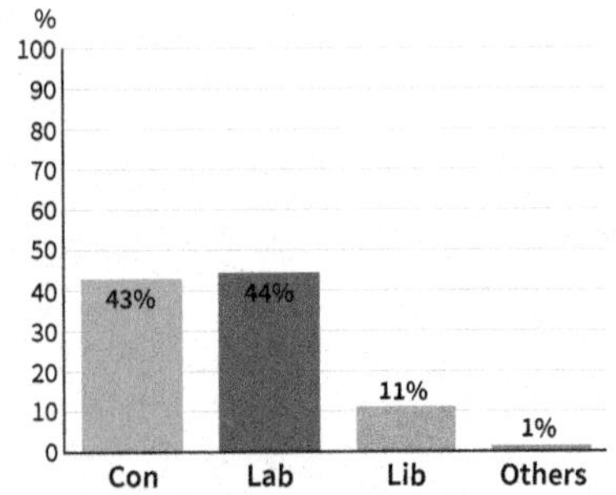

Figure 2.2: Votes won in the 1964 British general election; percentages have been adjusted to the nearest whole number. Ulster Unionist figures are included in Conservative totals.

ACTIVITY 2.1

Complete Table 2.1 as you read through this section on the Labour government of 1964–70. The first one has been started to get you going. Add as many rows as you want.

Wilson and the Labour governments

Wilson's ideology and leadership

Nothing in politics is inevitable. At first glance, Wilson's victory in 1964 may seem to have been so. However, Douglas-Home's incisiveness and modesty gave Labour a run for their money (see Figures 2.1 and 2.2). Labour had a very narrow majority. It was a very shocked and excited Wilson (with wife and eldest son) who went to Buckingham Palace on 16 October 1964 to see the Queen, and become Prime Minister.

Harold Wilson came from reasonably humble beginnings; his biographer describes his family as northern lower-middle class. He was a brilliant scholar, attending grammar school before achieving a first class degree from Oxford. His contemporaries at Oxford became his colleagues (Denis Healey) and opponents (Edward Heath) during his administrations. Wilson worked hard at university and this work ethic never left him. In fact, his style as Prime Minister was to interfere with his ministers' departments, causing irritation among them and leaving him open to criticism when things went wrong. Wilson liked to play his ministers off against each other. For example, the Department of Economic Affairs (DEA), led by George Brown, clashed badly with James Callaghan's Treasury. Both departments sought overall control of the economy, both men felt they were the superior of the other and Wilson kept them guessing. This was typical of Wilson and he became known as a slippery character. He found it hard to be loyal to any one particular minister, because he felt he was a cut above them and could do their job better. His closest confidante was Marcia Williams, his political secretary.

Wilson won the 1964 general election promising modernity. He was the youngest Prime Minister of the century, although with his pipe and raincoat he looked older. As leader of the Labour Party in opposition he was compared favourably to the American President, John F. Kennedy. His pedigree was of the left, but, in practice, he was pragmatic and his policies (if not always his rhetoric) tended to be centrist. He managed to combine a 'man of the people' persona with an image of dynamism. His idea was to get the country going again, through a planned economy underpinned by modern scientific thinking. He wanted to do away with privilege and replace it with purpose and drive. Britain was to be transformed into a modern, dynamic country: it would be forged in the white heat of a revolution. In short, Wilson's ideology appealed to people like him: middle class, intelligent and on the rise.

Problems faced	People involved	Action taken	Outcome
Problems with the pound	James Callaghan (Chancellor) Harold Wilson (PM) George Brown (DEA)	Describe the policy of devaluation avoidance followed by devaluation.	State the value of the pound and the impact on the government.
Industrial relations			

Table 2.1: Problems of the Labour government 1964–70.

Key personalities

Harold Wilson (1916–95) was leader of the Labour Party from 1963 to 1976 and Prime Minister from 1964 to 1970 and again from 1974 to 1976. He won four general elections (1964, 1966, Feb 1974 and Oct 1974) and lost once, to the Conservatives led by Edward Heath. He resigned from office in 1976 at the age of 60. He stated exhaustion but may have known about his early-onset Alzheimer's disease by then. Wilson was succeeded by James Callaghan. He was created Baron Wilson of Rievaulx in 1983 (after leaving the

House of Commons) and attended the Lords until a year before his death from colon cancer and Alzheimer's disease in 1995. Wilson wanted to be remembered for his role in the formation of the Open University.

Edward Heath (1916–2005) was leader of the Conservative Party from 1965 to 1975 and Prime Minister from 1970 to 1974. He won one general election (1970) and lost three to Harold Wilson's Labour Party. He was succeeded as leader of the Conservatives in 1975 by Margaret Thatcher. After losing the leadership, Heath remained an MP until 2001. He was the Father of the House between 1992 and 2001. Heath is most remembered for taking the UK into Europe on 1 January 1973.

James Callaghan (1912–2005) was leader of the Labour Party from 1976 to 1980 and Prime Minister from 1976 to 1979. He lost to Margaret Thatcher's Conservatives in the 1979 general election. Between 1964 and 1970 Callaghan held two ministerial posts: he was Chancellor of the Exchequer between 1964 and 1967 and Home Secretary between 1967 and 1970. He is best remembered for overseeing the devaluation of the pound in 1967. This cost him his position as Chancellor and he was moved to the Home Office in a swap with Roy Jenkins. He was the longest-lived British former Prime Minister and served in all four of the Great Offices of State.

George Brown (1914–85) was deputy leader of the Labour Party from 1960 to 1970. He missed out on becoming leader when Harold Wilson took over in 1963. Brown served under Wilson as Secretary of State for Economic Affairs between 1964 and 1966 and as Secretary of State for Foreign Affairs between 1966 and 1968. When Wilson could not contact him to talk about the pressure the pound was under in March 1968, he left the government. This followed several attempts at resignation, usually brought on by bouts of drinking.

Denis Healey (1917–2015) served as an MP for forty years, was Secretary of State for Defence between 1964 and 1970 and Chancellor of the Exchequer between 1974 and 1979. He lost out twice in attempts to become the Labour Party's leader. As Defence Secretary he cut spending on defence and recognised the UK's reduced capability to act as a police force around the world. He is remembered for announcing the withdrawal of troops from 'east of Suez'. He was the last of Wilson's 1964 cabinet to die.

Marcia Williams (1932– present) was Harold Wilson's private secretary in opposition. Once he became Prime Minister, she became his political secretary and head of the political office. Andrew Marr says that she 'helped build up his (Wilson's) morale, challenged his complacency and, until her apparent bullying became intolerable, probably made him a better politician than he would otherwise have been.'[1] Rumours of an affair between the two have never been proven and have been fiercely denied by both. She became Baroness Falkender (her mother's maiden name) in 1974 and in 2016 was still attending the House of Lords.

Roy Jenkins (1920–2003) was Minister of Aviation until the reshuffle of December 1965, when he became Home Secretary and oversaw the liberal reforms of the 1960s. Jenkins was moved to the Treasury in November 1967 after the devaluation of sterling. Along with Callaghan, Jenkins was a potential rival for the leadership of the Labour Party.

Barbara Castle (1910–2002) held three posts in Wilson's first two administrations: she held the post of Minister for Overseas Development for a year, then became Minister for Transport between 1965 and 1968, before becoming Secretary of State for Employment in 1968 (a post she held, along with the honorific title of First Secretary of State, until election defeat in June 1970). *In Place of Strife* is inextricably linked to her and its failure damaged her politically.

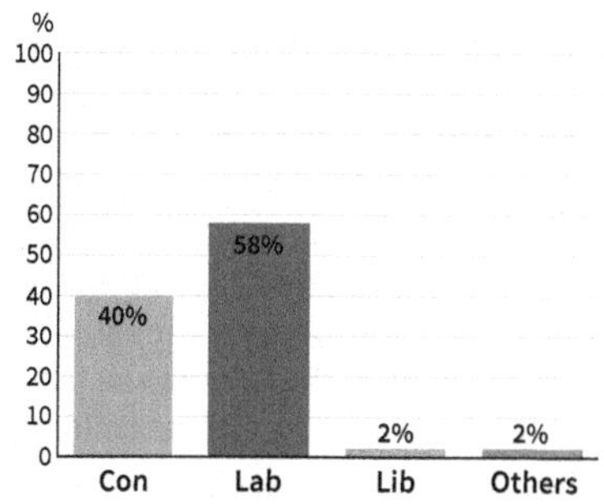

Figure 2.3: Seats in the House of Commons won in the 1966 British general election; percentages have been adjusted to the nearest whole number. Ulster Unionist figures are included in Conservative totals.

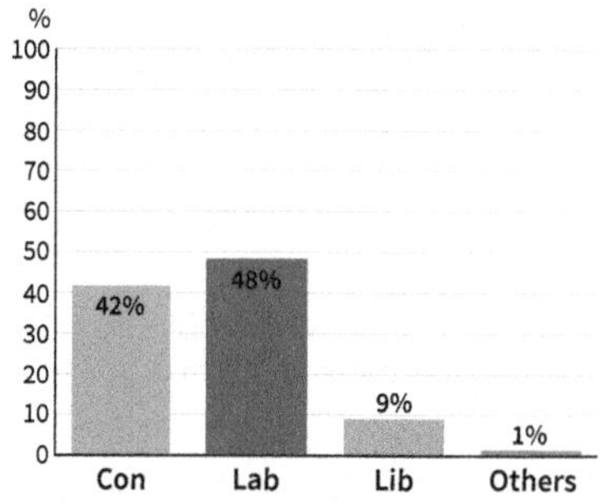

Figure 2.4: Votes won in the 1966 British general election; percentages have been adjusted to the nearest whole number. Ulster Unionist figures are included in Conservative totals.

Key terms

deflation: a measurement of the price level of goods and services and the opposite of inflation, deflation is when this measurement falls below zero. If the price of goods is rising too fast, deflationary measures, i.e. measures that decrease the price of goods, might be called for.

corporatism: the idea that the government, trade unions and businesses can sit together and discuss future policy in order to sort out issues like pay increases and strikes.

Cross-reference **Chapter 2** *Industrial relations*

Tony Benn (1925–2014) was a left-wing politician who first entered Parliament in 1950, and (with breaks) was an MP until 2001. Before the election victory of 1964, Benn inherited his father's peerage, which would have prevented him from remaining as an MP. His campaign led to the Peerage Act 1963. He entered government as Postmaster General and became Minister of Technology in 1966.

Economic policies and problems

'Sorry to leave such a mess, old cock'.[2] Not particularly encouraging words from the outgoing Chancellor of the Exchequer, Reggie Maudling, to the incoming Chancellor, James Callaghan. Labour had not been expecting the finances of the country to be in a mess. Their election manifesto promised increased spending on welfare, pensions and schools; this was immediately in jeopardy. The country seemed to be doing reasonably well: inflation was low, as was unemployment, but production in Britain was lower than its competitors. The major issue had been Conservative overspending, borrowing mainly from the Americans. The deficit, on arrival in office, was estimated by the Treasury to be £800m, but this overestimation was only discovered much later.[3] The drain on the finances was the expensive overseas bases, not the difference between imports and exports; without an understanding of this, there was no hope of a successful economic policy being formulated.

Callaghan and Brown introduced a surcharge on imports of 15% to try and raise some revenue. Obviously, this proved unpopular abroad and the fear of reprisals meant the surcharge was reduced to 10% within months and abolished altogether after a year. This did save £150m on imports but was not the solution to the government's problems. Callaghan's first budget had to be **deflationary**, but this would mean the government could not carry out its manifesto pledges. Income and petrol taxes were raised and corporation and capital gains taxes were to be introduced: these efforts were mildly deflationary.

Lord Cromer, the Governor of the Bank of England, was able to raise an aid package that saw the new government through the worst of 1964 and into 1965. In fact, exports began to outweigh imports and the books were becoming balanced. However, the aid package needed repaying and, if any more money was to be borrowed, foreign investors would want to see deflationary measures in place. The government were in a cleft stick: they had been elected on a platform that needed them to spend money, but the economy demanded that they did not.

Callaghan's 1965 budget introduced more deflationary measures that, in the absence of any better ideas from Brown, were accepted reasonably well. In the summer, the bank rate was cut by 1% (it had gone up by 2% the previous year) in order to give consumers (voters) some breathing space and to make the government more popular. In this way, the economy struggled along through the successful general election of 1966 and into 1967.

A key element in Wilson's government was the Department of Economic Affairs (DEA). It was established, under George Brown, in order to centralise planning. This was Labour's attempt at **corporatism**. Brown's task was to bring together government, unions and business in order to agree economic policy and strategy that would take the country forward. Brown did manage to write a National Plan that had voluntary agreements on prices and wages controls. This was a major achievement and down to his personality, but the Treasury, not wanting to lose control, stifled his efforts. The economy was in such a state that it was inconceivable that anything voluntary would work. By 1966 the DEA was dead in the water and Brown had been moved to the Foreign Office: the job he'd always wanted.

Devaluation

The one measure that might have delivered a stronger economy from the start was devaluation, but this would have been accompanied by a loss of prestige for the new government (which had a slender majority), so it was immediately ruled out. By 1967 it was being talked about much more seriously and in November action was needed. Britain was now indebted by £1500m and loans were not forthcoming: devaluation was the only option. It would mean the government going back on its promise, but there was no other choice and Callaghan had resigned himself to this option. A final begging telegram was sent to the US, asking for a loan and setting out the extent of the problem, but no one expected a positive response.

At the beginning of November, Wilson, Callaghan and Brown met for a drink at Number 10. They talked openly and honestly about a number of things and agreed that, if the telegram to America did not produce the right result, devaluation was the only option. It did not and devaluation was set for 18 November 1967. The announcement came just after 9 p.m.: the pound was devaluing from $2.80 to $2.40, a cut of 14%. Devaluation was accompanied by more deflationary measures, such as spending cuts on defence and the raising of the bank rate. For some it was not enough. As was expected, Callaghan resigned the next day and was replaced by Roy Jenkins.

Wilson delivered his famous 'pound in your pocket' speech the following day, saying that although the pound abroad was now worth less money, the pound in your pocket at home was still worth the same ('still alright'). He fooled nobody. Heath was able to reply to Wilson on television and accused the Labour government of failing in their duty of looking after the country's currency. He also pointed out that the Labour government had gone against its own policy: in 37 months they had denied 20 times that they would ever devalue the pound.

Under Jenkins the fortunes of the country did revive. Jenkins was happier to impose deflationary measures and taxes increased. This, together with a miscalculation by the Inland Revenue over the value of British exports, meant that he oversaw a surplus of revenue over government spending by 1969.

Industrial relations

A Labour government might reasonably be expected to have good industrial relations and be able to keep the trade unions on their side. Arguably, the unions share responsibility for the Labour defeat in 1970 and, in the longer term, they can blame themselves for their eventual demise under Thatcher in the 1980s.

Industrial relations were relatively calm in the period leading up to 1964, with fewer days lost through strike action in Britain than in any other western competitor, except West Germany.[4] Wilson hoped this would continue under his leadership and adopted a 'beer-and-sandwiches' approach to relations with the union leaders. He would invite them to Number 10 for a convivial chat over refreshments. Brown's voluntary incomes and wages policy, agreed with union leaders and employers, fell apart in 1966 with the strike by the National Union of Seamen (NUS) over weekend work and overtime rates. The seamen wanted a pay increase of 17%; pay had increased by 10% over the last year, making a mockery of Brown's policy of keeping increases to 3.5%. The government had to take a firm stance against the seamen.

ACTIVITY 2.2

Research a copy (audio or written) of Wilson's 'Pound in your pocket' speech. Discuss with a partner the good and bad points of it from the perspective of the Labour and Conservative parties.

Taking it further

Investigate the pattern of strikes in industry in Britain between 1960 and 1970 and the number of working days lost. Can you find any comparable data for some of the UK's competitors?

Key terms

white paper: this document presents the government's findings and intentions on a particular policy area. It does also allow for a degree of discussion before legislation is introduced.

wildcat strikes: action taken by members of a union, but usually without the knowledge or approval of the union leaders.

leak: information, which an organisation had officially decided to keep secret, released from the organisation to the press or other outsiders.

The ship-owners were ready to make a deal with the seamen but the government prevented them from doing so. Wilson, with information supplied by MI5, delivered a speech to the Commons, accusing several of the NUS leaders of trying to harm the nation. The speech shocked his Labour colleagues, because of its anti-union sentiment.

In a different speech Wilson went on to name eight NUS leaders as having associations with the Communist Party. This did end the strike, but at great political and economic cost to the government and to Wilson.

Economically, exports had fallen because of the strike, resulting in a loss of income for the government of £40m. This put pressure back on the pound, so the spectre of devaluation reappeared and, this time, did not go away. Politically, Wilson's actions horrified some of his colleagues and changed his relationship with the unions: now they did not trust him.

The trade unions

By far the most damaging piece of industrial relations was *In Place of Strife*, a government **white paper** setting out, in essence, that strikes would become more organised and regulated, and less spontaneous, and that the **wildcat strikes** favoured by some unions would cease. It is worth noting that the number of *actual* days lost through strikes was very low. However, the public perception of the problem and, therefore, the political problem for Wilson, was that these strikes were unacceptable. This perception was compounded when the strike rate really did increase in 1968. This called for action.

Barbara Castle was the minister charged with that action. In November 1968 she spent a weekend with her officials working on the initial draft of the document that was to become *In Place of Strife*. Amidst departmental **leaks**, the cabinet were split and it took several more meetings before Castle and Wilson got cabinet support. The public and press were largely impressed at the tough stance from the government against the unions. The unions needed convincing and they had a high-ranking minister, in the form of Callaghan, on their side. Despite being part of the cabinet, Callaghan voted against the white paper at Labour's National Executive Committee. This high treachery deserved strong action from Wilson, but none was forthcoming. To retrieve his reputation Wilson decided to implement some of the measures immediately, but came up against strong union opposition. Even Labour's backbench MPs were reluctant to back the document, as many of them (around 150) owed their jobs to union support.

Voices from the past

Harold Wilson

It has been apparent for some time – and I do not say this without having a good reason for saying it – that since the Court of Inquiry's report a few individuals have brought pressure to bear on a select few on the executive council of the National Union of Seamen who in turn have been able to dominate the majority of that otherwise sturdy union. It is difficult for us to appreciate the pressures which are being put on men I know to be realistic and responsible, not only in their executive capacity but in the highly organised strike committees in the ports, by this tightly knit group of politically motivated men, who, as the last General Election showed, utterly failed to secure acceptance of their views by the British electorate, but who are now determined to exercise back-stage pressures, forcing great hardship on the members of the union, and their families, and endangering the security of the industry and the economic welfare of the nation.[5]

Discussion points

1. Of whom is Wilson speaking when he refers to a 'tightly knit group of politically motivated men'?
2. Look back at the political background of men such as Wilson, Callaghan, Brown and Healey and discuss why this speech might have seemed shocking and to whom.
3. Was Wilson right to talk in such emotive political terms?

In Place of Strife caused serious problems for Wilson's government. Castle no longer trusted him, Callaghan was in open revolt, and backbench MPs would not support a paper that jeopardised their livelihood. Wilson set up an inner cabinet of seven and called the three main union leaders (Jack Jones, Vic Feather and Hugh Scanlon) to a weekend meeting at Chequers, the Prime Minister's country retreat. Barbara Castle, holidaying in Naples, flew in for the negotiations, but nothing came of them. Wilson and Castle were looking more and more isolated and, when Chancellor Jenkins felt he could no longer support the proposals, the government was doomed to failure. Wilson emerged from last-minute talks with the Trades Union Congress (TUC) declaring a settlement, but it was a capitulation and no one was fooled. Castle had failed to implement union reform and this had left the government looking weak. This was certainly one of the reasons for electoral defeat the following year. Moreover, the failure only made the unions stronger, ultimately leading to the disputes of the 1970s and their eventual emasculation in the 1980s.

Figure 2.5: Barbara Castle with *In Place of Strife*.

Date of strike and who is involved	What was the strike over?	What happened?	Action and outcome
September 1968 Girling Brakes	An oil valve was turned on by a member of the wrong union.	Gearbox assemblers walked out, causing a halt in production, which led to thousands of workers standing idle with some being laid off.	The government were impotent. Barbara Castle made a statement in the Commons outlining that she was setting up a court of inquiry. Four weeks later the workers returned.

Table 2.2: Industrial action 1964–70.

ACTIVITY 2.3

Research the amount of industrial action, 1964–70. Then complete Table 2.2.

Other domestic policies

Like Wilson's other policies, housing was touched by the white heat of technology. Ambitious targets were set, but never quite reached due to the pressure on the pound. The Labour government continued the trend for building high-rise tower blocks: they were cheap to build; stopped the urban sprawl into the countryside; and fitted in with modern ideas about architecture. Many council tenants moved into flats.

Wilson's ambitions in housing did not stop at tower blocks, but encompassed whole towns: new towns. The idea was not new: Letchworth (founded 1905) and Welwyn Garden City (founded 1920) were the first two garden cities. Attlee's government passed the New Towns Act in 1946, establishing fourteen towns designed to alleviate

Hidden voices

In Place of Strife

Three of the major proposals were:

- Unions should call ballots before a strike could be held
- There should be a 28-day cooling-off period before a strike can go ahead
- An industrial board would be set up by the government to impose a settlement.

Discussion point

Hold a class debate on the motion 'The proposals in *In Place of Strife* undermined the effectiveness of trade union strikes'.

pressure of population in their regions. Under the Labour government more new towns came into being and Milton Keynes was the most successful. Ironically, built to incorporate offices on the outskirts (to cut down congestion) and shopping in the centre (in pseudo-American style), Milton Keynes marketed itself as a leafy, green utopia. Sandbrook suggests that, 'far from representing a new mode of urban living, Milton Keynes in fact marked the triumph of suburbia'.[6]

Of all the amendments and new acts introduced by Wilson's government, he wanted to be remembered most of all for the Open University (OU). First mooted in 1963 in opposition, as the University of the Air, Wilson wanted to give a second chance 'to those who can profit from it, but who have been, for one reason or another, unable to go to a University or a College on leaving school ...'[7] The path to setting up the OU was not smooth, as Wilson faced opposition from Tony Crossland, his Education Minister, on the grounds that it was a waste of money. Wilson had to ensure that Callaghan set aside enough money for it, while the 1966 white paper received hostility from the *Times Educational Supplement* for being impractical. Nevertheless, Wilson persevered. The OU received its Royal Charter in July 1969 with its headquarters in Milton Keynes; its first undergraduates were admitted two years later.

Labour divisions

Figure 2.6: Ronan Point, in Newham in East London, built to help meet Labour's housing targets. A gas explosion brought down one corner of the building, killing four people. Inadequacies in construction methods were identified and public confidence in the safety of these tower blocks was shaken. This led to improvements in building legislation.

Wilson's leadership victory over Brown and Callaghan and subsequent election victory brought new divisions into the Labour Party. Not so much a split between left and right, as under Bevan and Gaitskell, but a contest between Brown and Callaghan, manufactured by Wilson. By placing Brown at the head of the DEA and appointing Callaghan as his Chancellor, Wilson set his two rivals against each other. In his autobiography, Callaghan points out that, despite his support for the setting up of the DEA, the three men found it difficult to agree a workable formula on how they should conduct their day-to-day business, because Brown and Callaghan had different priorities. He suggests that Wilson, as PM, should have had final say, but that this often took some time. It is clear that underneath a veneer of civility, Callaghan found working opposite Brown tiresome. Although they did reach an understanding, Wilson's hope of generating 'creative tension' did not go down well with his Chancellor.[8]

Wilson's cabinet was further beset by division between Jenkins and Callaghan. Neither man particularly liked the other. Jenkins thought Callaghan a 'bully' while Callaghan thought Jenkins 'arrogant'.[9] The result of their dislike played into Wilson's hands, as it kept two more possible leaders 'at' each other, rather than 'at' him. During the discussions over *In Place of Strife*, both men were mooted as successors to Wilson, but Jenkins's dislike of Callaghan prevented him from playing his hand out of fear of losing to his rival.

Overall, Wilson was able to use the antagonisms between his cabinet ministers to maintain his position as leader. They knew he was slippery, but were more frightened of a rival taking over and so were prepared to leave things as they were.

The beginnings of the 'Troubles' in Northern Ireland

A deeply divided province

The Government of Ireland Act (1920) formally recognised the six counties that would make up Northern Ireland (NI). The rest of the island would still be part of the UK, but the Irish War of Independence meant that an Irish Free State came into being instead (1922). Northern Ireland is predominantly Protestant, with a minority of Catholics, while the south is mainly Catholic. While it would be too simplistic to say that the 'Troubles' in NI started because of these religious differences, it would also be wrong to say that religion did not play a part in them. The religious labels were an outer manifestation of a clash of identities – Irish or British.

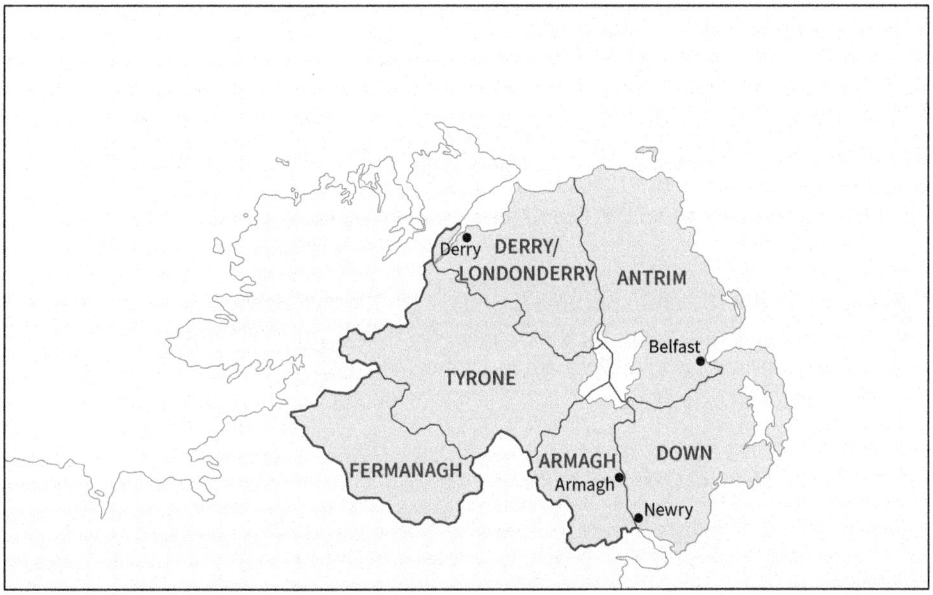

Figure 2.7: Northern Ireland.

It is fair to say that Northern Ireland did not register on Westminster's radar until the late 1960s. Governments, of whichever persuasion, felt that matters were best left in the hands of their elected representatives. The NI Prime Minister, Terence O'Neill (who was PM from 1963 to 1969), tried to introduce measures to bring Catholics and Protestants closer together. Furthermore, he attracted some big businesses to locate in NI, but this was weighted towards the capital, Belfast, in the east; the west remained relatively poor. Splits in NI society emerged along economic lines as well as religious: many working class Protestants were no better off than their working class Catholic neighbours. Unfortunately, the perception by these Protestants was that Catholics were seeking what they had, even though they had little. Resentment increased, and the man of the moment was Ian Paisley.

Key Protestant groups and personalities

Ulster is a term used by Protestants to denote the six counties of Northern Ireland. The original Ulster also included three counties now part of the Republic.

The **Royal Ulster Constabulary (RUC)** was NI's police force. It, too, was predominantly Protestant and heavily involved in the Orange Order.

The **Orange Order** is so named because of William of Orange, who was married to Mary (daughter of King James II). Crowned with her in 1689, he became King William III. Orangemen, members of the Orange Order, swear to uphold the Protestant faith. Marches take place annually to commemorate specific events and have sometimes resulted in violence.

The **Ulster Volunteer Force (UVF)** existed to try and combat Irish republicanism; they were the main opposition to the IRA. The UVF were responsible for many deaths, mainly of Irish Catholic civilians.

Terence O'Neill (1914–90) was from an Anglo-Irish family. He was educated at Eton and served in the Irish Guards during World War Two. He was the MP for the Bannside constituency between 1946 and 1970 and Prime Minister of Northern Ireland between 1963 and 1969.

Ian Paisley (1926–2014) was the leader of the Protestant Unionist Party between 1966 and 1970 and an evangelical minister from 1946 until his death in 2014.

Key Catholic groups and personalities

The **Irish Republican Army (IRA)** was founded in 1917 by members of previous Irish nationalist organisations. Dedicated to the independence and unity of the island of Ireland, it fought the British, then it fought in an Irish civil war. It then continued to operate as a terrorist organisation, campaigning for Northern Ireland to become part of an all-Ireland state. In the 1960s the movement divided: the Official IRA gradually faded from significance and the **Provisional IRA (PIRA)** maintained the 'armed struggle'.

Bernadette Devlin (b. 1947) became prominent in the civil rights movement in NI and was responsible for ensuring the People's Democracy march through Derry went ahead. She became an MP in 1969, but was jailed for her part in the Battle of Bogside.

Cross-reference **Chapter 3** *Bloody Sunday*

Growing violence

Paisley's rousing, anti-Catholic, speeches struck a chord with many Protestants in NI. His message stood in stark contrast to O'Neill's more moderate one. Violence began to creep into Northern Irish life. The state had the RUC and the B Specials (a heavily armed security force made up of Protestants); the Catholics had the IRA, although they had not been particularly active since the 1920s. The Protestants had the Ulster Protestant Volunteers (UPV), set up by Paisley and his apprentice, Noel Docherty. The latter was in charge of a further secret cell of paramilitary Protestants who, in collaboration with the Ulster Volunteer Force (UVF), were to be responsible for much of the violence to come. To add to this mixture a civil rights movement began – the Northern Ireland Civil Rights Association (NICRA) – that aimed to end discrimination against Catholics. NICRA's aims were loosely based on the American Civil Rights movement, the right for all citizens of Northern Ireland to be treated the same. However, instead of the persecuted minority being black, they were Catholic.

For many historians the killing of Mary Gould is considered the start of the 'Troubles'. Gould, a 77-year-old Protestant, died of burns acquired on the night of 7 May 1966. A group from the UVF targeted a Catholic pub, but got the wrong address and threw a petrol bomb through her window instead. A Protestant gang had killed an innocent Protestant woman! Further isolated attacks occurred and an innocent eighteen-year-old Catholic boy, Peter Ward, was killed outside a pub in Belfast. O'Neill spoke for the majority when he expressed his shock and anger at the murder and called for NI to consider whether they wanted violence, or law and order.

Tension was now close to the surface of Northern Irish society. During the 1967 marching season there were verbal attacks on O'Neill's weak leadership, and the Orange Orders distributed inflammatory literature. The civil rights movement staged a march in August 1968 that passed without violence. Because of this they planned another for October in Derry (Londonderry), designed to pass through Protestant areas and be deliberately provocative. Four hundred NICRA members defied a ban and marched through Derry, receiving the violent reaction they expected. O'Neill visited Westminster and was told to sort out the problems in NI. Upon his return he announced a five-point plan to calm down the Catholic community. This played into Paisley's hands and angered Protestants further. O'Neill, with his support in the government diminishing, played his last hand and gave a live television broadcast appealing for calm and order.

A splinter group of the civil rights movement, called People's Democracy (PD), ignored O'Neill's plea. The police told the group not to enter Derry for fear of possible violence, yet they marched on, encountering Protestant bricks, boulders and bottles. This battle

ACTIVITY 2.4

Research the history of the 'marching season' in Northern Ireland.

1. How did it arise?
2. Which groups are involved?
3. What happens during the marching season?

took place at Burntollet Bridge and images shown on television provoked further violence against Catholics in the Bogside area of Derry.

O'Neill called for a general election in NI and won, but it was a bitter fight. Paisley stood against him in his Bannside constituency. A bombing campaign in the spring of 1969 left much of Belfast without water and finished O'Neill off. The campaign was the work of the UVF, but Paisley stated that the IRA was clearly responsible. Paisley wanted O'Neill gone and a new leader in place: he got his wish when O'Neill resigned on 28 April 1969. James Chichester-Clark was the replacement, similar in pedigree and style to O'Neill.

In April, the PD's Bernadette Devlin defeated the Ulster Unionist candidate in a by-election, and the funeral of murdered taxi driver Samuel Devenney (beaten to death by the RUC) kept the mood tense throughout the spring. The Orange Marches of July did nothing to promote calm. The Apprentice Boys' march ignited into a full-scale battle. Over a three-day period in August 1969, fierce fighting broke out between the Catholics of Bogside in Derry on one side and the Protestant unionists and the RUC on the other. The state had finally lost control: fighting also broke out in Belfast, Armagh and Newry. Callaghan sent the British Army to quell the violence. They succeeded, and many soldiers commented on the friendly reception they encountered. With the army on the streets, and civil relations calming down, the 'Troubles' settled ... for the time being.

Event	Description	Outcome
Mary Gould's murder		
Peter Ward's murder		
NICRA march through Derry		
O'Neill's Crossroads speech		
PD march through Derry		
NI general election 1969		
Battle of Bogside		

Table 2.3: Events in the Northern Ireland Troubles.

ACTIVITY 2.5

Complete Table 2.3 by including a detailed description of the events listed (further research needed) and by considering the outcome in terms of impact on the British and Northern Irish governments as well as on Protestant and Catholic organisations and individuals.

The end of post-war consensus

While the period 1964–70 did not see the breakdown of the post-war consensus, there are signs that politicians and opinion-formers were beginning to question the way the country was being run, in the face of stiff international competition. Post-war Britain had been relatively prosperous, but when compared with her major overseas rivals – France, Germany, Japan and the USA – Britain was noticeably lagging behind. The idea that, economically, Britain was slipping led the left and right to question the post-war consensus. The Wilson government's answer was more state control. The formation of the DEA under Brown can be seen as one answer to Britain's economic decline. Another example was Anthony (Tony) Benn's leadership of the new Ministry of Technology.

Wilson's 1964 election promise to bring in an era of modernity forged in the white heat of technology was given shape in the new ministry. Benn, who replaced Frank Cousins in 1966, would have control over a vast array of resources in order to reshape modern Britain. Hi-tech industries would get support from MinTech, as the ministry became known, and the profile of the research and development of new ideas would be raised. Government would support business in raising the profile of cutting-edge technology, thus falling in line with Wilson's election promise. In practice, however, MinTech's achievements were limited.

Mergers were encouraged, although the merger of Leyland Motors with the British Motor Corporation in 1968 was a notable failure. The new company did not mount a perceptible challenge to international motor companies, being wound up in 1986 and signalling the end of British-owned mass car manufacture in Britain.

The breakdown of the post-war consensus did not fully start during the Wilson years, but the recognition that something new needed to be tried resulted in more state 'planning' embodied in the DEA and MinTech. The failure of both of these led to different approaches by subsequent governments.

Meanwhile, on the right, there were the first signs of free-market thinking from such figures as Enoch Powell and Nicholas Ridley, though for the time being they remained very much a tiny minority in the Conservative ranks.

Loss of the 1970 election

Wilson had a choice to make: should he call an election in October or June? June meant that there was less chance of trade figures getting worse, but October gave Wilson, and the Labour Party's fortunes, more chance to rise. He chose June and was rewarded with blue skies and brilliant sunshine. It was also a World Cup year, with England one of the favourites to win: the perfect time for a general election. The economy seemed to be going well, with trade figures in the black. What could go wrong? There are several answers to that question: Wilson's complacency, a drop in the trade figures and Heath's focus on the household budget.

It seems that Wilson was so pleased with his performance against Heath across the Despatch Box and on TV; so comfortable with his position as the leader of the Labour Party; and so happy with the trade figures, that complacency set in. After months trailing behind Heath, the Labour Party began the election campaign ahead in the polls, and stayed ahead until polling day. Wilson led an American Presidential-style campaign, where he was the focus of attention. Cheering crowds accompanied him on walkabouts, where he hardly talked about policy. Heath, on the other hand, managed to come across as aloof on film, although in their final TV broadcast it was considered that Heath came across better. The Labour Party thought this too little, too late – they would still win the election.

A factor that caused anxiety for the Labour Party was the trade figures, released a few days before the election. May's figures showed a deficit and Heath was able to step up his policy of targeting the housewife. He had been resilient in maintaining that he would win with this policy. He knew that devaluation had not made families richer and he kept telling whoever would listen. In the final analysis he was right. His chief whip, Willie Whitelaw, was preparing the way for Heath's successor, assuming he would lose. Heath and Wilson retired to listen to the result. As soon as the first result came in from Guildford, showing a swing of 5% to the Conservatives, Wilson knew he'd lost.

Liberal reforming legislation

Private Members' Bills

It is strange to think that the Labour government's most enduring legacy was its liberal reforms: ending capital punishment, divorce reform, legalisation of abortion and of homosexual relations. In fact, none of these were actually introduced into parliament by the government: they were all **Private Members' Bills**.

The end of capital punishment

There were a number of issues that Wilson was keen to allocate parliamentary time to, but felt were best left out of party politics. The abolition of capital punishment was one of them. The journey to abolition was not particularly straightforward and actually went against the wishes of the majority of the electorate. For most of the sixties, people simply did not want this law abolished. The Conservatives had introduced the Homicide Act 1957. This merely muddied the waters by making certain murders punishable by death, while others would be classed as manslaughter and receive a prison sentence. By the sixties the Conservatives were somewhat divided over the issue. Sidney Silverman was the Labour backbench MP who introduced the Murder (Abolition of the Death Penalty) Bill and its second reading was carried by 355 to 170 votes. This was not the end of the matter, as the Conservatives deployed a number of different tactics to try and stall its progress.

Key terms

Private Members' Bill (PMB): a bill introduced to parliament by a member of the House of Commons or Lords who is not in the government.

Firstly, they wanted the bill debated in the Commons, rather than in committee. The Labour and Liberal Parties worked together to defeat this. Secondly, the Conservatives presented a PMB that called for the bill to be recommitted to a committee of the whole house. This would mean that the bill would eat into valuable government time in the Commons, or would be dropped altogether. To stop this happening a resolution was passed that said the Commons should, unusually, meet on a Wednesday morning for this committee stage. Finally, when the bill was passed, the Lords added an amendment that said the Homicide Act of 1957 should come back into force after a period of five years, unless both Houses carried motions providing for permanent abolition.

The final debate on abolition had to take place before July 1970, so in the later stages of 1969 the issue came to parliament again. Between 1965 and the final debate in 1969 there had been some high profile murders whose perpetrators had escaped the death penalty. None eclipsed the Moors Murderers, Ian Brady and Myra Hindley, for wickedness and column inches. Their arrest came four weeks after the 'suspension' of the death penalty, so they were given life sentences instead. These and other murders kept the issue alive and meant that the MPs voting for abolition were going against their constituents' wishes. Opinion polls show that support for hanging among the public never dipped below 60% and went as high as 80% after crimes such as the Moors Murders.[10]

Wilson was advised to settle the debate before the general election of 1970, as it would not be in the interests of candidates to make abolition an election issue. He had to balance this argument against those who said that rushing it before Christmas might produce an unfavourable result – although both sides of the argument said this! The Conservatives tabled a censure motion, effectively claiming that there was no confidence in the government. The real problem was that both sides wanted to use the 1969 crime figures in their favour, but the figures were not yet available. Wilson appeased by allowing for a whole day's debate. In winding up the censure debate Callaghan promised that the crime figures for 1969 would be made available the next day, thus allowing a full and fair debate on abolition. Wilson notes in his autobiography that all three party leaders were in the abolitionist lobby and the vote to end the death penalty was carried by 343 to 185 in the Commons and by 220 to 174 in the Lords.

Figure 2.8: Ian Brady and Myra Hindley, the infamous 'Moors Murderers'.

There are two footnotes to the abolition story. The first is that, unfortunately, Sidney Silverman never got to see his bill become law, because he died in 1968. The second is that the Home Secretary most associated with the liberal reforms of this Labour Government, Roy Jenkins, was not Home Secretary when the bill was introduced in 1965 and had moved on from the Home Office to become Chancellor by the time it became law.

Divorce reform

Jenkins did have a hand in the reform of the divorce laws of the country. In fact, Marr calls him the 'single most influential politician of the sixties' for his role in the liberal reforms under discussion.[11] Prior to 1969 the law favoured the husband, in that reasons for divorce had to be proven. In essence, if a woman wanted to divorce her husband, she had to prove he was an adulterer. By 1937 improvements meant that the wife could add to the list of faults: drunkenness, insanity and desertion. These still needed to be proved and still placed the duty of proof on the woman. To make matters worse, divorce carried with it the whiff of social stigma, far more troubling for the woman than the man. Consequently, many women preferred to stay with unfaithful or violent husbands rather than risk becoming social pariahs. This position did not sit comfortably with Wilson's 'white heat' and it had to change.

Leo Abse, Labour MP between 1958 and 1987, introduced a PMB to try and permit divorce after seven years of separation. This failed, but it provided the basis for what became the Divorce Reform Act of 1969. Jenkins notes in his autobiography that the divorce laws were in urgent need of reform, because divorce involved 'both a great deal of unnecessary suffering and a great number of attempts to deceive the courts'.[12] He allowed time for debate in the Commons, giving the bill every chance of success – most PMBs fail because of a lack of time. The bill was passed in 1969, coming into effect on 1 January 1971. A marriage could now end if it had broken down irretrievably, no longer did the emphasis have to be on whose fault it was. It was often called a 'no-fault divorce' and, if both partners agreed, a divorce could be allowed after two years; or after five if only one partner wanted it to happen. This law showed that women were now equal partners in marriage.

Inevitably, within two years of the law coming into being, the number of divorces doubled. In fact, Peter Clarke (rather gloomily) traces the increase in divorce into the 1980s and suggests that the average duration of marriages regressed to the level of the 1820s![13]

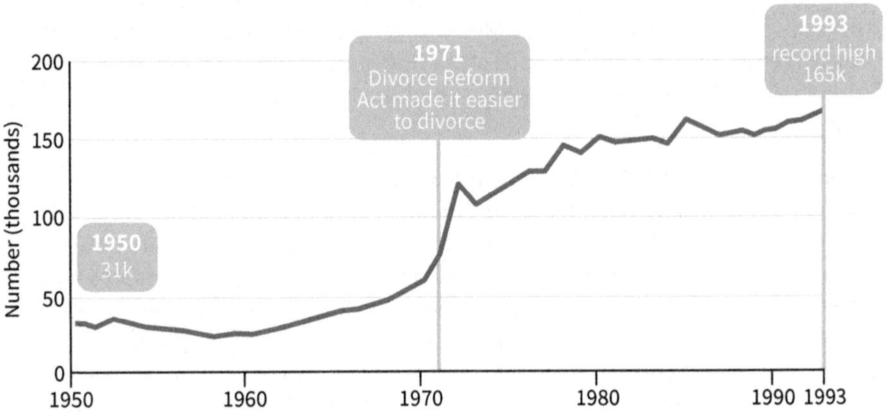

Figure 2.9: Historical trends in the overall number of divorces, 1950–93.

The legalisation of abortion

Another measure that allowed women more control over their futures was the Abortion Act 1967. Until this point abortion had been illegal, unless the mother's life was in danger. Before the act came into being the number of back-street abortions is widely acknowledged to have been around 100 000 per year. Many of these ended in further complications and permanent damage to the woman and even, in some cases, death. While some abortionists were competent, many were not, but frightened, isolated, young women – not knowing who to turn to and not wanting to make their plight public – went to these 'doctors' without complaint. If you had money you could buy good healthcare and privacy, although this did not guarantee success every time. Something had to be done to stop unwanted pregnancy from becoming a life-changing catastrophe.

The thalidomide crisis

In addition to the horrific number of botched abortions, there was a growing momentum for change as evidenced by a succession of unsuccessful bills between 1953 and 1966. The thalidomide drug, developed as a sleeping pill, had been thought to alleviate the symptoms of morning sickness and was given to pregnant women in the late 1950s and early 1960s. What subsequently became clear was that this drug had disastrous effects on the unborn child. Infants were born with malformations of the limbs, exhibiting as either no limbs or as short stumps. Abortions took place in order to stop babies with this condition being born. It seemed highly hypocritical to allow abortions for this, but prevent them for other reasons. Change followed.

David Steel

David Steel, a young Scottish Liberal MP who had won his seat in a 1965 by-election, introduced a bill to legalise abortion via the ballot for a PMB. One noticeable opponent of the bill was Leo Abse. Jenkins notes that he found it extraordinary to have to treat Abse as a hero when debating divorce reform, or the Sexual Offences Bill, but a 'hobgoblin' in debates over abortion. Support in the Commons meant that, despite several all-night sittings on government business, attendance was sufficient to push the bill through. Jenkins paid tributes to the young Scot, complimenting him on his 'exceptional courage' in seeing the bill through, despite not having a great party machine or a huge majority in his constituency, and being the 'baby of the house' (the youngest MP, 29 when the bill was passed).[14]

Abortion now needed the approval of two doctors, who deemed the abortion necessary because of medical or psychological need. The numbers of abortions rose, although it is hard to compare with pre-Abortion Act figures, because of the underground nature of the majority of them. What is clear is that access to legal, safe abortions through the NHS did not lead to an increase in promiscuity.[15]

The legalisation of homosexual relations

The Wolfenden Report, 1957 recommended that consenting adult homosexuals should be allowed to have sex in the privacy of their home. People were beginning to realise that homosexuality was not an illness that could be cured and punishment by incarceration was not the right answer. The report was backed by the *Daily Mirror*, *The Times* and the *Manchester Guardian*, but most of the dailies and weekend press rejected its message, with the *Sunday Express* calling it a 'pansies' charter'. Even Wolfenden was not offering full equality, only acceptance.[16] It would be another decade before the Sexual Offences Bill became law.

Following the publication of this report a group of distinguished people came together to support it. They became the Homosexual Law Reform Society. There followed a campaign to get the recommendations in the Wolfenden Report implemented: debate in parliament was followed by pamphlets and meetings, but it was clear the Conservative government was not planning to fulfil any of it. However, a new government was able to use the changing mood of the country.

Sandbrook suggests that, around the time of Wilson's first election victory, the public mood towards science and scientists was one of the utmost respect. Homosexuality was seen as a medical problem and should, therefore, have a medical solution – not a criminal one. Opinion polls pointed to a softening of attitudes towards homosexuals – not an attempt to understand, more one of pity. Homosexuals were ill and needed treating, not locking up. In addition, religious attitudes were changing too, with public support for reform from the Bishops of Bristol, London, St Albans, Birmingham and Exeter.[17]

Leo Abse, along with Lord Arran, became the main promoters of a new bill introduced in July 1966. Abse reasoned that, while most sections of society were seeing a relaxation in attitudes towards sex, homosexual men were not being treated with the same open-mindedness. One big issue was the fear that older men would prey on younger ones, especially teenagers. Abse conceded that the age of consent should be 21, thus avoiding including teenagers in the bill and keeping around 60 sympathetic Conservative members onside. For George Brown, it was of paramount importance to avoid corruption of the young – for this reason he opposed the bill. Further opposition came from those who still saw homosexuality as immoral.

Jenkins, as Home Secretary, was crucial to the success of the bill: he wrote that it would not have got through 'had not I or someone of a similar mind been Home Secretary'.[18] What Jenkins could provide was time and his authority. Most PMBs failed from a lack of willingness on the government's side to allow time for debate. Jenkins promised that this, and the other liberal PMBs, would be given sufficient time for debate. This was not always at the most convenient points in the day – in fact the bill was completed between 10.00 p.m. and 6.00 a.m. on 3 to 4 July. Furthermore, from the Despatch Box Jenkins could throw his considerable influence behind the bill, making it almost a certainty that it would pass. There was some opposition in the Lords, but without the worry of having to be re-elected, the peers passed the bill and it became law on 27 July 1967.

The law only applied to England and Wales, as opposition in Scotland and Northern Ireland was too great. Homosexuality only became legal in the 1980s in these two parts of the UK. Homosexual men greeted the law with relief, as they could now live their lives without fear of criminal prosecution.

Educational reform

The 1944 Education Act, introduced by Education Minister Rab Butler and thus commonly known as the Butler Act, put in place the Tripartite System of secondary education. Three types of school provided secondary education within the state system: grammar, technical and secondary modern schools. Entry to a grammar school was by way of an 11 plus examination, an IQ test that determined a child's schooling. Not all local authorities could afford to provide all three types of schools, so this test decided whether you went to the local grammar or were consigned to the local secondary modern – technical schools were rare. The secondary moderns lacked the prestige of the grammars and many of their pupils left school under the age of 16, while grammar school pupils stayed later and often went to university. By the time Labour came to power in 1964, there was a growing dissatisfaction with the education system and the 11 plus examinations.

Wilson moved Anthony Crosland from the DEA to become Education Minister in January 1965. Crosland was the product of the public school system and no fan of grammar schools. He was reputed to have sworn to destroy every 'grammar school in England. And Wales. And Northern Ireland'.[19] Crosland passionately believed in social equality. He is best known for his book, *The Future of Socialism*, written in 1955–56. In this, he argued that socialism needed to adapt to the modern world. Crosland wanted a fairer society, with a fair chance for everybody: the current education system did not provide this.

The 1944 Butler Education Act

The Tripartite System

Grammar	Secondary technical	Secondary modern
20% of children	5–10% of children	75% of children
GCE O levels	Less academic students	Most students sat CSE (from 1965), a few sat O levels
Preparing students for higher education	Preparing students to become scientists, engineers and technicians	Preparing students for less skilled jobs and home management

Figure 2.10: The Tripartite System introduced in 1944.

In addition to the new Education Minister's philosophy, we must add practical problems, such as money. Those born in the post-war baby boom now needed secondary education, but the country's schools were not fit for purpose. Local education authorities needed to make savings, so the choice between building two schools or one seemed no choice at all. The way forward was 'comprehensive' education: a system that would educate all pupils under one roof. There were many examples of sibling rivalry, where one sibling succeeded in getting into the grammar, while the other did not, creating resentment and jealousy that never healed. Marr points to a growing middle-class consciousness of disappointed parents whose offspring had failed to get into grammar school. These factors had already coalesced to make local authorities move towards a comprehensive system before Labour came to power; Crosland just accelerated the process.[20]

Educational reform under the Wilson government did not take the form of a new law, nor even an amendment to one; instead, it was based on the availability of money. Crosland's famous directive 10/65 said that money for new schools would only be forthcoming if those new schools were comprehensives. The process of change from grammar/secondary modern to comprehensive schooling, already started by the Conservatives, accelerated. By the time Wilson lost office, one-third of children were educated in a comprehensive school.

Did comprehensive schooling work? Wilson's promise was a grammar school education for all, but this was hopelessly optimistic. It was not realistic to expect every child to soak up an academic education, so what did he mean? He was really talking about schools providing a good education, in an environment that promotes learning. Given the difficulty in objectively measuring the performance of schools then, or now, it is hard to say whether the reforms provided a better education for the nation's children. What is clear is that, very quickly, the majority of pupils were educated in comprehensives and, in the words of Wilson's biographer, 'less privileged children in inner-city schools who had previously had the chance of a grammar school place at eleven were retained by the ghetto, and deprived of a possible escape route'.[21]

Finally, it is worth noting that the Open University (see the section 'Other domestic policies') was not the only change to higher education during the Wilson Years. The Robbins Report (published October 1963) led to the expansion of higher education

ACTIVITY 2.6

With a partner, conduct extra research into the education reforms and debate whether you agree or disagree with Ben Pimlott's assessment of the destruction of the grammar schools.

places and it fell to the Labour Government to implement and pay for its provisions. Lord Robbins chaired the committee tasked with the job of exploring why Britain only had 8% of the relevant age group in HE (Clarke, 1996 p. 288). A lower proportion, when compared with universities abroad, of undergraduates from families with the father in manual labour was the reason. A government commitment to provide grants for all in HE was one answer but there needed to be more places. More universities opened, concentrating on teaching rather than research.

There were many success stories and none more than the University of Sussex whose 'schools of study' provided excellent teaching in their field as well as purposeful cross-disciplinary work. Universities like East Anglia, Warwick and Lancaster increased the total number by 1968 to 56 with the total number of students doubling by 1970.

Social and cultural change

The expansion of the mass media

Television ownership in the sixties was high. Around 90% of homes had one and, with three channels to choose from (BBC2 was launched in 1964), the choice of what to watch was expanding. Increasing affluence and cheaper sets fuelled this growth, made more exciting by the latest innovations, such as the introduction of colour television programmes, used intermittently from the summer of 1967 and used more widely in the seventies as colour television sets became more common. The nature of the programmes also changed, as programme makers catered for a variety of audiences and the need to make their shows more exciting. News and sport remained the staple diet, but more exciting programmes were made, such as *The Prisoner*, a futuristic show set in 'the Village', that addressed themes such as freedom, personal identity and democracy. Comedy shows like *Monty Python's Flying Circus* (from 1969) pioneered the sketch show format and brought a very surreal style of comedy to television. The group Monty Python had been developing their style of comedy over the sixties as the six members had worked on various other comedy shows as writers and performers.

Private Eye was already an established satirical magazine by the time Wilson took over at Number 10. Hand in hand with this magazine was the TV programme, *That Was The Week That Was*, or *TW3*. Neither could be credited with changing the face of politics, but both annoyed Wilson. *Private Eye* had a column that purported to be written by Mrs Wilson, entitled *Mrs Wilson's Diary*, where all manner of trivia and titbits were espoused (including some rather bad poetry!). Interestingly, a play based on the diary faced censorship by the Lord Chamberlain before the Theatre Act came into force. Wilson felt that he was treated unfairly by the satirists and that he was genuinely popular among the public at large. The austerity package introduced in the summer of 1966 to stave off devaluation triggered some particularly savage treatment of Wilson in *Private Eye*. Furthermore, his refusal to denounce outright American policy in Vietnam, led to a cartoon showing Wilson licking Johnson's backside. While the majority of people may not have read or watched the aforementioned media, satire did sting the politicians, even if it did nothing to change their actions.

The Sun newspaper was launched in 1964 as a broadsheet with the slogan 'time for a newspaper, born of the age we live in'. This was a clear shot at appealing to those most likely to be a hit with the advertisers: women and teenagers. Sales of the first issue exceeded expectations, but *The Sun* soon came in for criticism for its lack of substance. News UK (Rupert Murdoch) bought the ailing newspaper in 1969 and turned it into a tabloid.

The growth in the mass media gave people more choice in what to watch and read, where to get their information from and how to spend their leisure time. This growth certainly helped fuel the changing attitudes in the sixties.

Growth in leisure activities

Hand in hand with the growth of the mass media went an increase in leisure activities. Fuelled by post-war necessity and a selection of specialised magazines and television programmes, do-it-yourself (DIY) continued to be a major pastime for the man about the house. As home ownership increased, so did hobbies like DIY. Perhaps the greatest leisure activity of the sixties was gardening and this was also supported by television programmes, such as *Gardeners' World*, the successor to *Gardening Club*. Here, Wilson's white heat of technology made an impact with the production of the Flymo hover mower, using hovercraft technology.

One important shift in leisure habits during the sixties was the change in holiday destinations. At home, the traditional seaside holiday trip to Blackpool, or a Butlin's Holiday Camp, was giving way to caravanning. The Caravan Club saw its membership double during the sixties and independent travellers experimented by visiting new places, such as Devon and Cornwall. A spirit of adventure may account for some of the increase in caravanning, but there were pragmatic reasons too. In Blackpool, for example, dumped raw sewage was washed onto the beach by the tide. At Butlin's and Pontin's Holiday Camps, moreover, there were clashes in moral outlook between visiting teenagers and more traditional families. The major threat to the traditional seaside vacation, however, came from package holidays abroad, as Spain became Europe's number one destination. Holidaying abroad was not as popular as it would later become (between 1966 and 1971 total holidays abroad rose from 4% to 8.4%), but the trend was upwards.[22] The leisure habits of the country were evolving: holiday destinations changed as people became more adventurous, or had more disposable income. Technological changes and increased media representation altered the ways in which people went about their traditional pursuits of DIY and gardening.

ACTIVITY 2.7

'The sixties were not all about swinging: for most families the home remained the focus of leisure time.' From your reading in this chapter, and your own research, write 500 words to say whether you agree with this statement.

The impact of scientific developments

On their mission to investigate goings-on in space, the crew of the *Discovery* have to contend with a sentient computer, HAL 9000, which is in complete control of the spacecraft. In order to preserve itself, HAL 9000 kills. This is the backdrop to Arthur C. Clarke's *2001: A Space Odyssey* – not real life, but, in 1964, one could have been forgiven for thinking that the scientific revolution would produce just such developments. From *Dr Who* to *James Bond*, science and gadgets were ubiquitous.

Scientific developments made an impact across a wide variety of areas, from the home to the hospital. Gardens benefited from hovercraft technology; while developments in photography, chemical engineering and transistor radio gifted to modern medicine better X-ray equipment, sulphonamides (antibacterial drugs) and hearing aids respectively. Not all scientific developments had life-changing impacts. For instance, one of the most useful developments of the sixties was polythene. Developed to insulate electrical equipment, polythene could also wrap or contain food. Another synthetic plastic, PVC, could be used in its non-rigid form for clothing, and plastic jewellery, miniskirts, handbags, boots, raincoats and furniture in bright, bold, colours became fashionable.

Figure 2.11: Vinyl clothing was highly fashionable.

The sixties also saw the recognition of the potential of computers and that they would play a huge part in business in the future, even if their manufacture and development was lacking. The government increased spending on non-military scientific research. Although she could not match the USA for spending, Britain outspent its European rivals in ensuring that science and scientists played a major role in a modern Britain.

The reduction in censorship

The first trumpet call of the permissive society had already been sounded in 1960 when Penguin Books were able to publish *Lady Chatterley's Lover* for the first time. The Theatres Act 1968 struck another blow to the old order. The role of approving plays for the theatre fell to the Lord Chamberlain, now more likely to organise the details of an overseas royal visit than provide the moral compass of a nation. The incumbent in the sixties was Lord Cobbold, a former Governor of the Bank of England and, to his credit, he was mightily relieved to see an end to his censorship role.[23]

Edward Bond's *Saved* provided the ammunition with which to challenge the existing censorship laws. *Saved* is a gritty play set in 1960's London, centred on a couple who fall in and out of love quickly and their associated friends and family. It portrays the reality of life on the dole and the frustration the characters felt with their lives. The leading female character, Pam, falls pregnant, but is not married – her baby is almost tortured to death by the father and his friends. The play was not allowed to run without severe cuts and, when it was shown to large private audiences, the Lord Chamberlain successfully prosecuted the producers.

This judgement, however, provided the impetus for backbench Labour MP George Strauss to launch a PMB which met with little opposition. There was already a select committee report in favour of abolishing theatre censorship to help the PMB on its way. Jenkins was, again, Home Secretary at the start of the bill's life, although not at its conclusion, and was credited by the Lord Chamberlain for its successful passage. The Theatres Act 1968 was another example of the liberal reforms of the sixties. While some plays, such as *Hair*, took advantage of the relaxation of censorship, there was no call to repeal the act.

Progress towards female equality

When Labour came to power in 1964 the role of women had hardly changed for decades. True, the kitchen might now have shiny white electrical goods, to take the tedium and hard work out of washing clothes and there might be a vacuum cleaner ready to take the strain out of keeping the floors clean. However, did this satisfy the women of the sixties? For some it would have done; women were spoken of as 'kitchen goddesses' and revelled in the role of homemaker, wife and mother. For many others, the sheer boredom of housework and the lack of prospects for women made them responsive to change.

The introduction of the female contraceptive pill in 1961 can be seen as a move towards equality, as far as sex is concerned. Initially the pill was only prescribed to married women, but it became available to single women in 1967. A survey by Geoffrey Gorer, conducted in 1969, highlights the importance of being able to have sex without fear of pregnancy for married and single women alike.[24] The pill gave women control over their own fertility and allowed them to pursue a career and have some form of financial independence. However, without the threat of pregnancy, men were sometimes more easily able to pressure women into having sex.

The Dagenham strike

Barbara Castle's role in bringing the Ford women's strike at Dagenham to an end convinced her of the need for action towards equal pay for women. The women working at the Dagenham plant were paid 85% of the men's wages, whereas at other Ford plants they received 92%. The problem was the government's prices and incomes policy, which would not allow such an increase, even if the employer did. To overcome this, Ford said they had reassessed the economic value of the women's work and Downing Street gave approval for the raise, despite Conservative opposition.

Now Castle had the bit between her teeth and wanted equal pay. The 1964 Labour Party Manifesto had called for a charter of rights for all employees, to include 'the right to equal pay for equal work'. The Trades Unions Congress followed this with a resolution in 1965 for equal pay for equal work.[25] The mood was moving in the direction of equality for women. In a final triumphant moment before the 1970 general election, Castle managed to squeeze proposals for equal pay into a Prices and Incomes Bill. She persuaded Jenkins to allow her to draw up proposals to phase in equal pay over the next five years. Castle suspected that Jenkins's approval for the measure came because he thought he would not be Chancellor during the next five years.[26] The Equal Pay Act 1970 came into effect in 1975 and helped pave the way for the UK's entrance into Europe, because the Treaty of Rome in 1957 had established this condition for its member states.

Changes in moral attitudes

Sandbrook has recently challenged Arthur Marwick's image of the the so-called permissive society of the 1960s.[27] That change took place can hardly be challenged: the reforms to divorce, abortion, homosexual relations, censorship and capital punishment, and the availability of the contraceptive pill for unmarried women, are all testament to that. However, these changes did not always chime with public opinion. Sandbrook's evidence is a *New Society* poll conducted in 1969: only 5% nominated 'easier laws for homosexuality, divorce, abortion etc.' as their favourite development, whereas half said theirs was an increase in the state pension. Furthermore, one of the most common objections was to the 'easier laws'.[28]

This challenge to permissiveness was personified in the person of Mary Whitehouse and the Clean Up TV Campaign she launched in 1964. Her strict moral code and evangelical outlook placed her in stark contrast to the popular image of the sixties. Whitehouse thought she was doing God's work and saw the BBC and, in particular, its Director General (Hugh Greene) as 'the one man who more than anyone else had been responsible for the moral collapse in this country'.[29] Her argument was with more than just the BBC: she railed against modern consumerism and mass culture and the effect they were having on traditional Christian values. In 1965 the Clean Up TV Campaign became the National Viewers' and Listeners' Association and it remained the most persistent voice against permissiveness.

The sixties can be seen as a time of great social change, as demonstrated by the number of liberal reforms enacted under the Labour government and Jenkins as Home Secretary, but it can also be seen as a time of conservative reaction to those changes.

ACTIVITY 2.8

Investigate some features of life in the 1960s, using the information in this chapter and further research of your own. Choose from among the following: increased TV ownership; new types of TV programmes; satire aimed at public figures; changing holiday habits; developments in computer technology; developments in medical technology; less censorship; the contraceptive pill; equal pay for women; changes in attitudes to divorce, to homosexuality, to abortion; the 'permissive society'; changes in popular music.

Youth culture and the 'permissive society'

Pete Townshend's magnificent *Quadrophenia* told the complex story of a **mod** named Jimmy. It included run-ins with that other youth group of the late-fifties and sixties, the **rockers**. Mods fighting rockers on a Bank Holiday at Brighton beach is an enduring image of youth culture from the sixties. Clashes were inevitable, but often overplayed in the media where newspapers used exaggerated language to describe the 'battles' between the two groups. Townshend's band, *The Who*, appealed to the mods as their fashion sense closely followed the mod style of Italian haircuts and Fred Perry shirts. The band, especially the drummer Keith Moon, could have walked out of an Andy Warhol pop art painting.

Clearly, the number one band of the sixties was the Beatles – four Liverpudlian lads groomed by Brian Epstein, their manager – who went on to conquer the world with their mixture of music and fashion. For a few short years, British music set the pace and London became the centre of fashion with designers, such as Mary Quant (fashion) and Terence Conran (home); hairstylists like Vidal Sassoon; photographers including David Bailey; actors and actresses like Michael Caine and Diana Rigg; models such as Twiggy; films like *James Bond* and cars like the Mini. Only American talent, for instance, Bob Dylan and Elvis Presley, could compete against the British invasion. This invasion was fuelled by the growth in disposable income for the teenagers and young adults of Britain. Everything became disposable and cheap, so the 7-inch single record replaced the 12-inch long-player and plastic replaced other manufacturing substances in clothing and homeware.

Key terms

The differences between mods and rockers were stark. A **mod** was a modern and smart youth, while a **rocker** had long hair and enjoyed the music of the previous decade.

It is worth noting that, with all of the changes in youth culture, the top ten albums of the sixties still included the soundtracks to *The Sound of Music* and *South Pacific* nestled among *Beatles* albums; and that Jim Reeves and Engelbert Humperdinck scored the highest selling singles of 1966 and 1967 respectively. For every *Goldfinger*, or *Thunderball*, there was a *Doctor Zhivago*.

Anti-Vietnam War riots

By the mid-1960s the threat from worldwide communism had diminished, making the justification for supporting the Vietnam War more difficult. Wilson had not wanted to support this war, but he hoped to be a restraining influence on America and sought a negotiated way out. Pimlott points to an increasing dissatisfaction among the left of the Labour Party that he failed to keep pace with their growing anti-war sentiment.[30] This movement also involved many of the young members who identified with their American counterparts. So why couldn't Wilson just disown the whole affair? The answer is quite simple: American loans kept the Welfare State afloat.

The anti-Vietnam War movement began to cause trouble after the 1966 election win. In his autobiography, Wilson tells of one nasty riot when visiting the university city of Cambridge in 1967. His car was attacked by a 'yelling mob of demonstrators'.[31] They damaged his car with staves, broke the radio and radiotelephone aerials, seriously injured a policeman, threw eggs and manhandled his wife, Mary, quite badly. The knock-on effect of this dissatisfaction was that disillusionment was sown across the party, support was eroded and membership fell. However, Sandbrook asserts that, while opinion was against Wilson and his refusal to withdraw what support he was giving America, it was not a major concern at the polling booth. 'Polls consistently found that, unlike students, ordinary voters did not care very much about foreign affairs and were much more concerned about the economy, the cost of living, immigration and crime'.[32]

The anti-Vietnam War riots in Britain were no match for their American cousins, but their effect on the Labour Party was significant. 'Ordinary voters' may have been more concerned about other issues, but over Vietnam the party of conscience lost touch with its soul'.[33]

Issues of immigration and race

Wilson's first Queen's Speech was notable because of its call to Sir Alec Douglas-Home to repudiate Peter Griffiths (MP for Smethwick) for his alleged racist campaign. The 1964 campaign to win the seat was ill-tempered. Smethwick had been the focus of post-Second World War immigration and the Conservative slogan used language that would later become completely unacceptable: 'If you want a nigger for a neighbour, vote Labour'.[34] Wilson stated that Griffiths should serve his time in the commons as a 'parliamentary leper'. Immigration and race would certainly play a part over the next six years.

The Commonwealth Immigrants Act 1962, introduced by the Conservatives, sought to limit the number of immigrants from the Commonwealth to those with a government-issued employment voucher. At the time Labour considered this act to be nothing more than anti-colour legislation. However, once in power, Labour strengthened this act in 1968, further restricting the right of entry. This was done in part to alleviate fears of the UK being swamped by Asian immigrants from Kenya. The initial act came about because of Kenyan independence, the 1968 act because the Kenyan government forced residents who were not citizens to apply for 'entry certificates'. This targeted Indian and Pakistani Asians specifically, as many chose not to become Kenyans on independence, preferring to keep their British passports. Callaghan, then Home Secretary, was worried about the Kenyan Asians and about the number of them that might arrive, estimating it could be around 200 000. There was growing concern among the British public, particularly in areas where the immigration would have greater impact, such as Bradford and Southall. The media whipped up a frenzy, and Callaghan had to do something. The 1968 act easily passed through both houses and became law on 1 March.

Callaghan believed that for a country to be healthy it must put in place laws to ensure that everyone is treated equally. He introduced a bill in April 1968 designed to do just that, but it got a mixed reception. Enoch Powell, Shadow Secretary of State for Defence, gave his famous 'Rivers of Blood' speech. In it, Powell forecast a gloomy future due to the high numbers of immigrants entering Britain. Heath sacked him from the **Shadow Cabinet** the next day. *The Times* said the speech used 'racial hatred' to get points across, but Powell received support from various industries, such as the dockers, who marched on Westminster. The Race Relations Act 1968 made it illegal to discriminate on grounds of colour, race, ethnicity or national origins. Callaghan later noted that 'in matters of race relations, we got it right. We were ahead of public opinion when Parliament passed the 1968 Act'.[35]

Labour's record on immigration and race relations is difficult to assess, because on one hand their Commonwealth Immigrants Act made it harder for immigrants to enter the country. Marr summarises the effect well by saying that the act, 'effectively slammed the door [on immigration], while leaving a catflap open for a very small annual quota'.[36] However, historians do point out that the Commonwealth Immigrants Act was popular with the voters as around three quarters supported the act, while Callaghan was seen as tough and decisive. On the other hand, The Race Relations Act was more successful and Callaghan's assessment of it, albeit with the benefit of hindsight, may be correct.

ACTIVITY 2.9

'The Race Relations Act has been a success for British society.' Set the Act in its 1968 context to analyse what it changed. Then, using your own experience, assess Callaghan's longer-term judgement, reached with the benefit of hindsight, that the Act 'got it right'.

Foreign policy

The Labour government had three big foreign policy issues to deal with between 1964 and 1970. Britain was not militarily involved in the Vietnam War, but America sought British support. Since a huge amount of financial help was coming from across the Atlantic, Wilson had to tread a fine line between offering support, but not men. No foreign policy is ever decided in a bubble and this period had other issues to contend with, not least another attempt at joining the European Economic Community. Finally, Britain had to realise that she could no longer afford to be a world player, and the withdrawal of troops east of Suez highlighted this, along with Wilson's failure to curb the activities of Ian Smith in Rhodesia.

Relations with and policies towards the USA: Vietnam

The number of American soldiers fighting in the Vietnam War escalated in the early sixties, so that by the time Wilson came to power Johnson, the American President, was deeply committed to a military conclusion. During his first few visits to America Wilson sought to broach the subject of Vietnam; Johnson wanted assurance of British support and Wilson wanted to give it, but did not want to commit British soldiers to any fighting. The war was unpopular at home, not only with certain sections of society, but also with members of the Labour left. Johnson wanted British soldiers in Vietnam and Wilson was not prepared to do this. However, he was prepared to help in other ways: he saw himself as an honest broker that would end the war by diplomacy.

Britain had co-chaired the Geneva Conference along with the USSR.[37] Wilson believed he had a special relationship with the Russians (who were not actually fighting in Vietnam). He believed he could talk to them and the two countries could collaborate, to offer a deal to bring the war to a conclusion. His position as co-chair precluded both military involvement and strong support of America and allowed him, on occasion, to publicly criticise American action.

Wilson tried several times to bring about a peaceful end to the war. In March 1965, his first action was to try and bring the USSR and the USA together in London, but the Americans didn't turn up and nothing came of it. In June, he suggested that a handful

Key terms

Shadow Cabinet: the alternative government consisting of senior members of her Majesty's Loyal Opposition, usually the second-largest party in the House of Commons. Each member of the shadow government is their party's spokesperson on a specific area of government policy and it is their job to monitor the actions, decisions and speeches of the actual minister, offer a critique and, where necessary, put forward alternatives.

of Commonwealth Prime Ministers should visit key capital cities in search of a peace formula, but this also failed. To finish the year Wilson sent Harold Davies, a junior minister and frequent visitor to Vietnam, to the Northern Vietnamese capital, Hanoi, to deal directly with Ho Chi Minh, but Davies was refused access to him.

Speak like a historian

Ben Pimlott

Pimlott explains well the difficulty Wilson faced in attempting to reach a settlement. Both the USA and the USSR/North Vietnam thought they could win by force and Britain was seen as being too close to America to be dealing honestly.

[A] war in which both sides are heavily committed and both expect to win is not one that can be ended by diplomatic means, especially if, as in the case of Britain and its representatives, the diplomatist is known to be in league with one side.[38]

Discussion point

Create a mind map to show the conflicted position in which Wilson found himself when dealing with the USA on the one hand, and the USSR on the other, on the issue of Vietnam.

A visit to Moscow in 1966 brought Wilson no nearer a settlement, which he put down to Russia's inability to influence events in Vietnam. Throughout all Wilson's diplomatic efforts, he should be commended for keeping British troops out of the conflict, while not jeopardising US financial support. He feared a split in the Labour Party were he to send troops. The Vietnamese New Year in February 1967 brought with it a four-day truce and the hope of negotiations and a longer period of ceasefire. The Soviet premier, Alexei Kosygin, was on a visit to Britain, providing the ideal opportunity to open discussions. With Wilson was Chet Cooper, a former chief of the CIA, acting on behalf of President Johnson. Over the course of the next few days, Wilson's impotence in directing any peace initiatives became apparent, as his efforts to steer a course to end the conflict failed.

Wilson and Kosygin had been discussing a plan that, in a first phase, would allow America to stop bombing and, in a second phase, would stop the movement of North Vietnamese troops into South Vietnam, thus allowing America to stop adding to their numbers. The plan, known as 'phase A/phase B', read:

(a) the United States will stop bombing North Vietnam as soon as they are assured that the infiltration from North Vietnam to South Vietnam will stop …

(b) within a few days (with the period to be agreed between the two sides before the bombing stops) the United States will stop further augmenting their forces in South Vietnam and North Vietnam will stop infiltration and movement of forces into the South.[39]

Cooper was confident that his President would approve and allowed Wilson to take a written document outlining the proposal to Kosygin that evening. The message was sent to Washington for confirmation. When none came it was sent a second time. Nonetheless, Cooper was confident that no news was good news and went to the theatre. His viewing was interrupted and he returned to the embassy, where he discovered that Washington was working on an alternative to phase A/phase B.

Wilson had been at a reception at the Soviet embassy where he handed the document to Kosygin, who received it well, and left the next day on a trip to Scotland.

Now at Number 10, Wilson, Cooper and one of Johnson's most trusted diplomats, David Bruce, congratulated themselves on their good work. Then the phone rang – Washington issued new instructions. These instructions changed the nature of phase A/phase B: it was not America, but North Vietnam, that was to make the first move, by stopping the movement of forces into the South.

The explanation seems to have been the second of Wilson's descriptions, although Bruce suggested it may have been the third. Wilson had come close to bringing the Vietnam War, if not to a conclusion then, certainly, to a position where a truce could be discussed. The Vietnamese New Year Truce gave an ideal opportunity to start discussions for peace; Wilson wanted to be the one who brokered the deal, but America was having none of it. Relations between the UK and the USA did not turn sour, but they were not quite the same afterwards.

Response to world affairs and relations with Europe

Wilson's premiership would see another attempt by a UK government to join the European Economic Community and European Coal and Steel Community. Ostensibly, the reason for this attempt was that the relationship with Rhodesia was causing strain on opinions towards Commonwealth, as well as the strained relationship with the USA over Vietnam. Wilson, more inclined towards the Commonwealth than towards Europe, could see that the future of the country was likely to be within a European community. Britain's economy needed new markets and the Commonwealth could not provide them. Maybe being part of a European trading zone would help the struggling economy. There was less opposition from the Conservative right and Labour left than before, because they had less support. Towards the end of 1966 George Brown attended a NATO ministerial meeting in Paris where, to his surprise, he was allowed an audience with General de Gaulle, the French President. Brown describes a friendly meeting, but de Gaulle would not budge on allowing Britain's entry into the Common Market. Brown says, 'It was at this meeting that de Gaulle made his famous remark about the impossibility of two cocks living in one farmyard with ten hens. He said that he had had a lot of trouble getting the five hens to do what France wanted, and he wasn't going to have Britain's coming in and creating trouble all over again, this time with ten'.[40] For de Gaulle, France was part of the Continent, while Britain's focus was the Atlantic Ocean and the United States. Nevertheless, to get the ball rolling, Wilson and Brown toured the six member countries to drum up support. Predictably, France proved difficult. Wilson returned from France charmed by de Gaulle and much more determined to enter the Common Market. He was able to persuade cabinet that Britain should make a formal application to join.

Cross-reference Chapter 1 *EEC and EFTA*

Wilson was determined to have full and open debate in both the cabinet and party, as well as in parliament. Without rushing his colleagues, he was able to make a statement on 2 May 1967 outlining that the government would begin the application process. The debate lasted three days and concluded with a vote, approving the application by 488 to 62. Wilson notes that this was the 'biggest majority on a contested vote on a matter of public policy for almost a century'.[41] A week later came a statement from de Gaulle, outlining the reasons for his opposition to the UK joining the EEC. Elaborating on what he told Brown, de Gaulle's main reasons were the UK economy, fear over change to the EEC and Britain's relationship with the USA and the Commonwealth. The first was a genuine concern: the pound was coming under increasing pressure. De Gaulle was also worried that the EEC would change beyond all recognition if the UK joined. In fact, he

Voices from the past

Harold Wilson

The group were furious and flabbergasted by the new instructions from Washington. In 1971, Wilson, now in opposition, wrote in his autobiography:

I was furious, I hope I can say icily so, though as the evening wore on the language in which I expressed myself was less and less parliamentary. The Americans who were with me in Downing Street were equally angry.

I said that there could be only three possible explanations. One, which I was reluctant to believe, was that the White House had taken me – and hence Mr Kosygin – for a ride. Two, the most likely, that the Washington hawks had staged a successful take over. Three – and here I paraphrase – that the authorities in Washington were suffering from a degree of confusion about a possible and unfortunate juxtaposition of certain parts of their anatomy, one of which was their elbow.[42]

Discussion points

1. Why might Wilson have been reluctant to think that the White House was taking him and Kosygin for a ride?
2. Can you explain what is meant by 'the Washington hawks'?

stated that the EEC would break up if the other five members imposed UK membership on France. Finally, de Gaulle commented that London showed a lack of interest in the Common Market, hinting that Britain's place was with Commonwealth and America. This 'velvet veto', as it was called by the British press, was a blow to Wilson's efforts. The final, unequivocal, veto came in November 1967 with a statement from de Gaulle one week after devaluation: a double blow for Wilson, but not unexpected. As already stated, Wilson was no idealistic pro-European so why, given the likely outcome, did he proceed with an application? It seems it may have been his determination to maintain party unity: '(Wilson) gave priority to the unity of the Cabinet and the management of the party, by allowing the application to proceed, knowing it was likely to fail'.[43]

ACTIVITY 2.10

From your reading in this chapter and your own research, compare the characters of de Gaulle and Wilson. Give reasons why they may (or may not) have found it easy to negotiate with each other.

Decolonisation, including 'withdrawal East of Suez' and Rhodesia

Decolonisation

Anthony Greenwood, Secretary of State for the Colonies, was told by Wilson to work himself out of a job as quickly as possible and, to his credit, Greenwood tried. He stated his position to the Defence and Overseas Policy Committee in May 1965: 'At this stage in our colonial history our main task must be to liquidate colonialism'.[44] Independence was to be given to those who wanted it and could sustain it. Of the remaining 31 dependent territories, Greenwood and his under-secretary, Eirene White, visited half of them in the first seven months of the administration. Despite the Colonial Office's zeal for independence, the Foreign Office put the brakes on with a series of objections ranging from the strategic to the pragmatic. There were fears that it would stimulate interference in newly independent states (Argentina might covet an

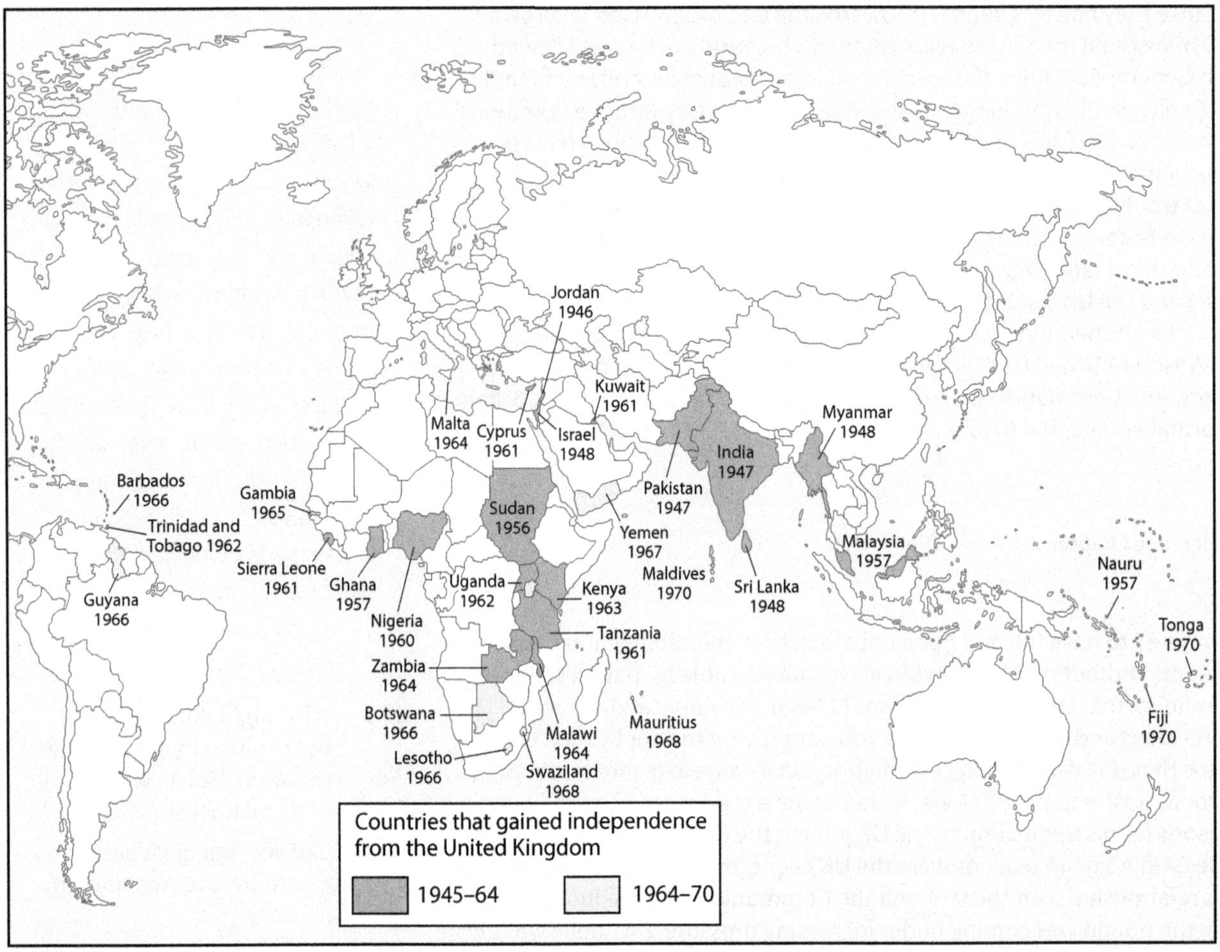

Figure 2.12: Decolonisation, 1964–70.

independent Falkland Islands), that strategically important islands around the world would be lost, and that there would be difficulty in deciding just who was ready for and capable of independence.

Withdrawal East of Suez

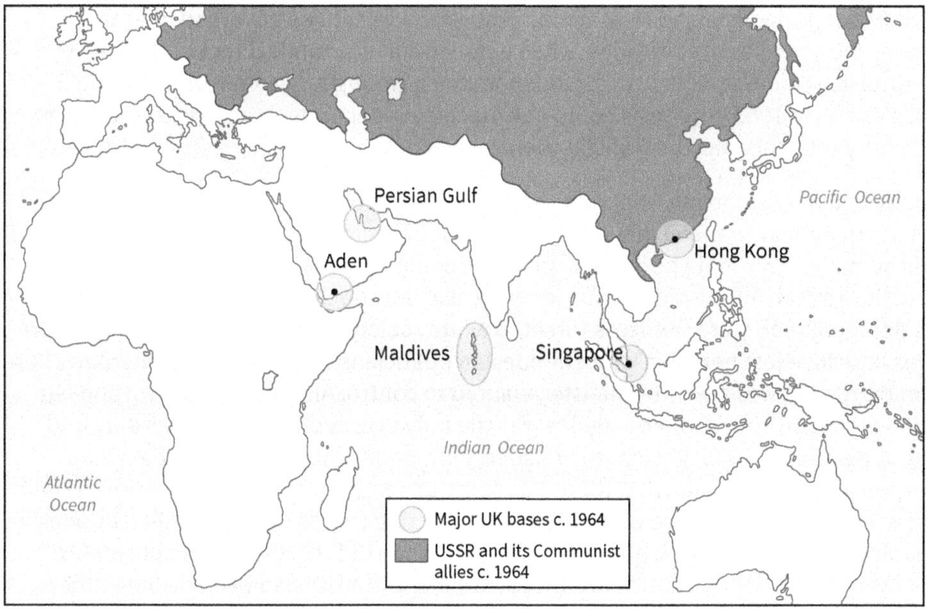

Figure 2.13: East of Suez.

The area around the Indian Ocean was known as 'East of Suez' and was dominated by British Imperial thinking, because the strategic importance of the area for trade and protection was huge. More importantly, America wanted Britain to keep up her presence in the area because America could not afford to expand its commitments due to the Vietnam War. Dean Rusk, US Secretary of State, suggested that America could not be the world's policeman alone and that Britain should continue to have a presence in the area.[45] These were lofty sentiments, but the reality was that Britain could not afford this policy. Callaghan was all for speedy withdrawal to offset the possibility of bankruptcy, while Healey and Brown could see the benefits of withdrawal, but were cautious over the speed. In the end Wilson and Healey (Secretary of State for Defence) tried to keep their options open, as they did not want to upset the Americans.

Eventually it was the country's finances that determined policy and a slow withdrawal was planned so that Britain could be out of the area by 1975–76. Devaluation in 1967 highlighted the ridiculous nature of Britain's assertions that it was still a world power. In addition, the change from Callaghan to Jenkins as Chancellor meant that now the highly critical Jenkins would exert more pressure to withdraw. Timing was now the issue: Jenkins was pushing for withdrawal from the Gulf by 1969 and East of Suez by 1970–71, based on economic necessity. Brown argued for delay, to offset the likelihood of a Communist uprising in Singapore. When Wilson had to tell President Johnson of the decision to withdraw he said that the British government was not acting in a 'Little England' spirit, but from 'a blend of exasperation at our inability to weather the successive economic storms of the past 20 years and determination, once and for all, to hew out a new role for Britain in the world at once commensurate with her real resources yet worthy of her past'.[46] It was becoming clear that Britain could no longer afford expensive overseas bases. The ending of several conflicts in the area (Indonesia and the Six Days War, for example) created propitious conditions for a slow withdrawal. This was the 'most important decision taken by the Wilson government in imperial and international policy'.[47]

ACTIVITY 2.11

Class debate on the motion: 'By the end of the 1960s, Britain's influence overseas was past history.'

Rhodesia

Rhodesia's unilateral declaration of independence (UDI), which stemmed from the Federation of Rhodesia and Nyasaland's collapse in 1963, highlights what can go wrong with colonial policy. Rhodesia had enjoyed a high level of autonomy since 1923 and had used this well to thrive as a manufacturer of iron and steel. In 1953 it had merged with two other British Central African states to form the Central African Federation (Rhodesia and Nyasaland): domestic affairs to be governed internally under the constituent territories; while defence and economic direction was led by central government. The push for independence among African territories led to its dissolution in 1963. Rhodesia could now become independent, as long as there was majority rule; this was the British government's policy.

There could never be majority rule – Rhodesian society, while not quite as segregated as South African, was still inherently racist. Public swimming pools were desegregated, but so many swimming pools were privately owned (by the white minority) that this had little effect. Mixed-race lavatories were also introduced and these two attempts at desegregation were seen as a threat to white society. To make matters worse, there was little love lost between white Rhodesian politicians and their UK counterparts. Ian Smith, the Rhodesian Prime Minister, wanted to control African nationalism and felt that white-controlled independence was the only way to do that. UDI was declared on 11 November 1965. Wilson was relatively impotent – he had ruled out a military response on the grounds that there was some uncertainty as to how the British public would react to fighting the whites. Moreover, getting troops into landlocked Rhodesia would have been a huge logistical challenge. Wilson did make efforts to prevent UDI by flying to Rhodesia, but this produced nothing. Once UDI had been declared there was little appetite shown for dealing, or original thinking as to how to deal, with the situation. Sanctions were also unlikely to work, as the supply of materials from the region would be disrupted and affect British industry.

Oil sanctions were imposed, but Rhodesia cut the supply of oil travelling through its land to Zambia, leading to an international effort to get oil to the latter. Wilson had to do something. He met Smith on board HMS *Tiger* in December 1966. Both men stated that they had the authority to make a deal. However, once on board, Smith began to renege on earlier promises and agreements, leaving Wilson to doubt his honesty and sincerity. This meeting is well chronicled and the result was a document that both men took back to their respective parliaments for approval. Wilson made an impassioned speech in the Commons, for which he received a rare standing ovation from his backbenchers, and the motion passed, not without some opposition from the Conservatives. Smith, however, could not carry his politicians and the Tiger document was rejected. The United Nations set up wide-ranging sanctions against Rhodesia and, in 1969, a Rhodesian referendum voted for a new republican constitution. Rhodesia remained an independent country ruled by a white minority until 1979.

Timeline 1964–70

Government and politics	Economics	Date	Society	Foreign affairs
October: Labour Party election victory with a majority of four seats	The DEA established with George Brown in charge	1964	BBC2 launched The Clean Up TV Campaign is launched	
Edward Heath replaces Sir Alex Douglas-Home as Conservative leader		1965	Murder (Abolition of Death Penalty) Act abolished the death penalty for murderers Tony Crossland's directive 10/65 issued, giving money to local government to convert to, or build, comprehensive schools	Independence granted to: The Gambia Maldives Rhodesian UDI November 1965
March: Labour Party election victory with a majority of 96 seats George Brown moved from the DEA to Foreign Affairs May: an Irish pensioner, Mary Gould, is killed by the UVF. This is seen as the start of the 'Irish Troubles'		1966	England football team win the World Cup	Independence granted to: Barbados Botswana Guyana Lesotho
Jim Callaghan replaced as Chancellor by Roy Jenkins Jim Callaghan becomes Home Secretary	Devaluation of the pound	1967	The contraceptive pill becomes available to single women Abortion Act allows women to have an abortion on the NHS Sexual Offences Act decriminalised homosexual acts between two men aged 21 or over	The Vietnam War ocurred during the entire duration of this administration The 'phase A/ phase B' debacle happened in February 1967 May-Nov application to join EEC turned down Independence granted to: Yemen
Enoch Powell's 'Rivers of Blood' speech led to his dismissal from the Shadow cabinet	Leyland Motors merged with the British Motor Corporation to form British Leyland	1968	Theatres Act reduces censorship on the stage Commonwealth Immigrants Act made it harder for memebers of the Commonwealth to come and live in the UK Race Relations Act made it illegal to discriminate against immigrants on the grounds of housing, employment or public services	Independence granted to: Mauritius Nauru Swaziland

ACTIVITY 2.12

1. Study the timeline. Events have been put into separate columns: which would you move to a different column and why?
2. Which developments have been omitted from the table that you think should be included? Explain why.

Government and politics	Economics	Date	Society	Foreign affairs
Government white paper *In Place of Strife* proposed	The DEA wound up	1969	Divorce Reform Act (came into effect in 1971) allowed couples to divorce after two years of separation	
		1970	Equal Pay Act introduces equal pay for women from 1975	Independence granted to: Fiji

Further reading

For a good overview of this period Andrew Marr's *A History of Modern Britain* is great. Written to accompany his documentary series (also worth watching), it is full of anecdotes that help to flesh out the politicians and main events. For a thorough analysis it is worth investigating Dominic Sandbrook's *White Heat*. He leaves no stone unturned in telling the complete history of these years. He also takes great pleasure in challenging some of the more traditional opinions of what happened. Finally, there are a wealth of autobiographies and biographies available from the major protagonists; Jenkins and Healey are often quoted as being two of the best of their kind, but Wilson had a wonderful way with words and is also very readable.

Practice essay questions

1. 'Wilson's announcement to withdraw troops East of Suez was the most significant part of his foreign policy.' Explain why you agree or disagree with this view.
2. 'Jenkins turned out to be the single most influential politician of the sixties.' (Marr p. 257) Explain why you agree or disagree with this view.
3. 'The sixties didn't really swing.' Explain why you agree or disagree with this view.
4. With reference to the sources and your understanding of the historical context, which of these sources is more useful in explaining the reasons for Labour's decision to devalue in 1967?

Source A

Source: Extract from Harold Wilson's 'Pound in your Pocket' speech to the nation on 19 November 1967

Tonight we must face a new situation, first what this means. From now on the pound abroad is worth 14% or so less in terms of other currencies. That doesn't mean of course that the pound here in Britain, in your pocket or purse or in your bank has been devalued. What it does mean is that we shall now be able to sell more goods abroad on a competitive basis. This is a tremendous opportunity for all our exporters and for many who have not yet started to sell their goods overseas but it will also mean that the goods we buy from abroad will be dearer and so for many of these goods it will be cheaper to buy British.

Source B

Source: Edward Heath speaking in the House of Commons on 22 November 1967 http://hansard.millbanksystems.com/commons/1967/nov/22/economic-situation#column_1324

Now I come to the point where the Chancellor said that devaluation would be justified—[Interruption.] This is the Chancellor's own statement and I want to read it to the House. The Chancellor said: It is true that there are circumstances in which a Government has no option but to devalue, namely, when internal costs and prices are so completely out of line with other countries that there is no other way of restoring a viable relationship. That is emphatically not the situation of Britain today. Has it become the situation in the last four months? I do not believe that it has. The Chancellor was right in July, and that is still the situation today. Those are the only circumstances in which the Chancellor believed that it was right for him to devalue for the benefit of this country. The Chancellor's own words were: That is emphatically not the situation of Britain today. The right hon. Gentleman concluded: Devaluation is not the way out of Britain's difficulties. He was absolutely right. If the Chancellor had not given such an overwhelmingly powerful analysis of the consequences of devaluation and pointed to the fact that there was no justification for it, why has he done it? Why have the Government devalued? The country and the rest of the world must draw their own conclusions from what has been happening.

Chapter summary

At the end of this chapter, you should have an understanding of the challenges faced by the British governments during a period of considerable change. In particular, you should have developed views on:

- the economic and political problems faced by Wilson and his colleagues
- the ways in which new legislation was making profound changes to British society
- the ways in which developments in science and technology were changing British culture
- Britain's altered role in international relations as British colonies gained independence.

Endnotes

1 Marr A. *A History of Modern Britain*. London: Macmillan; 2007. p. 240.

2 Marr A. *A History of Modern Britain*. London: Macmillan; 2007. p. 241.

3 Marr A. *A History of Modern Britain*. London: Macmillan; 2007. p. 241; Sandbrook D. *White Heat: a History of Britain in the Swinging Sixties 1964–1970*. London: Little, Brown; 2006. p. 92.

4 Wrigley C. *British Trade Unions since 1933*. Cambridge: Cambridge University Press; 2002. p. 43.

5 Hansard, vol. 730, 20 June 1966, cols. 42–43.

6 Sandbrook D. *White Heat: a History of Britain in the Swinging Sixties 1964–1970*. London: Little, Brown; 2006. p. 188.

7 Wilson, H. *The Labour Government 1964–1970: a Personal Record*. London: Weidenfeld and Nicolson; 1971. p. 534.

8 Callaghan, J. *Time and Chance*. London: Collins; 1987. p. 165–66.

9 Jenkins, R. *A Life at the Centre*. London: Macmillan; 1991. p. 441.

[10] Sandbrook D. *White Heat: a History of Britain in the Swinging Sixties 1964–1970*. London: Little, Brown; 2006. p. 340.

[11] Marr A. *A History of Modern Britain*. London: Macmillan; 2007. p. 257.

[12] Jenkins, R. *A Life at the Centre*. London: Macmillan; 1991. p. 181.

[13] Clarke, P. *Hope and Glory: Britain 1900–1990*. London: Penguin Books; 2007. p. 366–67.

[14] Jenkins, R. *A Life at the Centre*. London: Macmillan; 1991. p. 209.

[15] Sandbrook D. *White Heat: A History of Britain in the Swinging Sixties 1964–1970*. London: Little, Brown; 2006. p. 700.

[16] Buckle S. *The Way Out: a History of Homosexuality in Britain*. London: I.B.Tauris; 2015. p. 47–49.

[17] Sandbrook D. *White Heat: a History of Britain in the Swinging Sixties 1964–1970*. London: Little, Brown; 2006. p. 496.

[18] Jenkins, R. *A Life at the Centre*. London: Macmillan; 1991. p. 208.

[19] Crosland, S. *Tony Crosland*. London: Jonathan Cape; 1982. p. 148.

[20] Marr A. *A History of Modern Britain*. London: Macmillan; 2007. p. 247–48.

[21] Pimlott B. *Harold Wilson*. London: Harper Collins; 1992. p. 512.

[22] Sandbrook D. *White Heat: a History of Britain in the Swinging Sixties 1964–1970*. London: Little, Brown; 2006. p. 193–5.

[23] Jenkins R. *A Life at the Centre*. London: Macmillan; 1991. p. 211.

[24] Marwick A. *British Society since 1945*. London: Penguin Books; 1996. p. 169–73.

[25] Wilson Center Digital Archive www.unionhistory.info

[26] Castle B. *Fighting All the Way*. London: Macmillan; 1993. p. 427.

[27] Sandbrook D. *White Heat: a History of Britain in the Swinging Sixties 1964–1970*. London: Little, Brown; 2006. p. 341; Marwick p. 125.

[28] Sandbrook D. *White Heat: a History of Britain in the Swinging Sixties 1964–1970*. London: Little, Brown; 2006. p. 341.

[29] Barker D. Mary Whitehouse: self-appointed campaigner against the permissive society on television. *The Guardian*. 2001 November 24.

[30] Pimlott B. *Harold Wilson*. London: Harper Collins; 1992. p. 392.

[31] Wilson H. *The Labour Government 1964–1970: a Personal Record*. London: Weidenfeld and Nicolson; 1971. p. 445.

[32] Sandbrook D. *White Heat: a History of Britain in the Swinging Sixties 1964–1970*. London: Little, Brown; 2006. p. 383.

[33] Pimlott B. *Harold Wilson*. London: Harper Collins; 1992. p. 394.

[34] Sandbrook D. *White Heat: a History of Britain in the Swinging Sixties 1964–1970*. London: Little, Brown; 2006. p. 669.

[35] Callaghan, J. *Time and Chance*. London: Collins; 1987. p. 269.

[36] Marr A. *A History of Modern Britain*. London: Macmillan; 2007. p. 302.

[37] Further information on the Geneva Conference is available from: http://digitalarchive.wilsoncenter.org/collection/7/geneva-conference-of-1954.

[38] Pimlott B. *Harold Wilson*. London: Harper Collins; 1992. p. 390–91.

[39] Ellis S. *Britain, America and the Vietnam War*. Westport, USA: Praeger; 2004. p. 226.

[40] Brown G. *In My Way: the Political Memoirs of Lord George-Brown* London: Gollancz; 1971. p. 220.

[41] Wilson H. *The Labour Government 1964–1970: a Personal Record*. London: Weidenfeld and Nicolson; 1971. p. 390.

[42] Wilson H. *The Labour Government 1964–1970: a Personal Record*. London: Weidenfeld and Nicolson; 1971. p. 357.

[43] Hyam R. *Britain's Declining Empire: the Road to Decolonisation 1918–1968*. Cambridge: Cambridge University Press; 2006. p. 341.

[44] Hyam R. *Britain's Declining Empire: the Road to Decolonisation 1918–1968*. Cambridge: Cambridge University Press; 2006. p. 346–47.

[45] Hyam R. *Britain's Declining Empire: the Road to Decolonisation 1918–1968*. Cambridge: Cambridge University Press; 2006. p. 387.

[46] Hyam R. *Britain's Declining Empire: the Road to Decolonisation 1918–1968*. Cambridge: Cambridge University Press; 2006. p. 394.

[47] Hyam R. *Britain's Declining Empire: the Road to Decolonisation 1918–1968*. Cambridge: Cambridge University Press; 2006. p. 397.

3 The end of Post-War Consensus, 1970–1979

In this section, we will look at how first Heath's Conservatives and then Wilson's Labour came to power. We shall consider how they responded to the economic and industrial situation of the time. In addition, we shall look at the ways in which they responded to the developing crisis in Northern Ireland. We shall also study how the UK became a member of the EEC, looking into the way in which that fitted into other aspects of Britain's foreign policies. We shall, therefore, look into:

- Heath's government: Heath as leader; political and economic policies; industrial relations and the miners' strikes; the 'troubles' in Northern Ireland, including the Sunningdale Agreement.
- Labour governments of Wilson and Callaghan: political, economic and industrial problems and policies; problems of Northern Ireland.
- Society in the 1970s: progress of feminism; the Sex Discrimination Act; race and immigration; youth; environmentalism.
- Britain's entry into and relations with Europe; the state of the 'special relationship' with USA; attitudes to USSR and China.

Heath's government

When Douglas-Home resigned as leader of the Conservative Party in July 1965, an electoral process ensued. This was itself a novelty: previously, influential senior members of the party, nicknamed the 'magic circle', had privately consulted colleagues on who was likely to command the confidence of the party and the country and a name would 'emerge'. Discontent with how Douglas-Home had become party leader in 1963 had caused the introduction of leadership elections.

The three candidates were the Shadow Chancellor Edward Heath, Shadow Foreign Secretary Reginald Maudling and the Shadow Transport Secretary Enoch Powell. Maudling was by far the most experienced of the three, and the best known to journalists and the public at large. According to Robert Blake, Powell was not a serious candidate: 'he was putting down a marker for a future which has never come'.[1] In the event, Heath won a narrow outright majority and the other two candidates conceded defeat.

ACTIVITY 3.1

Find out more about each of the three candidates in the 1965 Conservative leadership contest. Make short notes on the contrasts between them. What do you think the outcome of the election tells you about the state of the party and its sense of direction?

Figure 3.1: Edward Heath.

Heath as leader

Heath's contrast with all recent Conservative leaders may have aided his candidacy. They had been part of the aristocracy, the gentry or the wealthy upper-middle class, with plenty of upper-class connections. Three had been to Eton and one to Harrow. Heath came from a working- or lower-middle-class background. He had attended Oxford University through a scholarship. A wartime career in the army led to his becoming a lieutenant colonel and being awarded the MBE (Member of the Order of the British Empire). He also passed top of the Civil Service exams.

Younger and without the social class labels of previous Conservative leaders, he was presented as a response to Wilson's appeal. He declared in 1974 that he was not a product of privilege, but of opportunity.[2] This experience of modest origins, personal success and seeing action in wartime affected Heath's aims and ideology. He believed in British membership of the EEC, and centrist social and economic approaches, priorities which aligned him with Macmillan.

As a leader, Heath did not have the success he had experienced as (for example) Chief Whip, where he had helped the party survive the stormy 1956 Suez crisis. His conviction that he was right made him impatient with the necessary process of persuading others. His humourlessness also isolated him in social gatherings. He was unmarried and childless, something that caused gossip both at the time and since.

Political and economic policies

The Selsdon Manifesto

Heath was keen on new ideas and fresh thinking. After losing the 1964 election, Home had asked him to take charge of policy development as chairman of the Conservative Research Department.

Voices from the past

Harold Wilson

This document was condemned by Labour Prime Minister Harold Wilson as the work of 'Selsdon Man', a phrase intended to echo the names of early forms of humans used by paleontologists, such as 'Neanderthal Man'.

Selsdon man is not just a lurch to the right. It is an atavistic desire to reverse the course of 25 years of social revolution.

What they are planning is a wanton, calculated and deliberate return to greater inequality.[3]

Discussion points

1. How far do you think Wilson's characterisation of the Conservative manifesto as 'a lurch to the right' was justified?
2. What aspects of its analysis of Britain's needs and proposed policies prompted Wilson's description?

In January 1970, the Shadow Cabinet met at the Selsdon Park Hotel in Surrey and drafted a **free-market** programme for the party manifesto for the next general election. It drew attention the economic problem of inflation, the political problem of a Liberal party by-election revival, and Labour's commitment to **state socialism.** The programme insisted that the Conservative Party must champion free enterprise and personal choice in order to play any useful role in British politics.

The manifesto urged 'a relatively low level of public expenditure'; an expansion of the private sector and opposition to nationalisation 'because it increases the power of the central government, removes a large part of British industry from the competitive disciplines of the market, and in so doing, misdirects and wastes precious capital resources'; and an end to prices and incomes controls.[4] It accepted the need for a Welfare State to care for the vulnerable and needy, but protested against the growing bureaucracy that this had created.

Key terms

free markets: unregulated or minimally regulated processes of buying and selling of goods and services.

state socialism: a version of socialism advanced, not by revolution, but by the progressive intervention of elected governments of the left to alter society and the economy. This is likely to include nationalisation of some, or all, of the larger means of production.

The 1970 general election

At the general election of June 1970, both the Conservatives under Heath and the Liberals with Jeremy Thorpe had new party leaders. This was also the first election in which people aged 18 and above could vote. The minimum age had been 21 in previous elections.

The result was a victory for the Conservatives, who increased both their vote and the number of seats they held in the House of Commons. They gained 77 seats, while Labour lost 76, giving the Conservatives a small majority.

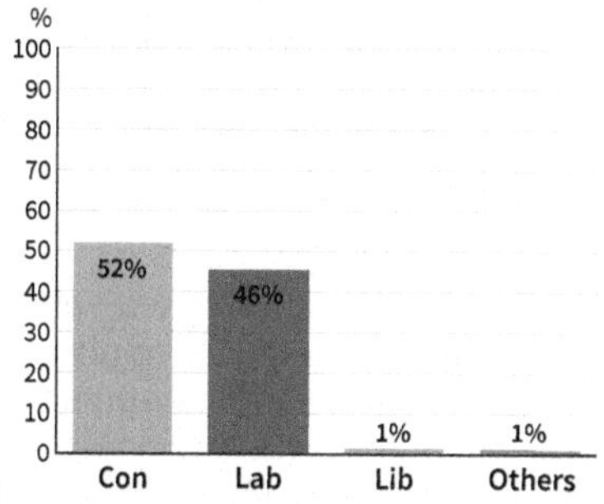

Figure 3.2: Seats in the House of Commons won in the 1970 British general election; percentages have been adjusted to the nearest whole number. Ulster Unionist figures are included in Conservative totals.

The U-turn

The Selsdon Manifesto had complained about 'the [Labour] Government's about-turns in economic policy'.[5] Within a short period, however, the Conservatives were to perform an 'about-turn' of their own.

Initially the government worked to put into practice its free-market agenda. Heath abandoned this policy direction because of increasing unemployment. Politicians remembered the economic depression, unemployment and poverty of the 1930s. There was considerable opposition to any return to such conditions, but also anxiety about the potential for social and political instability, should unemployment climb too high. The budgets of 1972–73 were the means of executing the U-turn.

The Barber Boom

At the beginning of 1972, the unemployment rate reached a million, double what it had been when the Conservatives came into office. Chancellor of the Exchequer Anthony Barber's response, dubbed a 'dash for growth', was to increase pensions and benefits, and reduce tax. In presenting his budget to parliament, he boasted it would add 10% to the UK's growth within two years, albeit it by adding £3.4 billion to the **public sector borrowing requirement (PSBR)**. The Keynesian intention of putting an additional £2.5 billion into the economy was to reduce unemployment and by early 1974 unemployment had been halved. The by-product was increased inflation.

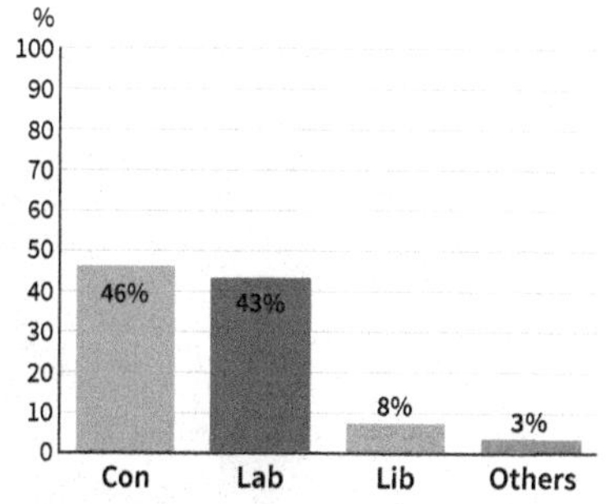

Figure 3.3: Votes won in the 1970 British general election; percentages have been adjusted to the nearest whole number. Ulster Unionist figures are included in Conservative totals.

Within 15 months Barber was forced to move to a deflationary budget to offset the unintended consequences of his inflationary one and to adopt a wages freeze. This triggered a strike by miners, who resented the limit on their freedom to negotiated higher wages and better working conditions.

Divisions among the Conservatives

Contrary to principles expressed in the Selsdon Manifesto was the nationalisation of Rolls Royce. This large manufacturing concern was facing bankruptcy. Its closure would add to the unemployment figures and the renown of the name was such that the firm's closure would also reflect badly on the health of British manufacturing as a whole. Despite talk of reducing the size of the state, the Conservatives took Rolls Royce into public ownership. When the Upper Clyde Shipbuilders were in danger of closing down that, too, was nationalised.

ACTIVITY 3.2

Make notes on the significance of the Conservative government's U-turn of 1972/1973, analysing whether it had a positive or a negative effect on the government's reputation.

The apparent lack of policy direction undermined Heath's standing. Iain Macleod died in 1970 and, in 1972, Reginald Maudling resigned, amid some scandal. The departure of Enoch Powell from the party in 1974 removed the remaining candidate from the 1965 leadership contest. The Conservatives lost two general elections in a row in 1974. Some outspoken remarks by Keith Joseph made his leadership candidacy unlikely so, in 1975, it was Margaret Thatcher who stood against Heath in a leadership contest.

Industrial relations and the miners' strikes

Key terms

public sector borrowing requirement (PSBR): the term used to describe the amount of money the government needed to borrow to make up the difference between what it could raise, e.g. through taxation and what it intended to spend, e.g. on services.

flying picket: striking worker who travels from place to place to demonstrate at the entrance to workplaces other than their own, attempting to dissuade other workers from going in to work.

Industrial Relations Act 1971

A key concern of the government was the power of the trade unions. Acting on a manifesto pledge, Employment Secretary Robert Carr introduced the 1971 Industrial Relations Act to specify what unions could, and could not, do. There was to be an Industrial Relations Court (IRC), which could impose a cooling-off period in disputes and demand ballots. A distinction was made between official strikes, organised by the elected leadership of the union and sudden, locally organised (or even unorganised), walk-outs. The TUC opposed the entire project with demonstrations and strikes. They were supported by the Labour party, despite the latter having attempted something similar in *In Place of Strife*. The plan was that unions would register with the IRC; they did not do so. The court did little. At one point it caused the arrest and imprisonment of five dockers' shop stewards for not appearing when summoned; this was an embarrassment to the government and the Official Solicitor obtained their release.

Miners' strikes 1972 and 1974

The Conservatives came to power claiming that inflation was a menace and that bringing it down was a priority. Yet during their time in office inflation went up. Whenever prices went up, unionised labour demanded higher wages and the award inevitably made their employers increase the prices of their goods or services to pay for the higher wages. This was an inflationary spiral.

The government itself was a major employer. One of its agencies, the National Coal Board, had been gradually reducing the size of the labour force as the industry itself shrank. It had done this without making redundancies, in exchange for which the National Union of Mineworkers had been avoiding a confrontation over declining levels of pay. This left the workforce discontented as, following years of improving pay relative to the average, miners had fallen back during the 1960s.

In 1971 the union boss Joe Gormley succeeded in negotiating a 14% pay rise. The following year a further pay demand was refused, leading to the first national coal strike since 1926. Through the use of **flying pickets**, the NUM quickly succeeded in creating a fuel crisis, with picket lines that members of other unions refused to cross. The power shortage was made worse by the winter weather and a state of emergency was declared. After seven weeks of striking, the miners accepted an improved offer from the NCB.

The high rate of inflation at this time undermined the pay rise. The government was attempting both to limit public-sector pay rises and recommend limits to the private sector, so was keen to avoid paying the miners more. Meanwhile, the 1973 oil crisis had pushed up the price of coal. NUM leaders were convinced their members deserved a pay rise and that the NCB, backed by the state, could afford one. The 1974 strike so reduced the availability of power that the government was forced to introduce a three-day working week to avoid running out of fuel.

Figure 3.4: NUM president Joe Gormley was not a left-winger, but was keen to get the best possible deal for his members.

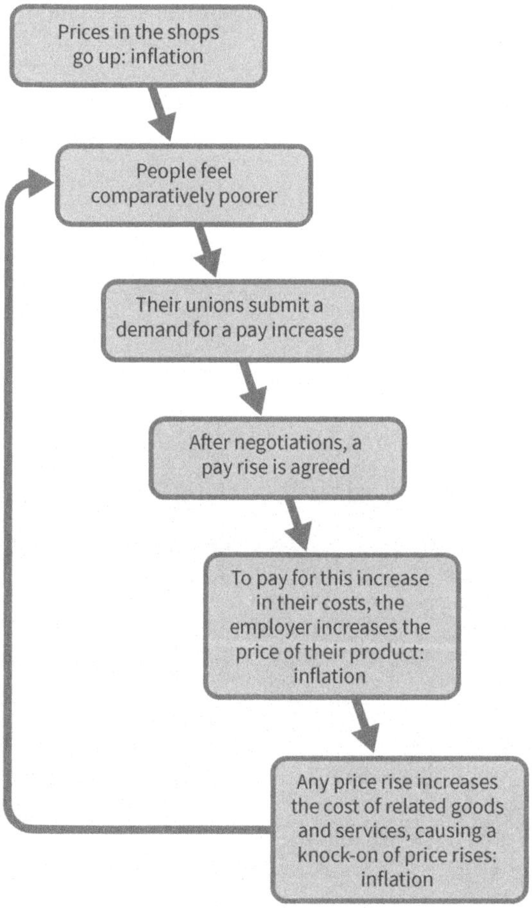

Figure 3.5: An inflationary spiral.

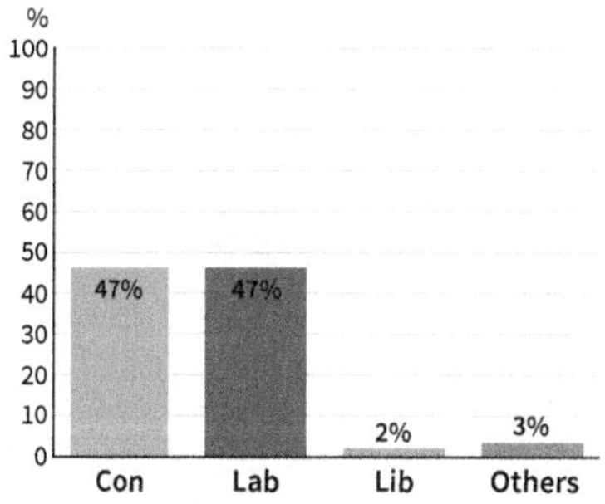

Figure 3.6: Seats in the House of Commons won in the February 1974 British general election; percentages have been adjusted to the nearest whole number. Ulster Unionist figures are listed as 'Others'.

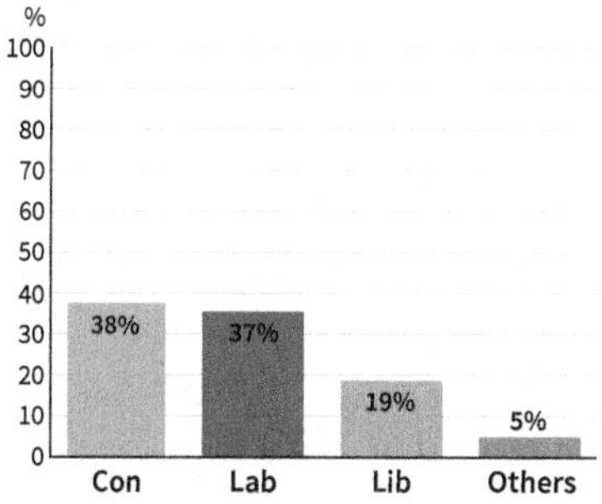

Figure 3.7: Votes won in the February 1974 British general election; percentages have been adjusted to the nearest whole number. Ulster Unionist figures are listed as 'Others'.

The February 1974 general election

The coal strike was the background to the February 1974 election. In an address to the country on television, Heath made inflation and standing up to strikers the central issues. In fact, the strike itself was conducted in a far quieter manner than the 1972 one. Moreover, a Pay Board report argued that the miners were paid less than comparable employees in other industries. This severely undermined the NCB and government's case. They suffered a further blow when the director general of the employers' organisation the Confederation of British Industry declared that he hoped the next government would repeal the Industrial Relations Act.

Former leadership contender Enoch Powell announced he would not stand for re-election on the Conservative manifesto. This was first because the election was fundamentally fraudulent, as the government was ready to give in to the miners after the election and second because the party had not stood by its free-market manifesto of 1970.

Labour made the case for increased central planning, including agreements with industry and the creation of a National Enterprise Board. Party leader Harold Wilson was careful to present a team, with James Callaghan, Denis Healey and others in the foreground of the campaign.

The Liberals made their leader Jeremy Thorpe prominent in the campaign. A poster placed his portrait alongside that of the Conservative and Labour leaders, inviting voters to 'Change the Face of Britain'.

The Conservatives (37.9%) and Labour (37.2%) gained very similar shares of the vote. The distribution of the votes gave Labour 301 seats to the Conservatives 297. Could

ACTIVITY 3.3

In the February 1974 general election the Conservative slogan was, 'Who governs Britain?' Labour's contrasting slogan was 'Let us work together'.

1. What message did each slogan seek to communicate?
2. How do they relate to the wider social and economic context?

> **Key terms**
>
> **internment:** a system of imprisonment without trial; historically following the arrest of the citizens of an enemy country during wartime, but used during the Troubles to hold individuals believed to be terrorists.
>
> **loyalist:** Protestant community in Northern Ireland with declared loyalty to the United Kingdom and the monarchy, specifically those willing to undertake militant activities to advance this point of view.
>
> **civil rights:** the constitutional rights of citizens by virtue of their being full members of society, likely to include the right to vote, form political parties and peacefully protest.

Heath remain in Number 10 through a coalition with the Liberals and an understanding with the Ulster Unionists? After negotiations, he resigned.

The new Labour government immediately awarded the miners a substantial pay rise and repealed the 1971 Industrial Relations Act.

The 'Troubles' in Northern Ireland

Figure 3.8: British soldiers deployed in Northern Ireland.

Ongoing violence

When Heath walked into 10 Downing Street, there were already British soldiers on Northern Ireland's streets. Home Secretary Reginald Maudling said, in an interview in 1971, that the government's intention was to keep the problems in Northern Ireland at 'an acceptable level of violence'.[6]

One response was a policy called **internment**, which John O'Beirne Ranelagh calls 'disastrous'.[7] In Operation Demetrius in August 1971, British soldiers arrested 342 people suspected by the police of being IRA members, or supporters. The arrests included people who had taken no part in IRA activities and at this stage no matching arrests occurred of **loyalists** with a history of violence.

Detainees were held without trial for long periods of time in an attempt, as Kenneth O. Morgan says, 'to separate the "men of violence" from the peaceful majority of the Catholic population'.[8] Some were interrogated. The arrests and detentions were followed by demonstrations, riots and violence.

Internment contributed to hostility toward the British authorities and radicalised those affected, worsening the situation.

The civil rights movement

The province contained a large minority of Roman Catholics, but the political institutions had been designed to exclude them from representation and participation. They were left vulnerable to discrimination in the fields of housing and employment. During the 1960s, groups such as the Northern Irish Civil Rights Association (NICRA), established in 1967, responded by raising issues of **civil rights**. The local political establishment feared any compromise would so weaken their own position that an unstoppable drift out of the UK and into Ireland would begin. There they would find themselves no longer a ruling majority, but a minority.

Demonstrations were called to protest the effective disenfranchisement and social and economic disadvantages suffered by Roman Catholics in Northern Ireland.

Londonderry was a controversial city; even its name was disputed. Historically 'Derry', it had been renamed 'Londonderry' in the 17th century to reflect its links with the City of London. Despite a majority Catholic population in the city, the majority on the city corporation was consistently Protestant and Unionist, due to **gerrymandering**. The citizens demonstrated in support of the civil rights movement and against internment. Deaths of civilians led to British troops being viewed, not as a protective force, but an army of occupation. There was rising support for the IRA.

Key terms

gerrymandering: deliberately planning an electoral system in order to exclude a given group and keep a different group in power indefinitely.

Cross-reference Chapter 2 *The beginnings of the 'Troubles' in Northern Ireland*

In 1968 a demonstration in Londonderry was planned. It was banned by the province's Minister for Home Affairs. Different participating organisations took different views and in the end it went ahead. It was met by a violent police response. Bystanders, not part of the demonstration, were treated as rioters. Further demonstrations followed and the Prime Minister of the province announced a number of reforms that would meet the demonstrators' demands. In 1969 a demonstration was threatened and attacked several times, revealing the hostility of the Protestant population and the unwillingness of the police to protect even a legal demonstration by Catholics.

The rising tide of civil unrest led to the resignation of the Northern Ireland prime minister; his replacement agreed to more of the demonstrators' demands.

Figure 3.9: Londonderry's 17th-century walls to defend English and Scottish settlers against Irish attacks. The Catholic Bogside area at their foot saw frequent violence during the Troubles.

Figure 3.10: The Rossville Street (Derry) Bloody Sunday mural showing Catholic priest Father Edward Daly leading as a wounded protestor is carried away from the Londonderry demonstration.

Bloody Sunday

In January 1972, the prime minister of Northern Ireland, Brian Faulkner, banned parades and marches for the year. Despite this, a demonstration was mounted and an estimated 10 000–15 000 people took part on 30 January 1972 in the Bogside area of Londonderry. A minority broke away from the main body of demonstrators and threw stones at soldiers manning barriers that had been set up to limit the route of the march. Soldiers responded with live ammunition, ultimately resulting in a total of 14 civilian deaths and numerous injuries.

The British army and government asserted that the soldiers had responded to gun and bomb attacks by people in the crowd assumed to be IRA members or supporters. When Home Secretary Reginald Maudling announced this in the House of Commons, Bernadette Devlin, a Catholic MP with a background in the civil rights movement, slapped him.

A report commissioned by Heath's government supported the army's description of events. It would be 37 years before another inquiry ruled that soldiers had lied and suppressed evidence. The demonstration had been illegal, following Faulkner's ban. There was a background of violence in which the IRA had indeed used bombs and guns to attack troops, as well as police and civilians. However, the 'Bloody Sunday' demonstration had not been marked by such attacks, and the troops' use of guns was finally ruled unjustified.

Attempts to resolve problems

According to Graham Spencer, 'Within six months [of Bloody Sunday], a secret meeting had taken place between the PIRA [Provisional IRA] leadership and Northern Ireland secretary Willie Whitelaw in London, but had failed miserably'.[9] The PIRA delegation included its chief of staff Seán Mac Stíofáin and future IRA and Sinn Féin leaders Gerry Adams and Martin McGuiness. They demanded that the future of Ireland (including Northern Ireland) should be decided by the people of Ireland as a whole. This was

Voices from the past

Bernadette Devlin

The MP for Mid Ulster at the time of Bloody Sunday was Bernadette Devlin. Elected in 1969 at the age of 21 (the youngest MP at the time, indeed one of the youngest ever), she was an eyewitness to events in Londonderry, but when she attempted to speak in the House of Commons the speaker refused to hear her. This is what she said:

On a point of order. I am the only person in this House who was present yesterday when, whatever the facts of the situation might be said – [Interruption.] Shut up! I have a right, as the only representative in this House who was an eye witness, to ask a question of that murdering hypocrite–[10]

Afterwards she was interviewed by various journalists in the street. Here is what she said:

A British Home Secretary got up and made what he called a statement. It did not have one substantiated fact in it. It lasted three minutes and at no stage did he even say 'I regret the fact that 13 people are dead' ... It wasn't an emotional reaction it was quite coldly and calmly done. I was the only member of Parliament who was in the chamber who was in Derry yesterday. I was fired on by the paratroopers and yet Parliamentary democracy was such that I was not allowed to speak ... What I achieved was simply delivering to the Home Secretary a simple, proletarian protest at the fact that he was responsible for the murder of 13 people ... We had 20 000 people marching on the streets, our streets; the streets belong to us, we have a right to be there, we had 3000 soldiers with no right to be there, enforcing by brutality and force of arms a law which a prime minister who has no mandate to govern any longer [Brain Faulkner] ... I'm just sorry I didn't get him [Maudling] by the throat.[11]

Discussion points

1. Comment on what you judge to be the strengths and weaknesses of Devlin's way of addressing the speaker and MPs, and journalists and the viewing public.
2. What do you think are the more notable things that she said and what is striking about the way she said them?

a refusal to recognise Northern Ireland as a political unit in itself, or as a part of the UK. In addition, the British government had to commit publicly to withdrawing from Northern Ireland by the beginning of 1975. Finally, all prisoners which the delegation counted as 'political prisoners' had to be released. The secretary of state for Northern Ireland, William Whitelaw, could not agree to these points.

In 1973, the government suspended the right to trial by jury for crimes to do with national security. The new **Diplock courts** were named after the judge who had written a report on responses to political violence that could act as alternatives to internment. The intention was to make it easier to convict the accused, when the government was concerned about both the intimidation of juries and about the covert sympathy of individuals, causing them to refuse to convict. To the Nationalists, the Diplock courts confirmed what the IRA had said: Northern Ireland was ruled by an unaccountable foreign government which had sent in an army of occupation.

The Sunningdale Agreement

In 1973, recognising that Northern Ireland presented a political problem, as well as a policing and security one, parliament agreed a devolution plan for Northern Ireland. An assembly would be elected by **proportional representation**, replacing the contested Stormont parliament, in which the Roman Catholics had little or no faith because they had little or no representation. (Law and order would remain with the government in Westminster.) A consultative (not a decision-making) Council of Ireland would allow members of the Irish government to meet members of Northern Ireland's devolved government and legislature. Constitutional parties on both sides of the sectarian divide supported the plan.

The negotiations led to an executive bringing together Unionists, the SLDP and the Alliance party. The Unionists rejected the idea of the Republic of Ireland having any role, but a deal was hammered out at a meeting at Sunningdale in Berkshire, between Heath, **Taoiseach** Liam Cosgrave and representatives of the three main Ulster parties.

It remained to be seen whether the party memberships would trust their leaders and what the paramilitaries and terrorists would do next.

Labour governments of Wilson and Callaghan

The Labour government that came to power in February 1974 was full of experienced ministers, people who had held office in Labour's 1964–70 administrations. The election had resulted in a **hung parliament**, so that Labour had no overall majority. Wilson could only govern if he kept his parliamentary party united and ensured that members of other parties supported Labour's measures. This meant that compromise and balancing of competing views was central to all government activity. Opportunities for radical change were likely to be few. Nevertheless, Labour's February 1974 manifesto had committed the party to a redistribution of wealth, making working people better off. Spending on education, health and housing rents would increase. All this meant that taxes on richer people went up, reversing some of what had happened under Heath.

Political, economic and industrial problems and policies

The Social Contract and its failure

The Labour party had been founded by the trade unions and the latter had been a key source of funding for the party from the beginning. The voting system assumed that union members were party members, but allowed the union leaders to vote on their behalf at conferences. As a result, a motion could be passed by vast numbers – once the boss of a large union had decided to support it. For as long as Labour was seen as able to manage the unions, then the connection was an electoral advantage. When the unions were seen as managing Labour, it became an electoral handicap.

ACTIVITY 3.4

Create a mind map to explain why the political situation in Northern Ireland became violent.

Key terms

Diplock courts: courts of law that sat in Northern Ireland from 1973 specifically to hear trials related to terrorist activity. Decisions about guilt or innocence were made by a judge instead of by a jury.

proportional representation: a system of voting in which the outcome in allocation of seats in a legislature resembles the proportional distribution of votes to political parties across the country. This contrasts with 'first past the post', in which each voting district chooses a single representative according to the casting of votes locally; this can produce distorted results, as parties popular across the country can achieve minimal or no representation, while those popular regionally can achieve relatively high representation.

taoiseach: Irish word meaning 'prime minister'.

hung parliament: one in which no party has a majority of MPs. Consequently, there has to be a period of negotiations which may lead to a minority government, or to a coalition government formed by two or more parties.

Key terms

social contract: a negotiated agreement whereby individuals and groups surrender certain rights in order to achieve certain benefits. Such an agreement is assumed by some political analysts to be the underlying basis of all societies. The expression was adopted by the 1970s Wilson government to describe a negotiated settlement with trade unions that would not be enshrined in statute, but would allow pay settlements to be moderated.

The question of how the government could reconcile its role and mandate with the role and mandate of trade union leaders remained an open one.

In July 1974, after winning the February election, the new Labour government kept its promise to repeal the Conservatives' 1971 Industrial Relations Act. In its place – and in place of the abandoned *In Place of Strife* – was the **Social Contract**. This had been hammered out in 1973 by Labour, in discussions with union representatives, and announced as policy in January 1974 as part of the election campaign. To take the project forward, Wilson appointed as Employment Secretary the left-winger Michael Foot.

Labour knew that, short of legislating to weaken the negotiating position of workers and their representatives in the unions (something they were philosophically unwilling and politically unable to do), inflation could not be controlled unless wage settlements were controlled. Settlements themselves could only be controlled if unions agreed to cooperate: this was the 'contract'. The unions agreed to play their part in exchange for improved social welfare, action to control prices and some freedom to negotiate wages.

Employers (which, because of nationalisation, had since 1945 included the government and its agencies, such as the NCB) could negotiate wage settlements more freely than under previous prices and incomes policies. At the same time, the TUC would exercise its authority to persuade unions to keep pay demands down – a practice known as 'wage restraint'. Limits would be imposed with a time lapse of a year between settlements, which also had to be justified by inflation having led to loss of buying power. The hope was that this would bring wage demands down to manageable levels and stabilise the situation. This should then allow a Chancellor of the Exchequer to anticipate future government spending and economic activity – something without which constructing a budget was impossible.

The Wilson government introduced new social security benefits, improvements in tenants' rights and an increase in the old-age pension. March 1974 saw the introduction of subsidies on food and housing. Rents in social housing (council houses and flats) were frozen. There would be greater attention to issues around the health and safety of people in work. These steps reflect the Labour philosophy of social justice and represent a commitment to using taxation to support the less well off. This is sometimes called 'redestributive politics'.

The Advisory, Conciliation and Arbitration Service (ACAS) was introduced to try to end industrial disputes, while Heath's Pay Board was abolished. There was a new National Enterprise Board and compulsory planning agreements with private industry. This was intended to empower the state to run the economy. Although well-intended by all sides, the Social Contract did not succeed: Peter Clarke regards the entire concept as 'vacuous'.[12] In the year that followed, inflation continued to rise, driven up by (and in turn driving up) wages. The Labour government decided it had no choice but to adopt an incomes policy.

James Callaghan

Between the two election victories of 1974 and the defeat of 1979, Labour formed governments under Wilson (1974–76) and James Callaghan (1976–79).

Unlike Wilson, a former economics don, Callaghan had never been to university: he had passed the exams, but been unable to afford to be a student. Instead, he had joined the civil service and gone on to naval service in the Second World War. Like Wilson, he had entered the House of Commons as part of the Labour landslide of 1945. Callaghan came into 10 Downing Street as the only Prime Minister to have served as Chancellor the Exchequer (1964–67), Home Secretary (1967–70) and Foreign Secretary (1974–76). Unlike most changes of office holder, Callaghan was not from the next political generation. Indeed, Wilson left office joking that it was time to make way for an older man.

Callaghan's very lack of higher education may have contributed to his concern with issues of education. Within months of becoming Labour leader and Prime Minister, Callaghan had addressed the subject in a speech given at Ruskin College, Oxford (an institution committed to giving a second chance to people who had not succeeded in school). This was unusual: prime ministers often gave speeches about law and order, foreign policy and the economy, but more rarely about schools. He described the primary school curriculum as a 'secret garden', one in which teachers followed their own instincts and in which governments took (or were allowed to take) little interest. Schools in general should prepare children for adult, working life and be more responsive to industry. Callaghan's call for a 'great debate' gradually bore fruit: several reports ensued, leading to a National Curriculum, following the Conservative 1988 Education Reform Act.

Callaghan was a strong supporter of the links between the Labour Party and the trade unions and had opposed the *In Place of Strife* proposals. He also opposed the **unilateralist** faction within the party. In the leadership election of 1976, six candidates stood. Callaghan initially came a close second to Michael Foot, emerging as winner in the second round, in which he was the centrist candidate, defeating both Foot and Denis Healey.

Devaluation and the IMF loan

Investors buy and sell currency, just as they do anything else of value, and they do so in anticipation of one currency increasing in value relative to another. In 1976, investors reached the conclusion that the pound was being traded for more than it was really worth; accordingly, more of them wanted to sell than wanted to buy, something which drove down the price of sterling.

The number of dollars you could buy for a pound sank and reached a record low in June 1976. The US Treasury Secretary concluded that the pound was now undervalued and offered a loan of $5.3 billion that would need repaying by December 1976.

The pound continued to be under pressure and the time for repaying the US Treasury loan approached. The government now turned to the **International Monetary Fund** (IMF) for a loan of $3.9 billion in September 1976. For such a large sum the IMF itself had to negotiate access to funds from the USA and Germany. Before agreeing to the loan, the IMF insisted on cuts in public expenditure so that the **budget deficit** would come down. Denis Healey as Chancellor had already proposed reducing expenditure and increasing taxes to balance the budget. He returned to the theme and, although colleagues were hostile to the procedure, no one was able to put up an alternative which commanded cabinet support. Even before Healey explained the plan to the House of Commons on 15 December 1976, he had to defend it to a hostile Labour Party conference in September: 'I am going to negotiate with the IMF on the basis of our existing policies ... It means sticking to the very painful cuts in public expenditure on which the Government has already decided. It means sticking to a pay policy which enables us, as the TUC resolved a week or two ago, to continue the attack on inflation'.[13]

Callaghan's speech to the same Labour Party conference also contained a warning that government thinking was moving away from the Keynesian idea that a country could spend its way out of a recession and increase employment, by cutting taxes and boosting government spending. It had only worked 'by injecting a bigger dose of inflation into the economy, followed by a higher level of unemployment as the next step'.[14] The policies being outlined were already laying ground for what would later be assumed to be 'Thatcherism'.

Key terms

unilateralist: one supporting the unilateral (one-sided) nuclear disarmament of, e.g. Britain, without attempting to negotiate a specific response from the Cold War enemy - the allies in the Warsaw Pact.

International Monetary Fund (IMF): founded in 1944 with the job of preventing monetary crises by looking after national currencies, including exchange rates and devaluations. A range of countries make funds available and individual countries can draw on the IMF's resources and advice. To that extent the Fund acts like a bank, with states and national governments as its customers.

budget deficit: the amount by which government (public) expenditure exceeds government income at any given time; this is treated separately from 'national debt', which is the deficit accrued over the longer term.

Key terms

summit: a meeting between heads of government, or heads of state, of different countries. It is preceded by a series of planning meetings between their advisers and officials, to ensure that when national leaders meet they are in a position to make wide-ranging decisions leading to the signing of treaties.

Cross-reference **Chapters 4 and 5**

With the IMF loan in place, the situation did improve. Interest rates came down. The pound started to regain some of its lost buying power. In the meantime, a new source of income started to arrive as North Sea oil started coming ashore in 1975. This began to affect the balance of payments, as Britain began to import less oil.

The winter of discontent

Trade union membership had hovered around 10 million for some years. By 1979 it had climbed to 13 million, around half the national workforce. Changes in the legal framework under Foot had left the unions in a stronger position. High membership gave them a sound financial basis and strong negotiating power.

Greater flexibility in pay negotiations had helped bring down the number of working days lost to strike action. However, in the winter of 1978–79, the number of strikes – particularly by public-sector unions seeking improved pay for their members – jumped.

The background lay in the Labour government's policy of keeping pay rises in the public sector under 5%, in their efforts to balance the economy and bring down inflation. As the gap between workers in the private and public sectors widened, so discontent grew. The problem was that some private-sector employers could afford to pay higher wages and were willing to do so. Car workers and transport workers both succeeded in negotiating rises well above the 5% limit. The unions wanted government to stay out of pay negotiations.

During a particularly cold winter, with bad industrial news on newspaper front pages, the Prime Minister was at an international **summit** in Guadeloupe. He was tricked by the press while out there and made a tactical error in dealing with press on his return. In Guadeloupe, he was photographed swimming in the tropical waters as though on holiday. Worse, on his return, he spoke to the press and, when asked about 'the mounting chaos in the country', replied 'Well, that's a judgment that you are making. I promise you that if you look at it from outside, and perhaps you're taking rather a parochial view at the moment, I don't think that other people in the world would share the view that there is mounting chaos'.[15]

The following day *The Sun* newspaper carried the headline 'Crisis? What crisis?' Callaghan had never used these words but, on top of the earlier photographs, they made it seem that the Prime Minister was out of touch – having been on a sunshine holiday when everyone else was cold and at work, and with no appreciation of the seriousness of the situation.

The number of public-sector and private-sector workers on strike went up and the strikes dragged on. To official strikes with union leadership were added unofficial ones, as different groups in different workplaces walked out. The strikes affected hospitals. Gravediggers struck, so the dead could not be buried. Rubbish collectors struck, so rubbish piled up in the streets, encouraging rats.

ACTIVITY 3.5

'Both Wilson and Callaghan made mistakes, but their achievements outweighed their lapses'.[16] How would you assess Wilson and Callaghan and their governments' records in the field of economic policy? Draw up a balance sheet, showing successes and failures, and assess how the two sides compare.

Figure 3.11: James Callaghan (centre) in Guadeloupe with (from left to right) the leaders of West Germany, the USA and France, 1979.

Labour had long sold itself to voters as a party which could handle trade unions and thus manage the economy: this period of strikes, dubbed the 'winter of discontent' in the media (it was a quotation from Shakespeare's *Richard III*), fatally undermined this claim. The government public standing seemed to have survived the 1976 crisis and the IMF loan. But, during the winter of 1978–79, opinion polls pointed to a marked change in voting intentions. The Conservatives came from behind to take a significant lead.

These political, economic and industrial problems contributed to opening out the divisions within the Labour Party. After the 1979 election, these divisions would become increasingly important.

Problems of Northern Ireland

The Troubles in Northern Ireland had not gone away. Peter Hennessy suggests it had become 'the greatest absorber of high-level prime ministerial time over the life of the government as a whole' during the Heath government.[17] Progress seemed to have been made by the government, but the Sunningdale Agreement itself was precarious and insecure. The work was undertaken by the Home Secretary, Maudling (1970–72) and Robert Carr (1972–74). Then, from 1972, the lead was taken by the newly created office of Secretary of State for Northern Ireland, William Whitelaw (1972–73) and then Francis Pym (1973–74).

The collapse of the Sunningdale Agreement

Although the leaders of the constitutional parties on both sides of the sectarian divide had signed up to the Sunningdale Agreement, the IRA campaign persisted. The compromises agreed did not limit either Unionist fears, or nationalist ambitions.

Within days of the agreement being signed, loyalist paramilitary groups had formed a coalition under the umbrella name of the 'Ulster Army Council'. Within weeks the Unionists voted against continued participation in the Northern Ireland Assembly.

Within months the loyalist Ulster Workers Council called a general strike, leading to a period of rioting.

The IRA now moved to attack targets on the British mainland, setting off bombs in pubs in Birmingham, Guildford and Woolwich, resulting in many casualties. Several people were quickly arrested and convicted in different group trials. After extended, slowly growing campaigns, their various convictions were overturned and they were released after serving 15–16 years in prison. No one else was ever brought to trial.

Elections to the Northern Ireland Constitutional Convention (NICC) were held in May 1975, using a system of proportional representation to ensure that a wider range of opinions and parties would be represented. One example of this (and symptomatic of what was happening within unionism) was that six different Unionist parties won seats; of these the largest was the grouping opposed to power sharing and to the NICC itself. The different parties could not reach agreement and the NICC lapsed.

It would take nearly 30 years of violence and negotiations to bring all parties back to a settlement not unlike the Sunningdale Agreement.

The effects of its failure

Kenneth O. Morgan says that the end of the Sunningdale Agreement and the failure of the NICC left Northern Ireland a place 'in which the violent men of the IRA and the Protestant 'Defence' organisations had the field to themselves'.[18] Some new optimism was created by the development, in 1976, of a grass-roots peace movement led by two Catholic women, Mairead Corrigan and Betty Williams. The movement began as a response to the killing of three children by a PIRA activist fleeing in a getaway car. It was expressed in demonstrations for peace, at first in Northern Ireland itself and then demonstrations of support around the world. In 1977 Corrigan and Williams received the Nobel Peace Prize.

The Maze prison

In 1971, republicans arrested during Operation Demetrius were interned at Long Kesh, in a collection of buildings left over from the Second World War. Of the initial 452 suspects, 104 were released because the authorities concluded they had no connection to terrorist organisations. Arrests continued and, by 1972, there were more than 900 internees. By the end of 1975, when internment ended, nearly 2000 people had been held without trial.

Special-category protests

What was the status of these prisoners and others who had been convicted of political violence? They did not see themselves as criminals. In addition, the acknowledged need to separate members of different paramilitary organisations imposed a difference on the authorities. During negotiations for a truce with the Provisional IRA, the Conservative government agreed it would allow a 'Special Category Status' and this was introduced in 1972. This allowed prisoners more free-association time, more visits, more food parcels and, crucially, the right to wear their own clothes rather than prison uniforms. The changes aligned the conditions in which they were held more with Prisoners of War under the Geneva Convention, than with that of criminals serving a sentence. Four years later, in 1976, the Labour government left this arrangement in place for existing detainees, but reversed it for new ones – who would serve their sentences in the newly built 'H-Blocks' on the Long Kesh site, which was now named Her Majesty's Prison Maze (HMP Maze). The first new prisoner refused to comply and wrapped himself in blankets for lack of anything else to wear. By 1978 there were nearly 300 prisoners taking the same course.

In addition, prisoners refused to cooperate with the usual regime of cleanliness – refusing to shower, refusing to empty chamber pots and even smearing excrement on the walls of their cells, forcing the authorities to move them from time to time, to steam clean the resulting filth. In 1980 and 1981, prisoners took the protests further, with extended hunger strikes, resulting in ten deaths.

Meanwhile, the decision was taken by the PIRA leadership to treat prison officers, like RUC officers and British soldiers, as targets for assassination; 19 were to die.

Taking it further

The period of the Troubles coincided with one of literary activity. What do poems such as Heaney's 'The Grauballe Man' or Ciaran Carson's 'Belfast Confetti' tell us about the conflict?

Society in the 1970s

Progress of feminism

Although women had been voting in general elections since 1918, they continued to be under-represented in parliament. In 1970, women made up 4% of the House of Commons; by 1979 this had had sunk to 3%.

Several women were able to become prominent across a wider range of fields than in previous generations: Jennie Lee and Barbara Castle were noted members of the Harold Wilson governments; Dorothy Hodgkin was a Nobel prize-winning scientist; Iris Murdoch and Doris Lessing won fame as novelists, Barbara Hepworth as a sculptor, Bridget Riley as a painter, Thea Musgrave and Elizabeth Maconchy as composers, Jacqueline du Pré as a cellist. However, Kenneth O. Morgan draws attention both to the fact that, by the 1960s, women made up about a third of the work force, and also that that they were largely grouped into a limited number of jobs, including secretarial and clerical, 'but the presence of women in public life, in politics, the law, the universities or the civil service was a limited one'.[19]

Second-wave feminism and Women's Liberation

It was only gradually that radical analyses of society, economy and culture returned to the position of women and its significance. When they did so, the language of the discourse drew on the well-established discussions of race and imperialism, so that the term 'Women's Liberation' was widely adopted. Women's campaigning did not achieve a mass membership on the model of political parties and the discussions were largely limited to educated white women from prosperous families. Reaching out to women who were poorer, less educated, or from ethnic minorities was difficult and not always recognised as being of importance.

Key individuals

Women's Liberation was, and remains, an international movement which campaigned and discussed a changing agenda of issues over a long period. Notable influences on British feminists in the 1970s included the British novelist Virginia Woolf's *A Room of One's Own* (1929) and *Three Guineas* (1938), French writer Simone de Beauvoir's *Le Deuxième Sexe* (*The Second Sex*, 1949) and American Betty Friedan's *The Feminine Mystique* (1963).

Australian-born, British-based, journalist and later academic Germaine Greer published *The Female Eunuch* in 1970. Inspired by earlier feminist writing, it became a best-seller and attracted a vast amount of media coverage. It argued that women were oppressed by men, that this oppression was exercised through the way society was organised and that it was internalised by women.

Different strands within the movement

Some women decided that the way forward was through education and communication. They set up magazines that would be an alternative to 'consumer' magazines, with their continual emphasis on cooking, knitting, shopping and personal appearance (*Spare Rib*, 1972), and publishing houses that specialised in women writers (Virago 1973, Onlywomen Press 1974).

Some protested against the 1970 Miss World competition in London. A beauty contest in which all the competitors were women and all the judges were men, it is not hard to see why this was the object of a hostile critique. The numbers involved were small and the public and press reaction was not altogether supportive.

In 1971, Erin Pizzey founded a refuge for women in west London. Chiswick Women's Aid was a practical response to the problems faced by women whose partners were violent, or threatening to them or their children. These were problems in which the criminal justice system was reluctant to become involved, as there was a widespread belief that the state had no role in private lives. Pizzey's work was praised, though her use of 'squatting' (occupying vacant domestic properties) was controversial.

The 1970 Equal Pay Act and the 1975 Sex Discrimination Act

In 1970, women earned a little over half of what men did. The Labour Party and the Trades Union Congress had both spoken in favour of equality of treatment and opportunity for women workers. The 1968 strike by women sewing machinists at the Ford car factory in Dagenham was about equal pay for different (but, in the strikers' view, comparable) work. The strike was successful and led to a political discussion that brought about the passing of new legislation, notably the 1970 Equal Pay Act.

Cross-reference Chapter 2 *The Dagenham strike*

By this time Britain had entered the EEC and the Treaty of Rome guaranteed equal pay for equal work, or work of equal value. The latter widened the concept of equality, something that was important since men and women often did different work. It also made matters complex, since establishing whether the work demanded sufficiently similar effort, education, training or skill was inevitably a matter of judgement, rather than simply measurement.

The 1975 Sex Discrimination Act protected men and woman against discrimination on grounds of gender or marital status. It affected the worlds of education and work (though not in Northern Ireland). It created the Equal Opportunities Commission, to which individuals could appeal if they wanted to bring their cases before the law courts or Employment Tribunals, in matters affected by both the Equal Pay and Sex Discrimination Acts.

Taking it further

The story of the Dagenham strike is shown in the film *Made in Dagenham* (2010). Watch the film, and discuss what the issues at stake were then and how different the issues are for women in employment now.

Race and immigration

Immigration rates

By the late 1950s, the non-white population of Britain was under 200 000. These communities tended to be centred on major ports, such as London, Cardiff and Liverpool.

Effects, attitudes and tensions

Although the numbers of new arrivals was certainly an issue at the time, the perceived differences between the immigrants and the existing population were also important. South Asian immigrants were often Muslim, sometimes Hindu or, more rarely, adherents of other religions. Immigrants spoke with different accents, dressed differently, ate different food and showed different behaviour patterns. This created a level of anxiety about Britain's future, even beyond the questions about jobs and housing.

The National Front

In the mid 1960s, the National Front (NF) was formed, primarily to oppose immigration. It adopted other right-wing and nationalist policies, being opposed to the United Nations, NATO, EEC and communism, and to the developing liberalising agenda that included legalising homosexual relations between men. It drew attention to crime statistics – arguing that the presence of immigrants had led to more robbery and violence – and to unemployment, which it also blamed on immigrant competition. The NF wanted, not merely to reduce or end immigration from Commonwealth countries in south Asia, the West Indies and west Africa, but to repatriate (send back) the immigrants who had already arrived in the UK. During the early 1970s NF membership continued to grow, though it struggled to find support outside its working class base.

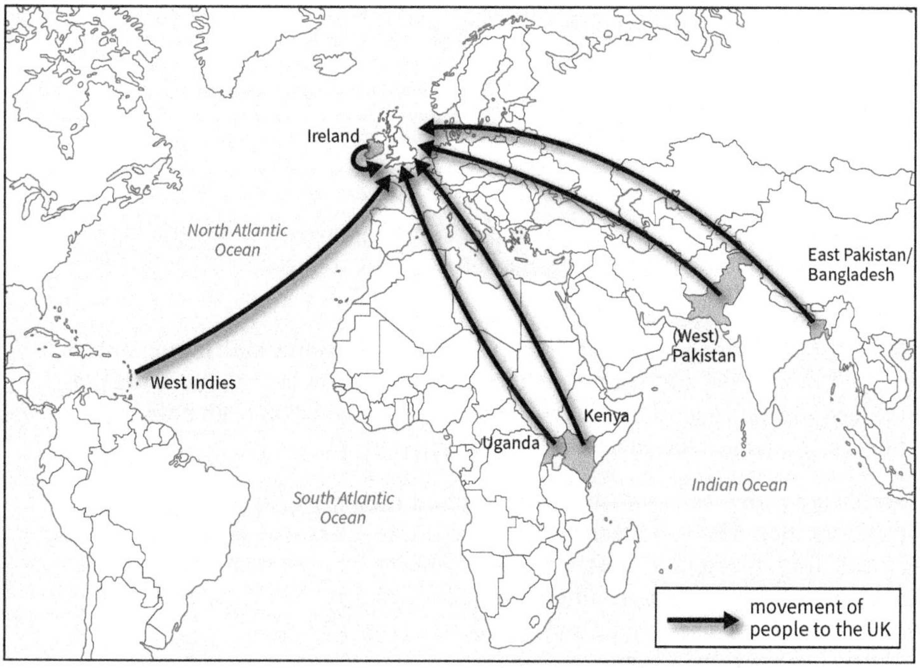

Figure 3.12: People travelled to Britain from several places in the world, notably south Asia, west Africa, West Indies and Ireland, as well as from Kenya and Uganda at a specific period.

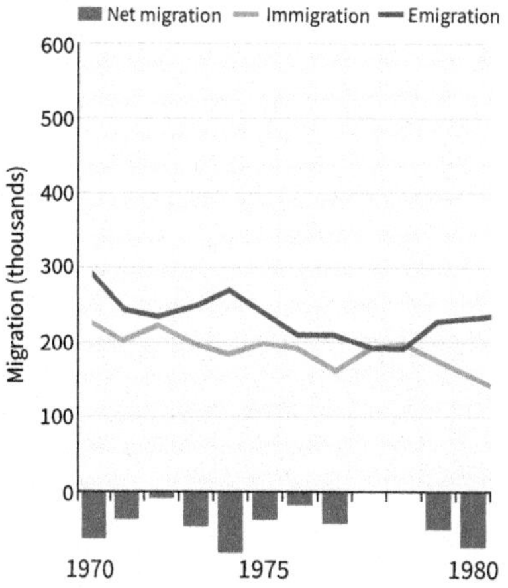

Figure 3.13: UK migration patterns, 1970–80.

Although a small party, it achieved double-digit results in some by-elections: at a 1973 by-election in West Bromwich West its candidate took 16.2% of the vote. Outside election campaigns, it maintained a profile by organising demonstrations. It naturally attracted the concern of existing parties and the interest of the media. The latter drew attention to the fact that some members (including prominent ones) had previously belonged to openly neo-fascist or neo-Nazi parties.

The NF was then undermined by divisions within the movement itself, but also by the response of Conservative leader Margaret Thatcher.

Cross-reference **Chapter 4** *Electoral success*

The Anti-Nazi League

In 1977 the Anti-Nazi League (ANL) was founded by members of left-wing parties, specifically to campaign against far-right organisations, individuals and policies. Much of its attention was devoted to the National Front, but it also drew attention to the activities of more openly neo-Nazi parties and groups. It had the support of various MPs, trade unions and pop groups, some of whom would appear at meetings and concerts in support of ANL, raising public awareness – and funds.

By the late 1970s, the NF was no longer the threat it had appeared to be and the ANL was formally ended, though other anti-fascist organisations continued to exist, or came into being, just as other far-right groups and political parties did.

Government legislation and response

The Conservative and Labour governments took similar approaches to the issues of the new arrivals. These can be summed up as first, immigration policy and second, race-relations policy. The belief was shared that, in Labour minister Roy Hattersley's words, 'Without integration limitation is inexcusable: without limitation integration is impossible'.[20] Both parties looked to pass some laws that would regulate the rate of arrival of immigrants and others that would regulate how people were treated.

Cross-reference **Chapter 2** *Issues of immigration and race*

The Conservative government passed the 1962 Commonwealth Immigrants Act, limiting access to those holding one of a limited number of government-issued employment vouchers.

The Labour government revised this with the 1968 Commonwealth Immigrants Act, reducing Commonwealth citizens' rights of entry to the UK to those born in Britain plus those who had a least one parent or grandparent who had been born there. Further restrictions followed in the 1971 Immigration Act.

Intermingled with these were attempts to outlaw racism on the basis that, once here, immigrants should be treated as citizens, not as foreigners. The 1965 Race Relations Act made discriminatory actions, such as refusing to serve someone in a bar or restaurant, or charging people different fees according to their race, a civil (but not a criminal) offence. It also established the Race Relations Board (from 1966) to hear and investigate complaints. Shops and boarding houses did not come into its remit. This was widened by the 1968 and 1976 Race Relations Acts. The 1976 Act extended the reach of the law into discrimination in employment, education and the workings of the state's own agencies. In 1976 the monitoring body was the Commission for Racial Equality.

Voices from the past

Margaret Thatcher

The inability of the NF to win seats in the House of Commons gradually undermined its popularity. Meanwhile, the newly elected leader of the Conservative party, Margaret Thatcher, carefully indicated she was sympathetic, not to the NF, but to the anxieties of its supporters. It has been argued that these words of hers in 1978 drew NF supporters back to the Conservative party in the 1979 election.

[W]e do not talk about [immigration] perhaps as much as we should. In my view, that is one thing that is driving some people to the National Front. They do not agree with the objectives of the National Front, but they say that at least they are talking about some of the problems ... If we do not want people to go to extremes ... we must show that we are prepared to deal with it.[21]

Discussion points

1. What do you think of Thatcher's approach to the NF, its supporters and the issue of immigration? You might want to read the quoted passage in context.
2. What kind of personality is she communicating, as well as what kind of policy?

Taking it further

Throughout this period, Irish immigration to the UK continued. Why might this have become controversial in the 1970s? Why do you think it didn't do so?

Tony Kushner calls chronicling of immigration, race riots and acts of parliament as 'providing a "pathological" view of black people in Britain. Black people arrive, create a "race problem", are opposed by public and then by state and finally rebel on the streets'.[22] What do you think he means?

Youth

Britain in the 1950s and 1960s had seen the development of a youth market: young people spending spare money in ways that defined their membership of different social groups. Whereas earlier, a musical choice might distinguish children from their parents, by the 1970s the youth market had become subdivided and choices showed membership of subcultures.

Prog rock and glam rock

Building on the sophistication of the lyrics and music of 1960s groups, such as the Beatles and the Kinks, progressive ('prog') rock groups, such as Pink Floyd and Genesis, recorded increasingly complicated performances. Songs were longer, and required the participation of more performers and a higher level of music technology.

Others performers emphasised the theatrical element in pop, wearing stage costumes and make-up. They would often adopt a stage name, as though separating their stage identity from the background. Thus David Jones performed as 'David Bowie', while 'Bowie' himself recorded as 'Ziggy Stardust', a stage character taking on the name and identity of a stage character, like a play within a play.

Punks

Late 1970s and early 1980s punk rock followed reggae's example, with lyrics which tended to be short slogans several times repeated – often shouted. The harmonic content was simplified to a small number of chords repeated many times, often without variation, loudly and very fast. Where Pink Floyd had recorded 'Money' partly in 7/4 time, punk rock stuck to the more traditional pop music 4/4. The result was music to which audiences could dance vigorously – something it would be hard to do with some prog-rock tracks.

This radical simplification was associated with the slowly growing unemployment figures by some commentators, who dubbed punk rock 'dole-queue rock', an aspect to which John Street draws attention, noting that unemployment was 'a trend to which the young were especially vulnerable'.[23] An examination of punk lyrics suggests that political analysis was not typical punk fare. However, the Sex Pistols 1977 single 'God Save the Queen' sneered at the monarchy and alleged the existence of a British fascist regime. The Clash's 'London Calling' and the Jam's 'Eton Rifles' did address political issues.

Other musical styles in the 1970s

In addition to these developments in music in the 1970s there were also: new wave or post-punk, including the Boomtown Rats and Ian Dury; folk, folk rock and electric folk, such as Fairport Convention and Steeleye Span, and heavy metal, such as Black Sabbath and Led Zeppelin.

In jazz, a notable development was jazz fusion (or simply 'fusion'); Soft Machine is a good example.

In classical music, Minimalism had not only become a prominent and controversial style, influenced by Americans Steve Reich and John Adams, but had begun to be heard in religious music by John Tavener.

Fashion

Designers and retailers were not slow in offering to affirm social-group membership through fashion choices. Punk was closely associated with torn clothes, with the head largely shaved, leaving an elevated, stiffened crest, sometimes coloured (style known as a mohican).

Hippies persisted with an alternative or anti-establishment style of living and music, emphasising long hair; a taste for prog rock or folk music; loose, often decorative and impractical clothes; vaguely revolutionary political views, especially an anti-war posture (influenced by the USA, which was in the middle of the long-running Vietnam War), and sometimes a mobile lifestyle, including travelling to different concerts and pop festivals. Tie-dyed tee shirts, or the smell of incense, such as patchouli, would tend to announce a hippie.

Skinheads wore Doc Marten boots and visible braces holding up trousers. They were more likely to adopt an aggressive manner and be drawn to right-wing groups with anti-immigrant, racist views.

Attitudes and responses

Each of these manifestations of younger people's tastes and choices attracted hostile media commentary in turn. A tendency to focus on the negative meant that hippie boys were not praised for pacifism, but criticised for effeminate hairstyles that risked head lice; skinheads were not praised for having short hair, but criticised for their association with football hooliganism. All drug-taking was heavily criticised. The pattern was an example of what sociologists and social historians call 'moral panic' – the feeling that a growing wickedness threatens the wellbeing of society.

Taking it further

1. Listen to some of the music of the period and make notes on what characterises the different pieces, groups and styles. Discuss the connections you see between them.
2. When American folk musician Bob Dylan appeared on stage in his first tour of the UK to use electric instruments, he was booed and one audience member shouted 'Judas!' Explain this response: what do you think was at issue?

Environmentalism

Pressure groups

Formed in 1926, the Council for the Protection of Rural England (CPRE) opposed **ribbon development**, and supported the development of **green belts**, national parks and the designation of areas of outstanding natural beauty. It has enjoyed the support of politicians, journalists and members of the royal family.

Friends of the Earth (FOE) was founded in the USA in 1969 and within a couple of years was active in the UK. Initially it concentrated on nuclear energy, before widening its remit to include issues around transport, waste and food production.

Greenpeace began in the USA in the early 1970s. It developed a wide-ranging critique of political, military, agricultural and industrial developments, based on their impact on things such as **biodiversity**. In 1972, volunteers sailed into the area where the

Key terms

ribbon development: the growth of urban areas by the development of additional buildings along the roads that go out from the towns and cities.

green belts: areas of countryside immediately around urban centres on which building is banned, or restricted, in order to prevent towns and cities growing outwards without adequate planning and to ensure town-dwellers have access to the countryside.

biodiversity: term describing the range of life forms currently present on Earth, much used in debates over human impact on the environment.

French military were conducting nuclear tests. Photographs revealing the violence used against the volunteers drew both press attention and public sympathy to the organisation. Later campaigns focused on whales and industrial effluent, but the tactic of **non-violent direct action** has been maintained.

The Ecology (from 1990 the Green) Party was founded in the mid 1970s. In the 1979 general election it won no seats, but its result was better than any of the smaller parties – behind the Liberals, but ahead of the National Front.

Aims, beliefs and activities

The beliefs that the four organisations cited have in common is that the effects of modern, western agriculture, industry and urbanisation need to be taken into account in all current and future decision-making. Some of the campaigning has been political and some at the level of large organisations (such as multinational companies), but some of it has been to do with emphasising lifestyle choices by individual consumers. Thus, CPRE and FOE both took part in the 1975 Consumer Congress, organised by the National Consumer Council, alongside charities to do with old age, housing and unemployment.

Government response

The environment was not considered a political priority by either politicians or voters in the 1970s. Any environmental legislation passed by previous governments had been stimulated by human need. The 1956 Clean Air Act had responded to urban air pollution, which had on occasion led to large numbers of deaths. The 1968 Town and Country Planning Act curtailed building on green belt land and areas of outstanding natural beauty. Although these were of significance, it should be noted that the CPRE had lobbied for such steps, a measure of their acceptability to the establishment.

Under Edward Heath, the Ministry of Housing and Local Government was replaced by the Department of the Environment, indicating potential for a widening and, in modern terms, a 'greening' of its brief.

Harold Wilson, always adept at noticing where opinion was moving, established the Royal Commission on Environmental Pollution in 1970 to advise government and parliament. For 40 years, this body reported on both rural and urban matters. Its 1970s reports addressed concerns about industrial and agricultural pollution, as well as issues around pollution in estuaries and coastal waters, air, and nuclear power.

In 1974, the Water (Control and Prevention of Pollution) Act was passed, with the intention of maintaining or restoring the health and cleanness of Britain's water – something of interest to more radical campaigning organisations, but also an issue that the CPRE could support.

Following the 1973 signing of an international convention on the trade, parliament passed the 1976 Endangered Species (Import and Export) Act to restrict the importation and exportation of certain animals and plants.

How issues were reported or reflected in popular media

The 1962 publication of American scientist Rachel Carson's *Silent Spring* attracted considerable attention in the UK, with its report on the effects of pesticides on the natural world. A subsequent campaign against DDT ran all through the 1970s, the pesticide being finally banned in the UK in 1984.

The 1972 publication of *Limits to Growth* similarly attracted media coverage. It offered a set of predictions about the future of the planet, drawing attention to its limited non-renewable resources. In addition to population, industrialisation, pollution and food production, it considered the depletion of resources. It was widely and vigorously discussed, as it brought into question the prevailing assumption that economic growth

Key terms

non-violent direct action: taking practical steps to advance a cause, including physically opposing an opponent, without the use or threat of violence, but sometimes going outside the law. This might include individuals or groups placing themselves in the way of vehicles to hinder, or draw attention to, e.g. the transportation of weapons or nuclear waste.

was a good thing, because it contributed to prosperity. On balance, the reception was hostile and many people took the view that the case had been overstated.

Outside controversies such as these two, media coverage of environmental issues tended to be infrequent. It was hampered for years by the fact that newspapers and broadcasters did not regard the environment as a continuing story and, consequently, unlike crime, politics, sport and foreign affairs, had no staff members who specialised in it. Individual stories would arise, but then blow over, leaving little trace. The natural world was usually left in the hands of a 'nature notes' columnist, except when there was a flood or an earthquake.

Key terms

maiden speech: first speech by an MP in a legislature, e.g. the British parliament.

Britain's entry into and relations with Europe

Edward Heath was a convinced European. His **maiden speech** in the House of Commons had been about proposals for the future of coal and steel in France and Germany. Apparently an obscure topic, the proposals in fact led to a set of industry agreements, which were a step towards the 1957 creation of the more ambitious EEC.

Cross-reference **Chapter 1** *EEC and EFTA*

From 1961, Heath had been Macmillan's negotiator in an attempt to join the EEC. During the 1970 general election, Heath neutralised the possibility of a controversy about relations with Europe, by declaring that he would not take Britain into EEC membership without the 'full-hearted consent' of parliament and people. As Prime Minister from 1970, he quickly reopened negotiations with the EEC. In 1971, with no President de Gaulle to veto the proposal and no suggestion that sterling would need to be devalued, Britain was accepted as a new member. Parliament passed the European Communities Act in the same year. This was a divisive issue. Some of Heath's own Conservative backbenchers were opposed and, in 1972, some demanded a referendum on membership, a move the Labour Shadow Cabinet decided to support. The Conservatives were divided, not only about EEC membership in general and about the terms that Heath had secured in particular, but also on the role of a referendum. Labour had its own divisions and pro-EEC Roy Jenkins resigned the deputy leadership over the Shadow Cabinet's decision. On 1 January 1973 Britain finally joined the EEC.

No referendum had occurred. Noting this fact, the Opposition made sure that, for the February 1974 general election, its manifesto promised that a future Labour government would both renegotiate Heath's terms of membership and then put the issue to the public to decide. This astute move displeased few and pleased many. It also allowed Wilson to avoid the party becoming visibly split over the question in the middle of an election campaign.

Accordingly, the Wilson government renegotiated, announced that the terms were greatly improved (they were in reality little changed) and organised the 1975 Referendum Act. The question determined by the Act was 'Do you think that the United Kingdom should remain part of the European Community (the Common Market)?'

The 'Yes' campaign was greatly aided by being supported by Labour's right and the Conservative left, plus the Liberals. These were individuals with compatible views of the world. Meanwhile, 'No' was hindered by being supported by Labour's left and the Conservative right, which found it impossible to work together: Labour's Tony Benn refused to appear on the same platform as Enoch Powell, now an Ulster Unionist. The outcome was clear: about two-thirds of those who voted supported remaining within the EEC.

ACTIVITY 3.6

Class discussion: There have been very few referendums in British history; they are associated with constitutional change. Each time there is a controversy about the question to be posed. In what ways do you think that the wording of the 1975 question may have affected the result?

The state of the 'special relationship' with USA

The idea that the UK and the USA have a 'special relationship' was famously asserted by Winston Churchill on a number of occasions. He argued that the relationship was essential to world peace. The concept endures because it reflects certain facts, since the two countries:

- were allies in the First World, Second World, Korean and Cold Wars
- use English as the majority language and the language of public affairs
- have comparable levels of economic development
- share certain values, such as the importance of democracy, the rule of law and civil rights.

Since the Second World War, UK governments have needed to keep in mind Britain's unique position (see Figure 3.14).

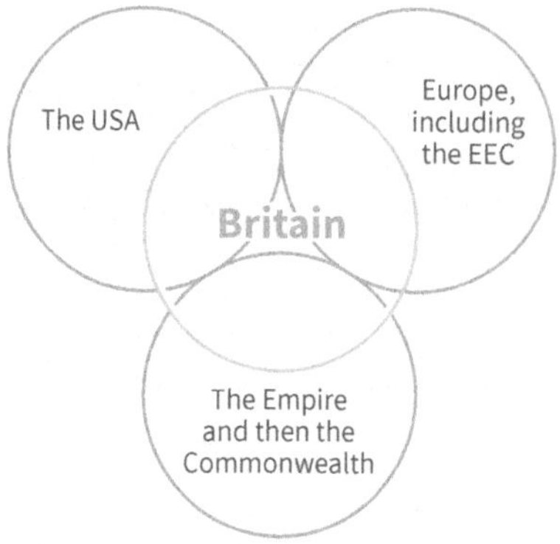

Figure 3.14: Britain's interactions with foreign powers.

Perhaps, for Wilson, the defining issue in relations with the US was the Vietnam War. President Lyndon B. Johnson had been keen to draw Britain in as an ally. Wilson was determined not to upset his own backbenchers by acceding. He was also keen not to upset the economy, recalling the impact of the Korean War on an earlier Labour administration. Besides, Britain had its own military commitments, not least fighting a Communist insurgency in Malaya. However, he balanced this refusal to join the war by refusing to condemn the US role in Vietnam, as many in the Labour party wanted.

Heath was perhaps the post-war Prime Minister who emphasised the relationship with the US the least. For him, the key issue was relations with the EEC. However, Niklas Rossbach argues that Heath and Nixon tried to convert the Anglo-American special relationship into a European-American one, as part of pursing the UK's EEC membership. In the event, Rossbach argues that the attempt failed and actually reinforced the existing diplomatic assumptions.

Alan Dobson argues that relations between Callaghan and, first, the Republican Gerald Ford and second, the Democrat Jimmy Carter, were good. Does the fact that Ford did not visit the UK during his term of office tell us something about the UK's importance to his administration? He was only US president for less than two and a half years, so we should be careful how we interpret the facts.

The impact of entry into the EEC on the 'special relationship'

Its name implies that the EEC was essentially an economic project and, certainly, its supporters believed that membership would support Britain's economic prosperity. However, it was also a politico-diplomatic one. Heath's government wanted Britain to exercise more influence in the world by working alongside European allies. Being part of NATO was the major element in British security policy during the Cold War, but membership of the EEC also has a Cold War context – the presence of the Warsaw Pact on the EEC's eastern borders only made the need for a cooperative and integrated western Europe to be more strongly felt. Few thought that joining the EEC would, or should, mean the end of close cooperation with the US. However, Heath, in particular, argued that Britain was at risk of being expected to back the US at every stage and get little in return: 'our job and Europe's job is to look after our own interests because what the Americans do is to look after their interests'.[24]

In the event, relations with the US survived UK membership of the EEC. Cooperation over defence remained as close as before. When, at the 1979 Guadeloupe conference, Callaghan appealed to Carter for help in the area of nuclear weapons – could the UK buy the American Trident weapon system? – Carter agreed to come up with an affordable deal.

ACTIVITY 3.7

Find out more about US presidents Nixon, Ford and Carter and also National Security Adviser, then Secretary of State, Henry Kissinger. Make short notes on their attitudes to:

- the Cold War
- the UK
- UK membership of the EEC.

Key terms

détente: French word meaning 'relaxation'; a term used in the history of the Cold War and by commentators at the time to describe the increased level of diplomatic contact between the USA and USSR and negotiations regarding nuclear weapons.

Strategic Arms Limitation Talks (SALT): a series of negotiations between USA and USSR.

Sino-Soviet split: a deterioration in diplomatic relations between USSR and China in the 1970s, in which the Chinese leadership both asserted its independence from Moscow and took a different view of Marxism on certain points.

The Cold War in the 1970s

The uncompromising face of Soviet foreign policy in the Cold War can be summarised as the Brezhnev Doctrine. It was set out in 1968 and stated that each Communist party had a responsibility to the people in its own country, but also to the international communist movement. In itself, this was not new: what mattered was that it was a coded threat. The USSR had already invaded East Germany in the 1940s and Hungary in the 1950s. In 1968 it sent Warsaw Pact troops into Czechoslovakia to overthrow a Czechoslovak government whose reforms it saw as a threat. The Brezhnev Doctrine was thus a clear statement that the Soviets' allies should expect to be told what to do and NATO should stay out of Soviet business.

The Cold War was a period of heightened international tension, as numerous countries remained in a state of readiness for the outbreak of a major war. When, during the 1960s and 1970s, politicians took steps to lower the tension, it was called **détente**. Superpower relations became less belligerent. This took various forms. Perhaps most important was that there was more discussion of arms control. Both the USSR and the USA needed this: the arms race was expensive and both had their economic problems.

In 1972 the **Strategic Arms Limitation Talks (SALT)** began, leading to an Antiballistic Missile Treaty and caps on the number of such weapons that each side could develop. In 1975, the Conference on Security and Cooperation in Europe led to the Helsinki Final Act, which was intended to recognise existing political borders, thus avoiding the threat of border disputes and opening doors to trade.

Meanwhile, in the UK CND was less active that it had been in the 1960s (and was to be again in the 1980s) and there was little desire by the British government to adopt a policy on nuclear weapons, or relations with the USSR, that differed from the American one. In this the Wilson-Callaghan administrations differed little from the Conservative ones. There was a left wing within the party which retained an optimistic, idealistic view of the USSR, but they were unable to take control of the party's foreign and defence policy at this point.

ACTIVITY 3.8

Find out more about key events in the Cold War in the 1970s and create a timeline. Remember to include the West's relations with both China and the USSR. Annotate your timeline, commenting briefly on the significance of the events and how they relate to the UK.

Attitudes to USSR and China

China had come under Communist rule in the 1940s, when Mao Zedong had led the party and its army to victory, both in the Second World War against Japan and against his political rivals. After a period of cooperation with Communist neighbours the USSR, relations between the two countries cooled as Mao refused to take orders from Moscow. The **Sino-Soviet split** was an event of enormous importance. The break between the Soviet Union and China meant that there were now three competing superpowers.

NATO and China

Richard Nixon was a career anti-communist. This stance had always been part of his political identity, so that while a Democrat president, or even a more liberal Republican, would beware of laying himself open to charges of being soft on Communism, Nixon felt insulated against such criticisms.

Nixon had three key reasons for wanting improved relations with China:

1. Any improvement in international relations is good for trade and the economy.
2. With the Sino-Soviet split, getting closer to China was a way of outmanoeuvring the USSR.
3. China was one of North Vietnam's backers and Nixon wanted to end the Vietnam War.

However, there was a major stumbling block. The Nationalist government of China and its forces, having lost the civil war, fled into exile in Taiwan. American governments since the Second World War had recognised them as the Chinese government. How could America recognise the Communists and abandon its allies in Taiwan?

Accordingly, his officials worked with their Chinese opposite numbers in preparation for a summit. The Assistant to the President for National Security Affairs, Henry Kissinger, secretly travelled to China to discuss the future. Meanwhile the United Nations was discussing China. The Chinese seat was occupied by the exiled Nationalists in Taiwan. The US argued that Communist China should be allowed to join, while Nationalist China should remain purely as Taiwan. In the event the vote was in favour of Communist China replacing the Nationalist representatives.

While secret meetings were taking place, China invited the US table-tennis team to visit. The 1971 event was nicknamed 'Ping Pong Diplomacy' by the world's media. In 1972, Nixon went to China for a week and met Mao just once. The latter was old and ill and said little, but what he did say laid out his views and requirements.

As Prime Minister, Edward Heath was keen to build the UK's own links to China. His Foreign Secretary, Alec Douglas-Home, visited the country in 1972 and Heath himself went in 1974 and 1975. The two sides discussed trade and largely avoided the topic of Hong Kong, an island that the UK had leased from China and was due to be returned in 1997. Suggestions that the deadline might be set aside were rebuffed, but Mao's successor Deng Xiaoping did accept that Hong Kong's success and value depended on its capitalist, free-market economy being left in place.

ACTIVITY 3.9

Nixon's visit to China has been turned into an opera, John Adams's 1987 *Nixon in China*. Taking account of the fact that it was written 15 years later, notice the words put into the protagonists' mouths by Adams's librettist. Make notes on what they tell you about attitudes to the visit after the event.

NATO and the USSR

Richard Nixon's meeting in Moscow with Communist Party secretary-general Leonid Brezhnev in May 1972 was important. Brezhnev had watched Nixon's February trip to China with anxiety: a better understanding between China and the US might leave the USSR diplomatically isolated. In addition, the Cold War was expensive. If the threat of war was reduced, all sides stood to gain. If, in addition, there could be more international trade, again, everyone benefited.

The first US President to visit Moscow, Nixon signed a set of agreements about limiting weapon stockpiles and trading in grain – the USSR continually failed to feed its people. This built on the achievements to date of the SALT. Further summits in 1973 and 1974 added little, but they did allow dialogue to continue. One problem was that Nixon's successor, Carter, raised issues of human rights, a matter which the Soviets did not want to discuss.

Did détente come to an end in the late 1970s? Certainly, the Soviet invasion of Afghanistan in 1979 meant that Red Army troops had gone beyond the limits established in 1945, something NATO regarded as menacing. Attempts to cite 'the spirit of Helsinki' and talk about human rights in the Soviet Union and its client states met with a frosty response.

ACTIVITY 3.10

'Was nothing at stake in general elections, were different party programmes false labels, was the party clash little more than a cover for rival personal ambitions?'[25] Review the policies and decisions of the Heath, Wilson and Callaghan governments: how different were they from one another? To what extent would you describe the 1970s as a period of political 'consensus'?

ACTIVITY 3.11

1. Study the timeline. Events have been put into separate columns: which would you move to a different column and why?
2. Which developments have been omitted from the table that you think should be included? Explain why.

Timeline 1967–79

Government and politics	Economics	Date	Society	Foreign affairs
Northern Irish Civil Rights Association (NICRA) established		1967		
June: Conservative victory in general election July: death of Iain Macleod January: Conservative Shadow Cabinet meets at Selsdon Park Hotel, Surrey Equal Pay Act Royal Commission on Environmental Pollution established		1970		
Robert Carr introduces Industrial Relations Act August: Operation Demetrius begins policy of internment	Nationalisation of Rolls Royce	1971	Immigration Act	Britain accepted as a new member of EEC Ping Pong Diplomacy
30 January: Bloody Sunday Resignation of Reginald Maudling	National coal strike Barber boom Nationalisation of Upper Clyde Shipbuilders	1972		European Communities Act Richard Nixon meets Mao Zedong Strategic Arms Limitation Talks (SALT) Nixon meets Brezhnev
Government introduces Diplock courts Sunningdale Agreement signed		1973	Social Contract agreed by Labour with unions	1 January: Britain finally joins the EEC Oil crisis Signing of CITES (Endangered Species)
Enoch Powell leaves Conservative Party February: general election won by Labour May: Ulster Workers Council called a general strike IRA set off bombs in pubs in Guildford (October), Birmingham (November) and Woolwich (November)	National coal strike Water (Control and Prevention of Pollution) Act	1974	March: government introduces subsidies on food and housing, and freezes rents in social housing July: Labour repeals 1971 Industrial Relations Act	

Government and politics	Economics	Date	Society	Foreign affairs
May: elections to Northern Ireland Constitutional Convention held National Enterprise Board established following Industry Act The Ecology (from 1990 the Green) Party founded		1975	Sex Discrimination Act	Referendum Act asks 'Do you think that the United Kingdom should remain part of the European Community (the Common Market)?' Conference on Security and Cooperation in Europe led to the Helsinki Final Act
Endangered Species (Import and Export) Act	Sterling crisis and International Monetary Fund loan	1976	Beginning of grass-roots peace movement in Northern Ireland led by two Catholic women Race Relations Act introduces Commission for Racial Equality	
The Anti-Nazi League (ANL) founded		1977	The two founders of grass-roots peace movement in Northern Ireland receive the Nobel Peace Prize	
	Winter of discontent (winter 1978–79)	1978		
		1979		Callaghan attends international summit in Guadeloupe; *Sun* headline: 'Crisis? What crisis?'

Further reading

Peter Clarke, *Hope and Glory, Britain 1900–2000*, Penguin 1996, rev. ed. 2004 is the final volume in the excellent *Penguin History of Britain*. Chapter 10 examines the 1970s. Kenneth O. Morgan, *The People's Peace, British History since 1945*, OUP 1990 is detailed and fair-minded. Vernon Bogdanor's Gresham College lectures on politics are excellent. http://www.gresham.ac.uk/six-general-elections includes a lecture on the February 1974 election. http://www.gresham.ac.uk/lectures-and-events/leadership-and-change-prime-ministers-in-the-post-war-world-winston-churchill offers lectures on all post-war prime ministers, including Wilson, Heath and Callaghan.

Practice essay questions

1. 'The Conservatives lost the February 1974 election solely over economic management.' Explain why you agree or disagree with this view.
2. 'Wilson's Social Contract stood no more chance of calming and regulating industrial relations than the Conservatives' Industrial Relations Act.' Explain why you agree or disagree with this view.
3. 'Bloody Sunday was the point at which the situation in Northern Ireland slipped out of political control.' Explain why you agree or disagree with this view.
4. 'The high level of immigration in the 1970s had a major impact on British society' Explain why you agree or disagree with this view.
5. 'Heath's reasons for Britain joining the EEC were idealistic; Wilson's reasons for holding a referendum were pragmatic.' Explain why you agree or disagree with this view.
6. With reference to the sources and your understanding of the historical context, which of these two sources is more valuable in explaining why Labour won the October 1974 general election?

Source A

Source: ***Britain Will Win with Labour***, October 1974 Labour Party Manifesto

[Following the February 1974 election] we have found ourselves faced in Parliament by a majority which could, and did, coalesce to frustrate the policies we had put before the nation ...

We have shown that as a Government we are prepared to take the decisions that are needed to achieve economic and social justice without which this country can never unite.

The policies we have followed over the past six months, the policies which the next Labour Government will follow, are policies to strengthen the Social Contract.

It is not simply, or narrowly, an understanding about wages. It is about justice, equality, about concern for and protection of the lower paid, the needy, the pensioner and the handicapped in our society ...

Source B

Source: ***Putting Britain First***, October 1974 Conservative Party General Election Manifesto

Over recent months, prices have been rising at an annual rate of over 20 per cent, and on present policies they will rise as much next year... Unemployment is rising rapidly, and the deficit in our balance of payments this year will be £4,000 million. By the end of the 1970s, on present forecasts, we are likely to owe £15,000 million for oil alone ...

If we do not solve our economic problems, our political difficulties will be made worse. And if we do not tackle our political problems, our economic problems will be insoluble.

Our main aim therefore is to safeguard the existence of our free society.

Chapter summary

At the end of this chapter you should be able to take account of the views of different historians of this period of British history and form your own views regarding:

- the similarities and differences between Heath's Conservatives and Wilson's Labour
- the economic and political challenges facing governments in the 1970s, including inflation and the role of the trade unions
- the extent and nature of changes in British society, including the growing immigrant population and the controversy regarding the changing status of women
- the foreign policy issues facing the British governments in this period, including relations with the EEC and USA, and the significance of the Cold War.

Endnotes

1 Blake R. *The Conservative Party from Peel to Major*. London: Heinemann; 1997. p. 298.

2 Dale I. *The Dictionary of Conservative Quotations*. London: Biteback; 2013.

3 Fielding S. *The Labour Governments 1964–1970 vol. 1: Labour and Cultural Change*. Oxford: Oxford University Press; 2003. p. 218.

4 The Seldsdon Group Manifesto http://www.selsdongroup.co.uk/manifesto.pdf

5 The Seldsdon Group Manifesto http://www.selsdongroup.co.uk/manifesto.pdf

6 Hamill D. *Pig in the Middle: the Army in Northern Ireland, 1969–84*. London: Methuen; n.e. 1986. p. 84.

7 O'Beirne Ranelagh J. *A Short History of Ireland*. Cambridge: Cambridge University Press; 1983, 1994. p. 272.

8 Morgan KO. *The People's Peace, British History since 1945*.Oxford: Oxford University Press; 1990, 2nd edn 1999. p. 332.

9 Spencer G. (ed.) *The British and Peace in Northern Ireland.* Cambridge: Cambridge University Press; 1983, 2015. p. 5.

10 Hansard, HC (series 5), vol. 830, 31 January 1972, col. 41.

11 'Interview with Bernadette Devlin' 1972, *24 Hours* BBC1, 31 January.

12 Clarke P. *Hope and Glory, Britain 1900–2000*. London: Penguin; 1996, rev. ed. 2004. p. 347.

13 Rosen G. *Old Labour to New, the Dreams that Inspired, the Battles that Divided*. London: Politico; 2005. p. 353.

14 Quoted by Fielding S. *The 1974–9 governments and New Labour*. In: Hickson K, Seldon A. (eds.) *New Labour, Old Labour: The Wilson and Callaghan Governments 1974–1979*. London: Routledge; 2004. p. 288.

15 Clarke C and James T. (eds.) *British Labour Leaders*. London: Biteback Publishing; 2015.

16 Tiratsoo N. *From Blitz to Blair: a New History of Britain since 1939*. London: Weidenfeld and Nicolson; 1997. p. 174.

17 Hennessy P. *The Prime Minister: the Office and its Holders since 1945*. London: Allen Lane/Penguin; 2000. p. 346–7.

18 Morgan KO. *The People's Peace, British History since 1945*. Oxford: Oxford University Press; 1990, 2nd edn 1999. p. 373.

19 Morgan KO. *The People's Peace, British History since 1945*. Oxford: Oxford University Press; 1990, 2nd edn 1999. p. 207.

20 Johnson P. (ed.) *Twentieth-Century Britain, Economic, Social and Cultural Change*. London: Longman; 1994. p. 419.

21 'Interview with Margaret Thatcher' 1978. *World in Action,* ITV, 30 January.

22 In Johnson P. (ed.) *Twentieth-Century Britain, Economic, Social and Cultural Change*. London: Longman; 1994. p. 412.

23 In Johnson P. (ed.) *Twentieth-Century Britain, Economic, Social and Cultural Change*. London: Longman; 1994. p. 470. Street also draws attention to the role of women performers in punk.

24 Quoted in Hennessy P. *The Prime Minister: the Office and its Holders since 1945*. London: Allen Lane/Penguin; 2000. p. 350.

25 Kavanagh D and Morris P. *Consensus Politics from Attlee to Major*. Oxford: Blackwell; 1989. p. 10.

PART 2: MODERN BRITAIN, 1979–2007

4 The impact of Thatcherism, 1979–1987

In this section, we will look at how the Conservative Party under Margaret Thatcher came to power in 1979 and then retained power at subsequent general elections. We shall consider how ideology affected policy. In addition, we shall look at the extent to which 'the government' can be regarded as a united or a divided force in politics and policy during this period. We shall study how ideology, unity and division can be found expressed in social, economic and foreign policy. Therefore, we shall look into:

- The Thatcher governments: Thatcher as leader, character and ideology; ministers; support and opposition; electoral success; internal Labour divisions and the formation of the SDP; Northern Ireland and the troubles.
- Thatcher's economic policies and their impact: monetarism; privatisation; deregulation; issues of inflation; unemployment and economic realignment.
- Impact of Thatcherism on society: sale of council houses; miners' strike and other industrial disputes; poll tax; extra-Parliamentary opposition.
- Foreign affairs: the Falklands; the 'special relationship' with USA; moves to end the Cold War; Thatcher as an international figure; attitudes to Europe, including Thatcher's policies; divisions within the Conservative Party over Europe.

The Thatcher governments

Thatcher as leader, character and ideology

Margaret Thatcher entered the House of Commons in 1959 as one of seven women sharing the Conservative benches with 246 men. She was a grocer's daughter and her origins were made prominent in her 1975 campaign for the Conservative leadership. Historian Richard Vinen calls the lower-middle-class label misleading: her upbringing was prosperous and her parents could afford to pay school fees. No reference was made to the, equally significant, fact that she was a millionaire's wife.

Thatcher came into government committed to a break with the post-war consensus, whereby much of the Conservative Party had been willing to accept the innovations of the 1945–50 Labour governments. Although 'Thatcherism' is a term much disputed by politicians, journalists and historians, it can be summarised as embracing:

- free markets
- monetarism
- privatisation
- cuts in public spending
- cuts in taxes
- emphasising individuals, not groups.

These are all complex and subtle matters, and we shall look at them one by one.

Key terms

wet: school slang for someone regarded as weak or ineffectual. During the 1980s, the Prime Minister called 'wet' members of her own government who did not adequately support her policies, implying they lacked political courage. Her more enthusiastic supporters in the cabinet became known as **'dry'**.

Ministers, support and opposition

Many of the ministers in Margaret Thatcher's first government were loyal supporters. In fact, one of the most loyal was the man who stood against her in the second round of the leadership contest in 1975, William Whitelaw. She appointed the former Northern Ireland Secretary Home Secretary and Deputy Prime Minister and he backed Thatcher loyally.

However, the Conservative leadership team was full of people whose careers had developed under Heath and his predecessors. They did not all warm to Thatcher's values, policies or approach.

Voices from the past

Margaret Thatcher

The phrase 'there is no such thing as society' was taken out of the context of this interview and frequently used by Thatcher's political enemies. Her words seemed to be a break with the post-1945 political consensus that the state had a responsibility to take care of children and unemployed, sick, disabled and retired people. Thatcher wanted to reduce the size of the state and thus lower the level of taxation. As things turned out, there was rather less change than she liked to boast and her opponents used to complain.

I think we have gone through a period when too many children and people have been given to understand 'I have a problem, it is the Government's job to cope with it!' or 'I have a problem, I will go and get a grant to cope with it!' 'I am homeless, the Government must house me!' and so they are casting their problems on society and who is society? There is no such thing! There are individual men and women and there are families and no government can do anything except through people and people look to themselves first. It is our duty to look after ourselves and then also to help look after our neighbour and life is a reciprocal business and people have got the entitlements too much in mind without the obligations.

Interview with Douglas Keay, ***Woman's Own***, September 1987

Discussion points

1. Why do you think this appealed to so many people?
2. Who was likely to disagree with Margaret Thatcher?
3. What do Thatcher's choices of words tell you about her views about 'society'?

According to historian Peter Clarke, Thatcher was not initially strong enough to exclude those whom she characterised as **wet**. She needed her first cabinet to be a balance of her supporters and those who were not her natural allies.

Over time, she was able both to increase the number of her ideological supporters and to promote them to more senior and influential positions in the government. Meanwhile, Heath left front-bench politics for good on losing the leadership, spending the rest of his Parliamentary career as a backbench critic of his party leader. Nevertheless, there continued to be influential members of the government who disagreed with the Prime Minister and, although Thatcher was famously able to dominate her cabinet, it would be a mistake to think that she always had her own way and faced down all opposition. Some Conservative opposition was in support of the concept of 'One Nation Conservatism' against what was seen as the free market's failure to support social cohesion.

The Westland affair

The divisions within the Thatcher government sometimes blew into crises. One notable example was the so-called Westland affair.

Westland was the only British company that made helicopters. In the mid 1980s, in financial difficulties and in need of money to survive, it entered negotiations with US firm Sikorski. Industry secretary Leon Brittan, taking an economic view of matters, was content with this development, arguing that the people to make the decision were the company's own management. Defence secretary Michel Heseltine took the view that defence implications mattered and suggested a European consortium could be put together to make an alternative bid. This was a choice between a **laissez-faire** and a **dirigiste** approach. It was also a choice between the US and the EEC. Unsurprisingly, the Prime Minister backed her Secretary of State for Industry.

In January 1986, deciding that his views were not being listened to, Heseltine walked out of a Cabinet meeting and announced his resignation to the press. As there was some suggestion that his position had been deliberately undermined by documents being secretly leaked, a fortnight later Brittan was forced to resign. This was in part to deflect attention from the Prime Minister, whose own position was being undermined – not by the helicopters, but by the allegations of undermining members of her own government by leaking. This provided an opportunity for Labour leader Neil Kinnock to attack the Prime Minister in the House of Commons, but the occasion turned out not to be one of his stronger performances.

Electoral success

The 1979 election

All three of the major parties had changed their leader since the 1974 election. The Liberal David Steel and Labour's James Callaghan had become their party leaders in 1976, while Thatcher had led the Conservatives since 1975.

The result of the 1979 general election is often referred to as a landslide. In terms of seats, that is certainly the case. But in terms of votes cast (a clearer measure of actual public support), the outcome is less clear cut (see Figures 4.1 and 4.2).

Although a Conservative victory, the results were not as clear as the distribution of seats makes it at first appear. Also (and this would prove increasingly important in future elections) the Liberal party possessed a level of support in the country, which its presence in the House of Commons did not properly show. This difference between seats and votes is worth watching in the subsequent elections. It acts as a corrective to those accounts that only notice the seats – which are an accurate guide to power in the Commons, but not to opinion in the country.

ACTIVITY 4.1

Find out more about the following government ministers and make short notes about what posts they held, their actions, and the topics and policies with which they were associated. Which were wet and which dry?

- Kenneth Baker
- Leon Brittan
- Peter Carrington
- Kenneth Clarke
- Michael Heseltine
- Michael Howard
- Geoffrey Howe
- Nigel Lawson
- John Major
- Cecil Parkinson
- Norman Tebbit
- William Whitelaw

Key terms

laissez-faire: an approach that prefers government to interfere as little as possible in business and the economy, leaving matters to managers and market forces.

dirigiste: an approach that assumes governments should make choices, including legislating, to achieve its preferred ends and using e.g. taxation to promote some developments and inhibit others.

The contrast is about more than economics: it is about what government is for and what society is.

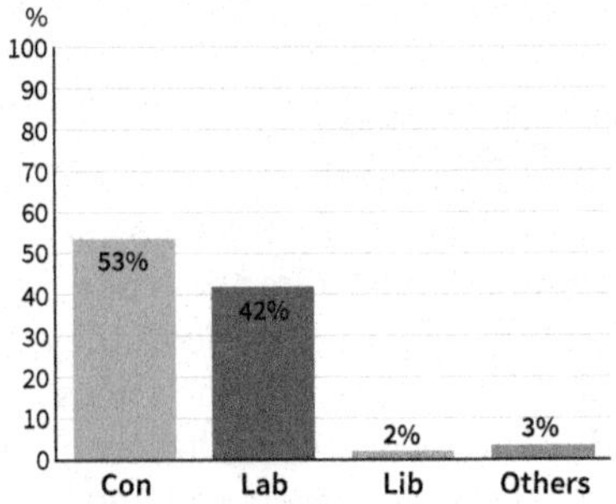

Figure 4.1: Seats in the House of Commons won in the 1979 British general election; percentages have been adjusted to the nearest whole number. Ulster Unionist figures are listed as 'Others'.

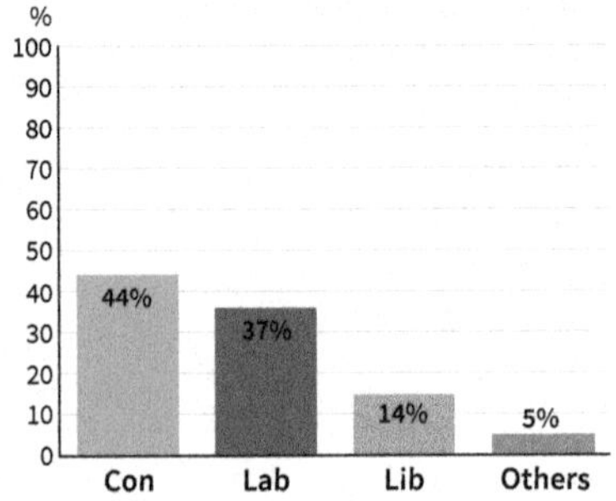

Figure 4.2: Votes won in the 1979 British general election; percentages have been adjusted to the nearest whole number. Ulster Unionist figures are listed as 'Others'.

The election gave Margaret Thatcher's first government a Commons majority of more than 40 seats, something that allowed them to introduce controversial measures and be reasonably sure of being able to get all of them passed.

Internal Labour divisions and the formation of the SDP

Following defeat in the May 1979 general election, James Callaghan resigned as Prime Minister and then, in October 1980, as Labour Party leader.

During the early 1980s, the differences within the Labour Party became more important than the shared ideology. The election of Michael Foot as the new party leader in November 1980 was controversial. Admired by the left wing of the party, he had little support from the right. His situation thus matched Thatcher's – in both leadership elections the vote among MPs had split the parliamentary parties and each leader needed to command the loyalty of the many who had opposed their candidature.

In reaction to Foot's election and the policy direction that followed, some of the right wing of the Labour Party formed the Council for Social Democracy (CSD) in January 1981:

- Bill Rogers was a Labour MP and former Transport Secretary
- David Owen was a Labour MP and former Foreign Secretary
- Shirley Williams was a former MP who had been Secretary of State for Education
- Roy Jenkins was a former MP who had served as a Labour Home Secretary and Chancellor of the Exchequer.

They led a growing group of MPs who argued that policies had moved too far to the left.

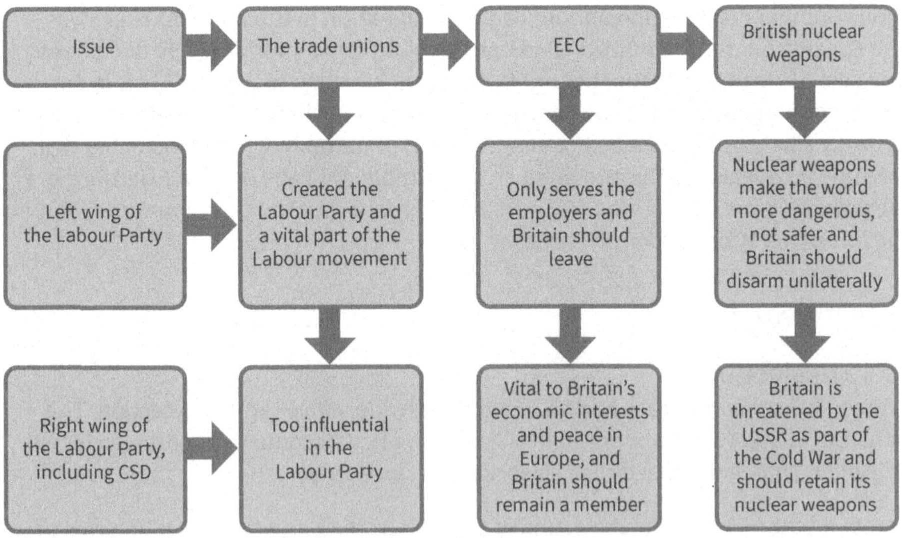

Figure 4.3: The CSD adopted views and policies that contrasted with those of Labour under Foot's leadership.

In March 1981, led by Jenkins, the four creators of the CSD founded the Social Democratic Party (SDP).

The 1983 election

By the time of the June 1983 general election, 29 SDP MPs sat in the House of Commons (28 former Labour, one former Conservative).

The 1983 Labour manifesto, *The New Hope for Britain*, committed the party to getting rid of Britain's nuclear weapons without negotiations; withdrawal from the EEC; abolishing the House of Lords; **renationalising** some key industries which the 1979–83 Conservative government had **privatised**; and ending council house sales. Each of these items had its enthusiasts and each would have benefited some people. But, as a manifesto, it had too little to offer and many of those MPs campaigning on the basis of these promises knew it. One even famously dubbed it the 'longest suicide note in history'.[1]

The Conservatives focused their attacks upon unilateral nuclear disarmament, judging it to be an unpopular policy but, more significantly, one on which party was not united. The (largely right-wing) press frequently emphasised Foot's informal, and thus unprofessional, manner and appearance, drawing the lesson that he was not a potential Prime Minister. The contrast was with Margaret Thatcher, fresh from victory in the Falklands War (a topic to which we turn later in this chapter).

The Conservative manifesto promised to reduce:

- inflation
- public expenditure
- taxes.

In addition, the elections of union officials and decisions over taking industrial action would both be made by secret ballots. British Airways and British Telecom would be privatised. Local councils' ability to increase the rates would be restricted or 'capped' and the Greater London Council (GLC; control of which Labour had succeeded in winning) would be abolished.

Labour's manifesto looked like a promise to spend money and put up taxes. The Conservatives seemed to be offering a manifesto for saving money and making money.

With Labour Party supporters now divided between the old party led by Foot and a new one led by Roy Jenkins, the vote was split, something of huge advantage to the Conservatives. Once again, the distinction between votes and seats is important to notice.

The Conservatives won an even bigger majority in House of Common seats than in 1979, but their share of the vote had actually come down. Although newspapers at the time emphasised the number of seats the parties had won, and commentators then and since have talked about the relative importance of the Falklands and the economy, the most important fact is that the Labour vote had split in two.

Also, inflation was now back down again and although unemployment was still high, it did not prove decisive for the electorate's choices. The unemployed were too few to be able to swing the result, even if they had all voted the same way – or, indeed, voted at all.

In the last days of the campaign, the Labour Shadow Education Secretary, Neil Kinnock, made a speech intended to move the electorate over to the issues of jobs and services – traditional Labour territory. In a long list of warnings, he ended up declaring, 'If Margaret Thatcher wins on Thursday, I warn you not to be ordinary. I warn you not to be young. I warn you not to fall ill. I warn you not to get old'.[2]

The speech did not turn around the election – matters had gone far too far for that – but it made Kinnock a household name. Within days of the election, Foot resigned as leader and the leadership election was then won by Kinnock.

Key terms

nationalisation: a **nationalised industry** is one owned by the state, and **nationalisation** is the process of taking it into public ownership.

privatisation: the process of moving a publicly-owned concern into the private sector, by selling shares in it.

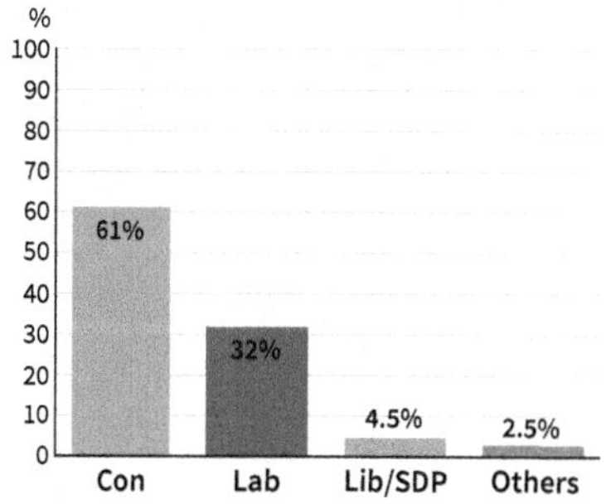

Figure 4.4: Seats in the House of Commons won in the 1983 British general election; percentages have been adjusted to the nearest whole number. Ulster Unionist figures are listed as 'Others'.

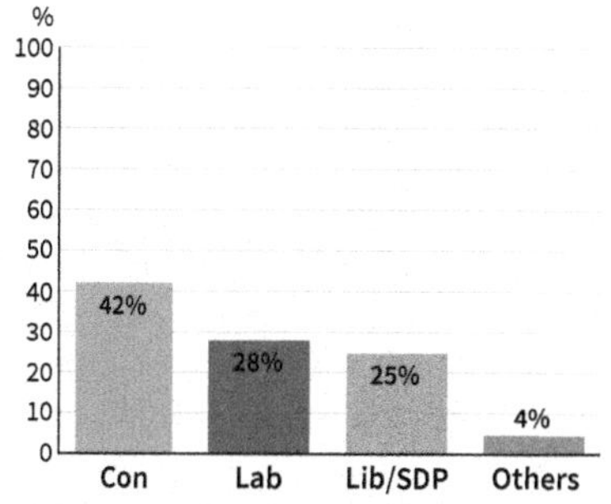

Figure 4.5: Votes won in the 1983 British general election; percentages have been adjusted to the nearest whole number. Ulster Unionist figures are listed as 'Others'.

Voices from the past

Denis Healey

Labour lost the 1983 election heavily. The party's deputy leader Denis Healey said afterwards:

The election was lost not in the three weeks of the campaign but in the three years which preceded it … in that period the Party itself acquired a highly unfavourable public image, based on disunity, extremism, crankiness and general unfitness to govern.[3]

Discussion points

1. Explain Healey's analysis.
2. When you have studied the rest of this chapter, reread Healey's analysis and make notes on what you think were the key reasons were for Labour's defeat in the 1983 general election.

ACTIVITY 4.2

Historian Richard Vinen says that Margaret Thatcher was 'lucky', but that there was more to her success than just luck. List some aspects of her electoral success, and make short notes on the ways in which they show either luck, or judgement, or both. When you have read the rest of the chapter, revisit this list and add to it successes from areas of policy.

The 1987 election

The Labour campaign in 1987 was more professional. Its manifesto had more connection with what ordinary people thought. In Neil Kinnock it had a confident leader (nearly 30 years younger than Foot) who had shown his leadership skills when opposing a left-wing faction within the Labour Party called Militant Tendency. Opinion polls registered his popularity. Yet Labour still lost the election.

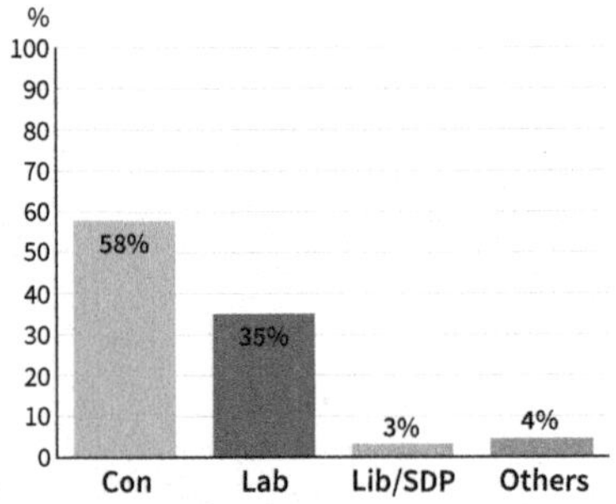

Figure 4.6: Seats in the House of Commons won in the 1987 British general election; percentages have been adjusted to the nearest whole number. Ulster Unionist figures are listed as 'Others'.

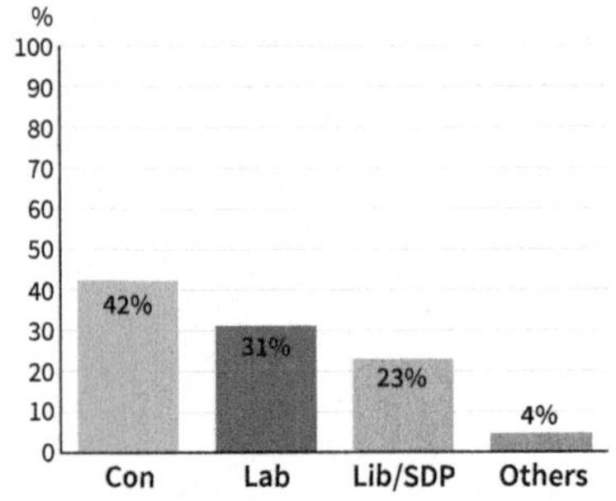

Figure 4.7: Votes won in the 1987 British general election; percentages have been adjusted to the nearest whole number. Ulster Unionist figures are listed as 'Others'.

Where Kinnock, like Foot, wanted to shed the UK's nuclear weapons, much of the party (including many of his own Shadow Cabinet) wanted to retain them. Many voters liked Kinnock; many agreed with several of the Labour manifesto policies. However, divided parties rarely thrive at elections.

Nevertheless, as in 1983, the decisive fact remained that opposition to the Conservatives was still divided between Labour and the Liberal-SDP alliance. The Liberal and SDP leadership reflected on the disappointing results of two elections and decided that part of the problem was the concept of an alliance and the confusion of a dual leadership. One consequence of the election was, therefore, that the two centrist parties merged, to form what was eventually called the Liberal Democrats.

Northern Ireland and the Troubles

The problems of Northern Ireland were brought home to the Conservatives even before they had won the May 1979 election. In March 1979, Conservative MP Airey Neave was killed by a time bomb planted in his car at Westminster by members of the Irish Republican Army (IRA). Neave had been the man who had organised Thatcher's campaign to be Conservative leader in 1975.

Most of the conflict had been fought out in Northern Ireland itself. Actions on the British mainland were highly unusual. A political assassination at the heart of the British political establishment was a considerable shock.

In August the same year, Prince Philip's uncle Earl Mountbatten was killed when his yacht, moored off the coast of Ireland, was bombed by IRA members. Two others on board also died and several were injured.

There were further attacks: December 1983 saw a bomb explode outside the famous London department store Harrods, with five deaths and several wounded. However, the IRA's most startling use of violence to supplement a political campaign was a bomb attack in October 1984.

The Conservative Party was meeting in Brighton for its party conference. The Prime Minister and numerous members of the government, along with party members and journalists in town to cover the story, were sleeping in the Grand Hotel when, on the night of 12 October, a bomb went off. Five people were killed, 31 were injured; the casualty list included household names. This was the nearest that conspirators had come to murdering the British government since the Gunpowder Plot of 1605. As with the Argentinian attack on the Falkland Islands, the Prime Minister's priority was defiance: the conference timetable was not altered. Thatcher's speech writers removed attacks on the Labour Party from her speech and substituted a response to the previous night's events. It had been (she declared) an attempt to 'cripple Her Majesty's democratically elected government' but 'all attempts to destroy democracy by terrorism will fail'.[4]

The Anglo-Irish Agreement

Contact with the Irish government acquired additional urgency. An agreement was reached in November 1985 and signed by the British Prime Minister and the Irish Taoiseach (prime minster). This stated, for the first time, that no change in the constitutional status of Northern Ireland could take place without the consent of the majority of its population. Since the Irish constitution had claimed from the beginning that the whole of Ireland was part of the Irish state, this was a major political development. The British government agreed that the Dublin government could put forward its ideas and concerns in relation to the north.

Unionism no longer spoke through one party. Already, in 1966, Ian Paisley had formed the Protestant Unionist Party, which in 1971 became the Democratic Unionist Party. It attracted support from a working-class base alienated by the existing Unionist Party's apparent willingness to cooperate over the Sunningdale Agreement. The Ulster Unionist Party itself went on to split over the Agreement. However, hostility to the Anglo-Irish Agreement was such that all unionist parties found themselves on the same side.

Given unionist hostility to a foreign government interfering in British affairs, this too was a major development. Fifteen Ulster MPs resigned their seats, in order to trigger by-elections in which the Anglo-Irish Agreement would be the topic at issue.

ACTIVITY 4.3

1. The year after the Brighton bombing, Margaret Thatcher stated that terrorists should be deprived of the 'oxygen of publicity'. What did Thatcher mean by this?
2. For six years, 1988–94, the UK media were banned from broadcasting the voices of Sinn Féin, IRA and certain other groups' members. Research the effectiveness of this and the tactics the media adopted to comply with the ban, while continuing to report the news.

Thatcher's economic policies and their impact

Margaret Thatcher's government came into power with an interlinked set of economic priorities. They wanted to:

- reduce inflation
- reduce the budget deficit
- reduce the size of the state
- reduce the power of the trade unions
- deregulate the **market**.

These were not separate articles, as we shall see.

Part of the background lay in discussions about the nature of the state: what could the state do well and what could it only ever do badly? Economist John Redwood (later a government minister) argued that in 1963 public expenditure had been 43% of GDP, by 1975 it had risen to 60% and at that rate 'the public sector will consume the whole of the gross national product by the end of this century'.[5] The government saw this as economically fatal. In addition, they believed that 'big government' took away from

Key terms

market: a place where people buy and sell goods. 'The market' is a shorthand reference to the totality of making, buying and selling. Market forces are the influence of the numbers of people bidding for goods (demand) and of those seeking to sell them (supply). When demand goes up, or supply falls, prices are pushed up as buyers compete. When supply goes up, or demand falls, prices drop.

individual enterprise and burdened the economy with bureaucracy, which demanded high taxes to pay for it, a further burden on business.

Figure 4.9: John Maynard Keynes.

Figure 4.10: Milton Friedman.

Monetarism

British economic policy since the Second World War, under both Labour and Conservative governments, had been heavily influenced by the work of economist John Maynard Keynes. Led by prominent Conservative Keith Joseph, Thatcher espoused Monetarism. To contrast Keynesian and Monetarist approaches to economics, we could loosely say that:

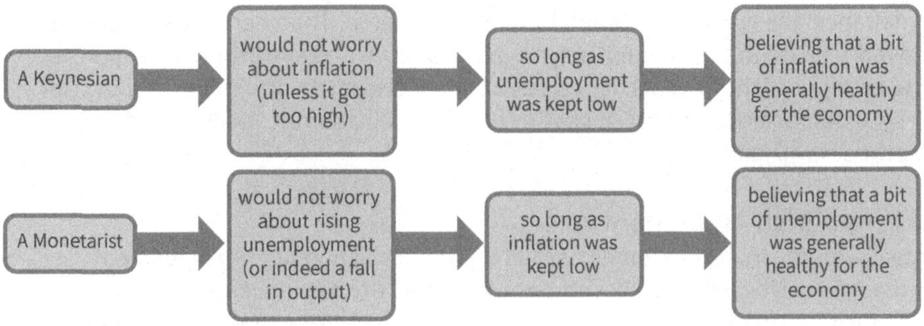

Figure 4.8: Keynesian and Monetarist economics.

Thatcher's first Chancellor of the Exchequer, Geoffrey Howe, reduced the standard rate of income tax from 33% to 30%, and the marginal rate for higher earners from 83% to 60%. In addition, the tax on unearned incomes came down from its highest rate of 98% to 75%. This of course reduced government income. To make up that loss Howe increased the rate of VAT from 8% to 12% (depending on the item being sold) to a flat 15%. This had controversial consequences:

- richer people paid less tax and poorer people paid more
- the cost of living went up.

Given the importance of inflation, the latter was clearly an economic problem, but Howe and his colleagues were confident it was a short-term one. The former was a social problem. However, the calculation was that, once inflation was beaten, everyone in work would be better off and the issue of differences in levels of prosperity

Voices from the past

Keynes and Friedman

John Maynard Keynes argued that governments should manage the economy with policies on prices and on incomes. When unemployment went up, government should spend money to create public-sector work, even if this meant they ran up additional debts. When things became more prosperous, they could scale back their involvement and put up taxes to pay off those debts.

Monetarists, such as **Milton Friedman**, wanted to see less regulation and lower taxes. Regulation slows business down and adds to its costs; lower taxes left people with more money to spend, which was good for business. Control of the money supply was a crucial government responsibility. Governments could decide how much money to allow to circulate, because printing more, or less, money influenced prices (and thus inflation), and so wage demands (and thus inflation). When central banks (such as the Bank of England) allowed too much money in circulation, inflation always followed.

Discussion points

1. Do some further research into Keynes's and Friedman's views. As a class, or in pairs, make the case for each economist in turn.
2. What are their priorities in each case?
3. How would you relate their ideas in general to the situation in the UK in the 1980s in particular?

Voices from the past

Geoffrey Howe

Geoffrey Howe served under Edward Heath and then ran against Thatcher in the second round of the 1975 Conservative leadership election. A quietly spoken member of the Shadow Cabinet, his criticism of Denis Healey had been brushed aside by the then Labour Chancellor as 'like being savaged by a dead sheep'. His reputation, first as Chancellor and then as Foreign Secretary, was technocratic. Nevertheless, it was his criticism of Thatcher in his 1990 resignation speech that set in train the series of events that ended her premiership.

Discussion point

Undertake some further research into Geoffrey Howe's budgets. What priorities do you think they reveal? Take into account economic matters, but also wider social ones.

was less important than increasing general prosperity. It was also assumed that if there was a fall in output, or a rise in unemployment or inflation, better control of the money supply would, over time, cure these.

As inflation rose, so Howe was forced to raise interest rates – from 12% to 14% in June 1979 and to 17% in December. This made borrowing expensive, something that affects both individuals and businesses. In the meantime, public spending was going in the wrong direction – in part because of the climbing numbers of unemployed people, who had to be paid out-of-work benefits, whereas if had they been in work, they would have been paying tax.

Figure 4.11: Geoffrey Howe.

Over time, inflation did come down and the policy of tax cutting was one to which his successor Nigel Lawson at Number 11 Downing Street remained loyal. Indeed, it was Lawson's 1988 budget that was the most famous for cutting taxes.

However, the cuts in direct taxes were balanced by an increase in other, indirect taxes. In addition, while cuts in public spending were indeed made, overall spending was pushed up by the rising rate of unemployment. The differences between Thatcher's economic policies and those of the preceding Callaghan government were not as great as the rhetoric makes them sound.

Privatisation

One aspect of the post-war political consensus was a belief in a mixed economy, whereby a large number of businesses would be privately owned (whether by the directors or by shareholders), but some **infrastructure** would be owned by the state. Public ownership was Labour Party policy, under Clause 4 of its constitution. During the period of Conservative governments in the 1980s and 1990s, shares that the government owned were sold:

1979–87	British Petroleum ('BP')
1984	British Telecom
1985–87	British Aerospace
1986	British Gas
1987	Rolls Royce
1988	British Leyland (as 'Rover Group')
1988	British Steel
1993	British Rail

Table 4.1: Government sell-offs.

Key terms

infrastructure: the structures that underpin social and economic activity, such as roads, railways, bridges and power supplies

monopolies: large companies with no competitors.

Voices from the past

Friedrich von Hayek

In 1944 Friedrich von Hayek published ***The Road to Serfdom*** while in exile in Britain. In this period, states as different as the UK, USA, USSR and Nazi Germany all had governments which intervened in the economy, a process which began in the First World War and had been encouraged by the Depression of the 1930s. Hayek argued that centralised decision-making could not cope with the myriad of unforeseen circumstances. His case was that economics should be left in the hands of individuals operating in a free market. Any other system either was tyranny, or would lead to tyranny. Commentators have often drawn links between Thatcher's government thinking and Hayek, but historian Richard Vinen doubts that they knew his work well (if at all), writing that it provided 'a convenient philosophical polish on things that Thatcherites wanted to do for reasons that had little to do with Hayek's thinking'.[6]

Discussion points

1. **In what ways do you notice the influence of Hayek on the Thatcher governments?**
2. **Consider Vinen's comments: what do you think?**

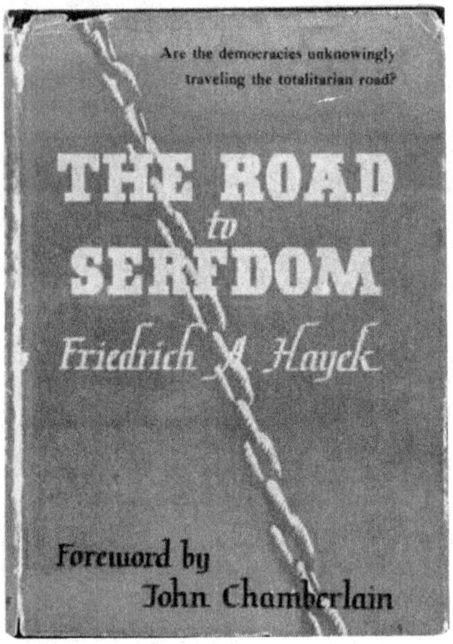

Figure 4.12: The first edition of *The Road to Serfdom.*

This sell-off was partly a matter of economics. For one thing, each sale was a fresh source of income, bringing large sums of money to the Exchequer. However, it was also a political and philosophical matter. Here the influence of Austrian economist and political scientist Friedrich von Hayek was significant. He had argued not only that centralised planning by governments was bound to fail, but also that when governments legislated for social equality, the process increased the power of governments at the expense of citizens. Interventionist governments were thus anti-democratic.

The first completed sale was of British Telecom. A large-scale advertising campaign was mounted to ensure that large numbers of people bought shares. These could easily have been sold to institutions, but the political decision was to build a share-owning democracy, in which large numbers of people owned shares in companies. This was clearly a political imperative for a Conservative government, as shareholders were statistically more likely to vote Conservative in elections. Also, widely distributed shares are harder to repurchase in renationalisation.

According to Peter Hennessy, Professor of Contemporary History: 'Once British Telecom was floated successfully in 1984, the boundaries of that highly disputed frontier – the public/private divide – were to be changed forever'.[7]

The process reduced the presence of the state in the economy: by the end, publicly owned corporations employed fewer than half as many people and contributed half as much to GDP.

Part of the philosophical logic was that privately owned companies face competition and must thus work to improve in order to retain market share. In fact, some of the large enterprises that were sold off were **monopolies**; they had no competitors. The government was forced to create independent authorities who would rule on whether, for example, price rises were justified. This was not really what the Thatcherites had wanted to achieve.

In addition, the creation of a large number of shareholders was a mixed success, as during the 1980s:

- The number of *individuals owning shares* trebled to nine million people.
- The number of *shares in the hands of individuals*, as opposed to large share-owning institutions, fell by a third.

Privatisation would be matched by the sales of council houses, a topic to which we shall turn shortly.

Deregulation

Deregulation means 'taking away the rules'. Typically, this means reducing the amount of government interference in the economy, cutting what is called 'red tape', or bureaucracy, by having fewer laws affecting what business can and can't do, thus creating a more 'free market'. The Thatcher government believed that:

- The market and private enterprise were fast and efficient.
- Government was slow and inefficient.

In 1982, the government did away with the 'Fair Wages Resolution', a long-standing agreement that government business would only go to employers who paid fair wages and offered decent working conditions. Following an attempt to reform and limit the old Wages Councils – which since 1909 had been establishing minimum rates for pay for specific industries – it took until 1993 to finally abolish them.

In 1983, the government negotiated an agreement with the London Stock Exchange regarding a complex case. The Office of Fair Trading had investigated the Stock Exchange, suspecting that the Stock Exchange's fixed minimum commissions system was illegal under the existing restrictive practices legislation. The old system had enforced a distinction between stockbrokers and stockjobbers:

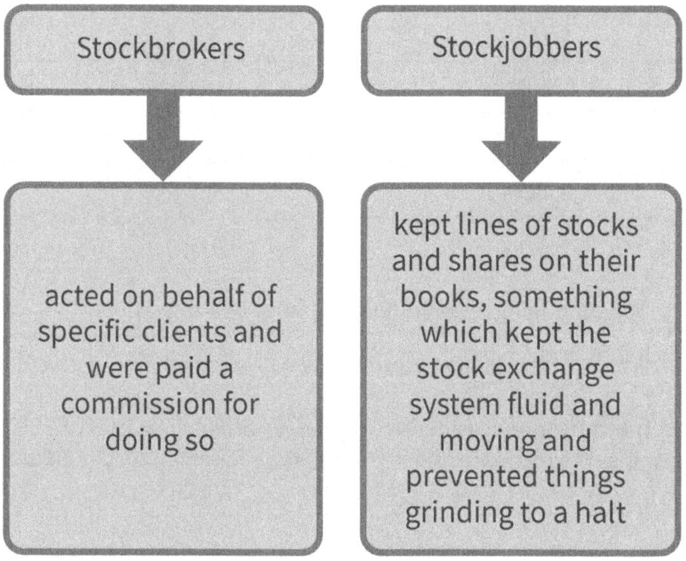

Figure 4.13: Stockbrokers and stockjobbers.

In addition, no one who was not a British citizen could be a member of the London Stock Exchange. Finally, brokers and jobbers were supposed to be independent, not members of a larger concern.

In October 1986 the rules changed in the **Big Bang**. The financial markets abandoned fixed commission charges. The broker/jobber distinction disappeared. The social class limitations of the Stock Exchange, maintained by established members, vanished. Old-established firms changed hands. International, and even foreign, companies chose to be listed on the London Stock Exchange, instead of elsewhere (even instead of in their own country).

During this process, the London Stock Exchange moved from individuals calling across a noisy room to achieve sales, to the use of computer screens and online trading.

Key terms

Big Bang: the name of the removal of several restrictive practices from the financial markets in 1986, which was seen as having created a new set of rules and expectations in the financial markets.

Removing some rules was intended to make trading in London quicker, easy and simpler and, therefore, more attractive. This was intended to make London the centre of the financial world, something that it achieved.

The same year, parliament passed the Financial Services Act, combining governmental regulation and self-regulation to provide a legal framework of accountability for the financial services industry. The Financial Services Authority was the equivalent of the regulators of privatised monopolies. Whether the outcome should be regarded as deregulation, or increased regulation, remains controversial.

Issues of inflation

Inflation was an important force driving the 1979 electoral success of Margaret Thatcher and her governments. Nevertheless, the first thing inflation did under the Conservatives was go up (Table 4.2).

Year	Inflation rate
1978	8.3%
1979	22%
1980	18%
1981	11.9%
1982	8.6%
1983	4.6%

Table 4.2: Inflation under the Conservatives.

Although these statistics look damaging, we should remember two things:

1. The inflation rate was already in the teens and climbing when Thatcher won the May 1979 election
2. These statistics reflect the consequences of the policies of earlier years, not of the year in which the statistic is recorded, since it takes time for any policy to take effect.

The initial budgets made the problem of inflation worse in the short term. In addition, the price of imported oil went up, pushing up inflation and worsening the balance of payments. As historian Robert Blake notes, 'By the summer of 1980 inflation was running at over 20 per cent and unemployment rose from 1.5 to 2 million between April and August'.[8] The Conservatives lost their lead in the opinion polls; the next election looked unwinnable. At the October 1980 party conference, Thatcher, referring to demands for a change in direction, declared:

'To those waiting with bated breath for that favourite media catchphrase, the 'U-turn', I have only one thing to say: "You turn if you want to. The lady's not for turning"'.[9]

Everyone understood the 'you turn'/'U-turn' joke; how many picked up the pun on the name of a once-famous play, *The Lady's Not for Burning*, is unclear. But the combination of the scriptwriter's humour and the politician's stubborn delivery was effective.

Unemployment and economic realignment

Conservatives whose views had been powerfully affected by the suffering caused by the mass unemployment of the 1930s (and also by the collaboration across social classes during the two world wars), prioritised employment.

Thatcherites feared that this priority was undermining the more important fight against inflation.

Figure 4.14: 'Labour isn't working' was the most famous poster of the 1979 election. With its punning slogan, it made unemployment an issue in the campaign.

Nevertheless, the 1979 election slogan 'Labour isn't working' suggested that bringing down unemployment would be a Conservative priority. Despite this, during the first Thatcher government, unemployment more than doubled.

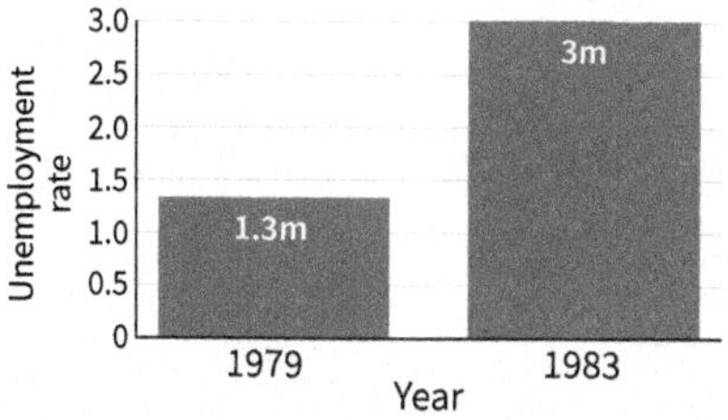

Figure 4.15: Unemployment 1979–83.

Most of the jobs that disappeared were:

- in the field of **heavy industry**
- held by men
- full time
- in unionised industries
- in the industrialised areas of south Wales, north England and the central belt of Scotland.

This was a personal disaster for the people involved, but it also showed that the balance of the British economy was changing, with:

- more women working
- more part-time workers
- more **light industry**
- more **service sector**.

Cross-reference Chapter 4 *People's March for Jobs*

You might have expected this to bring about a disastrous election result. As we have seen, 1983 did see the Conservatives' vote share fall, but only very slightly. Labour's leader Michael Foot had campaigned against the 'obscenity of mass unemployment'.

In 1981 and 1983 there were marches and demonstrations, but unemployment did not swing the 1983 election, for four reasons:

Key terms

heavy industry: the name for that area of manufacturing where large machinery makes large things happen, especially coal, steel, aircraft and cars.

light industry: uses smaller machines to make smaller things, such as clothing and electronics.

service sector: customers pay, not for a tangible product that they can drive or carry away, but for services based on education, training and skills. It includes hotels, restaurants, entertainment, lawyers, accountants and education.

1. There weren't enough unemployed voters to affect election results.
2. Most people were in work: 87% had jobs.
3. The numbers of unemployed had stopped rising. It had, perhaps, been the rise that had caused concern even to those in work, as the threat had seemed to be coming closer to them personally.
4. Unemployment was at its worst in areas that voted Labour. The issue might push up the Labour majority in those specific seats, but it didn't win them any additional seats, which was what they needed to form a government.

Cross-reference Chapter 5 *Race relations*

As unemployment rose, trade union membership fell. In 1981–83, trade union membership dropped by about 1.5 million; it dropped by a further 1.5 million during the remainder of the 1980s.

Peter Clarke notes that even the best year in the 1980s was worse than the worst year in the 1970s. The issue of unemployment did not go away in subsequent Thatcher governments, but understanding the figures became more complex, because the way in which the unemployment statistics were created changed. This meant that comparing like with like became impossible. What is sometimes called the 'headline' figure of unemployment (literally the one most likely to turn up in a newspaper headline) peaked in 1986 at 3.6 million. This was the worst since the Great Depression of the 1930s. By June 1990, it had declined to 1.6 million, but the changing method of counting made it harder for the Labour opposition to critique what was happening and for newspapers to report it accurately.

ACTIVITY 4.4

Margaret Thatcher declared in 1989 that 'You can't buck the market'. What did she mean? Organise a class debate around this, beginning with whether you agree, but more importantly going onto consider what the policy consequences are of agreeing, or disagreeing, with her declaration.

Figure 4.16: Norman Tebbit in 1981.

The impact of Thatcherism on society

The Thatcher government policies affected many aspects of society, including:

- housing
- industrial relations and strikes
- taxation and local government.

Each one of these issues created uproar in the House of Commons, discussion in the news media and violence on Britain's streets.

Sale of council houses

Margaret Thatcher's government thought that home ownership increased people's sense of citizenship and social responsibility. By contrast, council houses encouraged a culture of dependency on the state.

Voices from the past

Norman Tebbit

In April 1981, there were riots in the London district of Brixton. Encountering press suggestions that the cause of the riots lay in unemployment, Employment Secretary Norman Tebbit reminded a Conservative Party conference of his own relatively humble beginnings:

I grew up in the 1930s with an unemployed father. He did not riot. He got on his bike and looked for work, and he went on looking until he found it.

Speech to the 1981 Conservative Party conference

Discussion point

What are the different messages that Tebbit was communicating here?

In addition to these philosophical considerations, there was a tactical one: home owners tend to vote Conservative and tenants Labour. Increasing the number of home owners was likely to increase the number of Conservative voters.

Steered through parliament by Michael Heseltine, the 1980 Housing Act gave council tenants the legal right to buy the house or flat in which they were living. Not just that, but it offered discounts reflecting the years of rent paid. By 1987, about 1 million dwellings had been sold in the scheme. Labour found the issue difficult to deal with: it was in favour of social housing, but was embarrassed to be seen preventing people improving their circumstances.

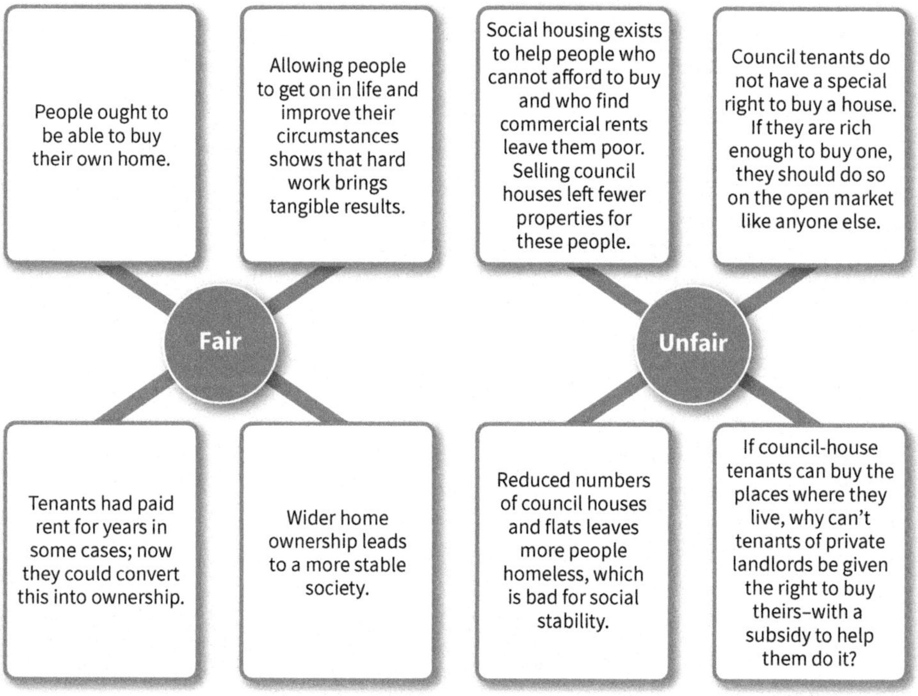

Figure 4.17: Was the sale of social housing fair?

Cross-reference **Chapter 5** *Conservative divisions*

ACTIVITY 4.5

What connections do you see between selling council houses and privatisation?

Key terms

Campaign for Nuclear Disarmament (CND): founded in 1957 to persuade public opinion, political parties and government that the UK should get rid of its nuclear weapons without waiting for the outcome of negotiations.

Figure 4.18: Michael Heseltine.

Voices from the past

Michael Heseltine

Michael Heseltine was Secretary of State for the Environment from 1979 to 1983. As such, he drove the policy on the sale of council houses and the response to the inner-city riots of the early 1980s. As Secretary of State for Defence between 1983 and 1986 he took the fight to the **Campaign for Nuclear Disarmament (CND)** and other anti-nuclear and pacifist groups. He resigned over the 'Westland affair' in 1986. Returning to government under John Major, he also returned to the Department for the Environment from 1990 to 1992. After the 1992 election, he was moved to the Department for Industry, where he preferred to use the old name 'President of the Board of Trade'.

Discussion points

1. Do some further research into Heseltine's career. What underlying principles do you think shaped it?
2. Could he have been described as 'wet' or 'dry'?

Miners' strike and other industrial disputes

In her memoirs, Margaret Thatcher wrote that she had beaten democratic socialism through the ballot box: 'undemocratic socialism ... would need to be beaten. I had never had any doubt about the true aim of the hard Left: they were revolutionaries who sought to impose a Marxist system on Britain whatever the means and whatever the cost'.[10]

This 'undemocratic socialism' was her way of referring to the political power of the trade unions. Historian Jim Tomlinson writes: 'Conservatives grounded much of their hostility to unions on their alleged impact on inflation'.[11] Nevertheless, much of the driving force in the policies towards the unions was to do with the issue of **governability**. Following the defeats of both Heath and Callaghan governments, the question was whether unions were powerful enough to prevent governments putting laws through parliament, and the police and judiciary enforcing them.

Secretary of State for Employment James Prior steered through the Employment Act of 1980. This outlawed **secondary picketing**, such a feature of the 1970s, and took steps to limit the **closed shop**.

Prior's successor Norman Tebbit took further steps with the Employment Act of 1982 to put employers in a stronger bargaining position. The 1982 Act:

1. Made it harder to sack someone for not being a trade union member.
2. Made it illegal for companies to agree a contract only with another company whose workforce were all union members.
3. Made it possible to sue trade unions, as well as individual trade union officials, where they were engaged in an illegal strike.
4. Narrowed the concept of a legal strike.
5. Gave employers the right to fire employees who were on strike.

Key terms

governability: the ability of governments to set policy directions, legislatures to pass laws and the criminal justice system to enforce them.

picketing: when a striking worker at the entrance to their workplace attempts to dissuade other workers from going in. **Secondary picketing** focuses not on the workplace that is the centre of the dispute, but that employer's suppliers, or the retailers who sell its products.

closed shop: a place of work where only union members can be employed.

Speak like a historian

Chris Wrigley

British historian Chris Wrigley makes the following comments on Tebbit's bold steps:

> With the 1980–93 legislation, the Thatcher and Major governments changed laws relating to trade unions in stages rather than in one big measure as the Heath government had done in 1971 ... Partly as a result of this approach, but probably because of the weakened economic circumstances of the trade unions and their lower public esteem after the strikes of 1979, there was less effective opposition.[12]

Discussion point

Why do you think the Thatcher government passed a series of employment acts where both Wilson and Heath governments had failed? Gather evidence on each of the three governments' attempts and have a class discussion.

The steel strike 1980

When steel workers went on strike early in 1980, the government funded a pay rise. Redundancies followed as the employer, British Steel, attempted to cut costs to remain commercially viable. The victory over pay strengthened the union; the redundancies weakened its reputation as a defender of its members' interests and also its own income base.

The miners' strike 1984–85

The government made clear that the size of the coal industry would be reduced; uneconomic collieries would close, miners would be made redundant. The National Union of Mineworkers (NUM) was determined to prevent the industry contracting and miners losing their jobs. The union balloted on strike action on three occasions in 1982–83 and on each occasion there was a strong majority against. To avoid a fourth defeat, NUM president Arthur Scargill allowed a local dispute to lead to a strike by the Yorkshire Area of the union. Other areas called strikes individually. Some areas opposed strike action, but when pickets arrived from other areas, union members refused to cross lines.

When the strike ended in March 1985, the miners returned to work having not achieved their aims. The result had weakened the position of the trade union movement in the country's economy, society and politics. Pits closed, miners were laid off and the NUM quickly lost half its membership.

There are seven key differences between the 1974 and the 1984–85 strikes. In 1984–85:

1. *The union was not united*: the Nottinghamshire miners, the best paid in the country, were least anxious about their future. They formed the Union of Democratic Mineworkers (UDM) and remained in work in large numbers.
2. *The Labour movement was not united*. Many Labour Party and trade union activists collected funds to support the strikers. Some unions acted in support: the National Union of Seamen opposed the import of coal. However, despite being the son of a miner himself, Labour Party leader Neil Kinnock sought to be even-handed, criticising both picket and police violence, and attacking the government's approach without defending Scargill.
3. *Coal stocks had been built up* in readiness at the power stations where it would be needed, not left at the pits where strikers could control it.
4. *The strike began in summer*, when demand for coal is lower, whereas Gormley had called the 1974 strike during winter, when demand is high.
5. The government had prepared the *legal ground*, passing the 1980 Prior Employment Act and Tebbit's 1982 Employment Act.
6. The government did not make the matter an *election issue*
7. Buoyed by success in *the Falklands War*, the government was committed (in the Prime Minister's own words from a 1984 speech she gave to Conservative backbenchers) to defeating the 'enemy within' having won against the 'enemy without'.

The Wapping dispute 1986–87

Over time, a number of corrupt and fraudulent practices by typesetters (also known as compositors) had grown up in the newspaper business. Newspaper proprietors did not challenge these, as newspapers cannot make up for lost sales – once a day has been spent in a dispute, that day's newspaper sales are gone for ever.

Under *The Times*'s new Australian-born owner Rupert Murdoch, plans were secretly laid to defeat the print unions. New technology meant that journalists could type their story direct into the newspaper design, rather than write the story on a typewriter and pass a piece of paper to others, who would then manually and mechanically make up the page in a process called 'hot metal'. Those currently doing the old jobs would be out of work. Management and unions could not reach agreement and, in January 1986, a strike was called. The management issued dismissal notices to the 6000 strikers.

Production of *The Times* and the company's other newspapers was moved from offices on London's Fleet Street to a new home in Wapping, where a new building, with new

ACTIVITY 4.6

Research the background, views and reputation of miners' leader Arthur Scargill and head of the National Coal Board Ian MacGregor. How important do you think their personalities, and those of government ministers, were to the conduct and outcome of the miners' strike of 1984–85?

technology, was waiting. For a year, the unions organised demonstrations, which were often rowdy. The police provided continual, often large-scale, supervision. In February 1987, the strike ended; the management had won.

The weakened unions

Failed strikes and rising unemployment both weakened the union movement. Membership fell by about 3 million during the 1980s, half of that fall occurring in just 24 months from 1981 to 1983. In 1990 the Employment Act ended the closed shop, a significant source of trade union power in some industries. Further legislation added to this in 1992.

Trade union leaders became less well known. In the 1970s and earlier, leading trade unionists were household names. Television comedy based around impersonating celebrities could frequently include imitations of prominent trade unionists, because the audience could be relied on to get the jokes. From the 1990s, fewer and fewer were recognisable and they were dropped by impersonators in favour of more recognisable figures.

Poll tax

ACTIVITY 4.7

Class discussion: the words Margaret Thatcher used most often in parliament were 'resource', 'negotiation', 'strike', 'wage' and 'productivity' (see http://www.hansard-corpus.org/). What does this tell you about the priorities she wished to communicate to MPs?

Until 1989–90, people in Britain paid a local property tax called the 'rates'. Homeowners felt its impact as they paid it directly; others felt it less as they paid it (if at all) as part of their rent. Homeowners were often Conservative voters and a group which the Thatcher government wanted to increase in size through the sale of council houses. This made their longstanding dislike for the 'rates' politically important.

This was the only tax directly controlled by local government. Millions of people were not contributing directly to the cost of local government (tenants notionally paid indirectly through their rent). At the same time, the turnout at local elections was very low, making the democratic status of the elected local councillors questionable.

A universal local tax would remove the injustice of the rates and might make more people vote in the elections in which local authorities are held to account for their actions. This idea formed part of the 1987 election manifesto. In the background was the fact that, with the perceived weakness of the parliamentary Labour Party, Labour local authorities were increasingly prominent in opposing government actions. This conflict even led to the government abolishing the Greater London Council in 1986.

The new tax was introduced in Scotland in 1989, and in England and Wales in 1990; it was never introduced in Northern Ireland. The job of driving the policy was in the hands of Michael Portillo. Officially named the Community Charge, everyone but its most ardent supporters called it the **poll tax**; even official government publications were forced to use the term, to be sure that people would understand what was being explained.

The poll tax was a political disaster for the government, for six key reasons:

1. Like the rates it was dependent on people staying in one place long enough for the tax to be collected. However, *tenants change address* more frequently than householders and so are harder to find and tax. This was a particular problem for local authorities with large numbers of students.
2. A campaign of non-compliance, with *large numbers of people not paying* or delaying payment, put numerous cases before the law courts; a small number of people went to prison.
3. The paperwork created by trying to find non-payers and enforce payment grew and the costs of implementing the tax grew.
4. The move from rates to a poll tax simply meant that large numbers of people who had previously not paid (or not noticed themselves pay) a local tax, now paid one. No one is pleased to see a *new and additional tax* imposed on them.

Key terms

poll tax: paid by every adult. Based on a 'head count', the term comes from an old-fashioned word for 'head'.

5. Despite the government's trying to make the tax lower for poorer people and higher for richer ones, the tax was widely seen as *unfair* by comparison with income tax, also a universal tax but based on the ability to pay because proportional to income.
6. It turned out to be, on average, much *higher* than predicted.

The fact that the tax was seen as unfair played into the wider criticism of the government as being *socially unjust*.

That final point was compounded by this tax coming on top of earlier decisions to reduce income tax and increase VAT, creating the belief (not unjustified) that rich people now paid less tax and poor people more.

Campaigning against the poll tax led to demonstrations and some of these became riotous. In March 1990 an estimated 200 000 people attended a demonstration in London's Trafalgar Square. In the disorder, the police charged the crowd with batons, there was fighting and more than 100 police officers had to be treated for injuries of various kinds.

The controversy was one element in the decision of Michael Heseltine to challenge Thatcher for leadership of the Conservative Party in November 1990. He did not beat her, but his challenge commanded sufficient support for her to be forced to resign.

Under her successor John Major, the poll tax was replaced by the **council tax**, a property tax that was a reformed version of the rates.

Cross reference *Council tax*

Extra-parliamentary opposition

Because of the perceived weakness of opposition within parliament, extra-parliamentary opposition, such as the anti-poll tax campaign, acquired an additional significance.

Anti-nuclear campaigns

In the 1980s a new theory of nuclear war developed and a new generation of nuclear weapons arrived in Britain. The intention was that, should a nuclear conflict begin, NATO would be able to strike first and in such a way as to prevent (or render ineffective) any Warsaw Pact response.

CND's membership increased. The minority that supported unilateralism grew larger. Hostility to the new generation of weapons actually became a majority view. Annual demonstrations now attracted quarter of a million people.

Large numbers of people took part in non-violent direct action, accepting arrest peacefully. Magistrates' courts found increasing numbers of ordinary people coming before them, some of whom went on to short periods of imprisonment. Peace Camps, where people lived in a permanent residential demonstration, usually close to the entrance of a military base, attracted considerable news coverage.

Section 28

Section 28 of the 1988 Local Government Act stated that local authorities should neither 'promote homosexuality', nor allow schools to teach 'the acceptability of homosexuality as a pretended family relationship'. Going against the post-war tendency towards steady **liberalisation** regarding human relationships, this was a response to the willingness of the Labour-run Greater London Council to provide loans or grants to gay and lesbian groups. In addition, schools had begun to adopt a

Key terms

council tax: a local tax introduced in 1993 to replace the poll tax.

liberalisation: a process whereby over time tolerance increases of differences in behaviour patterns and personal choices.

ACTIVITY 4.8

The most famous UK peace camp at the time was outside USAF Greenham Common. Influenced by the Women's Movement, this became a women-only camp. Organise a class debate around the issue of war, peace and gender, taking into account that the UK's head of state (Elizabeth II) and head of government (Margaret Thatcher) were both women at this time.

policy towards homosexuality modelled on those concerning race and gender. New campaigning groups were set up as a response, including Stonewall, while the existing Gay Pride rallies saw an increase in the numbers attending.

People's March for Jobs

In 1981 unemployed people walked from Liverpool to London, where there was a rally outside the GLC and the marchers lobbied MPs in parliament. The 1983 demonstration began in Glasgow; it too ended with a rally in London. Thousands attended, but not the hundreds of thousands the organisers had hoped for. These marches were designed to be compared with the Jarrow Hunger Marchers who, in 1936, had similarly walked from an area of high unemployment – the north of England – to London, to draw attention to their situation.

Faith in the City

Despite criticism that it was the 'Tory party at prayer', the Church of England came into conflict with the Thatcher government more than once.

Cross-reference Chapter 4 *The Falklands War, 1982*

Following the Falklands War, a service of celebration in London's St Paul's Cathedral avoided triumphalism. Archbishop of Canterbury Robert Runcie told the congregation that 'people are mourning on both sides of this conflict'. Taxed with the decision not to include *Onward Christian Soldiers* in the service, the Dean of St Paul's explained that the Argentinian forces were also Christian soldiers.

In 1985 *Faith in the City* was a report on urban life, drawing attention to the consequences of unemployment, poor housing, inadequate educational and social services, and racism. Its subtitle declared that this was 'a call to action by church and nation'. It explicitly examined both spiritual and economic poverty, and it required a response from both church and government.

The hostile Conservative response only added to the report's fame; *Faith in the City* was discussed in countless newspapers and news programmes. The politicians had failed to realise that a church is not a social club of well-behaved people.

Speak like a historian

Peter Clarke

In reviewing Thatcher's achievements, he balances different views but says finally:

Thatcher achieved her victories at a terrible cost, usually borne by others. By any test, from statistical surveys of relative incomes to the striking reappearance of beggars on the street, Britain became a more unequal society.[13]

Discussion points

1. What do you think of Peter Clarke's opinion?
2. In what ways do you think the Thatcher governments attempted to change society and to what extent do you think they succeeded?

Foreign affairs

The Falklands

Background to a crisis

The Falkland Islands lie in the south Atlantic, about 300 miles off the coast of Argentina. They were probably uninhabited until French and British explorers created small settlements there in the 18th century. In the 1830s, Argentina asserted that it had inherited a Spanish claim to the islands, which it called the Malvinas. Britain sent a Royal Navy ship to reassert British sovereignty and raise a British flag on the islands. The recently appointed Spanish governor abandoned plans to dispute the matter, since 80% of his small military force were British mercenaries who would refuse to fight their own countrymen.

Over the next 150 years, an English-speaking population of British descent gradually built up.

The Falklands War, 1982

In April 1982, Argentine forces landed on the islands. Heavily outnumbered, the small British garrison made as good a defence as it could, but the fight was quickly over. Another Argentine force landed on South Georgia, a separate set of smaller Atlantic islands to the south east.

The Argentine intention had been to put the British government in a position where it would be forced to accept the new situation. After all, the islands had been seized, and there were no clear strategic or commercial reasons for the UK to want them back. They had done their best to avoid British casualties in order to avoid the invasion itself creating a reason for a British military response.

News of the invasion came as a shock to the British government. The Foreign Secretary Lord Carrington accepted responsibility and quickly resigned. This was not altogether fair, since he had warned that an earlier government decision to save money by cutting back on the military connections with the Falklands would suggest Britain was losing interest in the islands. Thatcher formed a **war cabinet** and consulted with her military leaders. They advised that a naval task force could be created to sail to the islands to:

- engage Argentinian ships
- transport an army to retake the islands.

All of this required air support, but it also required political support.

For the Conservatives, the issue was sovereignty: British territory had been invaded and British people were now in the hands of a foreign government.

Labour officially supported the government. No party aspiring to form the next government wanted to send out a message that, if attacked, it would not put up a fight. The decision was made easier for the left-wing party by the fact that the enemy was a right-wing military **junta**.

The task force set sail in April and South Georgia was retaken without too much difficulty. The Falklands themselves proved a greater challenge, but an air campaign was followed by a landing in May. In June, after some fierce fighting, the Argentine forces surrendered. There had been more than 250 British deaths, while nearly 650 Argentinians had died in the war. About half of Argentinian deaths occurred when a single ship was controversially sunk.

1983: A khaki election?

In the weeks following the beginning of the South Atlantic Crisis, Margaret Thatcher's approval rating in opinion polls jumped. From being vulnerable to a leadership

Key terms

war cabinet: a small group, usually consisting of senior ministers and senior military commanders, which takes the decisions regarding the conduct of a war.

junta: Spanish word meaning 'committee' or 'administrative council'. In English, it is used exclusively to refer to the governing bodies of Latin-American military dictatorships.

ACTIVITY 4.9

Why do you think historian Peter Clarke has called the Argentinian leader General Galtieri the 'perfect enemy'?

Key terms

khaki election: one fought in the aftermath of a war.

challenge of the kind she had once mounted herself, she became almost beyond criticism. At the same time her government, which had seemed on course for certain defeat, was now about 20 percentage points ahead of both Labour and the Liberal/SDP alliance.

This has sometimes been referred to as a **khaki election**, one fought in the aftermath of a war. The argument is that the success in the South Atlantic delivered her a landslide. Figure 4.4 shows that there was certainly a landslide of seats. However, Figure 4.5 shows that the Conservatives actually suffered a slight loss of votes relative to 1979 (down 1.5% from 1979 – see Figure 4.2).

The Falklands War may have rescued the Conservatives from the acute unpopularity of the first half of their period of government, but it did not on its own decide the election.

The 'special relationship' with USA

Cross-reference Chapter 3 *The state of the 'special relationship' with the USA, Figure 3.14*

Different political leaders have emphasised one aspect or another of the delicate balance in the UK's international connections. Heath regarded the link to Europe as supremely important; his successor as Conservative leader, Thatcher, looked rather to the US. During her time in office there really did seem to be a 'special relationship', helped by the fact that the American president of the day held political views compatible with her own. Ronald Reagan had a background in right wing, anti-communist, cold war politics. On taking office he announced that 'In this present crisis, government is not the solution to our problems; government is the problem'.[14] Such an announcement can only have been music to the British Prime Minister's ears.

There were low points. The US responded to political instability in Grenada in 1983 by invading, declaring that the island was falling into the hands of pro-Soviet forces. A member of the Commonwealth, Grenada had Elizabeth II as its head of state. In the preceding days, and then hours, Thatcher had urged Reagan not to invade. He did not tell her that an invasion had begun.

Initially the US Secretary of State General Al Haig's attempts to negotiate a settlement to the 1982 Falklands crisis annoyed Thatcher, but, for the US, this was a war between two American allies. When Argentina turned down the attempts at peacemaking, the US felt free to ban arms sales to Argentina and both Houses of the US Congress passed resolutions supporting the USA siding with the United Kingdom.

Moves to end the Cold War

Beyond social and economic vision, the concern that brought Thatcher and Reagan together was, above all, the Cold War. Both believed in a strong defence being essential, accepting that the USSR was a continual military threat. The 1979 invasion of Afghanistan by Soviet forces did nothing to alleviate this continual anxiety.

In fact, the domestic politics of the Soviet Union underwent noticeable changes during the 1980s. The disastrous Afghan campaign contributed – as military disasters often do – but the continuing economic inefficiency and underperformance was important as well.

The man who had led party and country since 1964, Brezhnev, died in 1982. He was succeeded by former KGB head Andropov, who died after 15 months in post. The next general secretary of the party, Chernenko, only lasted 13 months. How, demanded Reagan, was he going to make progress with the USSR if its leaders 'keep dying on me'?[15] Clearly the Soviets thought the same and ended this run of old, dying men by appointing a man whom Andropov had promoted: Mikhail Sergeyevich Gorbachev. Born in 1931, he was a generation younger than his three predecessors and he took office in 1985 determined to change the country. Two Russian words that he used to describe what he intended to achieve became internationally known: **Perestroika** and **Glasnost**.

After meeting him, Thatcher told a BBC interviewer as early as December 1984, 'I like Mr Gorbachev. We can do business together'. This was not the language Prime Ministers usually adopted for describing their impressions of Soviet leaders.

> **Key terms**
>
> **Perestroika:** restructuring. The economic and political way the country worked would be remade. The USSR was not an economic success story and its people were unnecessarily poor.
>
> **Glasnost:** openness. The Soviet government and other leaders would be more open with the people as to what they were doing and why they were doing it. There were too many unnecessary secrets.

Thatcher as an international figure

With the Falklands War, Thatcher began to become more widely recognised around the world. Her argumentative presence at European council meetings quickly meant that she was a recognisable landmark. Her media appearances, when Gorbachev invited her to visit the Soviet Union, turned her into the western politician Soviet citizens knew best. In the Middle East, she became famous because of another war.

The First Gulf War

The First Gulf War (1990–91) was the result of an invasion of Kuwait by its larger neighbour, Iraq. The Iraqi leader Saddam Hussein had already conducted a major war against Iran and his regime had a poor human rights record. The invasion brought international condemnation and economic sanctions. Thatcher was in the USA at the time of the invasion, meeting President George Bush, who had been Reagan's Vice President. The Prime Minister advocated intervention; the President was more cautious, but, with Thatcher pushing military action, decided he agreed.

Several countries in the region were sympathetic to the plan to push Iraqi forces back out of Kuwait. The annexation of one country by another was almost unheard of in recent decades. Also, it was thought unsafe for Iraq to have control over so much of the world's oil supplies. The war itself did not last long. A substantial aerial bombardment was followed by ground troops. With the disorderly collapse of the Iraqi army, the military commanders realised that the road to the capital Baghdad was now open. The decision not to take that road, overthrow Saddam Hussein and institute political changes, was a political one.

Attitudes to Europe, including Thatcher's policies

The issue of 'Europe' divided the Conservative Party throughout Thatcher's (and then Major's) period in office. Loosely speaking, there were three views on the Conservative benches:

1. Be at the heart of Europe contributing to and being affected by the changes being debated in the EEC's councils
2. Remain, but minimise involvement in a fundamentally undemocratic institution
3. Leave the EEC altogether.

Kenneth Clarke and Michael Heseltine were Europhile, believing in the importance of the EEC for Britain's economy. In addition, they saw it as a force for political stability in Europe, helping avoid war between member states – it had, after all, grown out of the determination of France and (West) Germany to build strong economic, social and political links following the Second World War.

Margaret Thatcher herself was initially favourable toward the EEC. She voted in favour of the UK joining in 1973 and in the 1975 referendum on membership she supported the campaign for remaining within the EEC. As Prime Minister, she became known for arguing that the UK's payment to the EEC budget was too high. In this argument she was successful and the payment was reduced. Nevertheless, she signed the 1986

Single European Act, which led to barriers to trade being removed. Thatcher became more suspicious of the EEC when, in 1985, the presidency of the European Commission (an executive body) passed to French Socialist Jacques Delors, who spoke about the prospect of a single EEC currency. Addressing the TUC, in 1988, he emphasised the importance of legislation to protect employees' rights. It was after Thatcher's third election victory, in a speech given in Bruges in 1988, that she reassessed the European project and opposed further integration as being against the national interest. Henceforth Thatcher was identified with Euroscepticism. She declared in 1999: 'In my lifetime all our problems have come from mainland Europe and all the solutions have come from the English-speaking nations across the world'.[16] Clearly she had the Second World War in mind, contrasting the menace of Hitler's Germany with the support of Roosevelt's USA and the Empire's countries. Richard Vinen notes that Thatcher had not had a father or a brother in uniform in either of the two world wars, whereas many of the men in her early cabinets had fought. When young, they had often seen much of Europe (albeit under fire); she had not left the UK until she was 26. Their understanding of the importance of the EEC was inevitably different from hers.

Single European Act

As the EEC grew in importance, so Thatcher's dislike of it grew in strength.

The EEC had been based on the agreement reached in the 1957 Treaty of Rome. In 1986, this was revised in the Single European Act. The new Act:

- set out a timetable for creating a *single market*, removing remaining barriers to trade and enabling the free movement of people, goods and services across the EEC
- created the framework which would be developed into a *common defence policy*
- moved the decision-making principle from unanimity to *qualified majority voting*. This was because as the EEC grew in size (from the original six to 12 in 1986, with the likelihood of others joining in the future), decision-making became slower and more difficult, leaving the EEC inefficient.

According to Peter Hennessy: 'The passing of the Single European Act in 1986 [marked] a step (little noticed at the time) towards a Europeanised Britain ... and, incidentally, beginning to lay down the incendiary material which brought her premiership to an end five years later'.[17]

It was joint action by Geoffrey Howe, her Deputy Prime Minister and Leader of the Commons and her chancellor, Nigel Lawson, that is usually give the credit for persuading Thatcher to sign the Single European Act. This committed Britain to closer union.

Divisions within the Conservative Party over Europe

Some Conservatives put forward the argument that Britain had been persuaded to join a free-trade area with minimal political oversight, a **Common Market**. They were afraid that this collection of trading nations was developing into a state. Defending the unity, integrity and independence of the UK is one of the defining issues of Conservativism. Questions about Britain's membership of the EEC and the competencies of that association's agencies were bound to raise strong feelings.

The European authorities passed laws that regulated the way in which employers could treat employees and companies could trade. The EEC was, therefore, seen as interventionist at a time when Thatcher was steadily moving towards a less interventionist style of government. In a speech given in Bruges in September 1988, Margaret Thatcher expressed her discontent with the European project: 'We have not successfully rolled back the frontiers of the state in Britain, only to see them re-imposed at a European level, with a European super-state exercising a new dominance from Brussels'.[18]

Key terms

Common Market: a popular British name for the EEC that emphasised its economic role, and minimised its political and diplomatic one.

In fact, much of EEC practice was similar to what took place in the UK itself. Thatcher emphasised her hostility to EEC institutions acquiring additional powers, in a response to a question from Neil Kinnock in the House of Commons: 'Yes, the Commission wants to increase its powers. Yes, it is a non-elected body and I do not want the Commission to increase its powers at the expense of the House, so of course we differ. The President of the Commission, Mr Delors, said at a press conference the other day that he wanted the European Parliament to be the democratic body of the Community, he wanted the Commission to be the Executive and he wanted the Council of Ministers to be the Senate. No. No. No.'[19]

This was a logical position for her to adopt and entirely in tune with her political philosophy. However, the speech was a blow to those of her colleagues who were working to improve Britain's standing and increase its influence in the EEC, not least her own Foreign Secretary Geoffrey Howe. She could not have guessed that this outburst would set in train events that led to the end of her premiership four weeks later.

Timeline 1979–87

Government and politics	Economics	Date	Society	Foreign affairs
March: Conservative MP Airey Neave killed by an IRA bomb at Westminister May: Conservative Party under Margaret Thatcher wins general election August: Earl Mountbatten killed when his yacht is bombed by IRA	Inflation reaches 22%	1979		December: NATO agrees to deploy Cruise and Pershing II missiles in western Europe Invasion of Afghanistan by Soviet forces
James Callaghan resigns as Labour Party leader; Michael Foot new party leader October–December: first IRA hunger strike Thatcher tells October party conference 'The lady's not for turning' James Prior steers through the Employment Act	Sales of British Petroleum April to August: Unemployment rises from 1.5 to 2 million steel workers go on strike	1979–87 1980	Housing Act gives council tenants the legal right to buy the house or flat in which they were living April: riot in St Paul's, Bristol	
January: formation of the Council for Social Democracy March: foundation of the Social Democratic Party March–October: 2nd IRA hunger strike	First People's March for Jobs from Liverpool to London	1981	Riots in Brixton, London; Handsworth, Birmingham; Toxteth, Liverpool; Moss Side, Manchester	April: Argentine forces land on the Falkland Islands and South Georgia November: death of Soviet leader Brezhnev

ACTIVITY 4.10

1. Study the timeline. Events have been put into different columns: which would you move to a different column and why?
2. Which developments have been omitted from the table that you think should be included? Explain why.

Government and politics	Economics	Date	Society	Foreign affairs
		1982	Riots in St Paul's; Notting Hill Gate, London; Handsworth, Birmingham; Brixton, London; Toxeth Norman Tebbit's Employment Act	
May: general election Nigel Lawson becomes Chancellor of the Exchequer December: bomb explodes outside Harrods in London	March: miners' strike begins sale of British Telecom	1984		February; death of Soviet leader Andropov December: Thatcher: 'I like Mr Gorbachev. We can do business together.'
November: Anglo-Irish Agreement signed	March: miners return to work	1985	Riots in Handsworth, Brixton and Tottenham *Faith in the City* published	March: Soviet leader Chernenko died; succeeded by Gorbachev
	Sale of British Aerospace	1985–87		
Government abolish the Greater London Council	January: strike called at *The Times*, management dismisses 6000 people Sale of British Gas October: Big Bang, deregulation of financial markets Unemployment peaks at 3.6 million	1986		Single European Act
	Sale of Rolls Royce February: strike at *The Times* ends	1987	Margaret Thatcher accused of saying 'there is no such thing as society'	
	Sale of British Leyland (as 'Rover Group') Sale of British Steel	1988	Local Government Act, including Section 28	September: Margaret Thatcher criticises the European project in speech in Bruges
		1989–90	Poll tax introduced in Scotland, England and Wales	
		1990	March: demonstrations against the poll tax in London's Trafalgar Square	

Further reading

Peter Clarke, *Hope and Glory, Britain 1900–2000*. Penguin 1996, rev. ed. 2004 is the final volume in the excellent *Penguin History of Britain*. Make sure you get hold of the revised edition. You need Chapters 11–12. Richard Vinen, *Thatcher's Britain, the politics and social upheaval of the 1980s*. Simon and Schuster 2009 is balanced and clear. These books are both detailed and analytical. Robert Blake's *The Conservative Party from Peel to Major* (Heinemann 1997) is disappointingly partial and less scrupulous in the chapters added to cover the later period. Margaret Thatcher (*The Downing Street Years*), Nigel Lawson (*The View from No 11*) and Geoffrey Howe (*Conflict of Loyalty*) are among several political autobiographies describing events in the 1980s and 1990s. Each is worth reading, but each was written to justify the author's actions and so should be read with caution. They are all long, so use the contents pages and indexes to find specific topics. Vernon Bogdanor's Gresham College lectures on politics are excellent. http://www.gresham.ac.uk/six-general-elections includes a lecture on the 1979 election. http://www.gresham.ac.uk/lectures-and-events/leadership-and-change-prime-ministers-in-the-post-war-world-winston-churchill includes lectures on all post-war Prime Ministers, including Thatcher.

Practice essay questions

1. To what extent did the May 1979 British general election represent a change of political direction?
2. 'The priorities of the Thatcher governments 1979–90 were economic, not political or social.' Assess the validity of this view.
3. 'The Thatcher governments key opponent was neither Galtieri nor Scargill but inflation.' Assess the validity of this view.
4. To what extent did the Falklands War affect the 1983 British general election?
5. With reference to the sources and your understanding of the historical context, assess the value of these three sources to a historian studying the 1983 British general election?

Source A

Source: Neil Kinnock, speech in Bridgend, Glamorgan, on Tuesday 7 June 1983

If Margaret Thatcher is re-elected as Prime Minister on Thursday, I warn you. I warn you that you will have pain – when healing and relief depend upon payment. I warn you that you will have ignorance – when talents are untended and wits are wasted, when learning is a privilege and not a right. I warn you that you will have poverty – when pensions slip and benefits are whittled away by a government that won't pay in an economy that can't pay. I warn you that you will be cold – when fuel charges are used as a tax system that the rich don't notice and the poor can't afford.

I warn you that you must not expect work – when many cannot spend, more will not be able to earn … I warn you that you will have defence of a sort – with a risk and at a price that passes all understanding.

Source B

Source: Margaret Thatcher, speech in Harrogate, Yorkshire, on 26 May 1983

Labour's leaders are brave enough in the battle of words. Yet when it comes to the real battle for economic survival and lasting prosperity, they have no stomach for the fight.

Once again, their Manifesto confirms that in the end Labour always runs away. They are at it again in this Election; in full flight as fast as their legs will carry them. — They are running away from the need to defend their country. — They are fleeing from the long overdue reform of the trade unions. — They are running out on Europe. — And they are running scared that you might read and understand their Manifesto.

Above all, Labour is running away from the true challenge of unemployment. Its glib promise to create millions of new jobs - or rather, old jobs, or non-jobs- is no more than an evasion of the real problem that has long confronted us all.

Source C

Source: Liberal–SDP Alliance 1983 British General Election Manifesto

The Labour Party has not become more moderate ... The policies of nationalisation, attacks on private enterprise, withdrawal from Europe, with its devastating effect upon our exports and investment prospects, and alienation of our international friends and allies, are all enthroned and inviolate. Jobs and national safety would be at risk.

Mrs Thatcher offers no alternative of hope or of long-term stability. Some of her objectives were good. Britain needed a shake-up: lower inflation, more competitive industry and a prospect of industrial growth to catch back the ground we had lost over the years. But the Government has not succeeded. After a bad start it has got lower inflation, but the prospects even for the end of this year are not good. And the price paid has been appalling. British industry has seen record bankruptcies and liquidations. Unemployment has increased on twice the scale of the world recession.

Chapter summary

In 1979, Britain elected its first woman Prime Minister and the government that came to power changed the language in which politics, economics and society were discussed. But how much actually changed? At the end of this chapter you should be able both to take account of the views of different historians of this period of British history and to form your own views regarding:

- the significance of Margaret Thatcher's election as Conservative Party leader and then Prime Minister, including whether her governments represented a break with the political past
- the role played by divisions within political parties, notably the conflicts within the Labour Party and the formation of the SDP
- the approaches adopted to the continuing Troubles in Northern Ireland
- the nature of monetarism, privatisation and deregulation and extent to which economic policy was driven by theories and idealism
- changes in society and opposition to Thatcherism, notably the miners' strike and the poll tax
- relations with the wider world, including the Falklands War and membership of the EEC/EC.

Endnotes

1 Quoted in Pearce M, Stewart G. *British Political History, 1867–1990: Democracy and Decline*. London: Routledge; 1996. p. 525.

2 Harris R. *The Making of Neil Kinnock.* London: Faber and Faber; 1984. p. 208. Speech in Bridgend, Glamorgan, on Tuesday 7 June 1983. Thursday 9 June 1983 was polling day in the general election.

3 Heppell T. *Choosing the Labour Leader: Labour Party Leadership Elections from Wilson to Brown.* London: IB Tauris; 2010. p. 91, and in Sassoon D. *One Hundred Years of Socialism: the West European Left in the Twentieth Century*. London: IB Tauris; 2013.

4 Aitken J. *Margaret Thatcher: Power and Personality*. London: A&C Black; 2013. p. 413.

5 Blake R. *Conservative Party from Peel to Major*. London: Heinemann; 1997. p. 323.

6 Vinen R. *Thatcher's Britain, The politics, and social upheaval of the 1980s*. London: Simon and Schuster; 2009.

7 Hennessy P. *Muddling Through: Power, Politics and the Quality of Government in Postwar Britain.* London: Victor Gollancz; 1996. p. 294.

8 Blake R. *Conservative Party from Peel to Major*. London: Heinemann; 1997. p. 340.

9 Seldon A, Collings D. *Britain Under Thatcher*. London: Routledge; 2014. p. 98.

10 Thatcher M. *The Downing Street Years*. London: HarperCollins; 1993, 2011. p. 339.

11 Tomlinson J. *Thatcher, Monetarism and the politics of inflation*. In: Jackson B. and Saunders R. (eds.) *Making Thatcher's Britain*. Cambridge: Cambridge University Press; 2012. p. 62.

12 Wrigley C. *British Trade Unions since 1933*, (New Studies in Economic and Social History), Cambridge: Cambridge University Press; 2002.

13 Clarke P. *Hope and Glory, Britain 1900–2000*. London: Penguin; 1996, rev. ed. 2004. p. 400.

14 Reagan R. Presidential inaugural address. Speech presented 1981 January 20; Washington, USA. Available at: http://www.presidency.ucsb.edu/ws/?pid=43130

15 Wagner HL, Cronkite W. *Ronald Reagan*. Philadelphia, USA: Chelsea House; 2004. p. 16.

16 Thatcher M. Address to fringe meeting at Conservative Party conference. Speech presented 1999 October 5; Blackpool.

17 Hennessy P. *Muddling Through: Power, Politics and the Quality of Government in Postwar Britain.* London: Victor Gollancz; 1996. p. 294.

18 Senden L. *Soft Law in European Community Law*. Oxford: Hart Publishing; 2004.

19 Campbell J. *The Iron Lady: Margaret Thatcher from Grocer's Daughter to Iron Lady*. London: Penguin; 2012. Available at http://www.margaretthatcher.org /document/108234

5 Towards a new Consensus, 1987–1997

In this section, we will look at how Margaret Thatcher ceased to be Conservative Party leader and Prime Minister. We shall note the contrast made by her successor, John Major. We examine some of the changes that were taking place in society at this time and also some of the foreign policy issues and how they affected politics in Britain. We will look into:

- Fall of Thatcher and her legacy; Major as leader; economic developments, including 'Black Wednesday' and its impact; political sleaze, scandals and satire; political policies; approach to Northern Ireland; Conservative divisions.
- Realignment of the Labour Party under Kinnock, Smith and Blair; reasons for Labour victory in 1997.
- Social issues: the extent of 'social liberalism'; anti-establishment culture; the position of women and race relations.
- Foreign affairs: relations with Europe, including the impact of the Single European Act and Maastricht Treaty; interventions in the Balkans; contribution and attitude to the end of the Cold War.

Fall of Thatcher and her legacy

A key element in Thatcher's fall from power was the loss of her ministers' support. Heseltine had already resigned in 1986. Lawson generally succeeded in getting on well with the Prime Minister. However, she came increasingly to heed Alan Walters, her chief economic adviser 1981–83, and reappointed in 1989. Walters' role was to brief the Prime Minister directly and back her up in any dispute that might arise with the Treasury. His presence on the Prime Minister's staff signalled that Thatcher was determined to interfere in economic policy. Eventually, Lawson concluded he had lost the Prime Minister's trust and resigned in 1989.

After the 1983 election, Thatcher had moved Howe to the Foreign Office. An already tense relationship deteriorated and the issue of the UK's relationship with the EEC became a point of contention. At one point, Howe was telling the world that the government might consider joining a European currency, while Thatcher was announcing that was out of the question. His resignation letter was couched in moderate terms. However, in his 1990 resignation speech, Howe attacked Thatcher's approach to the European negotiations in which he'd been engaged. But, in doing so, he criticised her attitude to her cabinet colleagues: 'It is rather like sending your opening batsmen to the crease, only for them to find, as the first balls are being bowled, that their bats have been broken before the game by the team captain'.[1]

Thatcher's legacy

Assessing Margaret Thatcher's legacy is a complex process, not least because competing claims are put forward. As we have seen, some of what her governments undertook continued what had already been begun under the preceding Callaghan administration. Nevertheless, it is fair to say that the workplace and the labour market became more flexible and, therefore, able to respond to changing economic conditions. She also made a contribution to the end of the Cold War. Another element of her legacy is the divisions within the Conservative Party itself. The resignation of key ministers, such as Heseltine and Howe, reflected policy differences beyond the individual issues. These divisions would contribute to the Conservatives losing the 1997 election (and the two that followed).

ACTIVITY 5.1

Create a balance sheet, noting down aspects of Margaret Thatcher's record that you consider successes and those you judge failures. What qualifies them as successes or failures? What do you think her overall record adds up to?

Major as leader

John Major was a dramatic contrast to his predecessor, something which formed part of his appeal. He tended to speak slowly and quietly and in political parodies was shown coloured grey. Like Heath and Thatcher, he came from a notably lower social class than Churchill, Home, Eden, or Macmillan. Unlike Heath and Thatcher, he had never been to university (let alone Oxford) and his family had none of their respectability. His father had been a circus performer and Robert Blake describes his family life as 'shabby genteel'.[2] This, indeed, may have helped him win the leadership: a significant rival, the Foreign Secretary (and an experienced diplomat) Douglas Hurd had been to Eton – this may have been judged too patrician, a backward step and an electoral disadvantage.

Major's career had been directed by Margaret Thatcher. She had been persuaded to stand down partly on the basis that if she continued to campaign to be re-elected leader, Heseltine would win, but if she stood down, Major could be victorious. The question for voters (and for Conservative MPs) was whether Major would be his own man. 'I shall be a very good back-seat driver', Thatcher told the press. The comment was not malicious, but according to Major himself, 'it had a malign effect'.[3]

On being asked, in November 1990, to form a government, he said in a statement to the press outside 10 Downing Street: 'I want to see us build a country that is at ease with itself, a country that is confident and a country that is able and willing to build a better quality of life for all its citizens'.[4] This was a clear message that the politics of confrontation and division would be ended.

John Major became Prime Minister in November 1990, having been in the Cabinet for just three and a half years, with three months' experience as Foreign Secretary and about a year as Chancellor. In the opinion polls he had not been a front runner to succeed Margaret Thatcher: Heseltine was that, and Howe (who was not even running) and Hurd were also well ahead of him. Talk of a 'classless society' seems to have appealed strongly. According to Vernon Bogdanor, Major's key attraction to voters was about who he was not: in party leadership elections, he was not Thatcher in 1990 and not John Redwood in 1995; in the 1992 general election, he was not Kinnock.

Many commentators treat Major's term as a Prime Minister as a short break between the more durable Thatcher and Blair. In fact, he was the Prime Minister with fourth-longest continuous period of office in the 20th century, living at Number 10 Downing Street for more than seven uninterrupted years.

Nor should we think that his period in office was without events or achievements. Firstly, he maintained the unity of the UK at a time when various political forces were drawing its constituent parts further away from one another. Secondly, he kept Britain in the EEC – despite the vigorous campaigns by some of his backbenchers and some of his own cabinet members, to leave. Thirdly, he maintained the unity of a Conservative Party in which different views about Britain's relations with its European neighbours made it difficult to agree a common policy direction.

Economic developments, including 'Black Wednesday' and its impact

The Lawson boom and house prices

At the end of the 1980s and in the 1990s, house prices increased rapidly. This 'Lawson boom' contributed to a feeling of prosperity, since rising house prices made homeowners feel they were getting richer. Meanwhile, rising prices encouraged people to do everything they could to buy a property (see Figure 5.1):

- *fearful* that no property would be left that they could afford
- *hopeful* that, however burdensome the loan they took out, it would be justified when the value of the property they bought increased.

When house prices went down, many people were left owning property worth less than the loan they had taken out to buy it. This meant that if they became unable to keep up the payments on the loan and had to sell the house, the sale would not pay off the loan, leaving them both homeless and in debt. Because the value of property is known as 'equity', this new situation was known as **negative equity**. The numbers in the crisis tripled:

- Beginning of 1992: about 300 000 households in negative equity
- End of 1992: about 900 000 in negative equity.

Key terms

negative equity: when the value of a person's property (its equity) is less than the loan they took out to buy it, meaning that in the event of being forced to sell, they would still be in debt.

A vicious cycle became clear:

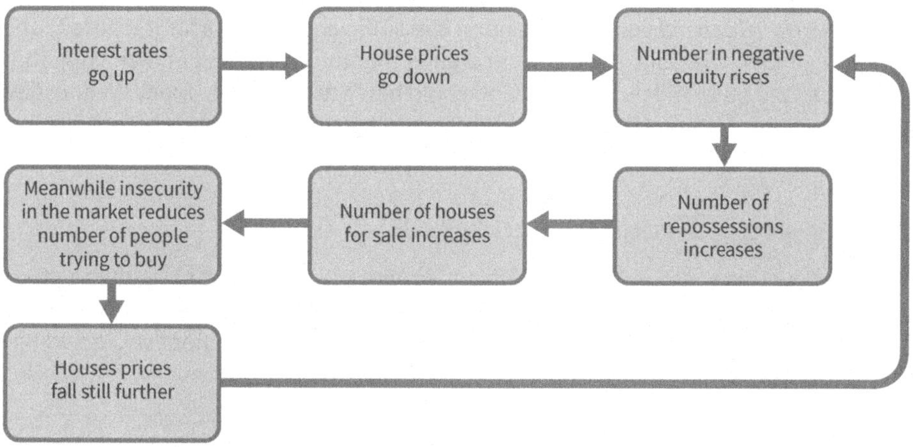

Figure 5.1: The vicious cycle of negative equity.

Key terms

run on the pound: the rapid selling of the British currency on money markets by investors who are afraid that it has become overvalued, that its value relative to other currency is about to drop and they need to sell in order to avoid losses. This process in itself then causes the pound to lose value.

'Black Wednesday' and its impact

Britain had joined the Exchange Rate Mechanism (ERM), part of EEC monetary policy, in October 1990. Thatcher was Prime Minister and had been persuaded by her Chancellor, John Major, and her Foreign Secretary, Douglas Hurd. The ERM tied the value of the pound to the value of other European currencies, the intention being stability and predictability. The problem was not everyone in the money markets believed that the links between currencies were based on economic reality.

On Wednesday 16 September 1992, there was a **run on the pound**. To defend its international valuation, the Bank of England put up interest rates to 15% and bought sterling on the foreign exchanges. As this did not work, the government was forced to withdraw sterling from the ERM, devaluing the currency. 'Black Wednesday' damaged the government's economic credibility.

Figure 5.2: Nigel Lawson.

In June 1993, Norman Lamont resigned as Chancellor, to be replaced by Kenneth Clarke. The latter worked to reduce government spending, and increase its income by raising taxes – though not income tax, on the basis that this was the one tax everyone noticed. The devaluation of the currency created by withdrawing from the ERM helped exporters, which in turn helped the balance of payments. British consumers were a little deterred from buying imported goods as they had just become dearer, while foreign consumers were a little encouraged to buy British goods as they had just become cheaper.

Joining and leaving the ERM, and the nature of a run on the pound, are complex issues about which economists, politicians and journalists take different views. Nigel Lawson had been in favour of joining the ERM when he was Thatcher's Chancellor, hoping it would help lock Britain into low inflation. Lawson's deputy, John Major, who became Chancellor himself, later persuaded Thatcher that the time was right to join the ERM. To Eurosceptics hostile to the EEC and ERM alike, this exit is dubbed 'White Wednesday' – because the UK should never have been in in the first place and the exit brought economic benefits, such as improved economic growth, lower unemployment and lower inflation. Not everyone agrees that these resulted from leaving the ERM.

But interest rates – which determined how much people's mortgages and other loans cost them – were an easy matter to assess. As borrowers received letters telling them how much the changed monthly payments were going to cost them, the government's popularity sank. October opinion polls gave Labour a 16-point lead. There would be

ACTIVITY 5.2

Find out more about devaluation and compare events in 1992 with those in 1967. Why do some economists regard it as bad practice, and why do governments do it?

further news stories, both good and bad, but Black Wednesday was a blow to the Conservative's credibility from which they never recovered.

Labour had argued it could negotiate with the trade unions: its failure to do so in the winter of 1978–79 caused voters to abandon it in sufficient numbers for it to lose four elections in a row. The Conservatives had argued that they were best at managing the economy, as the party of low inflation who could balance the books. Black Wednesday meant that voters lost confidence in them: it would be another 18 years before electors returned a majority Conservative government.

Political sleaze, scandals and satire

The Major government found itself in difficulties with the media and the public, when a series of news stories alleging wrongdoing by government ministers and backbenchers were published. These included scandals to do with money and dishonesty, including dishonesty under oath.

Sleaze and scandals

'Cash for questions' was the journalists' name for a process whereby MPs were paid by commercial businesses to ask questions in the House of Commons. The reason for asking a question should be that the MP judges it in the interests of their constituency (or the country as a whole) that they should do so. Accepting a fee to ask the question looks like taking a bribe. Neil Hamilton was the most prominent of those Conservative MPs accused of having been paid large sums to ask questions in this way.

'Arms to Iraq' was a scandal around a precision machine tools company, which was sold in 1989 because of financial difficulties and found itself with directors who worked for the Iraqi security services. The company began providing parts for the Iraqi weapons programme. The Ministry of Defence was found to have provided advice on how best to obtain export licences for material that was covered by legislation. The Minister for Defence Procurement Alan Clark was forced to admit that, when answering questions about the events, he had not told the whole truth. The enquiry, conducted by High Court judge Lord Justice Scott, uncovered what historian Robert Blake has, rather modestly, called the 'dubious conduct of ministers'.[5]

Former government minister Jonathan Aitken was accused of allowing a businessman to pick up his hotel bill. Worse, he lied in court about the matter (and had been preparing to have one of his children similarly lie): this is called 'perjury', a criminal offence. He had already lost his seat in Parliament; he now went to prison.

Tory party deputy chairman Jeffrey Archer resigned in October 1986, accused of having been a sex worker's customer and paying one £2000 in cash. Archer sued the newspaper that carried the story and, in 1987, won damages. In 1999 he was the Conservative candidate for the 2000 London mayoralty election. He never ran because, later in 1999, he was tried for perjury and perverting the course of justice. He went to prison and was expelled from the Conservative Party.

The government might have been able to distinguish between professional misbehaviour and private misdemeanour, clearly condemning bribes while brushing aside marital problems, but for one fatal step. In the 1993 Conservative Party conference, Major had called for a return to standards of decency with the sound bite 'back to basics'. This was seen as a call for higher (or perhaps more old-fashioned) moral standards. Following this speech, if ministers were found to have mistresses, illegitimate children, or sexual lives of interest to tabloid newspapers for other reasons, the matter became a political issue rather than one of personal embarrassment.

Satire

Such stories were inevitably picked up by satirists. Major's frustrations and supposed lack of imagination were both mocked in *Private Eye* magazine's 'The Secret Diary of

Voices from the past

Nigel Lawson

As Chancellor of the Exchequer from 1983, Nigel Lawson continued Howe's policy of moving from direct to indirect taxation. The deregulation of the financial markets took place during his time at the Treasury. The 'Lawson boom' helped halve unemployment at the price of doubling inflation, something he cannot have wanted, or expected.

The acid test of monetary policy is its record in reducing inflation. Those who wish to join the debate about the intricacies of different measures of money and the implications they may have for the future are welcome to do so. But at the end of the day the position is clear and unambiguous. The inflation rate is judge and jury.[6]

Mansion House Speech, 17 October 1985

Discussion points

1. Comment on Lawson's statement, relating it to financial policies under Thatcher and Major.
2. The subtitle of Lawson's autobiography is 'memoirs of a Tory radical'. What does he mean?

John Major', a parody of a popular book for children. He was represented in *Spitting Image*, initially with an antenna on his head to receive instructions from Thatcher and later as entirely grey. Political satire became a more notable element in the media and in political debate than it had been since the early 1960s. This may have been because the same party was in power for 18 years and because some voters had lost confidence that Her Majesty's Loyal Opposition could effectively oppose anything the government set out to do. In this its rise might be compared to the increasing importance of demonstrations and direct action.

Figure 5.3: The television programme *Spitting Image* presented physically distorted puppets that parodied the appearance of people in the news, with dialogue that parodied things they had said.

Cross-reference **Chapter 4** *Extra-parliamentary opposition*

Political policies

During the Scargill-led miners' strike, the NCB had, unsurprisingly, lost customers. Collieries were closed within months of the strike ending. The 1987 and 1994 Coal Industry Acts paved the way for mines to be privatised. This process was administered by Secretary of State for Industry Michael Heseltine.

Meanwhile, the electricity generators were also being privatised. Once out of public ownership, they could choose not to buy coal, making a bad situation worse. Even the Nottinghamshire miners were not immune, though some Conservative backbenchers showed loyalty, joining them in their protests. But this was now a declining industry and the NUM's break up, with the departure of the UDM, did nothing to help the employees' negotiating power.

Cross-reference **Chapter 4** *The miners' strike 1984–85*

Citizen's Charter

The **Citizen's Charter** was announced by Major in 1991. The project promised to increase accountability and responsiveness in the public sector, treating the public more like valued customers. Services would agree targets and be judged as to whether they were meeting those targets. Successes would be granted 'Charter Marks'.

Health and education were not being privatised, but the changes introduced clearly matched the privatisation agenda.

The health system was reorganised as an **internal market**. This meant that different units within the NHS were free to buy services from one another. The intention was to introduce market forces and, therefore, drive down costs and push up efficiency.

The reforms in education similarly had the driving motivation of reducing **bureaucracy**. The power of local authorities, to which state schools had historically been answerable, was reduced and schools had increasing powers devolved to them. Meanwhile the introduction of published performance league tables (an example of Citizen's Charter methods) was intended to empower parental decision-making. The watchword was 'choice'. This put parents in the position of customers, empowered to 'buy' services from the school of their choice. Education secretary Gillian Shepherd put together plans for what John Major in his autobiography calls 'hit squads', to take over the running of schools judged to be sufficiently underachieving.[7] In 1994, the **Teacher Training Agency** was created and in 1997 the **National Curriculum**. This was intended to standardise schools, teaching and learning and was, therefore, the complement, or contradiction, of 'choice', depending on how you interpret its implementation.

Key terms

Citizen's Charter: a guarantee of standards in the public sector, treating the public more like valued customers.

internal market: a relationship between the constituent parts of a large organisation which allows them to buy products or services from one another.

bureaucracy: the managerial paperwork associated with any larger organisation in both public and private sectors, especially those aspects of management popularly regarded as unnecessary.

Teacher Training Agency: body created in 1994 to provide additional training to teachers who were already in work, in order to ensure they were kept up to date with changes in educational policy and practice.

Key terms

National Curriculum: a standardised curriculum introduced in England, Wales and Northern Ireland (but not Scotland) in 1997, specifying the outline of what pupils should be taught at different ages in state schools.

National Lottery: a system of gambling in which part of the profits are used by the state to fund the arts, heritage, sport and 'good causes'.

Downing Street Declaration: a statement agreed by the Irish and British governments regarding the future of Northern Ireland.

Council tax

Understanding that the poll tax had been a major reason for Thatcher's fall from power, the new Prime Minister asked Michael Heseltine to become Secretary of State for the Environment again and dump the unpopular measure. In March 1991, Heseltine presented the idea of the 'council tax', which was intended to be fairer than either of the two preceding, unpopular systems:

- unlike the poll tax, it would be based on property values
- unlike the rates, it would be paid by everyone.

The places where people lived were assessed and grouped into different price bands, and the tax they paid depended on the band into which their home fell. No tax is ever going to be popular, but the Major–Heseltine success was in removing the poll tax from government plans and, therefore, from the list of things Labour could bring up against them in the next election. This was unlikely to be enough to turn the Conservatives' chances around overnight, but it was a step in the right direction for a party that wanted to retain power.

Other policies

In the field of law and order, the Home Secretary Michael Howard worked to reduce the freedom of judges when sentencing, by introducing a series of fixed and minimum sentences. At the same time Howard told the 1993 Conservative Party conference that 'prison works'. The prison population started to climb.

1993 also saw the introduction of the **National Lottery**. The sums raised by people betting paid for the prizes, costs and the profits of the administrators, but also donated large sums to the arts, heritage, sport and 'good causes'.

A further policy was announced by John Major at the 1993 Conservative Party conference. The Prime Minister drew attention to past divisions over Europe. He also noted the speed of change in society – something to which he might expect his audience to respond positively, given that Conservatives often prefer to postpone and minimise change, and question innovation. He praised what he called 'the old values – neighbourliness, decency, courtesy' and announced that it was 'time to get back to basics'.[8] His amplification on this, specifying individuals accepting responsibility and not passing it to the state, was a clear allusion to Thatcher's comment on 'society'.

Clearly intended to promote socially conservative values, it had disastrous political consequences, as it meant the decency, or otherwise, of politicians' private lives were of even greater significance, thus helping to trigger the issue of 'sleaze'.

Approach to Northern Ireland

Like his predecessor with the assassination of Airey Neave, Major had an early confrontation with the IRA. On 7 February 1991 the republican group launched a mortar attack on 10 Downing Street when the war cabinet was in session, discussing the Gulf War. Two shells missed their target, one landed in the back garden. Several people were injured, but no members of the government were hit.

In 1993, John Major and the Irish Taoiseach Albert Reynolds issued a joint statement, the **Downing Street Declaration**. It stated both that the people of Ireland had the right to self-determination and that the people of Northern Ireland had the right to choose whether that province should leave the UK and join the Republic of Ireland. In addition, it stated that the people of the island of Ireland had the right to solve problems in the north–south relationship by mutual agreement. The latter concept, that negotiations could take place within the island of Ireland, was important to republicans for whom the island was a 'natural' as well as a historically justified political unit. The Prime Ministers also stated that their governments would work towards a peaceful constitutional settlement and an end to political violence in

Northern Ireland. The negotiations were open to all parties, including parties linked to paramilitary organisations, once they had foresworn violence. This led to an IRA ceasefire the following year, which, in turn, brought about a matching ceasefire from the Combined Loyalist Military Command.

Unionists were suspicious, as they had been following the 1985 Anglo-Irish Agreement, but, as historian D. George Boyce writes, they decided to work with it, not to seek to undermine it.[9]

Conservative divisions

Although Major replacing Thatcher did alter the political dynamic to some degree and allowed individual policies to be dropped, some underlying divisions had been festering for many years.

The poll tax had been a fatal miscalculation by Margaret Thatcher, but its abandonment by Major and Heseltine neutralised the issue.

The deep divisions within the Conservative Party over relations with the EEC have plagued every leader before, and since, Thatcher.

The treaty signed in the Dutch city of Maastricht caused a substantial debate among Conservatives and a revolt by those backbenchers least sympathetic to the membership of the EEC.

In fact, the treaty contained a series of exemptions specifically for the UK, allowing the country to stay outside some of the new developments. These 'opt-outs' had been negotiated by John Major and his team, partly because they did not agree with the plans, but partly because they knew it would be hard to persuade their parliamentary colleagues to accept them.

The treaty was signed in February 1992, shortly before the general election; it would only take effect once parliament had ratified it, passing it into law. The foreseeable problem was those members of his own backbenches who were bound to vote it down.

In fact, the initial parliamentary response was positive, and a prompt ratification might have caused few problems. Postponing it meant that it came after a Danish referendum on Maastricht in June 1992, in which the Danes rejected the treaty (they accepted it in a second referendum following further negotiations). Conservatives opposed to Maastricht started calling for a British referendum.

At the second reading of the European Communities (Amendment) Bill, 22 Conservatives opposed the measure; the committee stage (in which the details would be gone through line-by-line) was postponed. The government attempted an intermediary stage in November, but this time more Conservatives voted against and some abstained. The debate seemed interminable and the opponents put forward a series of amendments intended to slow the bill's progress down – a staggering 600 in all. April 1993 saw opponents attempt to write the necessity of a referendum into the bill: this was defeated. The third reading was reached in May 1993; it was passed, but with 46 Tory rebels. Opposing your own government is not something MPs normally like to do; the size of the rebellion was a sign of the depth of the division and the strength of feeling.

The bill then had to grind its way through the House of Lords and then return to the House of Commons for further discussion. This process of readings, the two houses, the committee stage, amendments votes and so forth is, of course, the normal parliamentary procedure that any bill has to go through before it becomes an act of parliament and, therefore, law. What was unusual was the length of the process, the fierceness of the debating, the number of amendments and the size of the rebellion by the government's own side.

ACTIVITY 5.3

'The poll tax was to be a disaster of the first magnitude and contributed more than any other mistake to the fall of Margaret Thatcher in 1990.'[10] Discuss.

Voices from the past

John Major

Arguing in defence of the Maastricht Treaty, Major told the Conservative Group for Europe that:

> Fifty years from now Britain will still be the country of long shadows on county grounds, warm beer, invincible green suburbs, dog lovers and – to quote George Orwell – old maids bicycling to Holy Communion through the morning mist. And – if we get our way – Shakespeare will still be read even in school. Britain will survive unamendable in all essentials.[11]

Discussion points

1. What vision of Britain does this communicate?
2. How do you read the tone: nostalgia? Parody?

The process resulted in two clear outcomes:

1. The European Communities (Amendments) Act was passed, so Britain had now ratified the Maastricht Treaty
2. Conservative divisions on Europe were now clear to every voter. Voters don't like divided parties. The process of signing, debating and ratifying the Maastricht Treaty had done the standing of the Conservatives no good at all. It was another blow to their prospects in the forthcoming election.

Even after the 1992 treaty, the EEC continued to present the Major government with conundrums. How should they respond to the likelihood of a single currency? Supporters included the Foreign Secretary Douglas Hurd, Chancellor of the Exchequer Kenneth Clarke and Deputy Prime Minister Michael Heseltine (all of them previous leadership contenders). But there was widespread hostility to the whole idea in the Parliamentary party and the membership. As PM, John Major refused to rule out the UK's joining the single currency. However, in the 1997 election addresses, many individual Conservative candidates did so.

The Conservative leadership election 1995

Europe continued to be a divisive issue in Conservative politics. Conscious of the presence of hostile critics in the parliamentary party and the government, especially on this issue, John Major resigned as party leader in June 1995. This was in order to force a leadership election, challenging those who opposed his policies to 'put up or shut up'. In the event, only one did so and was heavily defeated. Others, perhaps mindful of Michael Heseltine's fate in 1990, were known to be considering standing in a second ballot. Major's victory was so crushing (he won 66% of the vote), no second ballot occurred.

Realignment of the Labour Party under Kinnock, Smith and Blair

Realignment of the Labour Party

Early in his leadership of the Labour party, Kinnock attracted positive press coverage for his response to the presence in the Labour Party of Militant. Like other parties, Labour contained a number of special-interest groups and groupings of MPs and others around particular shades of socialism. Militant was judged to be different and was dubbed a 'party within a party', with its own membership, its own newspaper and its own policy objectives. As it dominated Labour politics in Liverpool, the activities of the Liverpool City Council became controversial and formed part of an attack by Kinnock on the organisation at the 1985 party conference.

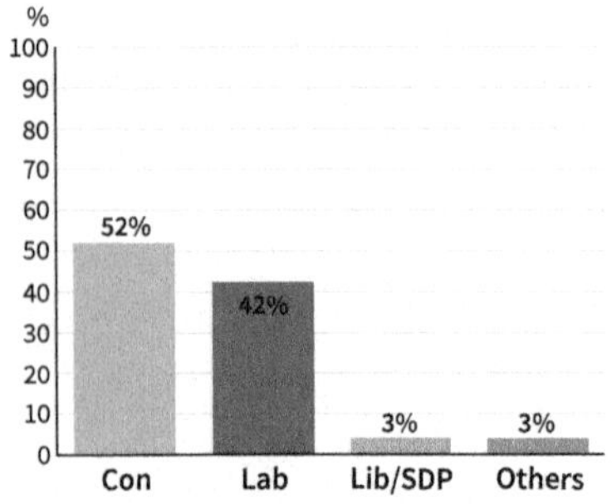

Figure 5.4: Seats in the House of Commons won in the 1992 British general election; percentages have been adjusted to the nearest whole number.

Going in to the 1992 general election, Labour was still led by Neil Kinnock. However, the Liberals and SDP, now merged as the Liberal Democrats (the 'Lib Dems'), and the Conservatives were both under new management with Paddy Ashdown and John Major respectively. Kinnock had agreed with Foot about some issues – he too had been a unilateralist – but, while securing the support of the party's left, he had taken its manifesto back to the centre ground. Polls and media predictions had led most people to expect a hung Parliament, or possibly a small Labour lead. In fact, the Conservatives won comfortably.

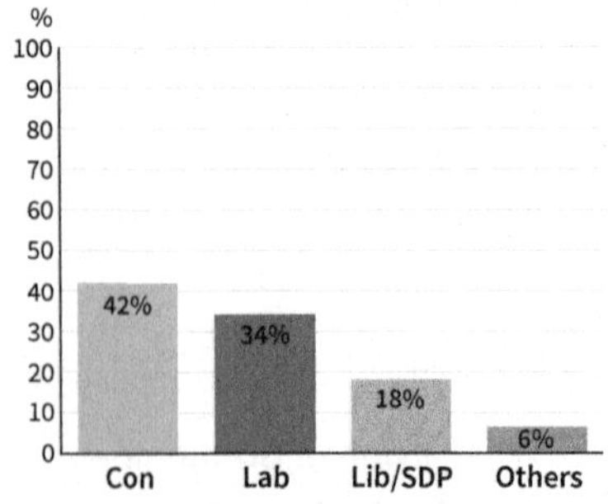

Figure 5.5: Votes won in the 1992 British general election; percentages have been adjusted to the nearest whole number.

Comparing these figures with those of previous elections, it is clear that the Conservative vote held steady, Labour improved its performance, the newly merged Liberal Democrat vote was slipping – but the anti-Conservative vote was still too divided for Labour to win.

Why Labour lost in 1992

According to Robert Blake, the election was memorable for Shadow Chancellor John Smith's declaration that he would increase the top rate of income tax; Major's decision to campaign by standing on a 'soap box' and address passers-by in the street; Kinnock's address to an eve-of-poll rally in Sheffield; and the fact that the opinion polls were wrong. Some commentators have even argued that the triumphalist tone of the Sheffield rally, in which Kinnock clearly thought victory was in sight, swung voters against Labour. However, Vernon Bogdanor has stated that an examination of the polls makes it quite clear that most people had made up their minds already and the television broadcast had no significant effect on the outcome.

The Sun newspaper was in no doubt of the reasons for the Conservative victory: 'It was *The Sun* wot won it' declared their headline, following the election results being announced. Certainly, that newspaper had run a tireless campaign of vilification against the Labour leader. But, again, Vernon Bogdanor is doubtful that this had more than a marginal effect on the results.

Despite their centre-left political similarities, there were clear differences between Kinnock and Foot. Kinnock was a moderniser, pushing for a more up-to-date approach to communication. In this he was opposed by many in the party and wider Labour movement. As historian Brian Harrison notes, Callaghan had already insisted he would not be 'packaged' in the 1979 election, while in 1988 Ron Todd of the TGWU attacked party modernisers with 'Filofaxes, sharp suits and clipboards'.[12] Benn complained that the 1992 election had been turned into a form of entertainment, insisting that earlier generations of campaigners would have been horrified. All seem to have clung to an ideal of plain-speaking which they clearly thought a characteristic of left-wing working-class politics, untainted by marketing.

ACTIVITY 5.4

Research the three items listed by union boss Ron Todd: Filofaxes, sharp suits and clipboards.

1. What were their associations and implications, and why was he hostile to their significance?
2. What does that hostility tell you about the ideas and ideals of the Labour movement at that time?
3. Write a short paragraph explaining the ideals that the statements of Callaghan, Todd and Benn suggest they shared. Consider aspects such as styles of speaking, social class and education.

Kinnock, Smith and Blair

Following the defeat of 1992, the Labour leadership went from Kinnock, to John Smith, to Tony Blair, with deputy leader Margaret Beckett taking over as acting leader on two occasions. That process of a resignation, a death and a temporary occupant of the post, meant three changes of leader in four years.

These changes were of more than just personnel, they affected the way in which the voting public saw the Labour Party. This reflects the potential in British politics for 'presidential' politics, within which some people's vote is strongly swayed by their view of the party leaders. As they decide how to cast their vote, they are most conscious of whom they want to put into 10 Downing Street. Neil Kinnock had been broadly liked and he had helped Labour become a party more people seriously considered supporting. But media hostility toward him, the issue of unilateralism and even, perhaps, his Welsh accent, had meant that he was not well thought of as a future Prime Minister. In Robert Blake's view, 'Major looked like a Prime Minister, indeed was one. Kinnock did not'.[13]

Kinnock, like Foot before him, resigned shortly after the results were announced. The Shadow Chancellor was elected the new party leader, with 90% of the vote. Smith was a broadly popular and respected figure, with a smiling, calm, manner, which was compared in the media to that of a family bank manager – and this time with a Scottish, not a Welsh, accent. Unlike Kinnock, Smith had ministerial experience, having worked in the Wilson and Callaghan governments, as well as the Foot and Kinnock shadow cabinets in opposition.

The situation looked promising for Labour: under Kinnock electoral support had gradually been climbing. With the well-liked and well-respected Smith as leader, would the next election be won by just one more step up in the popular vote – a policy of capitalising on the Conservatives' unpopularity and being uncontroversial, dubbed 'one more heave' at the time? Certainly Labour began enjoying some remarkably high

Figure 5.6: Neil Kinnock in 1992.

poll ratings – but so they had midway between the 1979 and 1983 elections. In the event, Smith died suddenly of a heart attack after less than two years in post.

Labour went through another leadership election, and Tony Blair won, with 57% of the vote.

'New Labour'

Under Blair, Labour moved further toward the centre ground of politics. Equality was downplayed in favour of social justice, a concept that Liberals and moderate Conservatives could readily support. Using the label (or slogan) 'New Labour', the party abandoned attacks on capitalism and embraced the free market. Labour also moved onto Conservative ground, by taking up the issue of law and order. Additionally, it became warmer on the subject of the EEC. Beyond policy, Labour became more sophisticated in its use of the media, the very 'marketing' activity treated with such hostility by an earlier generation of politicians.

ACTIVITY 5.5

Using the information in this section and in the previous chapter, as well as your own research, create a mind map to explain the New Labour landslide victory in 1997.

The concept of 'New Labour' was a practical response to the preceding years of continuous Conservative government and to a long-term pattern of Labour decline. Labour had not secured a clear-cut electoral victory since 1966. The architects of New Labour became convinced that they would never win again until they could attract the votes of aspirational 'Middle England'. For most politicians the overriding objective of their craft is to exercise power. Blair insisted that this was his purpose and that he did not enjoy being opposition leader. He had served his Parliamentary apprenticeship at the height of the Thatcherite ascendancy. His belief, shared by close associates, including Gordon Brown and Peter Mandelson, was that Labour must modernise if it were to survive and prosper. Much necessary work had been done before Blair became leader. Under Neil Kinnock much of the electorally toxic left-wing baggage of the early 1980s was abandoned. The process was consolidated under John Smith, but Blair and those who thought like him were frustrated by Smith's excessive caution and believed that the party must go further and faster. In particular, they held Smith's 'shadow budget' partly responsible for the loss of the 1992 election, because it had confirmed Labour's image as a 'tax and spend' party, not to be trusted with the nation's economy. Brown made 'prudence' a much-repeated watchword of his subsequent stewardship of the Exchequer.

Image was central to the New Labour project. A line had to be drawn under the past. Old Labour represented everything that was bad: 'the destructive influence of the trade unions, the dominance of the block vote at party conferences, the scourge of the hard left and Militant and the pettiness of the radical party activist'.[14] New Labour would create a New Britain – modern, youthful, progressive and dynamic. Out of this vision emerged the now much-derided concept of 'Cool Britannia'. Under Blair, Downing Street receptions were as likely to be populated by pop stars and sports personalities, as by ambassadors and captains of industry.

ACTIVITY 5.6

The new Clause IV pledged Labour 'to work for a dynamic economy, serving the public interest, in which the enterprise of the market and the rigour of competition are joined with the forces of partnership and co-operation ... with a thriving public sector and high quality public services'.[17]

1. What does the revised Clause IV tell us about the thinking of New Labour?
2. How does it compare with the old Clause IV of 1918?

Two symbolic moves defined Blair's early rise. In 1989, as shadow Employment Secretary, he announced that Labour would drop its support for the closed shop. *The Guardian* voiced its approval: 'A rigid insistence on total union membership offends against both civil rights and the temper of the times'.[15] Even more important was Blair's early decision as leader to change (in practice, to weaken) the celebrated Clause IV of Labour's constitution. In many ways this was unnecessary. But Blair saw 'modernising' Clause IV as important, to demonstrate just how far Labour had changed. In the words of one party official, 'It was a classic rebranding exercise. Announce that you are new and different, then demonstrably show that you are new and different by a very high-profile act'.[16] It would be unfair to dismiss the new statement as a mere commitment to political platitudes, but it certainly lacked the ideological conviction of its predecessor.

New Labour saw that the shaping of its image was not entirely within its own control. Indeed, it held the Conservative-dominated press partly responsible for Labour's exclusion from power since 1979. Memories of *The Sun*'s remorseless attack on

Kinnock in 1992 were deeply ingrained on New Labour minds, even if the newspaper's claim that it was '*The Sun* wot won it' was an exaggeration. Alastair Campbell, Blair's press spokesman and later Director of Communications and Strategy, was a key architect of Blair's election success and at least as influential as many members of the cabinet. Campbell sought to determine the political agenda in the media, and also to ensure a favourable reception for Labour and its policies. Strikingly, Blair accepted an invitation from Rupert Murdoch to speak to senior executives of News Corporation at a gathering off the coast of Queensland, Australia in July 1995. The supposedly invaluable prize at stake was *The Sun*'s support at the forthcoming election.

However, New Labour was about more than image. It was also a response to and part-acceptance of the Thatcherite revolution. Blair understood that most of the changes of the 1980s were irreversible and, indeed, that many had been beneficial. When the need was to satisfy the tribal instincts of a traditional Labour audience, Blair was fully capable of denouncing his Tory opponents. 'I can't stand these people ... being in government over our country', he declared at a special Labour Party conference in April 1995. Yet it was not always clear what, in their policies, he found so unacceptable. The primacy of the market, low direct taxation, control of inflation, privatisation, the acceptance of a globalised economy, restricted trade union power and, at least from his second term onwards, choice and diversity, were ideas that Blair did not so much accept as embrace. At times his admiration for Margaret Thatcher was undisguised and not just for being a strong leader who moulded her party in her own image. In 1996 he told an American newspaper that a future Labour government would fail if it were seen to be 'dismantling Thatcherism'. After taking office, he soon invited Mrs Thatcher to visit Downing Street. She reportedly declared that her legacy was safe in his hands, while Anthony Seldon argues that in Blair, 'rather than in any of the Tory leaders who succeeded her, she found her truest heir'.[18]

Figure 5.7: Tony Blair and Margaret Thatcher.

All of this required Blair to abandon much of the social democratic model that had dominated Labour thinking since 1945. However, he did not accept the Thatcherite alternative unreservedly. Blair believed Thatcher had paid insufficient attention to those who did not automatically thrive in a free-market economy. 'Self-help' was fine in theory, but took little account of those unable to help themselves. New Labour, therefore, would balance economic success with 'social inclusion', the market with the community. Thatcherite individualism had gone too far. 'I start from a simple belief,' said Blair in 1996, 'that people are not separate economic actors competing in the marketplace of life. They are citizens of a community. We are social beings, nurtured in families and communities and human only because we develop the moral power of personal responsibility for ourselves and each other'.[19] Here was a clear response to, indeed rebuttal of, Thatcher's much-quoted declaration that there is 'no such thing as society' – though the full context of her remark reveals that her overall message was considerably less brutal than the disembodied phrase implied.

The 'Third Way'

Figure 5.8: New Labour's Third Way.

The origins of these ideas, and even of the words used to describe them, are relatively easy to establish. For Blair, religious faith, though usually downplayed on the advice of his media guru Campbell, was all-important. A devout Christian, he had an abiding sense of what was right and an unshakeable confidence in his own judgement – even when, as was sometimes the case in regard to war, it conflicted with that of church leaders. More prosaically, Blair acknowledged the debt he owed to John Macmurray,

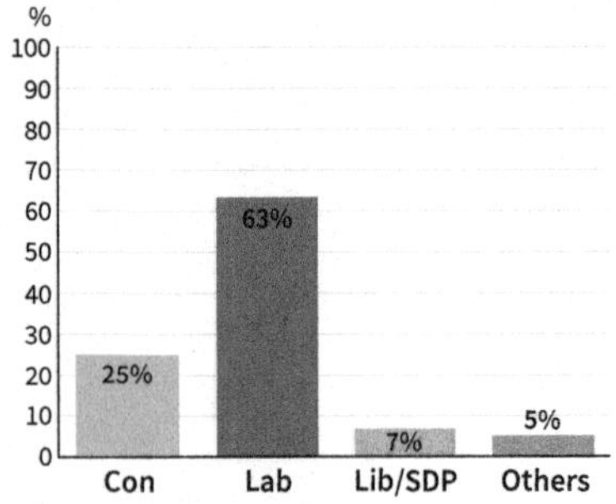

Figure 5.9: Seats in the House of Commons won in the 1997 British general election; percentages have been adjusted to the nearest whole number.

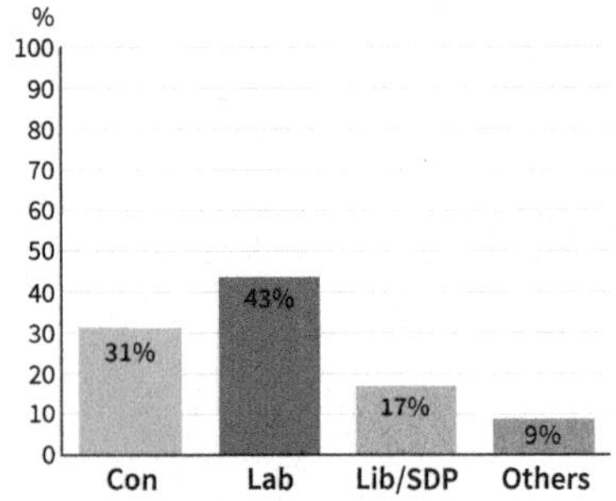

Figure 5.10: Votes won in the 1997 British general election; percentages have been adjusted to the nearest whole number.

a little-known academic, from whom he took up the idea of the central importance of community. The notion of the 'Third Way' was not new and had been popularised by Professor Anthony Giddens of the London School of Economics. Both Blair and Brown were fascinated by American politics, with Blair deeply impressed by Bill Clinton's skill in repositioning the Democratic Party during his successful bid for the White House (1992). A supposed common ideological commitment to the Third Way underpinned a close friendship between the two men and if Clinton had 'invented' the 'New Democrats', a corresponding rebranding of Blair's party followed naturally enough.

The important point is that New Labour sought to build on, rather than simply continue, Thatcherism. Blair's approach perhaps owed more than he ever conceded to John Major, or even to the former SDP leader and one-time Foreign Secretary, David Owen. It had been Major's ambition to project 'Thatcherism with a human face', while in the 1980s Owen had identified an 'electorally attractive political mix' if 'we could simultaneously break right on the market and left on social policy'.[20]

Reasons for Labour victory in 1997

While Labour had been gradually building support and increasing its credibility and electability, the Conservatives had been losing ground. The poll tax had not been forgotten. Black Wednesday and the disorderly withdrawal from the ERM was more recent, and had caused considerable loss of credibility. Labour looked united and full of ideas; the Conservatives looked and were divided.

In 1997, when the next election came, there was a 10% swing to Labour, which gained 146 additional seats giving them a total of 418. The Conservatives lost 178, seven cabinet ministers among them. They were left with 165 MPs, none of them from either Scotland or Wales, leaving them an England-only party. The Liberal Democrats gained 30 (but also lost two). This left Labour with a majority of 177, a situation comparable with the 1979 Thatcher victory. The changing fortunes of the parties was most dramatic in seats, but even in votes it is noteworthy.

This was clearly a major achievement by Labour and the change in their circumstances is clear in the significant increase in the percentage of votes won. Strikingly, the Liberal Democrats polled very slightly less well in votes, but better in seats, something that may reflect **tactical voting**. Hostility to the Conservatives appears to have trumped hostility to, or distrust of, one another – with Lib Dem and Labour supporters being willing to vote for one another's parties according to which looked most likely to defeat the Conservatives in individual constituencies.

That the tide was turning against them had already been made clear by the run of **by-election** losses (every one since 1990). The Conservatives had been damaged by continuing divisions on Europe. Memories of the poll tax may well not have gone away, while the ERM fiasco had left the party fatally wounded. Sleaze had also left its mark.

In Tony Blair Labour had found a leader who commanded interest and respect. Blair had also made it his business to reduce newspaper hostility, visiting Rupert Murdoch, who owned both the *Sun* and *The Times*. Labour had also been successful in promoting the Shadow Cabinet as a whole, so that several leading members of the party had become quite well known.

Key terms

tactical voting: supporting a candidate in an election, not because of agreeing with the party they represent, but because of their being the most likely to defeat a different party.

by-election: election taking place in a single constituency, not a general election, which takes place in all constituencies.

ACTIVITY 5.7

Why do you think Labour won in 1997? List the differences from the previous four elections, put them into order of importance and write short notes on each of them.

Social issues

The extent of 'social liberalism'

John Major's 1993 'back to basics' speech might lead us to think that his time in government was dominated by **social conservatism**. Certainly, it is a reminder that Thatcherism was seen, and saw itself, in moral terms not merely economic ones. In fact, the backward-looking nostalgia was balanced by a **social liberalism** that was increasingly mainstream. More people seemed to become more tolerant of a wider spectrum of behaviours, lifestyles and ways of being human.

Cross-reference **Chapter 4** *Section 28*

The results could be seen in changing attitudes to homosexuality. The 1960s had seen a partial decriminalisation of homosexuality. This had been led by parliament and the Wilson government; it had not been driven by, or succeeded in causing, a groundswell of public support. In the 1980s, 'Section 28' was Conservative Party policy and passed into law. Even at the beginning of the 1990s, a majority of British people were recorded as thinking that homosexuality was wrong. Yet, during the 1990s, the homosexual age of consent was lowered. It became possible for MPs, including cabinet ministers, to be openly gay because the mixture of fear, hostility and contempt had largely faded away.

Social conservatives were concerned to see the divorce rate in the early 1980s roughly double what it had been ten years earlier. In 1970, 1% of men and 1% of women were divorced; by 2000, it would be 8% men and 9% women. At the same time, the number of people living together without getting married was on its way up and, with that, the number of illegitimate births climbed.

The Tories had certainly faced difficulties over human relationships, but the basis of the 'sleaze' stories in the media was not so much sexual activity as perceptions of hypocrisy, the difference between the social views ministers and their backbenchers expressed publicly and their private lives.

Although a conservative Prime Minister, John Major spoke of a 'classless society'. He clearly had in mind something **meritocratic**. As a concept, this emphasis on achievement was compatible with Thatcherite individualism, as well as being something the Labour opposition would find it hard to discredit.

Key terms

social conservatism: respects social traditions such as marriage and the family, emphasises personal responsibility and in the criminal justice system prioritises punishment, as in Michael Howard's 1993 'prison works' speech.

social liberalism: expresses the importance of tolerance, balancing social justice and individual freedom; in the criminal justice system it prioritises education, therapeutic treatment and reducing reoffending.

permissive society: a journalists' phrase for describing a society in which a wider range of views and activities are permitted and regarded as socially acceptable.

bourgeois: French word originally meaning 'town dweller' but adopted in Marxist and left-wing circles to mean 'middle class'.

Voices from the past

Norman Tebbit

In 1985 Norman Tebbit gave a lecture asserting that the **permissive society** had blurred a series of distinctions.

Bad art was as good as good art. Grammar and spelling were no longer important. To be clean was no better than to be filthy. Good manners were no better than bad. Family life was derided as an outdated **bourgeois** concept. Criminals deserved as much sympathy as their victims. Many homes and classrooms became disorderly – if there was neither right nor wrong there could be no bases for punishment or reward. Violence and soft pornography became accepted in the media.[21]

Discussion points

1. List the criticisms Tebbit is making and do some background research.
2. To what areas of government policy does Tebbit's list refer?
3. What steps did the Thatcher and Major governments take which could be related to Tebbit's analysis?

Britain in 1997 was a more diverse society than it had been in 1979 and more tolerant of diversity. Racism, sexism, homophobia and anti-Semitism had not gone away, but the number of people whose views could be so defined had been falling and the number who would publicly express them had dropped dramatically. Intolerance had become socially unacceptable in a many parts of society.

Figure 5.11: Lady Diana Spencer, a kindergarten teacher, was thrust into the public gaze when her engagement to Prince Charles was announced.

Anti-establishment culture

The **establishment** – the people who own and run the country – generally includes not only politicians and senior civil servants, but also the heads of the armed forces, judges, bishops and wealthy industrialists, as well as royalty and aristocracy. The assumption is that these people have certain attitudes and attributes in common.

Anti-establishment culture is, therefore, the activities of those people who attack, oppose, mock and criticise the establishment. The 1990s saw the British royal family, the established Church of England and Westminster all weakened. This was a decline in the power and influence of the establishment, but also in the respect in which it was held. This development was part of what John Major was responding to in his 1993 'back to basics' speech.

However, the distinction between establishment and anti-establishment is subtle, complex and changing.

The royal family

As the daughter of an earl, Lady Diana Spencer was clearly a member of the establishment. Yet her 1981 marriage to the Prince of Wales, making her Diana, Princess of Wales, was still unusual in that heirs to the throne usually married foreign royalty. In 1986 the Queen's second son married the daughter of an upper-class, but non-noble, family. None of the four royal children married royalty, and only Prince Charles married a titled member of the aristocracy. The Princess of Wales's media image aligned her with celebrity culture and differentiated her from other members of the royal family. Her death in 1997 harmed the standing of the royal family in the short term.

The Church of England

As an **established church**, the Church of England is inherently part of the establishment. Yet it proved capable of taking anti-establishment steps, in publishing *Faith in the City* and in its handling of the post-Falklands War celebrations. The 1980s and 1990s saw part of the 20th century's decline in church attendance. The century opened with about 55% of children attending Sunday school; it ended with about 4% doing so. The issue of **disestablishment** was widely discussed in church circles, although no change was made to its status.

Key terms

meritocracy: a term popularised by the 1958 book *The Rise of the Meritocracy*. The book was, in fact, a warning that an elite which had reached power through personal achievement would feel little loyalty to, or responsibility for, those who had achieved less. Its author Michael Young was disappointed to see the word acquire a positive meaning and become a part of the vocabulary of the Blair government.

establishment: the collection of people who own and run the country, particularly those whose parents were also in a position of wealth and authority.

established church: a church with institutional links to the state, one guaranteed by law, or regulated by law.

disestablishment: the process whereby an established church breaks its ties with the state and its institutions.

Taking it further

Why do you think that church attendance has declined over the last 100 years? Some commentators point out that it matches the decline in membership of other organisations, such as political parties. What do you think this tells us about British society?

Cross-reference Chapter 4 *Faith in the City*

The House of Commons was naturally responsive to public opinion through the constituency party and electoral systems. The 1980s saw several MPs elected who might be dubbed 'anti-establishment'. However, sleaze affected not just individual MPs, but the standing in which politicians in general were held. This may have contributed to the growth of political parties, which challenged, not just other political parties, but the political system and its values.

In the 1964 election, Harold Wilson had succeeded on drawing on anti-establishment sentiment when he mocked 'the grouse-moor conception of national leadership', asserting that the right father, the right school and the right friends were not qualifications for joining government. However, Labour, an experienced party of government, was itself part of the establishment in many people's eyes. This fact pushed some towards revolutionary parties to Labour's left and others into the Green party.

Westminster

Green politics are manifestly anti-establishment, and the Green Party deliberately set out to organise itself differently. **Feminism** had challenged the assumption that men should rule over women. **Anti-racism** and **anti-imperialism** had challenged assumptions about white races ruling over black ones. In green politics, human abuse of the earth and the planet's other life forms could quite easily be analysed and criticised using the intellectual tools that had analysed sexism, racism and imperialism. The Green Party struggled to achieve representation in Parliament because of the first-past-the-post system (its first MP came in the 2010 general election). Even in the 1989 European elections, where it achieved 15% of the vote – making it the third largest party – it was still left without an MEP (its first MEPs came in the 1999 European elections). From 1993 it began winning seats in local councils.

Finally, it is important not to associate 'anti-establishment culture' purely with the left wing. Thatcherite politics had partly been an attack on the assumptions of the establishment: Lawson didn't subtitle his autobiography 'memoirs of a Tory radical' for nothing. In addition, we should not make the mistake of seeing the political satirists as anti-establishment: many of them had much the same education as establishment politicians and civil servants. By contrast, Thatcher and Major looked anti-establishment. She was a lower-middle-class woman, not an upper-middle-class man. He was state-school educated, never went to university, was once turned down in his application to be a bus conductor, and had experience of being unemployed.

The position of women

The 20th century had seen considerable changes in women's public and private lives, but it is important not to overstate the rate or extent of change.

Change	Continuity
Legislation in 1918 and 1928 gave women the vote and the right to stand for parliament, so they were treated the same as men in national and local elections.	Women were not treated equally in the choosing of parliamentary candidates. Selection committees largely preferred male candidates, making it difficult for women to enter parliament.
Legislation in the 1970s had made discriminating on the basis of gender illegal, including paying men and women differently if they were doing the same work.	Women were not treated equally in employment. They did not earn the same as men for comparable work.

Table 5.1: Change and continuity in gender discrimination.

Key terms

green: a political programme or view in which ecological issues, such as global warming, take priority over other issues, such as law and order, defence, social justice etc. – the issues on which most political parties expect to campaign.

feminism: a socio-political programme founded on the belief that women are suppressed and allowed less social, economic, political and cultural freedom and power than men. Feminism protests against that state of affairs and analyses the reasons for it.

anti-racism: a political programme or point of view which opposes treating people differently according to the supposed 'race' to which they belong, or making unfounded assumptions about individuals based on prejudice about the ethnic group with which they are associated.

anti-imperialism: political programme or point of view opposed to the invasion of a weaker country by a stronger one, or the imposition on it of a social, political, economic or cultural programme without the free agreement of the population.

Discriminating on the basis of gender was already illegal and the idea of men and women earning the same pay for the same work was well established by this period. The unsolved problem was that men and women did not always do the same work. Case by case, the principle of equal pay for comparable work was argued, established and tested. At the beginning of the 1970s, women's average earnings were still approximately 50% that of men. At the beginning of the 1980s, they had risen steadily to be 60% of men's. Rising pay was matched by rising involvement of women in trade unions. However, this rise in pay slowed and stopped at around two-thirds of men's average pay.

A change in the tax system, introduced by Nigel Lawson, meant that husbands were no longer responsible for their wives' tax returns. Previously, a married couple had been treated as an economic unit; now the marriage partners were treated separately. A small, but significant, step in the developing status of women in society, it can also be seen as reflecting the government's continuing emphasis on individuals over groups.

The 1980s were also the period in which access to higher education became more balanced. The newer universities had been co-educational from the beginning, but Oxford and Cambridge colleges had been created for men and it took time for them to open their doors to women applicants.

Although, clearly, Margaret Thatcher's achievement in becoming Prime Minister was admirable, it did not indicate a wider change in the political status of women. The presence of women in parliament did not change dramatically during Thatcher's time. Thatcher herself showed no interest in women's role in politics, promoting only a handful of women to government and only one (in fact, a member of the House of Lords) to cabinet. This brought accusations that, having ascended herself, she had done nothing to help other women follow her. John Major proved slightly more willing to promote women, including two in his cabinet.

Thatcher's gender may have had an effect on voting patterns. In the years since the Second World War, women had tended to vote Conservative in slightly greater numbers than men. During Thatcher's time as leader, women were only as likely as men to support her party, not more so.

ACTIVITY 5.8

1. Why was it that, after several years of closing the gap, women's pay was stuck at two-thirds of men's? Would you attribute it to the facts that:
   - more women worked part time
   - more women were reluctant to work longer hours (for family reasons)
   - more women took breaks in career or left the work force early (for family reasons)?
2. Find out more about the reasons behind the differences in pay. As a class, discuss whether they were fair or unfair.

ACTIVITY 5.9

Should feminists celebrate Margaret Thatcher's achievements? Research feminism and how different women, such as Camille Paglia, Andrea Dworkin and Beatrix Campbell have written about Thatcher. What are their arguments? What evidence do they present? Can you distinguish opinion from fact? What is your own opinion?

Race relations

In an interview on television while she was still leader of the opposition, Margaret Thatcher had declared that the British character had 'done so much for democracy, for law and done so much throughout the world that if there is any fear that it might be swamped people are going to react and be rather hostile to those coming in.'[22]

The word 'swamped', which she also used elsewhere in the interview, was much quoted and joined the list of Thatcher statements cited as evidence by her enemies – along with the supposed 'no such thing as society'. In the same interview, she explained that she understood why some people had begun voting for far-right parties, such as the National Front.

By contrast, Major's statement that he wanted to see a country that was 'at ease with itself', and a future offering a better life for 'all its citizens'[23] suggested that the approach to race relations would be different.

Since Enoch Powell's speech, misleadingly nicknamed 'rivers of blood' (and perhaps because of it), few politicians had been willing to discuss the questions of ethnicity, immigration and community. The existence of underlying hostility, prejudice and resentment became clear in a series of notable events.

The trigger for the 1981 Brixton riot was the increased presence of police offers in the area, part of a policy called (ironically) 'Swamp 81'. The intention was to respond to endemic street crime by stopping people on suspicion (or 'sus') that they might

ACTIVITY 5.10

The 1983 election had been unusual in displaying a poster of a black man in a business suit, with the slogan 'Labour says he's black. Tories say he's British'. The text went on to explain 'With the Conservatives there are no 'blacks', no 'whites', just people'. What messages do you think it was intended to communicate and what audiences do you think it was addressing?

be engaged in wrongdoing. The response saw buildings and vehicles burnt, and numerous people injured (particularly police officers). Lord Scarman, a judge, was tasked with writing a report on why the riots happened.

The Scarman Report examined issues around racial disadvantage, drawing attention to problems in employment and housing. It urged immediate action to remove the causes of disadvantage, to avoid similar disturbances in future. It also spoke out against the 'sus' practice of stopping and searching, since it targeted black people.

Figure 5.12: UK deprivation and riots in the areas of British cities with a significant black population in the 1980s: Bristol (St Pauls 1980 and 1982), Liverpool (Toxteth 1981 and 1982), Manchester (Moss Side 1981), Birmingham (Handsworth 1982 and 1985) and London (Brixton 1981 and 1985, Notting Hill Gate 1982, Tottenham 1985).

In 1993, a black secondary school pupil called Stephen Lawrence was murdered while he waited for a bus. Five suspects were arrested and the suggestion that the murder was racially-motivated was widely discussed. However, the suspects were released and there were no convictions for 20 years. There was a widespread suspicion that the police weren't taking the death of a black youth as seriously as they would have done that of a white person. A later report announced that the Metropolitan (London) Police were 'institutionally racist'. This was widely publicised and hotly discussed. Previously, the police response to criticism was often to say that individual officers had misbehaved, but the remainder were entirely dependable.

Taking it further

The 1999 MacPherson Report decided that the Metropolitan Police were 'institutionally racist'. This meant that the very way the institution was constituted and operated had inbuilt racism. Find out about these subtle and serious issues, what the words imply and what steps were taken to respond to the charge.

Key terms

ayatollah: a high-ranking Shia Muslim jurist, one who examines questions of Islamic law, and offers decisions and rulings.

fatwa: a ruling issued by an Islamic jurist.

In the meantime, three incidents drew attention to the Muslim community in Britain.

The first of these was the publication, in 1988, of *The Satanic Verses* – a novel taking its title from Muslim tradition and written by a Salman Rushdie, a British novelist from a Bombay (Mumbai) Muslim family. Seen as blasphemous, it provoked demonstrations and demands for its banning and was publicly burned in Bradford. The controversy spread outside Britain and there was a riot in Pakistan. Then the religious leader of Iran, **Ayatollah** Khomeini, issued a **fatwa** urging Muslims to kill Rushdie. The author was given police protection and moved to a secret place of safety. The affair was a challenge for British politics: it did not divide people along class or party lines. Labour MP Keith Vaz was prominent in a 1989 anti-Rushdie march through Leicester. Conservative MP Norman Tebbit was publicly hostile to Rushdie's 'acts of betrayal'. To some, the affair was an issue of freedom of speech, so Rushdie needed defending. To others, the host community needed to accommodate the views of the newly arrived Muslims.

Cross-reference **Chapter 3** *Figure 3.13*

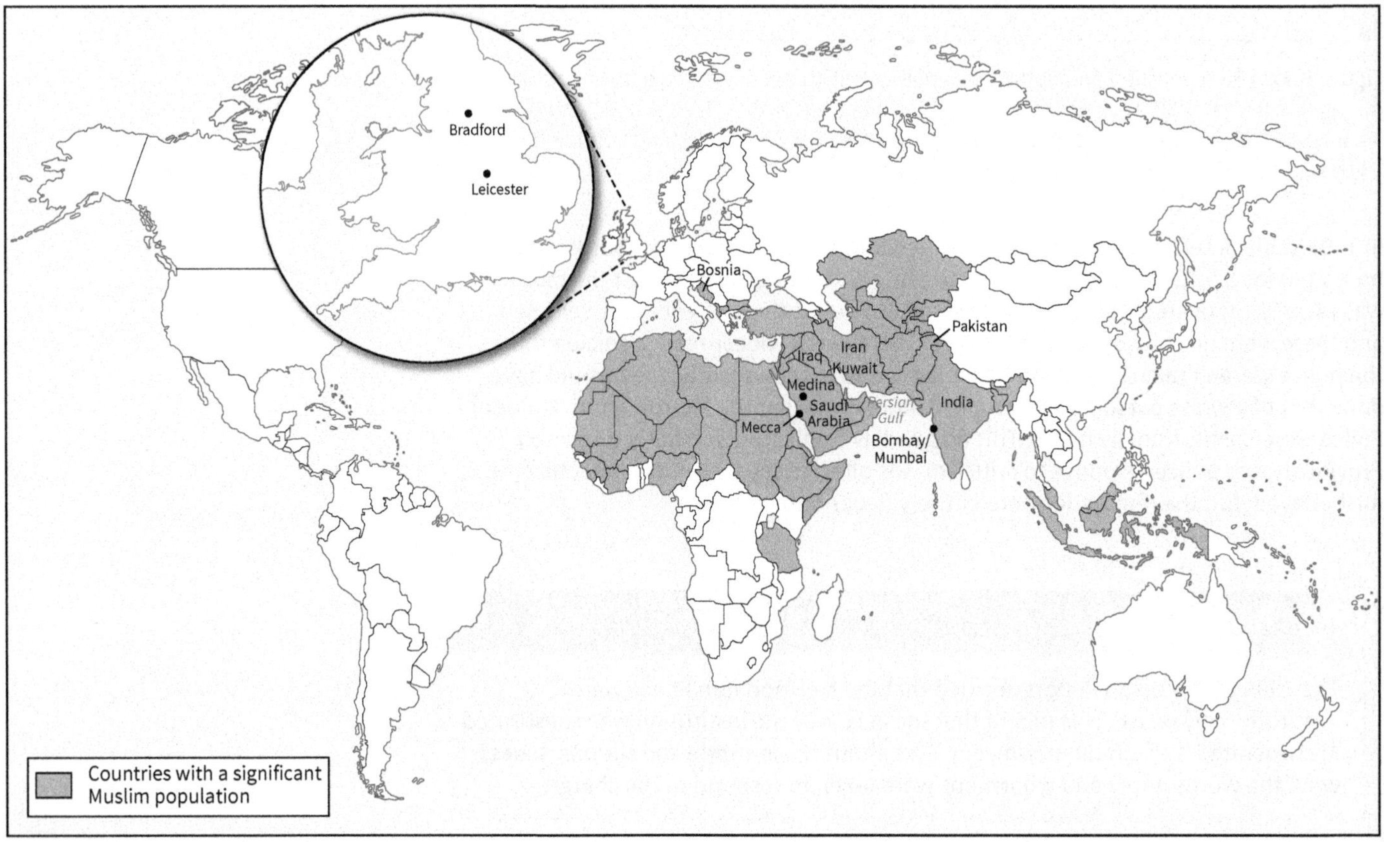

Figure 5.13: Events in the wider Muslim world affected people in the UK, just as a UK event, such as the publication of *The Satanic Verses*, had repercussions around the world. UK politicians had to be mindful of the historic links between many British Muslims and Muslim countries now in the Commonwealth.

The second event that increased the development of Muslim politics in Britain was the 1990-91 Gulf War. Despite the fact that the war had begun when a larger, more militaristic state (Iraq) had attacked a smaller one (Kuwait), the sight of western troops fighting a largely Muslim, Arab army seemed wrong. Also perceived as wrong was the fact that Saudi support meant western troops could be stationed in Saudi Arabia. They were in the peninsula which held the cities of Mecca and Medina, places of immense importance in the history and practice of Islam.

Cross-reference **Chapter 5** *Interventions in the Balkans*

Unrest in the Balkans was the third event. During the rising violence that contributed to, and stemmed from, the break-up of the state of Yugoslavia, one community that was victimised was the Muslim population in Bosnia. Following the 1980 death of its dictator, Josip Broz ('Tito'), the Communist Party's grip on power and the country's unity both weakened. Each of the regions that made up the Yugoslav Federation held multiparty elections in 1990. A sequence of conflicts and wars began. Muslims in Britain became aware of the crisis and noticed the initial lack of a western response. As with their lobbying against the Gulf War, the lobbying in favour of intervention to defend Bosnian Muslims was ineffective at first. This led to the feeling that the British state took no account of Muslim views.

During the 1990s, immigration continued to be a social and economic reality, but the pattern changed. Governments of the previous two decades had largely been debating the arrival of immigrants of African and South-Asian origins or descent. With the 1992 creation of a European Union in the Maastricht Treaty, the amount of migration between European countries rose significantly and Britain received gradually increasing numbers of European immigrants. From this point the controversy progressively became associated with the latter, as people with African or Asian ancestry became more widely accepted into British society.

Cross-reference **Chapter 5** *The Maastricht Treaty*

Taking it further

Class discussion: over time, the gender balance in higher education became more equal. In addition, the numbers of students from ethnic minorities began to match their percentages in society as a whole. Meanwhile, the social-class balance proved harder to modify: the women who went to university – and, within that, the women who went to Oxbridge – were from the same social classes as the men they sat next to in lectures. Why do you think that is?

ACTIVITY 5.11

List some of the ways in which society changed in the period between 1979 and 1997. What connections do you notice between the different changes? Consider the ways in which they challenge the structures of thought and action of political parties, trade unions and single-issue membership groups. To what extent do you think these were able to adapt to the changed social-reform agenda?

Foreign affairs

Relations with Europe

Studies of the Major government are not slow in pointing to its rapid ditching of the poll tax, as a way of abandoning an unpopular Thatcherite policy. In fact, the about-face on the EEC was just as marked. Major's early declaration was that, 'My aim for

Britain in the Community can be simply stated: I want us to be where we belong, at the very heart of Europe, working with our partners in building our future'.[24]

Key terms

Schengen Agreement: created in 1985 by five of the then ten members of the EEC. Britain was one of those that remained outside. The intention was to remove border checks to make trade and travel easier.

genocide: the attempt to kill an entire ethnic group, rather than individuals, specifically because of their ethnicity.

ethnic cleansing: the attempt to remove all members of an ethnic group from a territory, whether by exiling or murdering them.

Maastricht Treaty

EEC leaders signed a treaty in the Dutch city of Maastricht. Along with the earlier **Schengen Agreement**, the intention was to build on the 1986 Single European Act to make the EEC more efficient.

The treaty contained a series of exemptions specifically for the UK, allowing the country to stay outside some of the new developments. It thus allowed the UK not to accept:

1. **Monetary Union**: plans were being laid for the EEC to have a currency that would replace national currencies and be legal tender throughout the union. This would improve the ease of trade, but would reduce the ability of national governments to direct their own economic policy.
2. **Social Chapter**: this standardised employment legislation – including pay, health and safety, and workers' rights – across the EEC in ways that the Conservatives judged to be too interventionist, even though much of it would, in fact, have been familiar to employers. (It was later signed by a Labour government in 1997.)

Although there were steps towards greater integration of member states, British negotiators (including Major) had ensured there was no commitment to a federal European superstate, no move beyond the aspirational phrase 'ever closer union' from the 1957 Treaty of Rome.

The treaty was signed in February 1992, shortly before the British general election. Controversial in the UK, it also attracted considerable opposition in other countries. It was at first rejected by a referendum in Denmark (this formed the background to the financial turbulence which in turn led to the UK being forced out of the ERM on Black Wednesday).

Interventions in the Balkans

Following Tito's death in 1980, the internal strains within Yugoslavia began to show. The ethnic Albanian Muslim majority in Kosovo began to demand that their province be treated as a member republic, not as a part of Serbia, which had overall an Orthodox Christian majority. The leader of Serbia, Slobodan Milošović, demanded greater powers for Serbia, the largest and most populous of the six republics. Slovenia and Croatia elected governments with mandates to demand greater autonomy. Serbs in Croatia began to feel their position left them vulnerable – part of a majority in a united Yugoslavia, they were in danger of being a minority in a more autonomous or independent Croatia.

How should other countries react? The Americans decided that the Bosnian Serbs, in alliance with the Serbian government and army, were pursuing a policy of **genocide** (known in the Yugoslav context as **ethnic cleansing**). The intention was to kill, or drive out, non-Serbs from those areas in which Serbs were a majority, so that those parts of Bosnia could secede and join an enlarged Serbia. This was a view in which former Conservative Party leader Margaret Thatcher, Liberal Party leader Paddy Ashdown and former Labour Party leader Michael Foot agreed and with which Tony Blair would concur when he led Labour and Britain.

Figure 5.14: The six republics and the autonomous provinces of Yugoslavia until 1980.

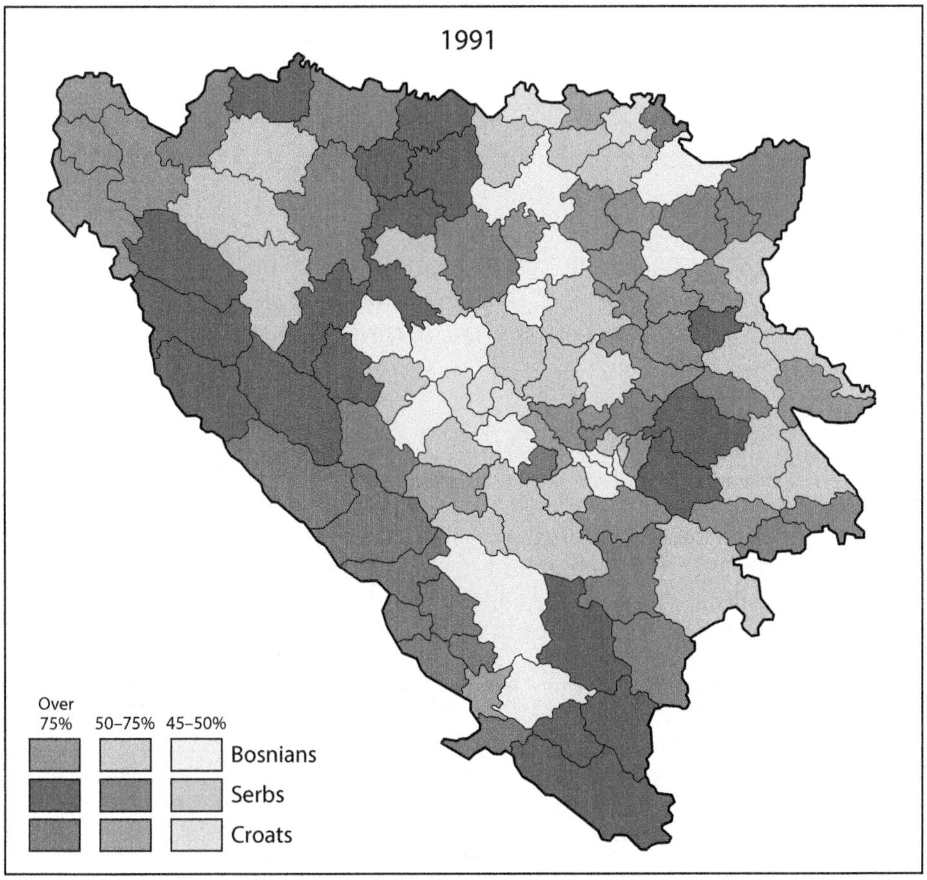

Figure 5.15: Ethnic distribution in Bosnia-Herzegovina before the war (1991). Maps easily show national borders, but these are often deceptive: different ethnic groups rarely lie neatly on different sides of any border, because people travel for reasons of family and employment. Notice the complexity in the attempts to show where Bosnia's Orthodox Christian ethnic Serbs, Roman Catholic ethnic Croats and Bosniak Muslims lived.

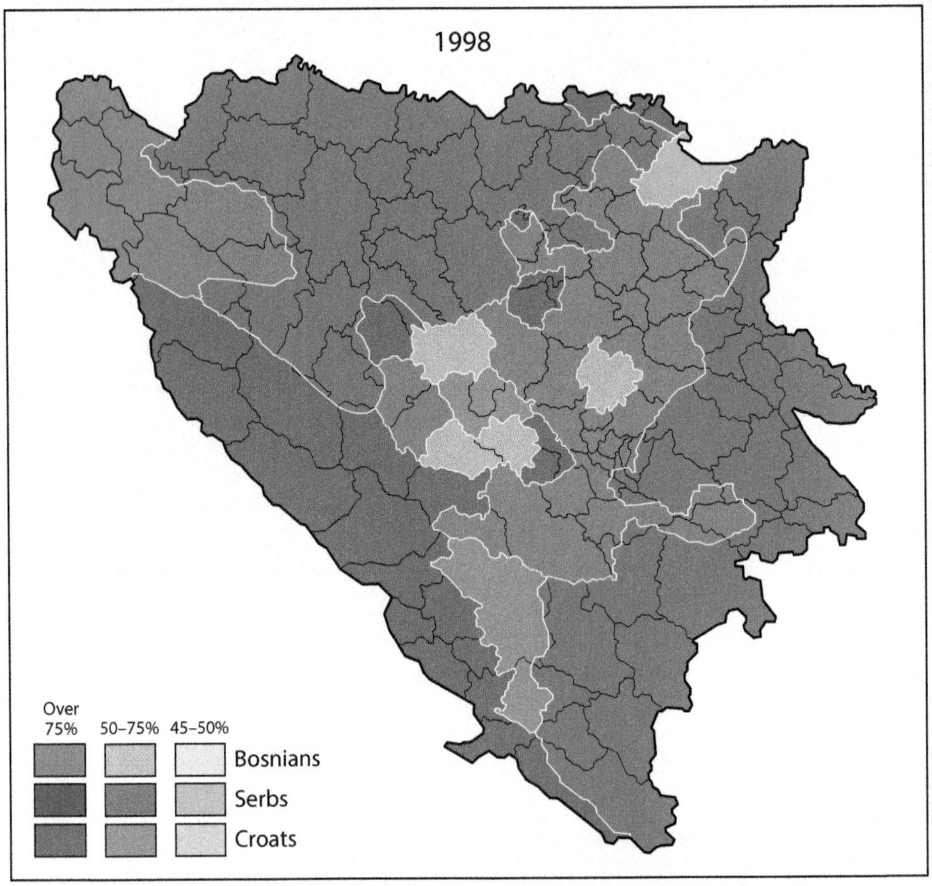

Figure 5.16: Ethnic distribution in Bosnia-Herzegovina after the war and ethnic cleansing (1998).

However, other countries watched developments with no intention of intervening in what were regarded as internal affairs. The United Nations began by regarding the conflicts as internal problems, something the UN stays out of. It took until 1999 for the UN to move to a different analysis.

Major and Hurd were agreed in staying out, despite the fact that the reports coming from the region made it clear that murderous crimes were being committed, of a kind little-seen in Europe since the Second World War.

American President, George H.W. Bush (father of a later President, George W. Bush) and his successor from 1993, Bill Clinton, worked to create an international intervention in Bosnia's crisis. Britain opposed the project. The killing took place while British negotiators worked to avoid involvement.

Two things happened to change this. First, central negotiations about the future of Yugoslavia were overtaken by regional decisions:

- 1991: Croatia and Slovenia declare their independence, followed by Macedonia
- 1992: Bosnia-Herzegovina declares independence; Yugoslavia reconstitutes itself out of Serbia (still including Kosovo) and Montenegro.

Four of the republics that had made up Yugoslavia were now recognised as independent states.

Second, a war that broke out in Bosnia involved Serbian and Croatian forces. This was something in which other countries and the UN could legitimately interest themselves. News that Bosnians had been murdered in large numbers by Serb forces was a major cause of a NATO bombing campaign that began in 1995, targeting Bosnian Serb forces.

The intention was to prevent the country being partitioned, with Serbia annexing Serb-majority areas to create a 'Greater Serbia'. A peacekeeping force took up its position in 1995–96, to enforce the Dayton Agreement – a peace settlement to which John Major was a signatory, alongside US, French, German and Russian leaders.

Contribution and attitude to the end of the Cold War

Margaret Thatcher became an internationally known figure, with a well-documented working relationship with the US Presidents Reagan and George H. W. Bush, and with Soviet leader Gorbachev. Major never achieved the same status, but he did have a solid working relationship with first Bush, then Clinton and with several European leaders.

Under both leaders, Britain worked closely with the United States. The 1979 deployment of Cruise and Pershing II nuclear missiles lay behind the increasing support for CND in the 1980s.

Cross-reference Chapter 4 *Extra-Parliamentary opposition*

However, the gap opening up between NATO and the **Warsaw Pact** was an economic one, far more than one of **matériel**. As western countries grew more prosperous, the economic problems in the Soviet Union and its client states worsened. It became clear that they were finding the Cold War unaffordable.

Margaret Thatcher's election in 1979 and Reagan's in 1981 had been preceded by another significant election – that of a Polish cardinal as Pope John Paul II in 1978. A pope from a Warsaw Pact country changed the political dynamic in Europe and significantly destabilised a strongly Catholic Poland.

Finally, the advent of Gorbachev and his attempted reforms made the USSR less threatening, but also hastened the collapse of the politico-military Warsaw Pact and then of the Soviet Union itself. The fact that Thatcher had shown herself willing to work with Gorbachev may have helped him be appointed Soviet leader.

Biographies of Thatcher emphasise her inexperience of foreign affairs on entering 10 Downing Street. In John Major's autobiography, he admits that, 'Of all the jobs in government, the Foreign Office was the one ... for which I was least prepared'.[25] He was only in that post for three months before becoming Chancellor of the Exchequer. This was unfortunate, given the fact that the international situation was in transition.

In November 1989, a year before Major came to power, the **Berlin Wall** had been torn down. During his first year in office, the Warsaw Pact was ended and then the USSR was formally dissolved. These were extraordinary, and largely unforeseen, developments. Richard Vinen points out that 'the 1979 election did not bring any sharp change in policy, which continued to revolve around nuclear weapons, NATO membership and the American alliance'.[26] The same is true of the elections that followed.

George H. W. Bush dubbed the situation the 'new world order'. Major's Foreign Secretary Hurd disagreed, saying in April 1994 that, 'We do not have a new world order. We have a traditional set of world disorders, and we are trying, case by case, and institution by institution, to equip ourselves to deal more adequately with these disorders'.[27]

Margaret Thatcher had been a Cold Warrior, standing with USA's Ronald Reagan. By contrast, John Major found himself as Britain's first post-Cold War Prime Minister. All foreign and military affairs had, for decades, been discussed with reference to the possible response of the Soviet Union. With no Warsaw Pact, the Gulf War, which Major

Key terms

Warsaw Pact: a military alliance comprising the USSR and several countries in eastern and central Europe, founded following the Second World War to counter the threat from NATO and maintain Soviet-sponsored governments in power in several countries where they had no popular mandate.

matériel: French word used in English to mean military hardware.

Berlin Wall: Cold War structure dividing East from West Berlin, built under USSR orders in 1961 and pulled down in 1989.

inherited, and the break-up of Yugoslavia had no Cold War dimension (the need to bear in mind Russian sensibilities was not in the same league).

ACTIVITY 5.12

1. Study the timeline. Events have been put into separate columns: which would you move to a different column and why?
2. Which developments have been omitted from the table that you think should be included? Explain why.

Timeline 1980–97

Government and politics	Economics	Date	Society	Foreign affairs
		1980-85	Riots in British cities	
		1985	Norman Tebbit's attack on the permissive society	
January: Michael Heseltine resigns from government over 'Westland affair'		1986		
	Coal Industry Act (1)	1987		
		1988	*Satanic Verses* (Salman Rushdie) affair begins	
		1989		November: Berlin Wall torn down
Lawson resigns as Chancellor		1989		
October: Howe resigns 22 November: Thatcher resigns John Major elected Conservative Party leader and Prime Minister	Britain joins the Exchange Rate Mechanism (ERM)	1990		Schengen Agreement August: start of Gulf War
		1990–91		Gulf War
7 February: IRA mortar attack on 10 Downing Street	March: council tax introduced to replace poll tax	1991		February: end of Gulf War Croatia and Slovenia declare their independence, followed by Macedonia
Conservative victory in British general election 16 September: Lamont resigns as Chancellor, replaced by Kenneth Clarke July: John Smith appointed Labour leader	Rapid growth of negative equity in housing market 16 September: 'Black Wednesday' c. 900 000 in negative equity by end of the year	1992		Maastricht Treaty signed Bosnia-Herzegovina independence Yugoslavia reconstitutes itself out of Serbia (still including Kosovo) and Montenegro Bill Clinton elected American president (took office in 1993)

Government and politics	Economics	Date	Society	Foreign affairs
John Major and the Irish Taoiseach Albert Reynolds issue Downing Street Declaration John Major tells Conservative Party conference it's 'time to get back to basics'		1993	Introduction of the National Lottery Stephen Lawrence murdered Home Secretary Michael Howard to Conservative Party conference: 'prison works'	
May: Labour leader John Smith dies July: Tony Blair appointed Labour leader	Coal Industry Act (2)	1994	Teacher Training Agency created	
June: John Major resigns as party leader, then re-elected		1995		NATO bombing campaign targets Bosnian Serb forces
		1997	National Curriculum introduced	

Further reading

John Major's *Autobiography* (HarperCollins 1999) is engagingly written and easy. It is complemented by Anthony Seldon's biography. Several books (e.g. Tiratsoo (ed.), *From Blitz to Blair*) have little to say about the Major government, treating it as a footnote to Thatcherism and leaving distinctions and differences unexamined. Robert Blake's *The Conservative Party from Peel to Major* has more detail, usefully lining up the key events and personalities, but offers little analysis. Peter Clarke's *Hope and Glory* continues to be balanced, fair minded and concise. Vernon Bogdanor's Gresham College lectures on politics are clear, detailed and balanced. Available at http://www.gresham.ac.uk/lectures-and-events/leadership-and-change-prime-ministers-in-the-post-war-world-winston-churchill. It includes lectures on all post-war Prime Ministers, including Thatcher, Major and Blair.

Practice essay questions

1. 'Margaret Thatcher was forced to resign as Prime Minister and Conservative Party leader in 1990 by domestic issues, not foreign affairs.' Assess the validity of this view.
2. To what extent did the change of Conservative party leader and prime minister, from Margaret Thatcher to John Major, represent a change of political direction?
3. To what extent was Tony Blair responsible for the Labour victory in the 1997 British general election?
4. To what extent did relations with Europe dominate British politics from the mid-1980s to the mid-1990s?
5. With reference to the sources and your understanding of the historical context, assess the value of these three sources to a historian studying the 1997 British general election.

Source A

Source: John Major, address to 1993 Conservative Party Conference in Blackpool, 8 October 1993

In housing, in the '50s and '60s, we pulled down the terraces, destroyed whole communities and replaced them with tower blocks and we built walkways that have become rat runs for muggers … In our schools we did away with traditional subjects – grammar, spelling, tables – and also with the old ways of teaching them. Fashionable, but wrong. Some said the family was out of date, far better rely on the council and social workers than family and friends. I passionately believe that was wrong.

Others told us that every criminal needed treatment, not punishment. Criminal behaviour was society's fault, not the individual's. Fashionable, but wrong, wrong, wrong …

It is time … to get back to basics, to self-discipline and respect for the law, to consideration for others, to accepting a responsibility for yourself and your family and not shuffling off on other people and the state.

Source B

Source: Tony Blair on arriving at 10 Downing Street, 2 May 1997

Today we have set objectives for new Labour Government – a world class education system. Education is not the privilege of the few but the right of the many.

We will work in partnership with business to create the dynamic economy, the competitive economy of the future. The one that can meet the challenges of an entirely new century and new age …

And it shall be a government, too, that gives this country strength and confidence in leadership both at home and abroad, particularly in respect of Europe.

It shall be a government rooted in strong values, the values of justice and progress and community, the values that have guided me all my political life. But a government ready with the courage to embrace the new ideas necessary to make those values live again for today's world — a government of practical measures in pursuit of noble causes.

Source C

Source: Liberal Democrat 1997 British General Election Manifesto

We are in politics not just to manage things better, but to make things happen. To build a more prosperous, fair and open society. We believe in the market economy as the best way to deliver prosperity and distribute economic benefits. But we recognise that market mechanisms on their own are not enough; that the private sector alone cannot ensure that there are good services for everyone, or promote employment opportunities, or tackle economic inequality, or protect the environment for future generations.

We believe in a society in which every citizen shares rights and responsibilities. But, we recognise that a strong country is built from the bottom, not the top; that conformity quickly becomes the enemy of diversity. And that the imposition of social blueprints leads to authoritarian centralised government. Liberal Democrats believe that power and opportunity, like wealth, should be widely spread.

Chapter summary

At the end of this chapter you should be able to take account of the views of different historians of this period of British history, and form your own views regarding:

- the similarities and differences between Thatcher's and Major's brands of Conservatism
- political challenges facing governments in the 1980s and 1990s, including sleaze and scandals
- the causes, extent and nature of the divisions in British political parties, for example, nuclear weapons and the Cold War and the EEC/EC
- economic crises, including 'Black Wednesday' and its impact
- the developing situation in Northern Ireland and the attempts of different governments to find a way out of the continuing violence
- the social-liberal, social-conservative and anti-establishment responses changes in society.

Endnotes

[1] Hansard, House of Commons, 6th series, vol. 180, col. 464.

[2] Blake R. *Conservative Party from Peel to Major*. London: Heinemann; 1997. p. 384.

[3] Major J. *The Autobiography*. London: HarperCollins; 1999. p. 200.

[4] Major J. *The Autobiography*. London: HarperCollins; 1999. p. 200–1.

[5] Lawson N. *The View from No 11: Memoirs of a Tory Radical*. London: Bantam; 1992. p. 480.

[6] Blake R. *Conservative Party from Peel to Major*. London: Heinemann; 1997. p. 402.

[7] Major J. *The Autobiography*. London: HarperCollins; 1999. p. 398.

[8] Stuart B. *The Conservative Party since 1945*. Manchester: Manchester University Press; 1998. p. 133.

[9] George Boyce. *Bigots in Bowler Hats? Unionism since the Downing Street Declaration 1993–95*. In: O'Day A. (ed.) *Political Violence in Northern Ireland: Conflict and Conflict Resolution*. Westport, USA: Praeger; 1997. p. 53, 55.

[10] Blake R. *Conservative Party from Peel to Major*. London: Heinemann; 1997. p. 371.

[11] Mr Major's Speech to the Conservative Group for Europe http://www.johnmajor.co.uk/page1086.html. Major discusses the speech, this passage, the media response to it and the wider context in Major J. *The Autobiography*. London: HarperCollins; 1999. p. 376.

[12] Harrison B. *The Transformation of British Politics 1860-1995*. Oxford: Oxford University Press; 1996. p. 241.

[13] Blake R. *Conservative Party from Peel to Major*. London: Heinemann; 1997. p. 396.

[14] Seldon A. *Blair*. London: Free Press; 2004. p. 247.

[15] *The Guardian*, 1989 December 19.

[16] Seldon A. *Blair*. London: Free Press; 2004. p. 216.

[17] Shaw E. *The Labour Party since 1945*. Oxford: Blackwell; 1996. p. 199.

[18] Shaw E. *The Labour Party since 1945*. Oxford: Blackwell; 1996. p. 451.

[19] Shaw E. *The Labour Party since 1945*. Oxford: Blackwell; 1996. p. 28.

[20] Owen D. *Time to Declare*. London: Michael Joseph; 1991. p. 599.

[21] Tebbit N. Back to the old traditional values. *The Guardian Weekly*, 1985 November 24.

[22] *World in Action* [television broadcast]. Granada Television; 1978 January 30. Interview with Margaret Thatcher.

[23] Major J. *The Autobiography*. London: HarperCollins; 1999. p. 269.

[24] Forman FN, Baldwin NDJ. *Mastering British Politics*. London: Palgrave Macmillan; 2007. p. 112.

[25] Major J. *The Autobiography*. London: HarperCollins; 1999. p. 111.

[26] Vinen R. *Thatcherism and the Cold War*. In: Jackson B. and Saunders R. (eds.) *Making Thatcher's Britain*. Cambridge: Cambridge University Press; 2012. p. 201.

[27] Hansard, House of Commons, 1994 April 25, col 21.

6 The Era of New Labour, 1997–2007

In this section, we will examine the New Labour era, dominated by the personality and ideology of Tony Blair and look at the troubles of the Conservatives, out of power for longer than they had been for quite some time. Peace came to Northern Ireland, and there were considerable changes in society and in Britain's influence in world affairs. We will look into:

- the Labour governments: Blair as leader, character and ideology; constitutional change; domestic policies; Brown and economic policy; Northern Ireland and the Good Friday Agreement
- the Conservative Party: leaders and reason for divisions; reason for electoral failures in 2001 and 2005
- social issues: workers, women and youth; the extent to which Britain had become a multicultural society
- foreign affairs: attitudes to Europe; the 'special relationship' with USA; military interventions and the 'war on terror'; Britain's position in the world by 2007.

The Labour governments

Blair as leader, character and ideology

Electoral history

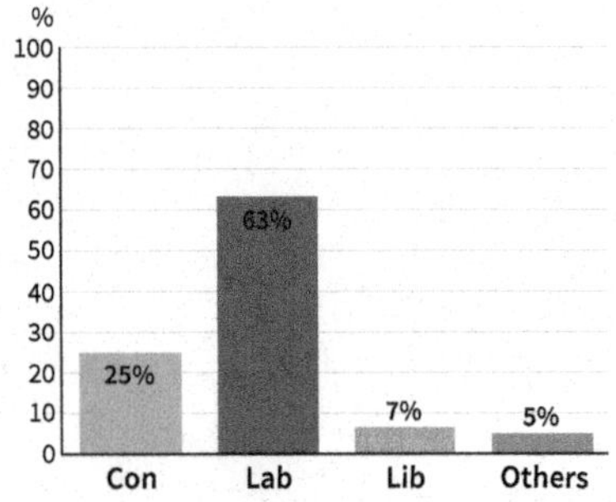

Figure 6.1: Seats in the House of Commons won in the 1997 British general election; percentages have been adjusted to the nearest whole number. Ulster Unionist figures are listed as 'Others'.

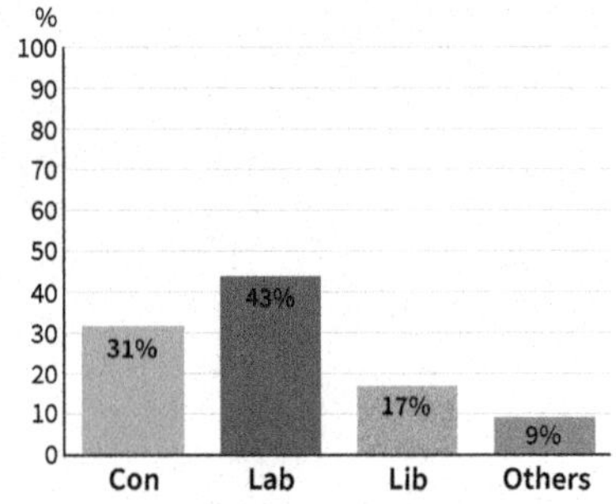

Figure 6.2: Votes won in the 1997 British general election; percentages have been adjusted to the nearest whole number. Ulster Unionist figures are listed as 'Others'.

In electoral terms Blair's performance as Labour leader is undeniably impressive. The party had never before succeeded in holding office for two successive full parliamentary terms. Indeed, prior to 1997 Labour had lost four general elections in a row. In 1983 (the year the youthful Blair was first elected to parliament) the party, standing on a manifesto described by one insider as the 'longest suicide note in history', had only narrowly held on to second place, ahead of the Alliance, in its share of the overall vote (see Figure 4.4). Its fourth loss in 1992 left it relatively close to the winning Conservatives in terms of Parliamentary seats, but still, in the eyes of many commentators, confined to the ranks of permanent opposition (see Figure 5.4). Yet Blair delivered Labour no less than three full terms in power, two of them following landslide election victories and the third on a perfectly comfortable majority. In 1997 the Labour Party ended up 13 percentage points ahead of the Conservatives and boasting an overall Commons majority of 179 seats.

It was victory on a scale even Blair found difficult to comprehend. Until the results were declared he retained contingency plans for a coalition with the Liberal Democrats, designed to ensure an anti-Conservative majority. In 2001 it was logical to expect the Conservatives to enjoy some recovery in popular esteem. Yet this was hard to discern. The result was almost a carbon copy of 1997. Labour's Commons majority was reduced only marginally. Finally, in 2005 Blair secured a record-breaking third victory on a reduced, but still very respectable, overall majority of 66. Blair served as Prime Minister for two and a half of Labour's three terms, before setting his own retirement date – itself a relatively rare achievement. During his premiership he outlasted four Tory leaders.

By any criteria this is a formidable record of achievement on the part of New Labour and Blair personally. However, its impact relies on the selective use of facts and statistics. Strikingly, even in 1997 Labour's share of the vote was lower than at any general election between 1945 and 1966, including the three successive losses of the 1950s (see Figures 1.2–1.7). Its total fell by 2.4 percentage points between 1997 and 2001, a bigger drop than any experienced by the Conservatives between 1979 and 1992 (see Figures 4.2, 4.5, 4.7 and 5.5). Labour's 2005 victory was on a lower overall vote than had been secured by any previous majority administration.

Indeed, the New Labour era witnessed a precipitous decline in British electoral participation. Average voter turnout at post-war elections had been around 75%. This dropped to just 59% in 2001 and 61% in 2005. If public confidence in New Labour declined sharply over its period in office, it was fortunate that the electorate showed a comparable lack of faith in the Conservative opposition. The vagaries of the country's voting system benefited Labour, by magnifying the scale of its electoral triumphs. Even so, elections in May 2007 – just months before Blair's resignation – saw Labour fall below the SNP in the contest for control of the Scottish parliament, secure its lowest share of the Welsh vote for almost 90 years and have fewer councillors and councils in England than at any time since the early 1970s. Blair presided over a marked decline in the number of Labour voters (and of party members). The party he handed over to Gordon Brown in 2007 was in a weaker position than the party he had inherited from John Smith, 13 years earlier. His personal popularity also fell sharply. At the time of Diana, Princess of Wales's death, in September 1997, Blair's approval rating stood at over 90%, making him the most popular Prime Minister since records began. Ten years later he was widely reviled, seen (even by many Labour supporters) as untrustworthy and dishonest. His successor and the candidates for the party's deputy leadership, vacated by John Prescott, all spoke of the need now to restore trust in government. In the words of a leading authority on electoral politics, 'Blair's electoral record combines record-breaking success with dramatic decline'.[1]

Nor is it clear that Labour's return to power in 1997 was entirely a function of New Labour's development into a highly effective election-winning machine. The Conservatives never recovered from the events of 'Black Wednesday' in 1992. Their undignified exit from the European Exchange Rate Mechanism (ERM) deprived them of their most important electoral asset – a reputation for economic competence. Before Blair was even elected leader in 1994, Labour had recorded a 23% lead in the opinion polls. There was a growing feeling, even without the Blair revolution, that the Tories had outstayed their welcome and that it was time for a change.

Character and ideology

The new Prime Minister enjoyed wide appeal. Happily married and with a young family, he seemed unlike the normal run of politicians and more someone to whom the average voter could relate. Here, it appeared, was a relatively young and relatively ordinary leader, who understood the concerns of and spoke the same language as, the man or woman in the street. When, in the first year of his premiership, Blair's whiter-than-white image was challenged by the Ecclestone affair – where suspicion arose that the boss of Formula One motor racing had secured an exemption from a forthcoming ban on tobacco advertising, in return for a donation to the Labour Party – the Prime Minister subjected himself to a television interview by the BBC's John Humphrys. Blair insisted that he would never do 'anything improper'. Indeed, he 'never had. I think most people who have dealt with me think I am a pretty straight sort of guy'.[2] The majority of the population appeared to believe him. Blair's ratings in the opinion polls remained high and the government enjoyed an unusually long 'honeymoon period'. However, over time and perhaps inevitably, the Prime Minister's image did tarnish. It was always in part the well-choreographed product of a highly professional public relations machine. After ten years in office and buffeted by the sort of events that had befallen every previous premier, it was only natural that far fewer electors were seduced by Blair's public image – open-necked shirt, tea mug in hand, estuary English. He was, after all, the product of a distinguished public school and Oxford University. It was his Conservative predecessor, John Major, and not he who had risen from a genuinely humble background.

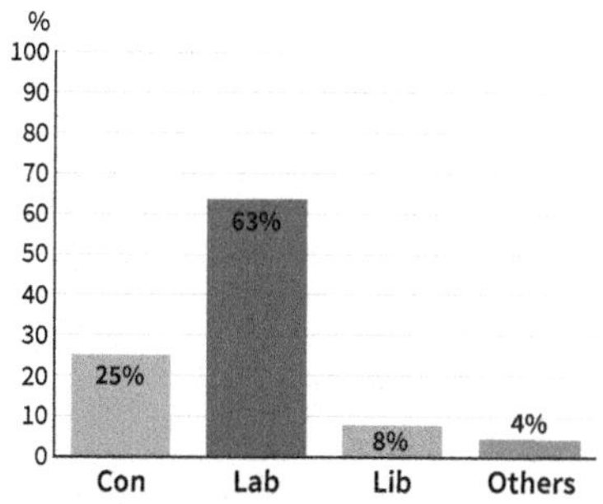

Figure 6.3: Seats in the House of Commons won in the 2001 British general election; percentages have been adjusted to the nearest whole number. Ulster Unionist figures are listed as 'Others'.

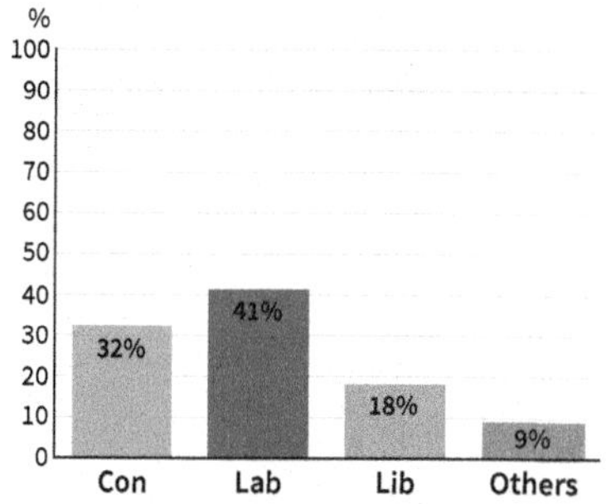

Figure 6.4: Votes won in the 2001 British general election; percentages have been adjusted to the nearest whole number. Ulster Unionist figures are listed as 'Others'.

Developing an ideology in opposition was one thing; deploying it in government quite another. Blair personally clung tenaciously to the mantra of 'New Labour', but found that practical politics, the 'art of the possible', required both compromise and pragmatism, as well as conviction. Over time, it probably became harder, not easier, to define what New Labour was all about. Some critics on the left suggested that the Prime Minister's philosophy was little more than a disguised form of Conservatism – a critique which did less than justice to a genuinely progressive strand in Blair's thinking. Certainly, the impact of New Labour in government was unlike the experience of any previous Labour administration. However, the difficulty of establishing a clear ideology is well illustrated in the fate of the so-called 'Third Way'.

The Third Way

In a 1998 pamphlet on the Third Way Blair defined the four values essential for a 'just society' as 'equal worth, opportunity for all, responsibility and community'.[3] Peter Riddell complained that the Third Way was infused with 'grand but often vague theories' and 'overreached itself by exaggerating its novelty and coherence'.[4]

Sir Christopher Meyer, Britain's ambassador in Washington, obliged to attend a Third Way seminar, was blunt: 'As I sat there, fighting off sleep in the conspicuous front row, it became ever clearer that the Third Way was less a coherent philosophy of government, more a tactic for election winning: how to hold your base and reach out to the centre ground at the same time. It is as old as the hills'.[5] Third Way language

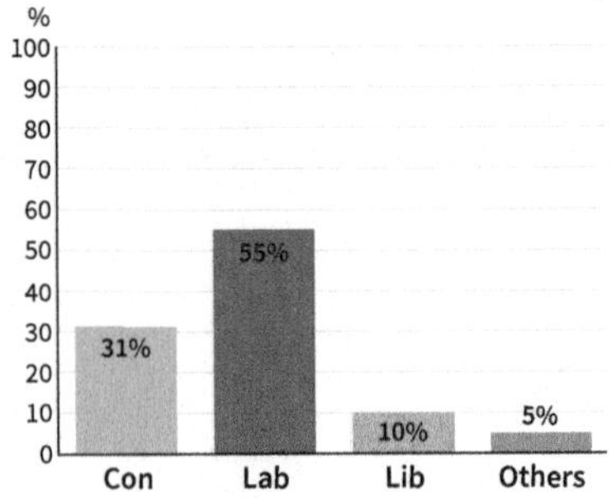

Figure 6.5: Seats in the House of Commons won in the 2005 British general election; percentages have been adjusted to the nearest whole number. Ulster Unionist figures are listed as 'Others'.

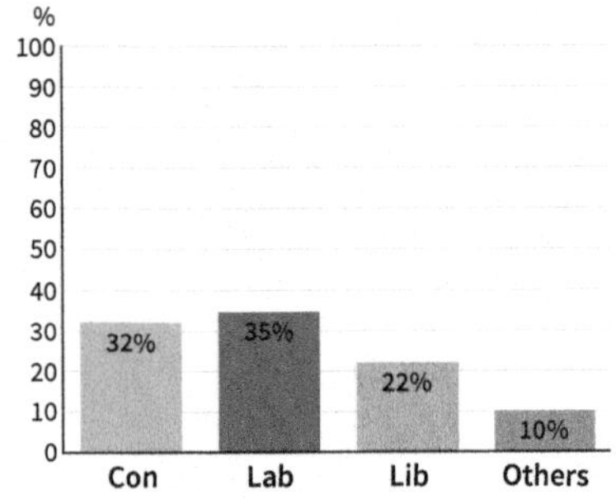

Figure 6.6: Votes won in the 2005 British general election; percentages have been adjusted to the nearest whole number. Ulster Unionist figures are listed as 'Others'.

was largely dropped after New Labour's first term in office. 'Whatever happened to the Third Way?' pondered Robin Cook in August 2001.[6]

Constitutional change

It was New Labour's declared intention to modernise the way Britain is governed. After the supposed (and sometimes actual) sleaze of the Major years, it was time for a thorough cleansing of the constitutional stables. The party's 1997 manifesto promised:

- referendums on Scottish and Welsh devolution and English regional government
- the election of mayors for London and other major cities
- hereditary peers would lose their right to vote in the House of Lords
- the European Convention on Human Rights (ECHR) would be incorporated into British law
- a referendum on electoral reform and legislation to ensure freedom of information and 'open' government.

It amounted to a substantial and ambitious reform programme. Much, but not all, of this was honoured and the nature of British government had changed substantially after Blair's ten years in power. Overall, however, critics identified a pattern of piecemeal and sometimes incoherent reform and a legacy of unfinished business.

Devolution

Devolution for Scotland and Wales was part of the unfinished business of Old Labour. The Callaghan government had tried and failed to introduce it in the late 1970s. Blair felt little personal enthusiasm, telling *The Scotsman*'s political correspondent during the 1997 election that 'sovereignty rests with me as an English MP and that's the way it will stay'.[7] Nonetheless, he accepted that devolution should be an early part of New Labour's legislative programme. Referendums were held in Scotland and Wales in September 1997. That in Wales – for an Assembly without tax-raising powers and able to enact secondary, but not primary, legislation – passed by the narrowest of margins. In Scotland, by contrast, the result was clear-cut. Nearly three-quarters of those voting said 'yes' to a Scottish parliament and 63.5% endorsed tax-raising powers. The Scottish parliament and the Welsh Assembly were duly created in 1998, coming into existence the following year.

Provisions were included which Blair was disinclined to extend to the Westminster parliament. Both new bodies had fixed terms of four years and were elected on a proportional voting system (PR). In the Scottish case this last stipulation was specifically designed to prevent the SNP (Scottish National Party) declaring a mandate for independence, on the basis of a parliamentary majority secured under a first-past-the-post system. In fact, the SNP, even under PR, defied this expectation and recorded an outright victory as early as 2011. Devolution was expected to kill off the growing Scottish desire for independence, but patently failed to do so, even though the **Barnett Formula** enabled Scotland to continue to enjoy a favourable financial settlement from the British Exchequer. New Labour took its eye off the political ball in Scotland, particularly after the death in 2000 of Donald Dewar – a leading architect of the devolution settlement and Labour's choice as First Minister in the Scottish parliament. The Westminster government contained a generous complement of Scots and it was striking that most of the party's leading lights chose to pursue their careers in London, rather than Edinburgh. After Dewar's death a complacent Scottish Labour Party soon lost the political initiative to the SNP. The Independence Referendum of 2014 showed that, while a clear majority of Scots still supports the Union, the issue of independence has not gone away. Indeed, the overwhelming success of the SNP in the 2015 British general election suggested that the long-term future of the United Kingdom remains in doubt.

In Wales, under devolution, Labour remained the dominant force. Independence for Wales remains a minority and, for the foreseeable future, unrealistic aspiration.

Key terms

Barnett Formula: a system devised in 1978 by Joel Barnett, Labour Chief Secretary to the Treasury 1974–79, to adjust funding to Scotland, Wales and Northern Ireland when changes are made to UK funding. Its practical effect is to ensure that spending per head is higher in Scotland than in England.

Even so, in areas of administration devolved to it, such as health and education, the Assembly's performance has sometimes attracted unflattering comparisons with the English experience. Blair personally seemed reluctant to accept the implications of devolution and used his influence to impose Alun Michael as First Minister, contrary to the Welsh party's wishes. Michael, however, resigned in 2000 rather than face a vote of 'no confidence' inside the Assembly.

The creation of devolved Scottish and Welsh administrations – particularly the former, given its more far-reaching powers – had obvious knock-on consequences for the governance of England. Now that Westminster MPs had lost the power to decide upon devolved issues as they affected Scotland, was it constitutionally acceptable that Scottish Westminster MPs could still vote upon the equivalent English issues? Furthermore, given Labour's traditional dominance in Scottish politics, it was possible that a future Labour UK government might only be able to legislate on English health and education issues courtesy of a parliamentary majority created by Scottish MPs. Herein lay the essence of the 'West Lothian Question', named after Tam Dalyell, the long-serving MP for West Lothian, who had articulated the problem while trenchantly opposing devolution.

New Labour may have hoped to resolve the 'English Question' resulting from its devolution strategy by establishing elected regional assemblies. The Deputy Prime Minister, John Prescott, published a white paper (2002) proposing a series of local referendums – beginning in those areas where the demand for devolution was apparently greatest. In practice only one was held, in north-east England, in 2004. This produced an overwhelming 78% vote against setting up a regional assembly. Prescott rapidly conceded that his policy was dead in the water. Plans for further referendums were abandoned. New Labour was more successful with proposals for elected mayors. Following a positive referendum, the Greater London Authority Act (1999) created the office of elected mayor and a 25-member assembly. Again, however, matters did not proceed quite as New Labour wished. In the resulting mayoral election, the decidedly Old Labour Ken Livingstone emerged victorious as an independent over the official Labour candidate. Livingstone was subsequently readmitted to the Labour Party and re-elected under his new colours in 2004. Elsewhere in the country most large councils rejected the mayoral option. Where contests went ahead, the voters' response offered little evidence of widespread popular endorsement of Labour's plans.

Electoral reform

Blair had to give consideration to the question of electoral reform from the very beginning of his party leadership. He was, by then, already exploring with Paddy Ashdown, leader of the Liberal Democrats, the possibility, not only of short-term electoral cooperation to defeat the Conservatives, but also the altogether more problematic issue of political realignment. Here, perhaps, was further evidence that Blair's roots were less firmly grounded in the Labour movement than he sometimes proclaimed. For the Liberal Democrats, some movement on PR was a prerequisite. Blair, however, repeatedly declared himself unconvinced by the argument. Nonetheless, in 1996, the two men asked Robin Cook and Robert Maclennan to lay the groundwork for a stable relationship, by exploring the possibility of cooperation on questions of constitutional reform.

The result of the 1997 general election changed matters decisively. With a 179 seat parliamentary majority, New Labour had no need of support from the Liberal Democrats, still less a formal coalition. Blair now argued that a formal merger of the two parties might be the necessary consequence of a change in the voting system.[8] He at least honoured his manifesto pledge to set up a commission on electoral reform, inviting the former SDP leader, Roy Jenkins, to chair it. In his report, published in October 1998, Jenkins proposed replacing the existing voting system with a scheme known as 'AV-plus'. The majority of MPs would be elected by single-member constituencies, using the **Alternative Vote**. This would retain the widely valued link

ACTIVITY 6.1

Find out more about the powers devolved to Scotland and Wales.

1. Why were there differences in the two countries?
2. Why were certain powers retained by Westminster?

Key terms

Alternative Vote (AV): a non-proportional voting system, whereby each voter indicates preferences on a list of candidates. The second preferences of voters whose first preference was for the eliminated candidate at the bottom of the poll are transferred. The procedure is repeated until one candidate secures at least 50% support.

between voters and their MPs. The remaining 100 or so MPs would be elected by a list system within wide geographical areas, to create a broadly proportional overall outcome. These proposals met with a lukewarm response from the Home Secretary, Jack Straw, apparently endorsed by the Prime Minister. To Lord Jenkins's dismay, no serious attempt was made to take matters further.

Parliament

The unelected House of Lords, in some ways a medieval anachronism, was an obvious target for an incoming administration with a reformist agenda, pledged to modernise Britain's institutions. However, New Labour's immediate programme was limited to removing hereditary peers from the Lords' membership. Bizarrely, an agreement between the new Lord Chancellor, Lord Irvine, and the leader of the Conservative peers, Viscount Cranborne, allowed for the retention of 92 hereditary peers. This deal – struck without the knowledge of the Tory leader, William Hague – understandably earned Cranborne the sack, but formed the basis of the House of Lords Act (1999). Thereafter, the process of reform stalled. A Royal Commission put forward possible options for a partially elected chamber, but progress was slow. This was, not least, because Blair was concerned that the enhanced legitimacy of even a partially elected chamber might challenge the supremacy of the Commons. Votes in both Houses in 2003 failed to produce a Commons majority for any of the proposed options. With Parliament deadlocked on the issue, no further progress was made before Blair stood down as Prime Minister.

	Commentary
Reform of the parliamentary working day at Westminster, from 1997	For the benefit of MPs with childcare duties.
Reforms to political party funding, 2000	Allegations in 2006, nevertheless, of peerages being awarded in return for political donations. Police investigation followed, in which a number of individuals including, unprecedentedly, the Prime Minister, were interviewed, but no charges laid.
Freedom of Information Act (2000)	Gave a right of access, with some exemptions, to information held by public authorities. More restricted than originally intended by the responsible minister, David Clark, whom Blair soon dismissed.
Human Rights Act (1998)	Enabled courts to declare that British public authorities had acted in contravention of the ECHR. Gave rise to a handful of questionable court judgements and a call in some quarters for a specifically British Bill of Rights, but led generally to a broadening and strengthening of the rights of individual citizens.
Constitutional Reform Act (2005)	Created a new Supreme Court to replace the Law Lords sitting in the House of Lords. The Lord Chancellor, whose post the government originally intended to abolish, ceased to preside over the upper chamber and lost his authority over the judiciary to the Lord Chief Justice. The position, later combined with that of Justice Secretary, became more avowedly 'political' and was opened up to members of the Commons for the first time since the 16th century.

Table 6.1: Other constitutional changes.

'Sofa government'

Blair introduced significant informal modifications in the day-to-day style of British government. These involved a substantial increase in the size and influence of the Prime Minister's political office, policy unit and press office. This created something like a Prime Minister's Department, staffed with unelected individuals answerable to Blair alone, in practice bypassing long-standing structures of governmental decision-making. The change began, understandably enough, during Blair's years as opposition leader when he surrounded himself with a small group of like-minded friends and trusted advisers. Perhaps because he had no previous ministerial experience - Blair's administration has been described as the least experienced Labour government since the first one in 1924 - he transferred the new structure to Downing Street.

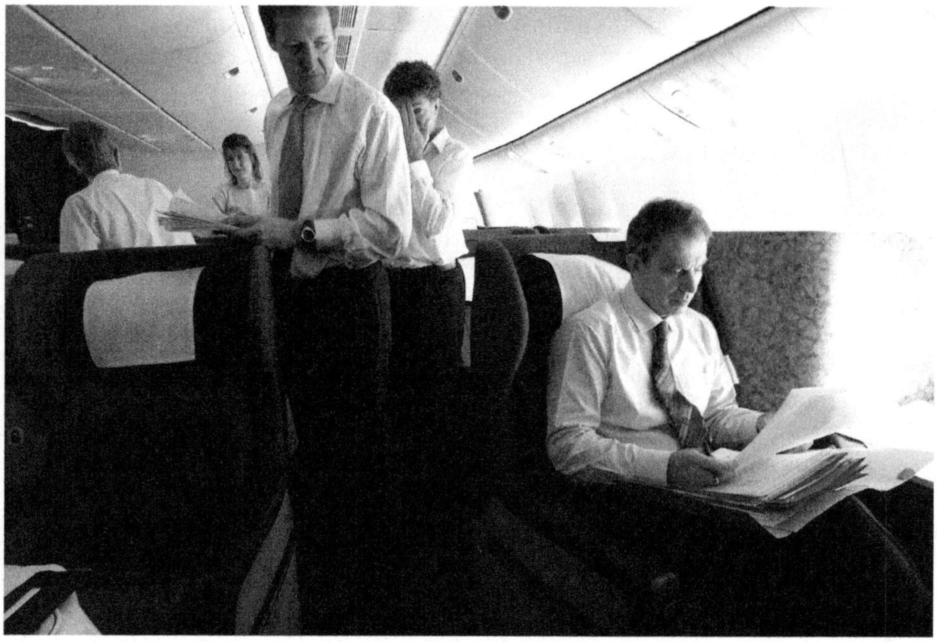

Figure 6.7: Who's in charge? Observers have commented on the lack of deference shown by many unelected officials towards the Prime Minister. Christopher Meyer's abiding memory is of Alastair Campbell 'standing over Blair, on some flight or other, gesticulating forcefully while the PM sat meekly in his seat like a schoolboy under instruction.'[9]

Alastair Campbell, Blair's press spokesman and later Director of Communications and Strategy, was 'arguably the most influential journalist that there has ever been in British politics'[10] and was, in the words of one displaced civil servant, 'more at the centre of the "big picture" than anyone else in the Cabinet'.[11] Jonathan Powell, appointed Chief of Staff in clear imitation of the American Presidential structure, was a central player in the Northern Ireland peace process. Philip Gould held no formal office, but was an important intellectual influence and election strategist. Anji Hunter was 'Special Assistant' and later 'Head of Government Relations'. Sally Morgan was Director of Political and Government Relations, 2001–05, and Andrew Adonis was Senior Adviser on Education and Public Services, 2003–05, before being elevated to the Lords and junior ministerial office.

The formal powers of the British premiership are ill-defined and, since the First World War, many incumbents have sought to extend them as far as they could. Yet it may be suggested that Blair took this process to new heights. As one insider put it, 'there was never any intention of having collective Cabinet government'.[12] It was not that the cabinet ceased to exist. But, recalled Robin Cook, 'Tony does not regard the Cabinet as a place for decisions. Normally he avoids having discussions in Cabinet until decisions are taken and announced to it'.[13] Senior civil servants and cabinet ministers were, understandably, concerned and historians will long debate the new style's impact on the key episodes of Blair's government. Nor did it escape official censure. In his report on the role of intelligence in the Iraq War, Lord Butler pointed an accusing finger at so-called 'sofa government' – ad hoc meetings where important decisions were taken informally, without properly minuted discussions, or adequate paperwork.

Domestic policies

Speaking in 1997, Blair predicted that he would head 'one of the great, radical, reforming governments in our history'.[14] Whether this ambition had been achieved after ten years in power is debatable. Certainly, Blair's first term was a disappointment, not least to himself. Fearful of repeating the mistakes of 1992, New Labour's 1997 manifesto gave an impression of major policy changes, without offering a great deal of detail. This also reflected a failure since 1994 to plan out a domestic policy agenda. In reality, the new government's priority was to win an historic second term. This strategy compelled caution, the avoidance of mistakes and the necessity to establish a reputation for governing competence and responsibility. Furthermore, any genuinely bold initiatives would probably fall foul of the pre-election decision to retain existing Conservative expenditure plans during the government's first two years.

All this was understandable enough. However, given his enormous parliamentary majority, a united and largely subservient party and a favourable economic climate, Blair's best opportunity for genuine radicalism was thereby lost. A second landslide victory in 2001 gave New Labour another chance. The second term certainly saw greatly increased expenditure on public services. However, critics have argued that Blair still failed to give enough long-term thought to his policy objectives. Too many of those around him were focused on immediate approbation in the media, at the expense of strategic policy planning. The perception spread that New Labour was all about 'spin' and presentation, rather than genuine substance. This was unfair, but helped to erode the government's grounding in popular support. In addition, new factors arose to impede its progress. The 9/11 crisis and subsequent wars in Afghanistan and Iraq understandably diverted Blair's priorities. Brown's ambitions to succeed to the premiership increasingly translated into an obstructive lack of cooperation in dealings with the present incumbent. Additionally, it became ever clearer that the thrust of Blair's reforms ran against the grain of traditional Labour values and objectives. Overall, contrary to normal experience and notwithstanding the ongoing debate over the succession and an increasingly disgruntled parliamentary party, it seems that Blair was most successful in delivering his agenda during his final years in office.

ACTIVITY 6.2

'Whether Blair's sofa government will ultimately be seen as part of a long-term transition to a more presidential style of government, or as a disastrous aberration from well-established good practice remains to be seen.'

1. Evaluate the benefits and disadvantages of 'sofa government'.
2. How would you feel if this style became the norm for UK governments during your lifetime?

Education

His first government's priorities, Blair promised in 1995, would be 'education, education, education'. His commitment was insistent, but did not necessarily presage a major change of direction. Under the influence of Andrew Adonis, Blair accepted the main policies of the outgoing Tory government – the national curriculum, a regime of testing and regular inspections and financial delegation to schools, away from local education authorities (LEAs). To these Blair added 'targets' to ensure that improvements in school standards were not just projected, but achieved. Not surprisingly, he often found greater resistance to these policies among his own backbenchers than from the Conservative opposition. Perhaps New Labour's greatest change, at least from the party's own past, was its celebration of different types of school, so as to maximise parental choice. The idea that standards mattered more than structures sounded reasonable enough, but stuck in the craw of Labour traditionalists, who regarded the implementation of a universal comprehensive system as an end in itself. Alastair Campbell's assertion that the days of the 'bog-standard'[15] comprehensive were over signalled the change.

ACTIVITY 6.3

Who do you think were the most important figures in the Blair administration? Organise a classroom role-play debate between a minister and one of Blair's team of advisers and consider the differing perspectives of the two figures.

Taking it further

Research the new types of schools that emerged under New Labour: specialist schools, academies, trust schools. Find out:

1. What was distinctive about each?
2. Was there wide support in parliament?
3. Was there wide public support?

New Labour saw good schooling as a key element in its broader goal of social inclusion and, at the end of the two-year spending freeze, Chancellor Brown provided significant extra funding. Current expenditure on schools rose from £21.43 billion in 1997–98, to £34.36 billion in 2005–06. Funding for school building more than doubled over the same period. Changes to teachers' remuneration, designed to introduce performance-related pay, had the practical effect of creating a longer, more generous, salary scale. This additional expenditure seemed to lead to better performance. Statistics suggested consistently higher pupil attainment in both primary and secondary schools. Yet reasons for scepticism persisted. Critics argued that pupils were being better prepared year by year for specific tests. Was it really credible that A-level candidates were getting cleverer each year – as the ever-improving figures suggested? The dissatisfaction of both employers and universities with the educational attainments of school-leavers pointed in a different direction. Strikingly, increasing numbers of parents struggled with the financial burdens of private education at a time when the state system was supposedly showing such marked improvement. Meanwhile, educationalists worried that schools were coming to resemble exam factories, whose positions in league tables had become the be-all and end-all of their existence.

For the most part, higher education took a back seat to schools during the Blair years, despite having incurred severe funding cuts under the Conservatives. The Education Secretary, David Blunkett, drew selectively upon the recent Dearing Report, to impose up front yearly fees on university students. The government made an unexpected announcement of an ambitious, if arbitrary, target participation rate of 50% of the population going to university by age 30. This raised further questions about where the necessary funding would come from, especially when the government went into the 2001 election with a commitment not to introduce 'top-up' fees. Amid criticism that many graduates emerged with degrees of questionable value, New Labour stressed that university expansion must serve the needs of the national economy. In his second term, Blair soon realised that 'top-up' fees would be necessary if British higher education was to remain competitive in a global market, though Brown suggested publicly that higher fees would deter potential students from poorer backgrounds. In the event, a late change of heart by the Chancellor helped the government win the crucial Commons division in 2004 with a majority of just five votes. The new scheme allowed for deferred, rather than up-front, payment, with bursaries for those from low-income families. Even now, university income remained significantly lower than deemed necessary by Dearing. A growth in income from overseas students was one compensating factor.

Health

One of New Labour's striking slogans during the 1997 election was that there were just '24 hours to save the NHS'. Given the almost universal affection in which the NHS is held by the British people, it was a compelling message, albeit essentially hyperbolic electoral rhetoric. Yet, given the 1997–99 spending restrictions, Blair's first term witnessed few dramatic changes. Policy until 1999 was largely left to the distinctly 'Old Labour' Secretary of State for Health, Frank Dobson. There was a feeling in Blair's circle that NHS reform was, for the moment, too big an issue and should be left until the second term. However, in January 2000, apparently without consulting Brown, Blair used a television interview to announce that health spending would be increased to the average level of the EU. The NHS Plan was well received and figured prominently in the government's 2001 election strategy.

Furthermore, at least until he was blown off course by unforeseen developments in the international arena, Blair was determined that his second term would be the time for delivery. In his reshaped government, trusted and competent ministers were placed at the head of the relevant departments and given an assurance of remaining in post for the duration. In the event, of the ministers in question – Estelle Morris at Education, Stephen Byers at Transport, David Blunkett at the Home Office and Alan Milburn at Health – no one managed to stay the course. Blair seemed to have forgotten Harold Macmillan's old adage that the biggest impediment facing governments in the implementation of their programmes was, quite simply, 'events'.

The increase in health spending was, on the surface, spectacular. Expenditure in cash terms tripled – from £30 billion in 1997 to £90 billion in 2007. Despite this, though extra money was certainly needed and produced visible improvements, few saw these as commensurate with the money poured in. Milburn wanted to free hospitals from central control, devolving power to them as 'foundation' hospitals, while encouraging provision from the private sector. Patient choice would be paramount, with money following the patient. Blair reminded Labour traditionalists that a system created in the late 1940s was probably not appropriate for the 21st century. Increasingly he promoted the notion of 'competition' in the health service – anathema to many of his colleagues because of the simplistic equation with 'privatisation'. For the Prime Minister, therefore, it was inevitably an uphill struggle. As early as 1999, he had spoken of the scars on his back resulting from his efforts to reform the public services. Life was no easier in the second term. Brown seemed unconvinced by the direction of policy. At the 2002 party conference Blair claimed that 'we're at our best when at our boldest'[16] and insisted that he was looking to renew, not betray, the public services. The wording of Brown's speech to the following year's conference was carefully chosen. 'We are best', he urged 'when we are Labour'.[17] The omission of the word 'New' was not accidental.

Overall, Blair bequeathed unfinished business regarding the NHS. International comparisons could be misleading and the effects of increased funding were not always easily measured. Improvements in heart disease and cancer survival rates were part of an international trend going back to the early 1990s. Britain's own successful breast cancer screening programme started in the 1980s. Almost certainly, the extra money would have had more effect if reforms had been fully implemented before it was injected. Appropriate changes in working practice could have dramatic, yet inexpensive, results. Accident and Emergency Unit waiting times were reduced by treating patients with minor injuries quickly, instead of making them wait until patients with more serious injuries had been dealt with. Some serious health issues, such as obesity and the consequent explosion of diabetes, remained to be tackled. If most electors believed that the NHS was stronger after the Blair decade, there was no room for complacency. Problems including an ageing population, inflation in medicine and equipment costs and huge extensions in the range of treatments potentially available, lay outside the control of any government. Others, including the future cost to the NHS of the **Private Finance Initiative** hospital building programme, were essentially New Labour's own creation.

Key terms

Private Finance Initiative (PFI): a way of creating a 'public-private partnership' by funding public infrastructure projects through private capital. Likely to involve high long-term repayment costs.

Law and order

Blair had made an early impression as Shadow Home Secretary with his sound bite, 'tough on crime, tough on the causes of crime'.[18] He aimed to dispel Labour's image as a party that failed to match the Conservatives in their readiness to punish those who broke the law. The experience of his working-class Sedgefield constituency convinced him that the poor suffered most from crime and that law and order ranked high among the electorate's priorities. New Labour was certainly active in the field with, it should be said, a greater emphasis on the first half of Blair's maxim. More than 40 acts of parliament dealing with criminal justice and penal policy were placed on the statute book. One estimate suggests that more than 3000 new criminal offences were created. At times New Labour seemed eager to appropriate the populist agenda of the *Daily Mail*. By the end of Blair's premiership, the government could boast a significant reduction in the rates of crime. However, the accuracy of such statistics was hotly debated, partly because of variations in the way crime is recorded and partly because of continuing popular perceptions of the *threat* of crime, irrespective of what published figures imply. Furthermore, crime reduction is an international phenomenon, variously attributed to such diverse causes as harsher sentences and the removal of lead from petrol!

After 9/11, traditional law and order issues were compounded by new concerns over international terrorism. New Labour's difficult task was to strike an appropriate balance between the party's longstanding commitment to civil liberties and the need to maintain public safety. A Commons defeat in November 2005 over the government's attempt to include, in its Terrorism Bill, provision for detention without trial for up to 90 days, suggested that Blair had not got the balance right – or at least had not convinced his own party on this matter. Forty-nine Labour MPs voted against the proposal. Meanwhile, increased immigration from the expanded EU, under its freedom of movement provision, and the failure of the Home Office to get a grip on asylum applications, led to further unease. The Blairite Home Secretary, Charles Clarke, had to resign in April 2006 over his department's apparent inability to deport convicted foreign criminals.

Brown and economic policy

Brown and Blair

It was a paradox of Blair's premiership that a man who developed the presidential style of government, to an extent never before seen in British history, had, at the same time, to share authority over his administration with his most senior cabinet colleague. Blair and Gordon Brown were both central to the New Labour project. Brown's politics were more firmly rooted in the Labour tradition and he probably had a somewhat different idea of the sort of society Labour should ultimately create – one in which traditional Labour values of fairness and equality were firmly entrenched. Nevertheless, the two men shared the same analysis of where the party had gone wrong in recent decades and what needed to be done to return it to power.

Moreover, their careers had moved forward in tandem. They were personal friends and had entered parliament together in 1983. Their talents soon led to front-bench appointments and then to election to the shadow cabinet. However, until the leadership vacancy created by John Smith's death in May 1994, Brown was regarded as the senior member of the partnership. His, most agreed, was the superior intellect and, as Shadow Chancellor, his position in Labour's hierarchy was clear. This situation was not fixed. Brown's abrasive, sometimes gloomy, personality had already begun to make enemies within the parliamentary party; meanwhile, Blair's affability had won friends. In any case, Blair's decision to seek the leadership permanently changed the relationship between the two leading architects of the modernisation project. Equally, Brown regarded as nothing less than treachery the decision of Peter Mandelson, the third member of the New Labour triumvirate, to jump ship and support Blair's candidacy.

Much has been written about the celebrated dinner at the Granita restaurant, Islington, on 21 May 1994, at which Blair and Brown reached an accord about the way ahead. What was agreed is unlikely ever to be authoritatively established. The meeting produced no formal written record and the versions later put out by the two camps differ in significant respects. What is clear is that it was agreed that Blair, and not Brown, would stand for the leadership. More contested is Brown's belief that, in return for this act of self-denial, Blair would stand aside for him midway through a second term of Labour government. It seems unlikely that Blair would have offered such a specific commitment, though his subsequent career revealed a singular capacity to leave interlocutors with the impression he had said what they wanted him to say. If Blair did make such a promise, it is likely that his will to stick by it was eroded by his perception of Brown's tactics during the Labour government, hindering Blair's achievement of his policy goals. Equally problematic is Blair's alleged surrendering of authority over vast tracts of a future Labour government's economic and social policy, creating, in Anthony Seldon's words, 'a very different kind of premiership to anything previously known in British history; to a significant extent it would be shared'.[19]

At all events, while the Blair-Brown axis at its best could still deliver huge advantages for New Labour, with increasing frequency it came to paralyse Blair's premiership. At times the relationship became poisonous, each man seemingly reluctant to look at the other directly. By early 1998 Brown's team was briefing that the Chancellor was, in practice, the government's chief executive, Blair merely its nominal chairman. The Prime Minister's camp soon countered that, for all his intellectual distinction, Brown was 'psychologically flawed'. Brown used his authority to devise economic policy within his own circle without consulting Blair who, it was rumoured, was not up to the sort of complex issues involved. Brown's secrecy, until the last moment, over the contents of the 1999 budget, caused particular irritation to his Downing Street neighbour. The Chancellor also succeeded in extending the range of government policy falling within his autonomous remit.

With hindsight, it was probably unfortunate for Blair that he did not face Brown in a contested leadership in 1994. This, and the probability that he would still have emerged victorious, would have made it altogether more difficult for Brown and his followers to retain their sense of grievance and thwarted entitlement.

The European currency (the euro)

A key Blair ambition was to take Britain into the European single currency. Granted his wish for Britain to be at the heart of the European project, this was for him a primarily political judgement. As early as November 1997, however, Brown succeeded in making membership of the euro dependent on five *economic* tests:

1. Had the UK achieved economic convergence with Europe?
2. Was the UK flexible enough to adapt to the change of currency?
3. How would UK investment be affected?
4. What would be the impact on the UK's financial services sector?
5. What would be the likely impact on employment and growth?

The elasticity of these tests ensured that the final decision would rest, not upon objective evaluation, but upon his own wish. Under the influence of his adviser, Ed Balls, Brown became increasingly sceptical about the euro and, though the five tests were periodically revisited, Blair eventually accepted that his hope of British participation was dead in the water.

The Exchequer

While still in opposition, the Brown-Blair partnership worked well enough. Both agreed that a key priority should be to dispel Labour's image as a party that would inevitably increase both taxation and borrowing, to finance its expenditure plans. Accordingly, they agreed upon a formal commitment not to increase existing rates of income tax and to stick to the Major government's spending limits during Labour's first two years in power. This was wise in electoral terms, but, inevitably, circumscribed the policy goals that a first-term Labour government could achieve. In fact, overall government expenditure as a percentage of the national economy did not return to the level reached in the last year of Major's government until Blair had already served five years as Prime Minister. As Peter Sinclair put it, 'tax policy in the Blair years was not just remarkably conservative; it was strictly Conservative in key respects'.[20] An economist arriving from Mars, suggested Peter Riddell, would reasonably have concluded that the same government had been in power in Britain throughout the second half of the 1990s.[21]

Yet if the New Labour government signalled continuity in tax and spending policy, Brown did make two important decisions during his first month in office. The announcement that the Monetary Policy Committee of the Bank of England would take over responsibility for setting interest rates was widely applauded. Too often Chancellors had cynically used this means to manufacture short-term booms for party political/electoral advantage. In return for surrendering this power, however, Brown clearly intended to transform the Treasury into a policy department with overall responsibility for domestic administration. Brown's second initiative was that the Bank of England should surrender its regulatory powers over the City to a newly created Financial Services Authority. This reflected Brown's admiration, shared by Blair, for the American neo-liberal model of deregulation and incentivised capitalism – a model which, by the end of Brown's chancellorship, had, in the IMF's opinion, elevated Britain's attractiveness as a venue for foreign capital to that of the Cayman Islands.[22]

Brown was in office for ten years, and was, apparently, remarkably successful. Notwithstanding his deteriorating relationship with Number 10, he operated in the manner of an overmighty medieval baron, beyond the reach of even the king. His removal from the Exchequer was occasionally mooted, with a possible transfer to the Foreign Office, but never materialised. His ability to deliver the goods was his greatest protection. In the comprehensive spending review of July 1998, Brown announced his plans for the period after the government's two-year freeze. These included £40 billion of extra spending over the following three years, especially on health and education. Though the Chancellor's largesse required so-called **stealth taxes** and was frequently 'spun' and even triple-counted, it was the single most important economic decision of the New Labour era, opening the way for the public sector investments of the government's second term.

Overall, Brown's tenure witnessed a decade of continuous, reasonably steady, growth. He had one great advantage denied to previous Labour governments. On vacating Downing Street, Major claimed that 'the incoming government would inherit the most benevolent set of economic statistics since before the First World War'. Easily dismissed as the self-serving plea of a defeated Prime Minister, this was essentially true. Following ejection from the ERM, the Conservatives had stumbled upon a successful economic strategy that had already produced nearly five years of sustained improvement, leaving the Tories expecting, but never receiving, the electoral benefits of a **feel-good factor**. For all that, under Brown living standards continued to rise, while unemployment moved downwards, inflation never got out of control, interest rates remained low and the pound strengthened by around 14%.

It was unlike the experience of any previous Labour Chancellor. Able to produce a seemingly endless stream of figures and statistics and brooking no criticism, Brown convinced many observers that the 'prudent' Chancellor had finally broken the cycle of 'boom and bust'. Of course, this was nonsense. No Chancellor, however gifted, could escape the economic cycle, nor fully protect the country from a downturn in the globalised world economy. Furthermore, since 2008, many of Brown's 'achievements' have been viewed in a different light. Besides his too light regulation of the banks, critics suggest that he borrowed to excess, allowing the annual deficit and, therefore, the accumulated debt, to rise remorselessly. By failing to build a budget surplus in good times – 'mending the roof while the sun was shining' – he left Britain's economy more vulnerable than it needed to be to the international banking crisis. Additional Brown decisions, such as scrapping pension dividend tax credits in 1997 – with consequences for the viability of many company pension schemes – and the 1999 sale of a substantial part of Britain's gold reserves at what proved to be deflated prices, now seem ill-advised. For all that, whether Brown should be judged as one of the

Key terms

stealth taxes: taxes whose impact is indirect and which are not immediately perceived by voters as affecting them financially.

feel-good factor: an idea, based upon the belief that economic prosperity is the single most important determinant of voting behaviour, that electors will reward an incumbent government if they sense that their own standard of living is rising.

most accomplished Chancellors of modern times, or else as one whose stewardship bears heavy responsibility for the years of austerity and spending cuts that followed, is probably a question whose answer must yet be deferred.

Northern Ireland and the Good Friday Agreement

If Northern Ireland continues to enjoy relative peace and stability, history may judge the settlement of the 'Troubles' as Tony Blair's most significant achievement. The 'peace process' of course was just that – a process rather than an event – and important work had been done before New Labour came to power. The Anglo-Irish Agreement (1985) marked the first formal recognition of the Republic of Ireland's right to be interested in and consulted about Northern Ireland. Major's government had built upon this foundation, pursuing constructive negotiations with successive Irish Taoiseachs, but had become increasingly hamstrung by its weak parliamentary position and the consequent need not to alienate Unionist opinion. Whatever had been achieved already, the work of the Blair government was crucial and, in contrast to his limited role in the affairs of Scotland and Wales, this was a matter where Blair personally was heavily involved and which, as he told Bill Clinton shortly after the 1997 election, he intended to make a priority of his administration.

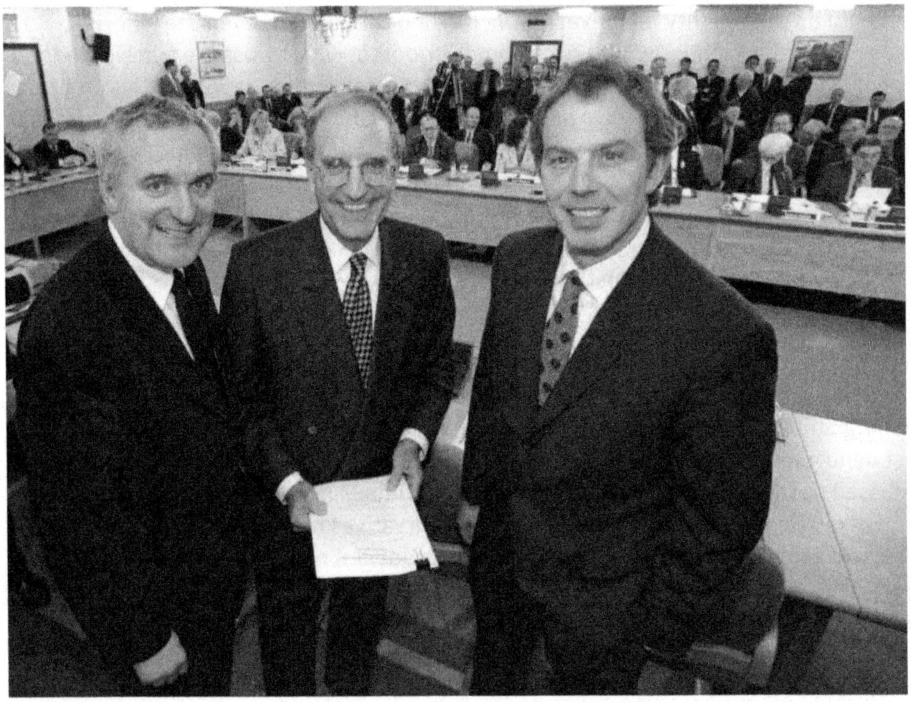

Figure 6.8: Blair's informality and 'blokeish' personality proved critical in bringing the contending parties together and forging an agreement. Irish Taoiseach Bertie Ahern, (left) is shown here with former US Senator George Mitchell (centre) and Prime Minister Tony Blair (right).

Belfast was the venue for Blair's first official trip outside London after becoming Prime Minister. There, he insisted that he believed in and valued the Union. Any settlement would have to respect the will and consent of the Northern Irish people. This was hugely important. Had Blair maintained Labour's traditional policy of Irish unity by consent, it is unlikely that meaningful dialogue with Northern Ireland's Unionist majority would have been possible. Negotiations chaired by the former American senator, George Mitchell, eventually produced the Good Friday Agreement of 10 April 1998. Blair made a dramatic intervention, arriving in Belfast to break an apparent deadlock threatening the entire negotiating process. He never lost confidence in his own powers of persuasion and his ability to reconcile the irreconcilable. At the same time, he seemed unaware of his capacity for self-parody. 'Now is not the time for sound bites', Blair declared before adding, to the toe-curling embarrassment of his audience, 'I feel the hand of history upon our shoulders'.[23] The agreement:

- restored devolution to Northern Ireland on the basis of a power-sharing assembly at Stormont
- allowed for a North-South Council to improve cross-border cooperation
- committed Dublin to dropping its constitutional claim to the six counties of Northern Ireland
- committed the paramilitary forces to decommissioning their arms
- promised the release of 'political' prisoners
- included an undertaking to reform Northern Ireland's police service.

A bumpy road still lay ahead that would see the replacement of the moderate Ulster Unionist Party (UUP) and Social Democratic and Labour Party (SDLP) as the main standard-bearers of the Unionist and Nationalist causes, by the more extreme Democratic Unionist Party (DUP) and Sinn Féin. The Omagh bombing, four months after the agreement, was a stark reminder that terrorist violence had not gone away. Prevarication over decommissioning continued at least until July 2005, when the IRA formally declared that their weapons would be put beyond use and that the IRA's aims would, thereafter, be pursued by peaceful means. The Stormont Assembly was twice suspended and direct rule from London reimposed. For all that, the broad framework of the Good Friday accord remained and, in the last weeks of his premiership, Blair had the satisfaction of seeing the veteran DUP leader, Ian Paisley, and the former IRA commander, Martin McGuinness of Sinn Féin, take office as First Minister and Deputy First Minister of the province.

The Conservative Party

Leaders and reasons for divisions

The state of the Conservative opposition materially contributed to the Blairite ascendancy. With just 165 MPs after the 1997 electoral debacle, its worst performance since 1906, the party was in a sorry state. Several talented individuals, including Michael Portillo, had gone down to electoral defeat. Many who survived had still not reconciled themselves to the way in which Thatcher had been ejected from the leadership seven years earlier. The party remained deeply divided, especially over Europe, which had plagued Major throughout his time in office. New Labour's media machine had been highly successful in painting the Tories as not only divided, but incompetent and corrupt as well. It was a sign of the times that the outgoing government had lost the backing of several of its traditional cheerleaders in the press.

Following such a catastrophic defeat, it was inevitable that Major would stand down from the leadership, even though his personal standing remained higher than his party's. He had probably tired of the thankless task of trying to hold his disputatious party together. His decision to spend the day following the election watching cricket spoke volumes. In his place, the surviving Conservative MPs appeared to make a wise choice in the selection of the youthful William Hague. Here, they believed, was a man to hold his own with Tony Blair. Hague's rise through the party, since first addressing the annual conference as a teenager, had been meteoric. Highly intelligent and a brilliant debater, he was the archetypal self-made man. In contrast to the public school-educated Blair, Hague was a product of the comprehensive state system. He took over with a clear commitment to modernise the party.

However, Hague operated in unfavourable circumstances and his overall performance proved disappointing. New Labour enjoyed an extended honeymoon with the electorate, while Blair's personal standing remained high. This was the era of 'Teflon Tony'. The economy prospered, while the Tories' own credentials for economic management remained tarnished by association with Britain's expulsion from the

ERM. Labour had taken time to recover from the nadir of 1983 and it was unrealistic to expect an immediate Conservative bounce back under Hague.

Yet to these intractable difficulties, Hague added his own mistakes and misjudgements. The quest to modernise was soon overtaken by an attempt to consolidate the party's core vote. Underlying tensions between modernisers and consolidators became more apparent with Portillo's return to the Commons, following a 1999 by-election. Immediately appointed Shadow Chancellor, Portillo put forward a more overtly modernising agenda than many of his colleagues were comfortable with. Rather than focusing on the electorate's priorities of health, education and transport, Hague reverted to such traditional Conservative preoccupations as law and order, immigration and Europe. In committing the party to oppose joining the euro over the next two parliaments, he largely succeeded in burying what would otherwise have been a divisive issue in his own ranks. But, encouraged by Tory successes in the 1999 European elections, Hague elevated Euroscepticism to a prominence it did not enjoy among the wider public. In opposing the government's determination to repeal 'Section 28', which had prohibited local authorities from 'promoting' homosexuality in schools and elsewhere, Hague failed to sense the changing popular mood. His support for Tony Martin, the Norfolk farmer who shot an intruder, laid him open to charges of crude populism. His endorsement of the novelist Jeffrey Archer, later convicted of perjury, as Tory candidate for London mayor, smacked of political naivety. Though he landed several telling blows at Prime Minister's Questions (PMQs), Hague failed to convince voters that he was a Prime Minister in waiting. Almost certainly, the leadership had come too soon. In his later career as Foreign Secretary under David Cameron (2010–14), Hague acquired a political gravitas that had been lacking in his earlier incarnation as leader.

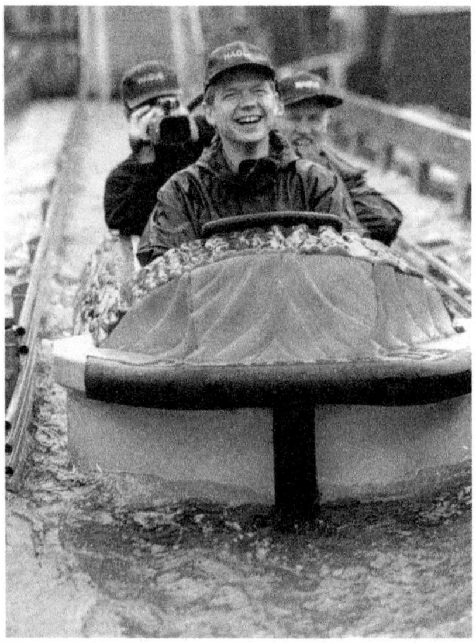

Figure 6.9: William Hague's efforts to present a contemporary, down-to-earth image in his public appearances were sometimes embarrassing rather than reassuring.

Hague resigned immediately following the Conservatives' worse than expected performance in the 2001 general election. The selection of his successor was conducted under new rules, whereby the parliamentary party chose two contenders – Ken Clarke and Iain Duncan Smith – to be presented to the full party membership for a final decision. The latter emerged victorious by a clear majority – 61% to 39% – a result deriving almost entirely from the candidates' respective views on Europe. The talented and experienced Clarke was a committed Europhile and advocate of the single currency, at a time when the membership had become deeply sceptical. Duncan Smith could claim a democratic legitimacy denied to all his predecessors, but this was not matched by support inside the parliamentary party, where he had attracted the votes of only a third of Conservative MPs. It was a handicap he never overcame. New Labour was still riding high, developing a reputation for governmental competence on the basis of economic growth, expanding employment and low inflation. In its second term, moreover, the government began a policy of significant new investment in the public services. Duncan Smith's fate clearly depended on his performance as party leader. It proved to be significantly worse than Hague's.

Many Tory MPs doubted whether their new leader had the intellectual capacity for the job. He was ill at ease on the opposition front bench and no match for Blair's increasingly assured performances at PMQs. Plausibly, in response to New Labour's presentational slickness, the Conservatives needed to offer a more homespun alternative. However, Duncan Smith's projection of himself as the 'quiet man' of British politics invited ridicule, rather than additional voter support. The Tory image remained, as even their Chairman put it, that of the 'nasty party'.[24] The shadow cabinet, in which Clarke and Portillo declined to serve, looked more right-wing than its predecessor and, in opposing adoption by homosexual couples, Duncan Smith, like Hague over Section 28, failed to move with changing social mores. In many ways the problem was that New Labour occupied much of the ideological ground that a more self-confident Conservative Party would have claimed as its own. Lacking room to manoeuvre, Duncan Smith's Tories drifted to the right.

The Conservatives continued to languish in the opinion polls and failed to profit from Blair's mounting unpopularity over Iraq. With Duncan Smith offering the government his support on this issue, disgruntled voters turned instead to the Liberal Democrats. With major donors deserting the party; growing discontent at Conservative Central Office; and even the whips' office close to rebellion, it was no surprise when, in October 2003, Tory MPs forced a vote of confidence which Duncan Smith lost by 90 votes to 75. Like Hague, he did much in the years that followed to rebuild his political reputation, but the conclusion seems inescapable that Duncan Smith had few of the skills needed in an effective opposition leader.

Determined to avoid another contested leadership election and, perhaps, worried that the membership might again make the 'wrong' choice, Conservative MPs reverted to something like the 'customary procedures' last seen in the 1960s. They ensured that Michael Howard now emerged as leader by unchallenged acclamation. Howard was an experienced politician and effective speaker, with a reputation for toughness – especially on questions of law and order – but his focus was on party unity, rather than modernisation. Policy initiatives were few and largely unsuccessful. He lacked popular appeal and was easily associated in the public mind with the failures of the later Thatcher years and the discredited Major government. He never fully recovered from the barbed jibe of his former Home Office colleague, Ann Widdecombe, that there was 'something of the night' about him. Howard engineered a few effective tilts at Blair's expense. For example, in December 2003 he insisted that, as the product of a grammar school, he was not going to be lectured to by a public school-educated Prime Minister on the merits of wider access to university education. Overall, however, he never got the better of Blair, who played upon the idea that Howard was fundamentally an opportunist whose political moves were dictated by short-term tactics, rather than conviction. Like Hague, Howard mistakenly used the evidence of European election results to dictate his priorities for the subsequent general election. Howard's claim that public services could be maintained on a lower level of expenditure failed to convince and his appointment of Oliver Letwin as Shadow Chancellor proved unfortunate. As in 2001, the party relied on its core vote and the hope that disgruntled voters would not back the increasingly unpopular Blair.

Howard announced his resignation as soon as the results of the 2005 general election were confirmed. His most significant contribution to his party's history may well have been to delay his actual departure for several months, during which his preferred candidate for the succession, David Cameron, was able to consolidate his position. Only then did control of the party pass into the hands of younger politicians, committed to a strategy of modernisation – detoxification, even – and understanding that, if they were to regain power, the Conservatives could no longer rely on the sort of traditional right-wing policies foregrounded since 1997. Cameron's celebrated put-down of Blair in the Commons in December 2005 – that 'he was the future once' – might have been taken from Blair's own drawer of sound bites, but it was a symbolic moment and, fortunately for the Tories, it reflected a growing public mood.

Reasons for electoral failure in 2001 and 2005

Neither in 2001, nor 2005, did the Conservatives come remotely close to ousting Tony Blair from Downing Street. Indeed, the two results are among the worst in the party's long history (see Figures 6.3–6.6). Talk of Tory 'recovery' seems misplaced. Indeed, Conservative weakness over the period served to exaggerate New Labour's ascendancy. The government's popularity had steadily declined, notwithstanding continuing parliamentary majorities. However, it had lost votes to the Liberal Democrats, rather than to the main opposition party.

Once renowned for electoral professionalism, the Conservatives went into the 2001 and 2005 contests with a less impressive 'product', less well 'marketed' than that of New Labour. Though much of the Thatcherite legacy remained intact, it was New Labour that had appropriated that legacy and many of the votes that accompanied it. In both elections the Conservatives overplayed the European card. Hague's pledge to 'save the pound' rang somewhat hollow, given that his own stated position did not guarantee sterling's long-term survival. The Tory campaign in 2005 was widely judged the least effective of the three major parties. Condemned for its 'dog-whistle' approach, appealing subliminally to the electorate's less attractive instincts, it came close to adopting the agenda of the right-wing tabloid press. New Labour had delivered much with which the electors felt comfortable, so although the Prime Minister's personal standing declined, the lack of a viable alternative enabled it to be re-elected for an unprecedented third term.

Social issues

Workers, women and youth

On balance, the Blair decade was a good time for British workers – though not for those institutions, the trade unions, that had for so long sought to protect their interests. In opposition, Blair had insisted that 'there will be fairness not favours for employers and employees alike. The Labour government is not the political arm of anyone today other than the British people.' In many ways, this was a startling declaration. The trade unions had been present at the party's birth at the beginning of the 20th century, their role variously interpreted as midwife, or parent. Just under a century later, that relationship was abruptly terminated. It was time, Blair said, to 'forget the past'.[25] From this position he never wavered. He was 'determined to eradicate … the destructive and debilitating culture of the Old Labour movement where trade unions used their financing of the party and their block votes at the annual conference to dictate what Labour should carry out when in government'.[26] Convinced that the close trade union link damaged the party electorally and also that a flexible labour force had to make its own way in a highly competitive international market, Blair would not turn back the clock. The era of 'beer and sandwiches at Number 10' would not be reinstated and the trade union legislation of the Thatcher and Major governments would be retained.

The new politics were enforced in a benign economic climate, which enabled a number of developments:

- Take-home pay rose steadily and so did living standards, though much of this was based on personal debt.
- While not responding to union clamor to repeal 'anti-union' laws, the government did oversee several improvements in individual workers' rights, for example, reducing the qualifying period before protection against unfair dismissal could be claimed.
- The European Working Time Directive fixed maximum working hours for around three million employees, but there were few moves towards pay equalisation.
- Several leading New Labour figures declared that they were relaxed about inequality. The 'filthy rich' were welcomed: Britain needed to encourage entrepreneurial success to facilitate a dynamic and successful economy.
- New Labour, and particularly its Chancellor, did, however, care about the low-paid and wanted to eradicate child poverty. The National Minimum Wage was introduced in 1999, initially at £3.00 per hour for 18–22-year-olds and £3.60 for older workers, setting a new threshold below which those in work should not fall. Previously opposed by the Conservatives on the grounds that it would cost jobs, it soon won widespread acceptance, becoming a fixed feature of the labour market.
- Equally important, though ultimately more controversial, Working Tax Credits (WTCs) were introduced in order to provide an automatic top-up to the low incomes of working families, and were partially inspired by President Clinton's welfare-to-work policies in the US. Over succeeding years, the cost of WTCs rose exponentially and was seen by many commentators as unsustainable.

ACTIVITY 6.4

Class debate on the motion 'Working Tax Credits encourage the continuation of low pay and subsidise employers at the expense of tax-payers.'

Women

Women benefited disproportionately from New Labour's reforms, essentially because they constituted a majority of workers in those low-pay categories the government sought to help. Indeed, perhaps for the first time, women were accepted as an integral part of the workforce, rather than as an add-on to a male-dominated sector. The government pursued a family-friendly workplace agenda. Paid maternity leave was significantly increased and the National Childcare Strategy allowed for progress in a field where Britain lagged behind the rest of the EU. By 2000, 73% of mothers with children under 13 were in work. Despite earlier legislation, a gender pay gap persisted, which New Labour failed to close. However, many women benefited from the decision to grant divorcees a share of their ex-husbands' occupational pensions. Meanwhile, New Labour did its bit for gender equality by substantially increasing the number of female MPs. Partly as a result of all-women shortlists – subsequently ruled illegal – for the first time more than 100 women entered parliament at the 1997 election, a large majority of them Labour. Soon dubbed 'Blair's Babes', they were sometimes criticised for being too subservient to the leadership, but at least the Commons had taken a significant step to more accurately representing the general population.

Youth

New Labour was also aware of the particular problems facing young people. Under the 'New Deal' programme, the government targeted those 17–25-year-olds neither in work nor education. They were offered one-to-one advice to get a job, failing which they had to take up one of four options – education, job training, working on an environmental project or helping a voluntary organisation. One survey suggested that, by mid-2000, around 160 000 young people had been found jobs at least six months quicker than would otherwise have been the case. Here was clear evidence that New Labour was not ideologically wedded to market forces. Young workers also benefited from the minimum wage, though at a lower rate than enjoyed by older people. Employers, however, continued to complain that the young often lacked the skills needed in a modern, competitive economy.

Cross-reference Chapter 6 *Education*

The government perhaps put too much emphasis on widening participation in higher education, at the expense of encouraging practical skills for those best suited to a non-academic pathway. Nonetheless, popular concern over the issue of unemployment declined during Blair's premiership, from 39% in 1997 to just 8% ten years later.

A multicultural society?

Immigration had long been an issue in British politics. From the 1960s, however, many of the worst examples of racial prejudice had seemingly been eradicated – partly by legislation, but, more importantly, by growing tolerance and understanding among the indigenous population. Happily, Britain had come a long way from the 'No blacks, no Irish, no dogs' signs in the lodging houses of the 1950s. Just 3% of the population ranked immigration among their leading concerns at the time of the 1997 general election. Nonetheless, the enquiry into the 1993 murder of the black teenager, Stephen Lawrence, revealed worrying evidence of 'institutional racism' in the Metropolitan Police. Under New Labour, moreover, the issue of multiculturalism – its successes, its failures, its very desirability – became hotly debated. This was partly because of evidence that integration had not proceeded as smoothly as some believed, partly because of unexpectedly high EU immigration and partly as a response to terrorist atrocities, most obviously the London bombings of July 2005.

There were racially motivated riots in Burnley, Oldham and Bradford in 2001. These shook the prevailing complacency about the extent of genuine integration in Britain's northern towns and cities. Increasingly it appeared that within these locations ethnic and indigenous communities existed side by side – but separately. A latent discontent emerged from the ranks of the white population where it was felt that positive discrimination in favour of people of Asian origin was serving to disadvantage those who described themselves as 'white British'. Not surprisingly, politicians of the far right were quick to exploit these tensions and enjoyed some success in local elections. For a while, rising support for the extremist British National Party was a cause of particular concern. The atrocities of 7 July 2005, when suicide-bomber terrorists caused multiple deaths on the London Underground and a bus, provoked further soul-searching, especially when it became apparent that the perpetrators were British-born Muslims, brought up and educated in this country. Whatever else, 'multiculturalism' had self-evidently failed, in these cases at least, to instil a sense of British values. The need to counter a feeling of alienation was clear.

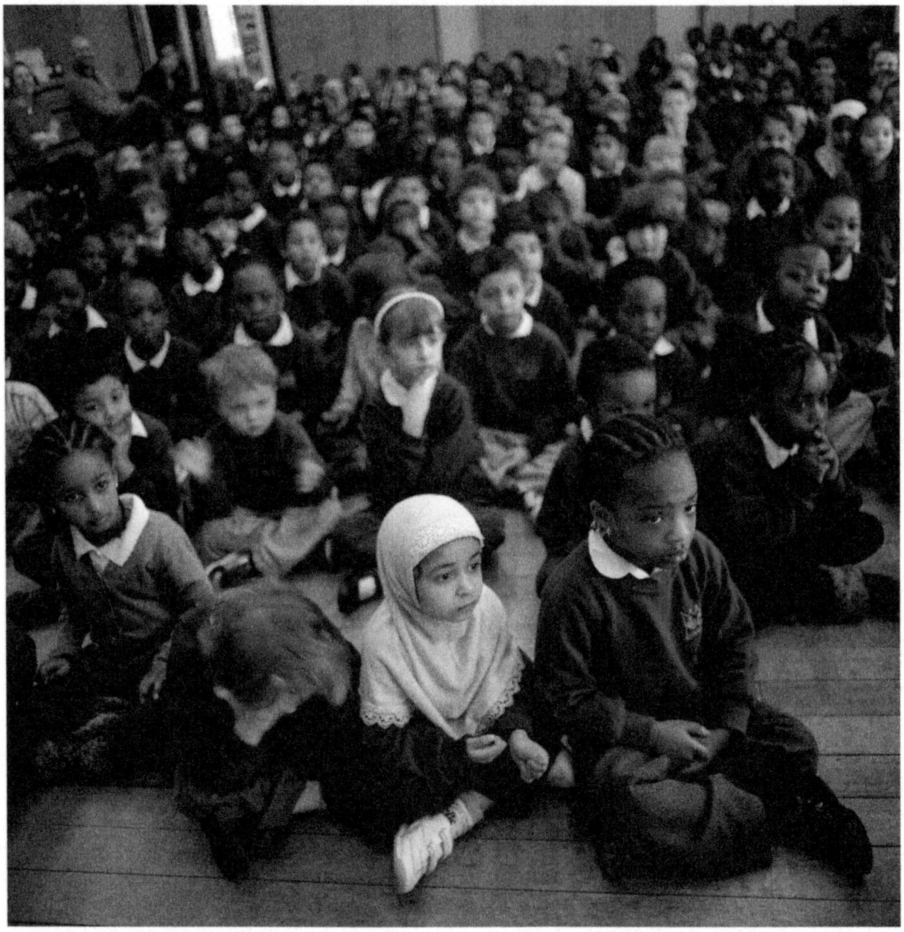

Figure 6.10: Multicultural Britain in the early 21st century.

Elsewhere, problems derived from high concentrations of migrant labour (partly from the EU), putting intense pressure on local services, including schools and hospitals. Indigenous residents objected to the rapid cultural changes overtaking their communities and complained, sometimes on the basis of no more than anecdotal evidence, that new arrivals were taking away jobs or, worse still, 'living on benefits'. Sporadic inter-community tensions resulted, which the mainstream parties could not ignore, especially in the light of rising support for a new political force, the United Kingdom Independence Party (UKIP), which gave prominence to these anxieties. Overall, if Blair had hoped to remove immigration from the realm of political controversy, he failed. By the end of his premiership, 44% of the population ranked immigration control as their issue of greatest concern, though – strikingly – less than 20% saw it as a major factor in their own area.

For all of that, on the ground there was strong evidence that Britain was, indeed, becoming a multicultural society and that, for the most part, this was accepted, often welcomed, by the general population. The longer-term response to home-grown Islamic extremism suggested considerable common ground between British Muslims and the wider community. This included the desirability of full integration in British society, the recognition of women's rights as equal citizens and the need to accept British laws and institutions. In one of his last speeches as Prime Minister, Blair argued that respect for diversity must be balanced by acceptance of 'common, unifying, British values'. If not yet a consensus view, Blair's sentiments reflected the opinions of a growing body of British citizens.

Foreign affairs

Attitudes to Europe

Blair came to power promising to place Britain at the centre of the European Union. The issue of European integration had come close to destroying John Major's government and, though Major had skilfully negotiated a number of opt-outs, he left office amid the widespread perception that Britain had become Europe's awkward partner. Not surprisingly, the arrival of New Labour was widely welcomed on the continent as opening up a possible new beginning. However, two factors were bound to impede Blair's ambitions. First, the most important element of the European project at this time was the introduction of the single currency. Blair's inability, in the face of Treasury opposition, even to place the option of British participation before the electorate in a referendum, made the idea of British leadership in Europe somewhat far-fetched. If Blair hoped to win popular support for the euro, his best chance probably lay during the government's initial honeymoon period, but that chance was lost in the face of Brown's assertion of his financial authority.

The euro	Introduced in Europe on 1 January 1999. Blair was keen to join, but Brown was opposed.
Relationship with the USA	Blair saw the UK as the USA's no. 1 ally. Europe saw this as lack of commitment to Europe.
Worker migration	Numbers of workers arriving from other member states were higher than foreseen. Blair could have opted for transitional restrictions but failed to do so until 2007.
Common Agricultural Policy	Blair was outmanoeuvred in negotiations. The CAP symbolised the leader status of France and Germany within Europe and favoured German, and especially French, farmers. Blair failed to reduce it in the interests of British farming.
The war in Iraq	Britain collaborated in Iraq with the USA. France, in particular, was strongly opposed to the war.

Table 6.2: Britain and Europe – the tensions.

The second impediment is well-captured in the words of Blair's first Foreign Secretary, Robin Cook: 'It is a fixed pole of Tony Blair's view of Britain's place in the world that we must be the Number 1 ally of the US'.[27] While Blair hoped this might enable Britain to act as a bridge between Europe and America, on the continent it was viewed with suspicion, bearing witness to a fundamental lack of Europeanism on Britain's part. The two most important European leaders, President Chirac of France and Germany's

Chancellor Schroeder, became increasingly wary of the British government's intentions. The Iraq War would painfully illustrate the point.

Cross-reference **Chapter 6** *Brown and Blair*

As in several other areas, Labour's stated European policy goals in 1997 were not significantly different from those of the Conservatives. The one exception was the Social Chapter. Tone and style were all-important and the signing of the Social Chapter soon after the government took office was widely seen as an indication of New Labour's good intentions. The government was also fortunate that the question of enlargement was high on Europe's agenda. This was something that both Conservative and Labour parties could embrace enthusiastically, because the greater the EU's extent and diversity, the less likely was an eventual federal outcome. During Britain's presidency of the EU in 1998, accession negotiations got underway with a first group of six countries, mostly from the former communist bloc. Blair made a serious miscalculation in not taking up the option of transitional restrictions on the free access to Britain of workers from the new member states. In the event, far more of these migrants arrived than had been anticipated. It marked the start of a political hot potato, which was to remain at the forefront of Britain's concerns. As the subsequent accession of Romania and Bulgaria approached in 2007, Blair decided to impose the permitted temporary restrictions. Britain also had some early success in advancing the full implementation of the single market. Despite earlier agreements, serious impediments to genuinely free trade persisted, especially in areas such as financial services where Britain was strong.

Perhaps the most surprising indication of British 'leadership' in Europe came with the Saint-Malo Agreement (1998), when Britain and France laid the foundations for the European Security and Defence Policy. Britain had hitherto been nervous about extending EU competence into the field of defence, fearing the resulting complications for NATO. This, however, was the high point of Blair's relations with Chirac, which deteriorated steadily thereafter. Indeed, in October 2002, during negotiations on Common Agricultural Policy (CAP) reform, Chirac is reported to have told Blair: 'You have been very rude and I have never been spoken to like this before'.[28] Blair understood that CAP reform was bound up in the overall question of the EU budget and that any progress on the former would probably require concessions from Britain over the rebate negotiated by Mrs Thatcher. Blair was outmanoeuvred at the European Council meeting in December 2005, when he accepted a modest cut in the rebate *without* a formal agreement on reducing the CAP. If he aimed to break the Franco-German duopoly that had dominated Europe for so long, this was a clear indication of his failure. As with Chirac, relations with Schroeder also cooled, after early hopes of a partnership forged around Blair's version of social democracy. Ironically, his two closest friendships with European leaders were with 'Conservatives' – Aznar of Spain and Italy's Berlusconi – a further indication that he was more interested in getting things done, than in conforming to ideological or party political constraints. Yet there were many who, perhaps wisely, would have advised Blair to give the controversial Italian premier a wide berth.

Cross-reference **Chapter 6** *War*

If 1998 and 2001 Anglo-American bombing raids on Iraq raised eyebrows in several European capitals, Britain's role – joined at the hip with the US – in the Iraq War of 2003 was disastrous from the point of view of Blair's European ambitions. A low point was reached when, on 10 March 2003, Chirac let it be known that France would veto any second UN resolution. At that moment, a key element in Blair's efforts to legitimise American military policy fell to the ground. Though relations improved somewhat in the years that followed, especially once Chirac and Schroeder left the political stage, the impact of the Iraq War on New Labour's Europe policy was profound and long-lasting. If Blair still nurtured any hope of defying Brown and taking Britain into the euro, the corrosive effects of the War on his domestic credibility made a referendum on the issue unthinkable. Speaking in the second year of his premiership, Blair had set out his goals: 'It means realising once and for all that Britain does not have to choose between being strong with the US, or strong with Europe; it means having the confidence that we can be both'. [29] His premiership revealed just how difficult this self-imposed mission was. Blair never managed to reconcile the concept of Europe as Britain's long-term destiny with loyalty to America as its immediate priority. Perhaps his greatest failure, however, was that, after ten years in power, the British people were no closer to wholeheartedly embracing Europe than in 1997. He was probably fortunate that French and Dutch rejections of a proposed constitutional treaty in 2005 saved him from having to hold a referendum on it in Britain – a reference to the popular will he would, very probably, have lost.

The special relationship

Given Blair's conviction that the 'special relationship' remained the cornerstone of British foreign policy, it was not surprising that New Labour struck up a good working relationship with the Democratic President, Bill Clinton. Blair and Brown both visited the US on several occasions in the early 1990s. They were drawn to the American economic model and struck by the success of Clinton's 1992 campaign, in attracting the sort of middle-of-the-road voters essential to Labour's return to power. Clinton and Blair got on well and the President expressed pleasure at the outcome of Britain's 1997 general election: 'I'm looking forward to serving with Prime Minister Blair. He's a very exiting man, a very able man'.[30] President and Prime Minister found common ground in the 'Third Way', offering an intellectual veneer to their respective brands of progressive politics. Relations became somewhat strained during the Kosovo crisis (1999) and Blair was alienated by revelations of Clinton's sexual indiscretions. Nonetheless, his success in persuading Clinton to speak at Labour's 2002 annual conference was a highlight of his premiership.

Figure 6.11: Clinton and Blair at the 2002 Labour Conference.

What is surprising is that Blair managed to strike up an even closer relationship with Clinton's Republican successor, George W. Bush, whose political views lay some way to the right of Britain's Conservative Party. Even the presence in Bush's administration of an unusually hard-line (and unprecedentedly powerful) Vice President and a Defence Department dominated by the so-called '**neo-cons**', failed to deter Blair from his determination to show that he could work with the Republican President. Ironically, Blair's initial concern was not that Britain might be dragged into unlooked-for foreign adventures, but that an isolationist President might withdraw from the international defence obligations upon which Europe relied. If popular British perceptions of Bush as an ill-informed buffoon were somewhat overdrawn, the new White House did little to endear itself to its traditional friends. Over a range of policies, Bush alienated most of America's European allies.

Key terms

neo-cons: a right-wing American political movement that became particularly influential in the Republican administrations of President George H. W. Bush and President George W. Bush. It starts from the premise that, in a dangerous world, only the US has the power to make it a better place and advocates intervention in pursuit of democracy and American values.

Seduced, like so many of his predecessors, by the special relationship, Blair was ready to pay a heavy price for continued American friendship, even at a cost to his personal standing in Britain and Europe. He believed that, by staying close to Bush, he could influence him and, if need be, restrain him from policy excesses. Disagreements between the two men would only be voiced in private. However, observers increasingly doubted whether, in the last resort, Blair would really stand up to the President. Bush was grateful for Blair's support, but was probably always inclined to do what he and his senior advisers wanted. The Blair–Bush axis was not, of course, a partnership of equals and, as Cook noted, Blair 'is programmed to respect power not to rebel against it'.[31] Contrasts were drawn with Margaret Thatcher who, notwithstanding her close relationship with Ronald Reagan, 'would still stamp her feet and protest when she did not like what his administration did'.[32]

The terrorist attacks on New York's twin towers on 11 September 2001 ('9/11'), transformed matters. Blair's statement on the resulting crisis was clear. It would not, he insisted, be a battle between the US and terrorism, but between the free, democratic world and terrorism. In that contest Britain would stand 'shoulder to shoulder with our American friends'.[33] Perhaps because of their shared Christian faith, Bush and Blair increasingly spoke in messianic tones, as if now engaged in a moral crusade, a struggle between good and evil. With hindsight, it appears that Blair had taken a path that would lead to British involvement in the Iraq War.

Speak like a historian

J. Kampfner

John Kampfner, an award-winning journalist, has worked as a foreign correspondent in Moscow and Berlin. He has also written well-received books on Boris Yeltsin's Russia and Robin Cook.

[Bush] signed into law subsidies for US farmers that violated all the tenets of free trade that Blair so passionately advocated. He imposed tariffs on foreign steel producers that set off a bitter trade row with Europe. Most damaging, however, for Blair's efforts to portray the administration in a positive light was its refusal to ratify the establishment of the International Criminal Court unless US forces were given a blanket immunity from prosecution.[34]

Discussion points

1. Find out more about the policies of George W. Bush and the ways in which they created difficulties for Blair in Europe.
2. Account for Blair's continuing determination to stay close to the American President.

Military interventions and the 'war on terror'

Origins

Blair sent British forces into battle five times in six years. There was nothing in his background that anticipated the militaristic emphasis of his premiership. Indeed, as a boy at his Edinburgh public school, Fettes, he had opted for community service, rather than joining the Combined Cadet Corps. Those who took seriously Cook's insistence on an ethical dimension in New Labour's foreign policy, were unlikely to have been thinking of 'ethical wars'. Nonetheless, Blair's ideas on Britain's world role were clearly evolving by the time he became Prime Minister. Speaking in Manchester shortly before the 1997 election, he declared that for 'century upon century it had been the destiny of Britain to lead other nations'. Furthermore, that destiny 'should be part of our future. We are a leader of nations or nothing'.[35]

The most important statement of Blair's world view came in a speech in Chicago in April 1999. His theme was the circumstances in which it would be legitimate for the international community to intervene in the internal affairs of a sovereign state. Blair argued that those intervening must be sure of their case and convinced their own interests were engaged; diplomatic options must have been exhausted; there would have to be achievable goals; and the commitment would need to be for the long-term and include the task of rebuilding. There were problems with this approach. Foreign Office lawyers worried about the implications for international law and the UN. Furthermore, while Blair's thinking was not identical to that of the American neo-cons, there was sufficient overlap for them to begin to coalesce. However, for Blair, here was the philosophical underpinning for what became known as the doctrine of humanitarian intervention.

This was not simply a case of abstract thinking. Blair was also learning from the real world. The speech was delivered during a crisis in Kosovo, an Albanian enclave in the process of being 'ethnically cleansed' by Slobodan Milošević's Serbs. Blair rapidly concluded that, to avert disaster, there was no alternative to the deployment of ground troops. While Downing Street probably exaggerated Britain's role in securing a successful outcome, Kosovo gave Blair confidence in the correctness of his own analysis. The only casualties among western forces were two helicopter pilots killed in a training accident. Applauded on the world stage, Blair saw Kosovo as a model for humanitarian intervention, founded on moral principles. A similar success in Sierra Leone in 2000, which seemed to have saved the former British colony from catastrophic civil strife, confirmed his self-confidence. Even the 2001 invasion of Afghanistan, in response to 9/11, and the rapid fall of the Taliban government, seemed to follow the same pattern – though subsequent Anglo-American disagreements over the problems of 'nation-building' and peacekeeping should have sounded a warning note. 'On each step-up', concludes Seldon, Blair 'became stronger and more assured of his own judgement'.[36]

War

'Iraq was the pivot on which the Blair decade swung'.[37] More than anything else, the war shaped judgements about Blair's government and the Prime Minister personally. While assessments must remain provisional, it is likely to be seen as the biggest single mistake of his premiership. Taking into account the traumatic impact of 9/11 and the outlook of key figures in the Bush administration, including Vice President Cheney and Defence Secretary Rumsfeld, who saw Iraq as unfinished business from the first Gulf War (1991), it was probably inevitable that America would now act against Saddam Hussein, even though no significant connection was ever demonstrated between the Iraqi dictator and the attack on the twin towers. Bush's 'axis of evil' speech showed that he believed Iraq was too dangerous for the existing policy of containment to be continued. By the spring of 2002 he spoke of 'regime change'.

ACTIVITY 6.5

Class debate on the motion: 'Blair's assessment of Britain's position in world affairs was neither accurate nor defensible.'

Taking it further

Research the First Gulf War. Chart the deterioration of relations between the Arab and the Western worlds in a timeline of events from 1991 to 2001.

Blair seems to have been swept up in this evolving situation. He certainly saw terrorism, backed up by 'weapons of mass destruction' (WMD), as an existential threat to western democracy that could only be dealt with militarily. In addition, he clearly enjoyed, post-9/11, being fêted in the US, regarded as America's best friend and the President's closest ally. If conditions were laid down – on the establishment of a broad coalition; the need to exhaust a UN route to a settlement; efforts to tackle the longstanding Middle East problem which, Blair believed, partly explained the rise of Islamic terrorism – these appear to have been pursued as desirable goals, rather than red lines to be insisted upon. Speaking at the Crawford summit in April 2002, Blair proclaimed a doctrine of pre-emption. The 9/11 attack showed it was no use waiting to be hit if you saw a threat coming. Saddam posed such a threat (even though, objectively, he was weaker than during the First Gulf War) and, if the US found itself fighting in defence of democratic values, 'we fight with her'.[38]

On 24 September 2002 the British government published a report based on the findings of the Intelligence Services. 'Iraq's Weapons of Mass Destruction – The Assessment of the British Government' became one of the most controversial landmarks on Britain's path to war. The dossier suggested that 'some of Iraq's WMD could be ready for use within 45 minutes' and that Saddam's 'WMD programme is active, detailed and growing', giving rise to understandably alarmist newspaper headlines. The 45-minute claim, however, related only to tactical battlefield weapons that could not be used against the west. If the cautious and qualified conclusions of the intelligence agencies had not actually been misrepresented, then 'every last drop of intelligence was squeezed from the relatively thin raw material to portray the dossier, and hence the justification for war, as strongly as possible'.[39] With the passage of time, an increasing number of British citizens concluded that Blair knew that Saddam had no WMD, but had lied in order to take the country to war. Cook was more charitable. The Prime Minister's 'sin was not one of bad faith but of evangelical certainty'.[40]

Blair deserves credit for persuading Bush to seek UN backing for military action, but the resulting Security Council Resolution 1441 was less than satisfactory. While declaring Saddam in 'material breach' of previous UN resolutions and warning of 'serious consequences' if he failed to comply, this was not the form of words that the UN usually used when sanctioning military action. It thus 'fudged the trigger for war', allowing countries such as France and Russia to claim that a breach of 1441 would not give the green light for war.[41]

On 15 February 2003 London witnessed possibly the largest demonstration in British history, as up to two million people from across Britain joined a 'stop the war' rally. On 7 March the UN weapons inspector, Hans Blix – who was heading a UN Monitoring, Verification and Inspection Commission to determine whether Saddam was in breach of existing UN resolutions – declared that he was making considerable progress, that he had failed to identify any WMD, but that he needed more time to complete his mission. Blair, however, was not deflected. Cook resigned from the government; the International Development Secretary, Clare Short, agreed to remain for the time being, in spite of her opposition to the war. Though the consent of parliament was not constitutionally necessary, Blair – still the great communicator – spoke passionately in favour of the course upon which he was set. The vote was won comfortably, thanks to Conservative support, but 139 Labour MPs rebelled. The war began on 19 March. However, the Prime Minister's problems were only beginning.

Military victory was quickly achieved and, objectively, the overthrow of a cruel and oppressive regime offered a measure of vindication to Anglo-American policy. But the anticipated 'Baghdad bounce' did not translate into a significant improvement in the government's standing. The first problem was the failure to discover *any* WMD. Increasingly, the government sought to shift its ground. The removal of a brutal tyrant was a worthy achievement and had rendered the world a better place. However, critics had become wary of New Labour's media management skills. 'To discover a new humanitarian basis for war now that we find [Saddam] had no weapons to disarm does not … merely move the goalposts, but transports the entire football field, stadium and all'.[42] Allegations that the government had 'sexed up' the pre-war intelligence led to a full-scale row with the BBC and to the tragic suicide of government scientist David Kelly. However, the greatest tragedy of the Iraq invasion lay in America's failure to give any serious thought to the tasks of reconstruction. That responsibility, denied to the UN, lay with the US Defense Department, whose head, Donald Rumsfeld, rapidly became a figure of ridicule in Britain. Fundamental mistakes were made, not least the 'De-Ba'athification' of Iraqi society, which deprived the country of any viable bureaucratic infrastructure. Blair seems to have gone along with the American belief that there would be no eruption of conflict between Shia and Sunni Muslims, once

Voices from the past

Robin Cook

Extract from his resignation speech, House of Commons, 17 March 2003:

What has come to trouble me most over past weeks is the suspicion that if … Al Gore had been elected, we would not now be about to commit British troops. The longer that I have served in this place, the greater the respect I have for the good sense and collective wisdom of the British people. On Iraq, I believe that the prevailing mood of the British people is sound. They do not doubt that Saddam is a brutal dictator, but they are not persuaded that he is a clear and present danger to Britain. They want inspections to be given a chance, and they suspect that they are being pushed too quickly into conflict by a US Administration with an agenda of its own. Above all, they are uneasy at Britain going out on a limb on a military adventure without a broader international coalition and against the hostility of many of our traditional allies.[43]

Discussion point

Assess Cook's speech as a critique of the Iraq War. Which features of Blair's policy does it seek to question?

Saddam's controlling hand was removed. In fact, it proved impossible to stabilise Iraq, which fell into a state of chaos and anarchy.

In 2004 Anthony Seldon wrote this: 'If Iraq settles quickly into a peaceful democratic nation, if the world becomes a safer place, if no terrorist bombs in Britain follow the 3/11 [2004] attack in Madrid, if WMD proliferation slows, then the view of the war and of Blair's judgement will change'.[44] More than a decade later, it is clear that this best-case scenario failed to materialise. The consequences for Tony Blair's reputation need no further comment.

Britain's position in the world, 2007

It would be difficult to argue that Britain's standing in the world was significantly stronger in 2007 than ten years earlier. On the credit side, the country was probably a more 'typical' EU member than under Major, not least because enlargement had done something to dilute the prevailing Franco-German predominance. However, Blair's hopes for a directing role within the EU had proved illusory, and the country seemed no nearer making the fundamental choice between Europe and the US regarding its role in the world. The government paid laudable attention to pressing world issues, such as climate change, third-world poverty and debt relief. Blair's performance at the 2005 Gleneagles G8 summit, interrupted by terrorist attacks in London, was widely applauded. But the Iraq War proved a spectacular own goal. Not only was Blair's personal standing badly damaged – it always seemed unlikely that in retirement his efforts as a Middle East peace envoy would meet with success – but Britain's status in the region was probably lower than at any time since Suez in 1956. Blair apparently believed that the world would come to see the Iraq War his way; it never did. Still struggling as Blair left office with the aftermath of conflicts in both Afghanistan and Iraq, Britain was, self-evidently, badly over-extended. Additionally, though it was difficult to prove, many believed that Blair's adventurism had left the country more, not less, vulnerable to terrorist attack. As for the close relationship with the US, which Blair had prioritised, it was, as in the past, heavily dependent on personalities. Bush left office in January 2009 and there were few signs under his successor of anything approaching the Blair–Bush 'love-in'. All told, this was, at best, a mixed record, leaving Britain as uncertain of its international role as in 1997.

ACTIVITY 6.6

1. Study the timeline. Events have been put into separate columns: which would you move to a different column and why?
2. Which developments have been omitted from the table that you think should be included? Explain why.

Timeline 1997–2007

Government and politics	Economics	Date	Society	Foreign affairs
May: New Labour sweeps to power with landslide majority. Blair Prime Minister; Brown Chancellor; Cook Foreign Secretary John Major resigns as Conservative leader to be succeeded by William Hague July: IRA restores cease-fire Government announces plans for elected London mayor and assembly August: Death of Diana, Princess of Wales September: Scottish and Welsh devolution referendums	May: Bank of England given responsibility for setting interest rates Financial Services Authority assumes responsibility for regulation of 'the City' July: Brown's first budget includes 'windfall' tax on privatised utilities November: Brown sets five economic tests for euro membership	1997		
April: Good Friday Agreement on Northern Ireland August: Omagh bombing kills 28 October: Royal Commission on Lords reform established under Lord Wakeham Welsh Secretary, Ron Davies, resigns Jenkins Report on electoral reform published	February: Working Tax Credits introduced	1998		February: Blair's first visit to United States as Prime Minister December: Saint-Malo Agreement
May: Labour largest party in the Scottish and Welsh elections 65 Labour MPs rebel over welfare reforms June: Conservative gains in the European elections October: Mandelson returns to government as Northern Ireland Secretary Deal over removal of all but 92 hereditary peers from House of Lords	March: Brown introduces 10p income tax rate April: National Minimum Wage introduced at rate of £3.60 per hour July–March 2002: Brown sells off substantial part of Britain's gold reserves	1999	February: Macpherson Report accuses Metropolitan Police of 'institutional racism' September: ban on gay servicemen and women lifted	January: euro introduced in 11 countries; Britain remains outside April: Blair's Chicago speech on 'humanitarian intervention' June: Kosovo conflict ended
January: Wakeham Commission recommends partially elected second chamber February: Northern Ireland Assembly suspended May: Livingstone elected London Mayor October: death of Donald Dewar November: Freedom of Information Act passed	March: Significant extra funds announced for NHS July: £43 billion for public services over next three years announced	2000	January: Blair commits to increasing NHS spending to EU average November: age of homosexual consent reduced	May: British troops sent to Sierra Leone

Government and politics	Date	Society	Foreign affairs
January: Mandelson resigns as Northern Ireland Secretary June: general election, Labour returned with slightly reduced majority. Straw Foreign Secretary Hague resigns as Conservative leader, succeeded by Iain Duncan Smith	2001		January: George W. Bush becomes US President September: terrorist attack on New York twin towers October: Allied invasion of Afghanistan
October: Bill Clinton addresses Labour's annual conference. Blair says Labour is best when it is boldest	2002		January: Bush's 'Axis of Evil' speech April: Crawford Summit September: Camp David Summit Government issues 'Iraq Weapons of Mass Destruction' dossier November: UN Resolution 1441 passed
June: Lord Falconer replaces Lord Irvine as Lord Chancellor September: Brown tells party conference Labour is best when it is 'Labour' October: Duncan Smith replaced by Michael Howard	2003		February: huge anti-war demonstration in London March: 139 Labour MPs vote against war in Iraq Iraq war begins
November: referendum in North-East rejects devolved administration	2004	July: top-up university fees introduced	
March: Constitutional Reform Act sets up Supreme Court May: general election, Blair wins third term on substantially reduced majority. Howard announces his resignation July: London bombings IRA announces it has put its weapons beyond use November: government defeated in Commons over 90-day detention orders December: Cameron becomes Conservative leader	2006		July: Gleneagles Summit December: Blair accepts reduction in Britain's EU rebate
March: scandal breaks out over honours for public donations April: Charles Clarke resigns as Home Secretary over Home Office failings	2006	November: Education and Inspections Act	July: Israeli invasion of Lebanon October: Blair imposes temporary restrictions on immigrants from Bulgaria and Romania
May: Ian Paisley becomes Northern Ireland First Minister June: Blair resigns; Gordon Brown becomes Prime Minister	2007		

Further reading

The books written, or edited, by Anthony Seldon, referenced in the notes, offer detailed and expert analysis of the Blair premiership. In addition, two books by the journalist Andrew Rawnsley provide a well-informed (and sometimes lurid) narrative of the inner workings of New Labour: *Servants of the People* (London, 2000) and *The End of the Party* (London, 2010). Several of the key figures in the story have written their memoirs, including Tony Blair, *A Journey* (London, 2010), Peter Mandelson, *The Third Man* (London, 2010) and Jack Straw, *Last Man Standing* (London, 2012). Alastair Campbell has published his contemporary diaries: *The Blair Years* (London, 2007).

Practice essay questions

1. What was 'new' about New Labour during Blair's premiership?
2. How successful was Tony Blair in his aim to make Britain a leading and fully committed member of the European Union?
3. 'Blair's attachment to the "Special Relationship" with the USA was unrealistic and ultimately, a disaster for him and Britain.' Assess the validity of this view.
4. With reference to the sources and your understanding of the historical context, assess the value of these three sources to an historian studying the modernisation of Clause IV of the Labour Party's constitution.

Source A

Source: Tony Blair. ***A Journey: My Political Life***. London: Hutchinson; 2011. p. 75–76

Clause IV was hallowed text repeated on every occasion by those on the left who wanted no truck with compromise or the fact that modern thinking had left its words intellectually redundant and politically calamitous. Among other things, it called for 'the common ownership of the means of production, distribution and exchange'. When drafted in 1917 by Sidney Webb ... the words had actually been an attempt to avoid more Bolshevik language from the further left. Most of all, of course, it reflected prevailing international progressive thought that saw the abolition of private capital as something devoutly to be desired. What was mainstream leftist thinking in the early twentieth century had become hopelessly unreal, even surreal, in the late-twentieth-century world in which, since 1989, even Russia had embraced the market.

Source B

Source: Tony Benn. ***Free at Last! Diaries 1991–2001***. London: Arrow Books; 2003. p. 298

Blair is going round the country arguing for his new Clause 4, and he came out with a new draft about fairness and opportunity and binding people together, and so on. It was quite incredible. Absolute Liberal, SDP, Tory-wet stuff. When the left advocates constitutional change, it is divisive and an arid constitutional struggle. When Blair does it, it's marvellous, it's essential; anyone who disagrees with it follows the old hard-left shibboleths ... [Among Benn's local party committee in Chesterfield] [t]here were one or two wobblers, but the overwhelming majority were furious with what Blair had done and felt we should confirm Clause 4 ... Walworth Road is apparently going to send a pack and a ballot form; we're not going to be guided by that, we'll put our own question and that question is: 'Do you want to keep Clause 4 and possibly add other things, as may be decided at Conference?'.

Source C

Source: Alastair Campbell. ***The Blair Years.*** London: Hutchinson; 2007. p. 11

By now, he [Blair] had also let me know, and sworn me to secrecy, that he was minded to have a review of the constitution and scrap Clause 4. I had never felt any great ideological attachment to Clause 4 one way or the other. If it made people happy, fine, but it didn't actually set out what the party was about today. It wasn't the politics or the ideology that appealed. It was the boldness. People had talked about it for years. Here was a new leader telling me that he was thinking about doing it in his first conference speech as leader. Bold. … He knew that in terms of the political substance, it didn't actually mean that much. But as a symbol, as a vehicle to communicate change, and his determination to modernise the party, it was brilliant.

Chapter summary

By the end of this chapter you should be in a position to understand and assess:

- the nature and central ideas of New Labour
- the main changes introduced by the Blair government across a wide range of policy areas
- the reasons for New Labour's electoral ascendancy and its eventual decline
- the importance of the government's foreign policy and the main problems it encountered.

Endnotes

1 Seldon A. (ed.) *Blair's Britain*. Cambridge: Cambridge University Press; 2007. p. 39.

2 *The Guardian*. 1997 November 17.

3 Seldon A. (ed.) *Blair's Britain*. Cambridge: Cambridge University Press; 2007. p. 411.

4 Seldon A. *Blair*. London: Free Press; 2004. p. 380.

5 Meyer C. *DC Confidential*. London: Weidenfeld & Nicholson; 2005. p. 95.

6 Cook R. *The Point of Departure*. London: Simon & Schuster; 2003. p. 37.

7 Seldon A. (ed.) *Blair's Britain*. Cambridge: Cambridge University Press; 2007. p. 492.

8 Ashdown P. *The Ashdown Diaries 1997–99*. London: Penguin; 2001. p. 30.

9 Meyer C. *DC Confidential*. London: Weidenfeld & Nicholson; 2005. p. 198.

10 Rosen G. (ed.) *Dictionary of Labour History*. London: Politicos; 2001; cited Seldon A. *Blair*. London: Free Press; 2004. p. 294.

11 Seldon, A. *Blair*. London: Free Press; 2004. p. 302.

12 Seldon A. *Blair*. London: Free Press; 2004. p. 437.

13 Cook R. *The Point of Departure*. London: Simon & Schuster; 2003. p. 115.

14 Seldon A. *Blair*. London: Free Press; 2004. p. 694.

15 Campbell A. *The Blair Years*. London: Arrow Books; 2007. p. 501.

16 Seldon A. *Blair Unbound*. London: Simon & Schuster; 2007. p. 115.

17 Seldon A. *Blair Unbound*. London: Simon & Schuster; 2007. p. 226.

18 Sopel J. *Tony Blair: the Moderniser*. London: Michael Joseph; 1995. p. 156.

19 Seldon A. (ed.) *Blair's Britain*. Cambridge: Cambridge University Press; 2007. p. 645.

20 Seldon A. (ed.) *Blair's Britain*. Cambridge: Cambridge University Press; 2007. p. 201.

21 Seldon A. (ed.) *Blair's Britain*. Cambridge: Cambridge University Press; 2007. p. 5.

22 Seldon A. (ed.) *Blair's Britain*. Cambridge: Cambridge University Press; 2007. p. 216–17.

23 Seldon A. (ed.) *Blair's Britain*. Cambridge: Cambridge University Press; 2007. p. 519.

24 The *Guardian*. 2002 October 7.

25 Ludlam S and Smith M. (eds) *New Labour in Government*. Basingstoke: Palgrave Macmillan; 2001. p. 120.

26 Seldon A. (ed.) *Blair's Britain*. Cambridge: Cambridge University Press; 2007. p. 219.

27 Cook R. *The Point of Departure*. London: Simon & Schuster; 2003. p. 102.

28 Seldon A. (ed.) *Blair's Britain*. Cambridge: Cambridge University Press; 2007. p. 539.

29 Seldon A (ed.) *The Blair Effect*. London: Little, Brown; 2001. p. 310.

30 Seldon A. *Blair*. London: Free Press; 2004. p. 369.

31 Cook R. *The Point of Departure*. London: Simon & Schuster; 2003. p. 104.

32 Seldon A. *Blair*. London: Free Press; 2004. p. 620.

33 Kampfner J. *Blair's Wars*. London: Simon & Schuster; 2003. p. 114.

34 Kampfner J. *Blair's Wars*. London: Simon & Schuster; 2003. p. 172.

35 Kampfner J. *Blair's Wars*. London: Simon & Schuster; 2003. p. 3.

36 Seldon A. *Blair*. London: Free Press; 2004. p. 385.

37 Boulton A. *Tony's Ten Years* London: Simon & Schuster; 2008. p. 113.

38 Kampfner J. *Blair's Wars*. London: Simon & Schuster; 2003. p. 167.

39 Seldon A. *Blair Unbound*. London: Simon & Schuster; 2007. p. 139.

40 Cook R. *The Point of Departure*. London: Simon & Schuster; 2003. p. 221.

41 Meyer C. *DC Confidential*. London: Weidenfeld & Nicolson; 2005. p. 257.

42 Cook R. *The Point of Departure*. London: Simon & Schuster; 2003. p. 294.

43 Hansard, House of Commons, vol. 401, col. 728, 17 March 2003.

44 Seldon A. *Blair*. London: Free Press; 2004. p. 603.

Glossary

A

Alternative Vote A non-proportional voting system, whereby each voter indicates preferences on a list of candidates. The second preferences of voters whose first preference was for the eliminated candidate at the bottom of the list are transferred. The procedure is repeated until one candidate secures at least 50% support.

Anti-racism A political programme or point of view which opposes treating people differently according to the supposed 'race' to which they belong, or making unfounded assumptions about individuals based on prejudice about the ethnic group with which they are associated.

Anti-imperialism Political programme or point of view opposed to the invasion of a weaker country by a stronger one, or the imposition on it of a social, political, economic or cultural programme without the free agreement of the population.

Ayatollah A high-ranking Shia Muslim jurist, one who examines questions of Islamic law, and offers decisions and rulings.

B

Balance of payments The relationship between the value of a country's exports and imports, measured in terms of goods and services. A 'favourable balance' is achieved if the value of exports exceeds that of imports.

Bank rate The rate of interest at which the Bank of England lends money, which in turn determines the rate at which the high street banks lend to the public. Increasingly used in the 1960s to cool an overheating economy.

Barnett Formula System Devised in 1978 by Joel Barnett, Labour Chief Secretary to the Treasury 1974–79, to adjust funding to Scotland, Wales and Northern Ireland when changes are made to UK funding.

Benelux countries A shorthand way of referring to Belgium, the Netherlands and Luxembourg.

Berlin Wall Cold War structure dividing East from West Berlin, built under USSR orders in 1961 and pulled down in 1989.

Big Bang The name of the removal of several restrictive practices from the financial markets in 1986, which was seen as having created a new set of rules and expectations in the financial markets.

Biodiversity Term describing the range of life forms currently present on Earth, much-used in debates over human impact on the environment.

Bi-partisan Common to the two leading political parties.

Bourgeois French word originally meaning 'town dweller' but adopted in Marxist and left-wing circles to mean 'middle class'.

Budget deficit The amount by which government (public) expenditure exceeds government income at any given time; this is treated separately from 'national debt', which is the deficit accrued over the longer term.

Bureaucracy The managerial paperwork associated with any larger organisation in both public and private sectors, especially those aspects of management popularly regarded as unnecessary.

By-election Election taking place in a single constituency, not a general election (which takes place in all constituencies).

C

Campaign for Nuclear Disarmament (CND) Founded in 1957 to persuade public opinion, political parties and government that the UK should get rid of its nuclear weapons without waiting for the outcome of negotiations.

Citizen's Charter A guarantee of standards in the public sector, treating the public more like valued customers.

Civil rights The constitutional rights of citizens by virtue of their being full members of society, likely to include the right to vote, form political parties and peacefully protest.

Clause IV A clause in the Labour Party constitution that committed Labour to the common ownership of the means of production, distribution and exchange – in other words, the progressive nationalisation of British industry.

Closed shop A place of work where only union members can be employed.

Common Market A popular British name for the EEC that emphasised its economic role and minimised its political and diplomatic one.

Conspicuous consumption Economic situation in which non-essential goods are being bought in greater numbers and value than is the norm.

Consumerism An economic situation founded on the continuing sale and purchase of consumer goods.

Core vote That section of the electorate upon which a party can reliably count for support, often associated with a particular class or social group.

Corporatism The idea that the government, trade unions and businesses can sit together and discuss future policy in order to sort out issues like pay increases and strikes.

Council tax A local tax introduced in 1993 to replace the poll tax.

D

Deflation A decline in the prices of goods and services over time. The opposite of inflation.

Détente French word meaning 'relaxation'; a term used in the history of the Cold War and by commentators at the time to describe the increased level of diplomatic contact between the USA and USSR and negotiations regarding nuclear weapons.

Devaluation A formal move taken by government in a period of fixed exchange rates to reduce the value of its currency in relation to those of other countries. It has the practical effect of making exports more competitive. The pound was devalued in this way in 1949 and 1967.

Diplock courts Courts of law that sat in Northern Ireland from 1973 specifically to hear trials related to terrorist activity. Decisions about guilt or innocence were made by a judge instead of by a jury.

Dirigiste approach Assumes governments should make choices, including legislating, to achieve its preferred ends and using e.g. taxation to promote some developments and inhibit others. The contrast is about more than economics: it is about what government is for and what society is.

Disestablishment The process whereby an established church breaks its ties with the state and its institutions.

Downing Street Declaration A statement agreed by the Irish and British governments regarding the future of Northern Ireland.

Dry More enthusiastic supporters in Margaret Thatcher's cabinet. See entry for Wet.

E

Establishment The collection of people who own and run the country, particularly those whose parents were also in a position of wealth and authority.

Established church A church with institutional links to the state, one guaranteed by law, or regulated by law.

Ethnic cleansing The attempt to remove all members of an ethnic group from a territory, whether by exiling or murdering them.

Eurosceptic Individuals doubting the value of EEC membership, regarding it as a threat to national sovereignty and prosperity.

F

Fatwa A ruling issued by an Islamic jurist.

Feel-good factor An idea, based upon the belief that economic prosperity is the single most important determinant of voting behaviour, that electors will reward an incumbent government if they sense that their own standard of living is rising.

Feminism A socio-political movement founded on the belief that women are suppressed and allowed less social, economic, political and cultural freedom and power than men. Feminism protests against that state of affairs and analyses the reasons for it.

First-past-the-post electoral system Voting system whereby the individual who tops the poll in each constituency is elected and no account is taken of the percentage of the poll secured by each party in the region or country as a whole.

Flying picket Striking worker who travels from place to place to demonstrate at the entrance to workplaces other than their own, attempting to dissuade other workers from going in to work.

Free markets Unregulated or minimally regulated processes of buying and selling of goods and services.

G

Genocide The attempt to kill an entire ethnic group, rather than individuals, specifically because of their ethnicity.

Gerrymandering Deliberately planning an electoral system in order to exclude a given group and main a different group in power indefinitely.

Glasnost 'Openness' – used to describe changes in the politics of the USSR under Gorbachev.

Governability The ability of governments to set policy directions, legislatures to pass laws and the criminal justice system to enforce them.

Green A political programme or view in which ecological issues, such as global warming, take priority over other issues, such as law and order, defence, social justice, etc. – the issues on which most political parties expect to campaign.

Green belts Areas of countryside immediately around urban centres on which building is banned, or restricted, in order to prevent towns and cities growing outwards without adequate planning and to ensure town-dwellers have access to the countryside.

Gross national product The total value of all the goods and services produced in one year by the residents of a country, including income from overseas investments. 'Gross domestic product' excludes overseas investments.

H

Heavy industry That area of manufacturing where large machinery makes large things happen, especially coal, steel, aircraft and cars.

Hire-purchase agreements Means of buying goods through a series of part-payments over a period of time, generally at a higher overall cost than for ordinary purchase.

Hung parliament One in which no party has a majority of MPs leading to a period of negotiations, which may lead to a minority government, or to a coalition government formed by two or more parties.

Hustings Literally, the platform from which a candidate gives his election address. Now used more generally to describe election campaign activity.

I

Inflation A process of continual price rises and of the falling value of money, usually measured by the Retail Price Index and, more recently, by the Consumer Prices Index.

Infrastructure The structures that underpin social and economic activity, such as roads, railways, bridges and power supplies.

Internal market The relationship between the constituent parts of a large organisation which allows them to buy products or services from one another.

International Monetary Fund (IMF) Founded in 1944 to prevent monetary crises by looking after national currencies, including exchange rates and devaluations. A range of countries make funds available and individual countries can draw on the IMF's resources and advice, rather like a bank.

Internment A system of imprisonment without trial; historically following the arrest of the citizens of an enemy country during wartime, but used during the Troubles to hold individuals believed to be terrorists.

J

Junta Spanish word meaning 'committee' or 'administrative council'. In English, it is used exclusively to refer to the governing bodies of Latin-American military dictatorships.

K

Keynesian economics Economic theory based on the writings of the Cambridge economist, J.M. Keynes, which dominated thinking from the Second World War until the 1970s. In essence, it involves a belief that government should use economic policy to iron out the fluctuations of the market, in order to control the level of employment and maximise productive efficiency. Regulating demand can encourage growth when necessary, or hold it back when there is danger of the economy overheating.

Khaki election One fought in the aftermath of a war.

L

Laissez-faire approach One that prefers government to interfere as little as possible in business and the economy, leaving matters to managers and market forces.

Leak Information that an organisation had officially decided to keep secret, released from the organisation to the press or other outsiders.

Liberalisation A process whereby over time tolerance increases of differences in behaviour patterns and personal choices.

Light industry Uses smaller machines to make smaller things, such as clothing and electronics.

Loyalist Protestant community in Northern Ireland with declared loyalty to the United Kingdom and the monarchy, specifically those willing to undertake militant activities to advance this point of view.

M

Maiden speech First speech by an MP in a legislature, e.g. the British Parliament.

Market place where people buy and sell goods. 'The market' is a shorthand reference to the totality of making, buying and selling. Market forces are the influence of the numbers of people bidding for goods (demand) and of those seeking to sell them (supply).

Matériel French word used in English to mean military hardware.

Meritocracy Popularised by the 1958 book *The Rise of the Meritocracy* – a warning that an elite which had reached power through personal achievement would feel little loyalty to, or responsibility for, those who had achieved less. The word acquired a positive meaning and become a part of the vocabulary of the Blair government.

Mod A modern and smart youth in the 1960s.

Monopolies Large companies with no competitors.

N

National curriculum A standardised curriculum introduced in England, Wales and Northern Ireland (but not Scotland) in 1997, specifying the outline of what pupils should be taught at different ages in state schools.

Nationalised industry One owned by the state.

Nationalisation The process of taking an industry into public ownership.

Negative equity When the value of a property (its equity) is less than the loan taken out to buy it, meaning that, in the event of being forced to sell, the owner would still be in debt.

National Lottery A system of gambling in which part of the profits are used by the state to fund the arts, heritage, sport and 'good causes'.

Neo-cons A right-wing American political movement, particularly influential in the Republican administrations of President George H. W. Bush and George W. Bush. It advocates intervention in a dangerous world in pursuit of democracy and American values.

New Right Term used to describe those Conservatives who followed Margaret Thatcher and Keith Joseph in their belief that the party should abandon much of the post-war settlement and re-establish its free market, small state credentials, giving priority to the elimination of inflation, even if this meant higher unemployment.

Non-violent direct action Taking practical steps to advance a cause, including physically opposing an opponent, without the use or threat of violence, but sometimes going outside the law. This might include individuals or groups placing themselves in the way of vehicles to hinder, or draw attention to, e.g. the transportation of weapons or nuclear waste.

North Atlantic Treaty Organisation (NATO) A military alliance created following the Second World War to counter the threat of the USSR and its allies and retain the involvement of the USA in Europe.

O

One Nation Conservatism The name, appropriated from Disraeli, was used by a small group of new Conservative MPs in 1950 to describe their support for the sort of moderate, reforming Toryism which encouraged social cohesion and avoided divisive policies. Now used more generally to describe the left wing of the Conservative Party.

P

Perestroika 'Restructuring' The economic and political way the country worked would be remade. The USSR was not an economic success story and its people were unnecessarily poor.

Permissive society A journalists' phrase for describing a society in which a wider range of views and activities are permitted and regarded as socially acceptable.

Picket A striking worker who stands at the entrance to their workplace, attempting to dissuade other workers from going in.

Political consensus Significant overlap, or similarity, in the policies of the leading parties (or, more usually, their leaders) producing a noticeable continuity in governmental practice.

Poll tax Tax paid by every adult. Based on a 'head count', the term comes from an old-fashioned word for 'head'.

Private Finance Initiative (PFI) A way of creating a 'public-private partnership' by funding public infrastructure projects through private capital. Likely to involve high long-term repayment costs.

Private Member's Bill (PMB) A bill introduced to parliament by a member of the House of Commons or Lords who is not in the government.

Private sector That part of the economy that is owned and run by private interests, rather than the state, usually along capitalist lines.

Privatisation The process of moving a publicly owned concern into the private sector, by selling shares in it.

Proportional representation System of voting in which the outcome in allocation of seats in a legislature resembles the proportional distribution of votes to political parties across the country.

Public Sector Borrowing Requirement (PSBR) Term used to describe the amount of money the government needs to borrow to make up the difference between what it can raise, e.g. through taxation and what it intends to spend, e.g. on services.

R

Ribbon development The growth of urban areas by the development of additional buildings along the roads that go out from the towns and cities.

Rocker Youth in the 1960s with long hair who enjoyed the music of the previous decade.

Run on the pound The rapid selling of the British currency on money markets by investors who are afraid that it has become overvalued, that its value relative to other currency is about to drop and they need to sell in order to avoid losses. This process in itself then causes the pound to lose value.

S

Schengen Agreement 1985 agreement between five of the then ten members of the EEC to remove border checks to make trade and travel easier.

Secondary picketing Focuses not on the workplace that is the centre of the dispute, but that employer's suppliers, or the retailers who sell its products.

Service sector Customers pay, not for a tangible product that they can drive or carry away, but for services based on education, training and skills. It includes hotels, restaurants, entertainment, lawyers, accountants and education.

Shadow cabinet The alternative government consisting of senior members of her Majesty's Loyal Opposition, usually the second-largest party in the House of Commons. Each member of the shadow government is their party's spokesperson on a specific area of government policy and it is their job to monitor the actions, decisions and speeches of the actual minister, offer a critique and, where necessary, put forward alternatives.

Sino-Soviet split Deterioration in diplomatic relations between USSR and China in the 1970s, in which the Chinese leadership both asserted its independence of Moscow and took a different view of Marxism on certain points.

Social conservatism Respects social traditions, such as marriage and the family, emphasises personal responsibility and in the criminal justice system prioritises punishment.

Social contract A negotiated agreement whereby individuals and groups surrender certain rights in order to achieve certain benefits. The expression was adopted by the 1970s Wilson government to describe a negotiated settlement with trade unions that would not be enshrined in statute, but would allow pay settlements to be moderated.

Social liberalism Expresses the importance of tolerance, balancing social justice and individual freedom; in the criminal justice system it prioritises education, therapeutic treatment and reducing reoffending.

Socialism A political philosophy holding that economic activity should be communally owned and geared towards the needs of society as a whole, rather than the individual. In the British tradition the necessary transformation has generally been seen as a gradualist, rather than revolutionary, process.

State socialism A version of socialism advanced, not by revolution, but by the progressive intervention of elected governments of the left to alter society and the economy. This is likely to include nationalisation of some, or all, of the larger means of production.

Stealth taxes Those taxes whose impact is indirect and which are not immediately perceived by voters as affecting them financially.

Strategic Arms Limitation Talks (SALT) A series of negotiations between the USA and the USSR.

Summit A meeting between heads of government, or heads of state, of different countries. It is preceded by a series of planning meetings between their advisers and officials, to ensure that when national leaders meet they are in a position to make wide-ranging decisions leading to the signing of treaties.

T

Tactical voting Supporting a candidate in an election, not because of agreeing with the party they represent, but because of their being the most likely to defeat a different party.

Taoiseach Irish word meaning 'prime minister'.

Teacher Training Agency Body created in 1994 to provide additional training to teachers who were already in work, in order to ensure they were kept up to date with changes in educational policy and practice.

U

Unilateralist One supporting the unilateral (one-sided) nuclear disarmament of, e.g. Britain, without attempting to negotiate a specific response from the Cold War enemy – the allies in the Warsaw Pact.

W

War cabinet A small group, usually consisting of senior ministers and senior military commanders, which takes the decisions regarding the conduct of a war.

Warsaw Pact A military alliance comprising the USSR and several countries in eastern and central Europe, founded following the Second World War to counter the threat from NATO and maintain Soviet-sponsored governments in power in several countries where they had no popular mandate.

Wet School slang for someone regarded as weak or ineffectual. Margaret Thatcher called 'wet' members of her own government who did not adequately support her policies, implying they lacked political courage. Her more enthusiastic supporters in the cabinet became known as 'dry'.

White paper This document presents the government's findings and intentions on a particular policy area. It does also allow for a degree of discussion before legislation is introduced.

Wildcat strikes Action taken by members of a union, but usually without the knowledge or approval of the union leaders.

Bibliography

Aitken J. *Margaret Thatcher: Power and Personality*. London: A&C Black; 2013.

Ashdown P. *The Ashdown Diaries 1997–99*. London: Penguin; 2001.

Benn, T. *Free at Last! Diaries 1991–2001*. London: Arrow Books; 2003.

Blair, T. *A Journey: My Political Life*. London: Hutchinson; 2010.

Blake R. *Conservative Party from Peel to Major*. London: Heinemann; 1997.

Boulton A. *Tony's Ten Years*. London: Simon & Schuster; 2008.

Brivati B. *Hugh Gaitskell*. London: Richard Cohen; 1996.

Brown G. *In My Way: the Political Memoirs of Lord George-Brown*. London: Gollancz; 1971.

Buckle S. *The Way Out: a History of Homosexuality in Britain*. London: IB Tauris; 2015.

Bullock A. *Ernest Bevin: Foreign Secretary*. London: Heinemann; 1983.

Butler D. and Stokes D. *Political Change in Britain*. London: Macmillan; 1974.

Campbell A. *The Blair Years*. London: Arrow Books; 2007.

Campbell J. *Nye Bevan and the Mirage of British Socialism*. London: Weidenfeld and Nicolson; 1987.

Campbell J. *The Iron Lady: Margaret Thatcher from Grocer's Daughter to Iron Lady*. London: Penguin; 2012.

Callaghan J. *Time and Chance*. London: Collins; 1987.

Castle B. *Fighting All the Way*. London: Macmillan; 1993.

Catterall P. (ed.) *The Macmillan Diaries, vol. II*. London: Macmillan; 2011.

Clarke C and James T. (eds.) *British Labour Leaders*. London: Biteback Publishing; 2015.

Clarke P. *Hope and Glory, Britain 1900–2000*. London: Penguin; 1996, rev. ed. 2004.

Cook R. *The Point of Departure*. London: Simon & Schuster; 2003.

Crosland S. *Tony Crosland*. London: Jonathan Cape; 1982.

Dale I. *The Dictionary of Conservative Quotations*. London: Biteback Publishing; 2013.

Driver S. and Martell L. *New Labour: Politics after Thatcherism*. Cambridge: Polity Press; 1998.

Dutton D. *Douglas-Home*. London: Haus; 2006.

Eccleshall R. (ed.) *English Conservatism since the Restoration: an Introduction and Anthology*. London: Routledge; 2002.

Ellis S. *Britain, America and the Vietnam War*. Westport, USA: Praeger; 2004.

Fielding S. *The Labour Governments 1964–1970 Vol 1: Labour and Cultural Change*. Oxford: Oxford University Press; 2003.

Forman FN, Baldwin NDJ. *Mastering British Politics*. London: Palgrave Macmillan; 2007.

George S. *An Awkward Partner: Britain in the European Community*. Oxford: Oxford University Press; 1998.

Gresham College. *Six General Elections*. Available at http://www.gresham.ac.uk/six-general-elections

Gresham College. *Leadership and Change: Prime Ministers in the Post-War World – Winston Churchill*. Available at http://www.gresham.ac.uk/lectures-and-events/leadership-and-change-prime-ministers-in-the-post-war-world-winston-churchill

Hamill D. *Pig in the Middle: the Army in Northern Ireland, 1969–84*. London: Methuen; n.e. 1986.

Harris R. *The Making of Neil Kinnock*. London: Faber and Faber; 1984.

Harrison B. *The Transformation of British Politics 1860-1995*. Oxford: Oxford University Press; 1996.

Healey D. *The Time of My Life*. London: Penguin; 1990.

Hennessy P. *Muddling Through: Power, Politics and the Quality of Government in Postwar Britain*. London: Victor Gollancz; 1996.

Hennessy P. *The Prime Minister: the Office and its Holders since 1945*. London: Alan Lane/Penguin; 2000.

Hennessy P. *Having It So Good: Britain in the Fifties*. London: Penguin; 2006.

Heppell T. *Choosing the Labour Leader: Labour Party Leadership Elections from Wilson to Brown*. London: IB Tauris; 2010.

Hickson K and Seldon A. (eds.) *New Labour, Old Labour: the Wilson and Callaghan Governments 1974-1979*. London: Routledge; 2004.

Howe G. *Conflict of Loyalty*. London: Macmillan; 1994.

Hyam R. *Britain's Declining Empire: the Road to Decolonisation 1918–1968*. Cambridge: Cambridge University Press; 2006.

Jackson B and Saunders R. (eds.) *Making Thatcher's Britain*. Cambridge: Cambridge University Press; 2012.

Jay D. *Change and Fortune: a Political Record*. London: Hutchinson; 1980.

Jefferys K. *Retreat from New Jerusalem: British Politics 1951–1964*. Basingstoke: Macmillan; 1997.

Jenkins R. *A Life at the Centre*. London: Macmillan; 1991.

Johnson P. (ed.) *Twentieth-Century Britain, Economic, Social and Cultural Change*. London: Longman; 1994.

Kavanagh D and Morris P. *Consensus Politics From Attlee To Major*. Oxford: Blackwell; 1989.

Kampfner J. *Blair's Wars*. London: Simon & Schuster; 2003.

Kynaston D. *Austerity Britain*. London: Bloomsbury; 2008.

Kynaston D. *Family Britain*. London: Bloomsbury; 2010.

Lapping B. *End of Empire*. London: Paladin; 1985.

Lamb R. *The Failure of the Eden Government*. London: Sidgwick & Johnson; 1987.

Lawson N. *The View from No 11: Memoirs of a Tory Radical*. London: Bantam; 1992.

Lloyd T. *Empire, Welfare State, Europe: English History 1906–1992*. Oxford: Oxford University Press; 1993.

Ludlam S and Smith M. (eds.) *New Labour in Government*. Basingstoke: Palgrave Macmillan; 2001.

Macmillan H. *Riding the Storm*. London: Macmillan; 1971.

Major J. *The Autobiography*. London: HarperCollins; 1999.

Marr A. *A History of Modern Britain*. London: Macmillan; 2007.

Marwick A. *British Society since 1945*. London: Penguin; 1996.

Marwick A. *The Sixties: Cultural revolution in Britain, France, Italy, and the United States, c. 1958–c. 1974*. Oxford: Oxford University Press; 1998.

Meyer C. *DC Confidential*. London: Weidenfeld & Nicolson; 2005.

Morgan J. (ed.) *The Backbench Diaries of Richard Crossman*. London: Hamish Hamilton and Jonathan Cape; 1981.

Morgan KO. *The People's Peace, British History since 1945*. Oxford: Oxford University Press; 1990, 2nd edn. 1999.

O'Beirne Ranelagh J. *A Short History of Ireland*. Cambridge: Cambridge University Press; 1983, 1994.

O'Day A. (ed.) *Political Violence in Northern Ireland: Conflict and Conflict Resolution*. Westport, USA: Praeger; 1997.

Owen D. *Time to Declare*. London: Michael Joseph; 1991.

Pearce M and Stewart G. *British Political History, 1867–1990: Democracy and Decline*. London: Routledge; 1996.

Pimlott B. *Harold Wilson*. London: Harper Collins; 1992.

Pimlott B. (ed.) *The Political Diary of Hugh Dalton*. London: Jonathan Cape; 1986.

Ramsden J. *The Winds of Change: Macmillan to Heath, 1957–75*. London: Longman; 1996.

Rosen G. *Old Labour to New: the Dreams that Inspired, the Battles that Divided*. London: Politicos Publishing Ltd; 2005.

Rosen G. (ed.) *Dictionary of Labour History*. London: Politicos; 2001.

Sampson A. *Anatomy of Britain*. London: Hodder and Stoughton; 1962.

Sandbrook D. *Never Had It So Good: A history of Britain from Suez to the Beatles*. London: Little, Brown; 2006.

Sandbrook D. *White Heat: a History of Britain in the Swinging Sixties 1964–1970*. London: Little, Brown; 2006.

Sassoon D. *One Hundred Years of Socialism: the West European Left in the Twentieth Century*. London: IB Tauris; 2013.

Seldon A. (ed.) *The Blair Effect*. London: Little, Brown; 2001.

Seldon A. *Blair*. London: Free Press; 2004.

Seldon A. *Blair Unbound*. London: Simon & Schuster; 2007.

Seldon A. (ed.) *Blair's Britain*. Cambridge: Cambridge University Press; 2007.

Seldon A and Collings D. *Britain Under Thatcher*. London: Routledge; 2014.

Self R. *British Foreign and Defence Policy since 1945*. Basingstoke: Palgrave Macmillan; 2010.

Senden L. *Soft Law in European Community Law*. Oxford: Hart; 2004.

Shank M. *The Stagnant Society*. London: Penguin; 1961.

Shaw E. *The Labour Party since 1945*. Oxford: Blackwell; 1996.

Shepherd R. *Iain Macleod*. London: Hutchinson; 1994.

Sopel J. *Tony Blair: the Moderniser*. London: Michael Joseph; 1995.

Spencer G. (ed.) *The British and Peace in Northern Ireland*. Cambridge: Cambridge University Press; 1983, 2015.

Stuart B. *The Conservative Party since 1945*. Manchester: Manchester University Press; 1998.

Tanner D, Thane P and Tiratsoo N. (eds.) *Labour's First Century*. Cambridge: Cambridge University Press; 2000.

Thatcher M. *The Downing Street Years*. London: HarperCollins; 1993, 2011.

Turner J. *Macmillan*. Harlow: Longman; 1994.

Tiratsoo N. *From Blitz to Blair: a new history of Britain since 1939*. London: Weidenfeld and Nicolson; 1997.

Vinen R. *Thatcher's Britain: the Politics and Social Upheaval of the 1980s*. London: Simon and Schuster; 2009.

Wagner HL and Cronkite W. *Ronald Reagan*. Philadelphia, USA: Chelsea House; 2004.

Wilson H. *The Labour Government 1964–1970: a Personal Record*. London: Weidenfeld and Nicolson; 1971.

Wrigley C. *British Trade Unions since 1933*. Cambridge: Cambridge University Press; 2002.

Young JW. (ed.) *The Foreign Policy of Churchill's Peacetime Administration, 1951–1955*. Leicester: Leicester University Press; 1988.

Young JW. *Winston Churchill's Last Campaign: Britain and the Cold War 1951–55*. Oxford: Clarendon Press; 1996.

Acknowledgements

The authors and publishers acknowledge the following sources of copyright material and are grateful for the permissions granted. While every effort has been made, it has not always been possible to identify the sources of all the material used, or to trace all copyright holders. If any omissions are brought to our notice, we will be happy to include the appropriate acknowledgements on reprinting.

The publisher would like to thank the following for permission to reproduce their photographs (numbers refer to figure numbers, unless otherwise stated):

Page 1: Trinity Mirror / Mirrorpix / Alamy Stock Photo, **Figure 1.1:** Fox Photos / Getty Images, **Figure 1.10:** George Marks/ Getty Images, **Figure 1.12:** Pictorial Press Ltd / Alamy Stock Photo, **Figure 1.14:** Glasshouse Images / Alamy Stock Photo, **Page 37:** Heritage Image Partnership Ltd / Alamy Stock Photo, **Figure 2.5:** Keystone / Getty Images, **Figure 2.6:** Rolls Press/Popperfoto / Getty Images, **Figure 2.8:** Bettmann / Getty Images, **Figure 2.11:** Trinity Mirror / Mirrorpix / Alamy Stock Photo, **Page 69:** Hulton Archive / Getty Images, **Figure 3.1:** Mary Evans Picture Library / Alamy Stock Photo, **Figure 3.4:** Keystone Pictures USA / Alamy Stock Photo, Figure 3.8: Alain Le Garsmeur / Getty Images, **Figure 3.9:** Design Pics Inc / Alamy Stock Photo, **Figure 3.10:** Oli Scarff / Getty Images, **Figure 3.11:** AFP / Getty Images, **Page 99:** Bettmann / Getty Images, **Figure 4.9:** Everett Collection Historical / Alamy Stock Photo, **Figure 4.10:** Everett Collection Historical / Alamy Stock Photo, **Figure 4.11:** Aardvark / Alamy Stock Photo, **Figure 4.14:** Pictorial Press Ltd / Alamy Stock Photo, **Figure 4.16:** Geoff Bruce / Getty, **Figure 4.18:** Trinity Mirror / Mirrorpix / Alamy Stock Photo, **Page 128:** Peter Jordan / Alamy Stock Photo, **Figure 5.2:** Hulton Archive / Getty Images, **Figure 5.3:** Trinity Mirror / Mirrorpix / Alamy Stock Photo, **Figure 5.6:** Allstar Picture Library / Alamy Stock Photo, **Figure 5.7:** WENN UK / Alamy Stock Photo, **Figure 5.11:** Anwar Hussein / Getty Images, **Page 157:** Jeff Overs / Getty Images, **Figure 6.7:** Trinity Mirror / Mirrorpix / Alamy Stock Photo, **Figure 6.8:** An Chung / Getty Images, **Figure 6.9:** PA / PA Archive/Press Association Images, **Figure 6.10:** Corbis, **Figure 6.11:** Scott Barbour / Getty Images

Index

CPSIA information can be obtained
at www.ICGtesting.com
Printed in the USA
LVOW02s1034110716
495849LV00017B/391/P

9 781107 57308